FIRE FORCE

ATSUSHI
OHKUBO

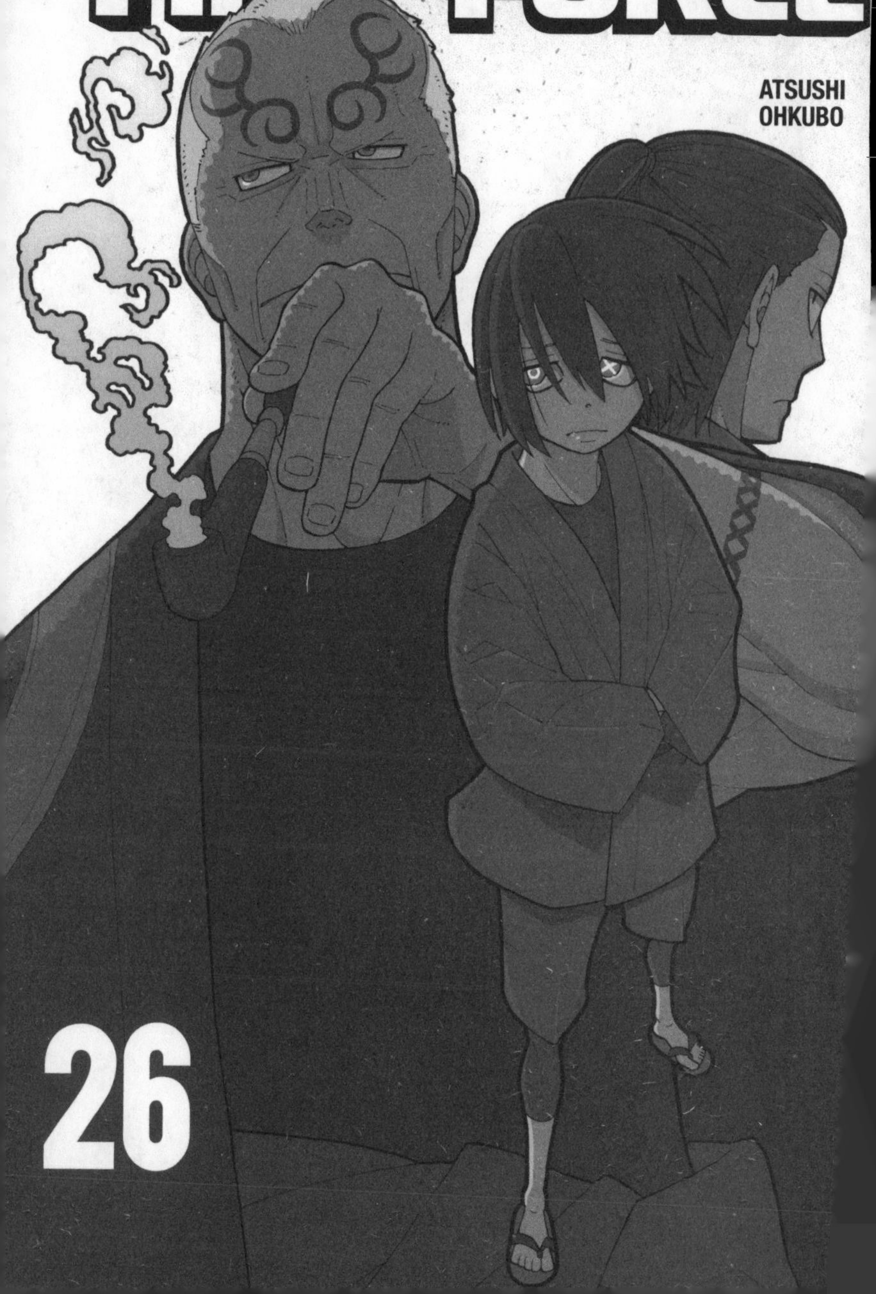

26

rin”.

to

to you.

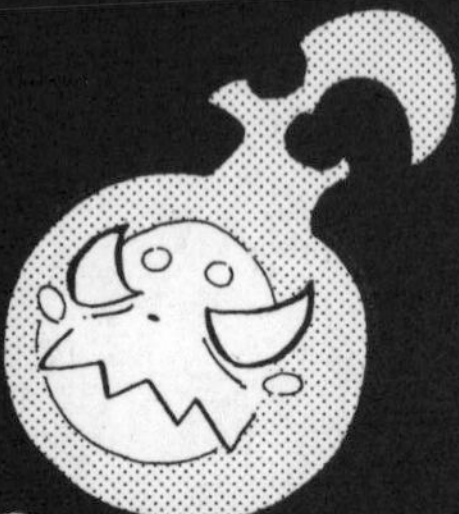

VOL.26

ATSUSHI OHKUBO

“Nichi

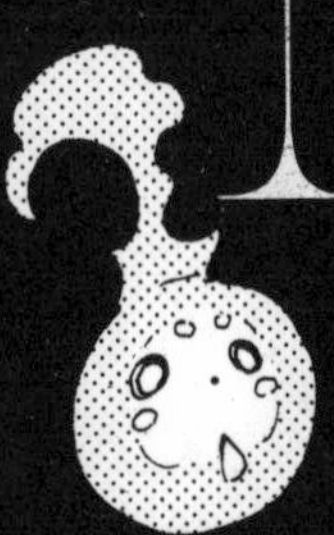

I want

give back

FIRE FORCE

SPECIAL FIRE FORCE COMPANY 8

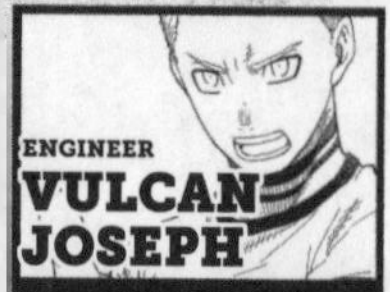

ENGINEER
VULCAN JOSEPH
The greatest engineer of the day, renowned as the God of Fire and the Forge. He inked some tattoos on the ankles of Shinra's alter-ego.

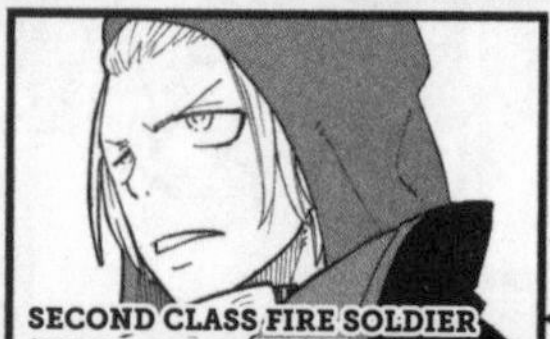

SECOND CLASS FIRE SOLDIER (THIRD GENERATION PYROKINETIC)
ARTHUR BOYLE
Trained at the academy with Shinra. He follows his own personal code of chivalry as the self-proclaimed Knight King. He's a blockhead who is bad at mental exercise. He's a weirdo who grows stronger the more delusional he gets. He noticed something was different about Shinra and explained that Shinra was acting exactly like the devil in the training academy rumors.

WATCHES OUT FOR

TRUSTS

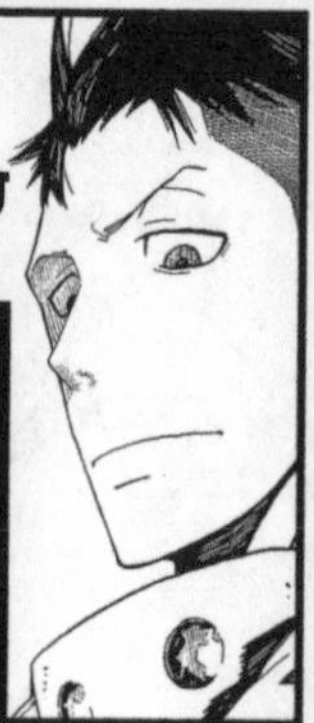

CAPTAIN (NON-POWERED)
AKITARU ŌBI
The caring leader of the newly established Company 8. He has no powers, but uses his finely honed muscles as a weapon in a battle style that makes him worthy of the Captain title. Even when Shinra's personality changed, he refused to abandon him and waited for Shinra's return.

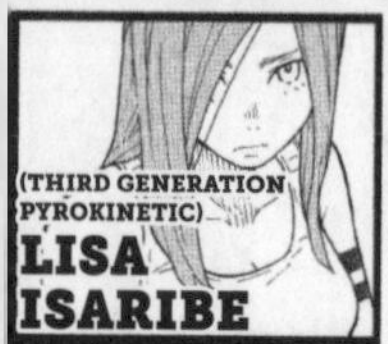

(THIRD GENERATION PYROKINETIC)
LISA ISARIBE
Formerly a spy sent by Dr. Giovanni, she is now a member of Company 8. She controls tentacles of flame.

IDIOT!!

WATCHES OUT FOR

TRUSTS

STRONG BOND

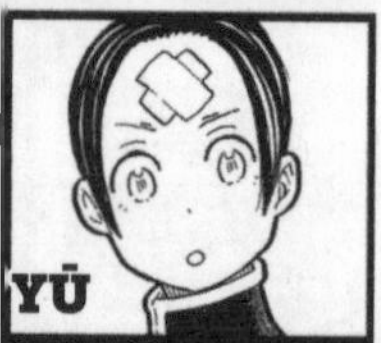

YŪ
A self-proclaimed apprentice of Vulcan's. Has now recovered from the injuries inflicted by Dr. Giovanni.

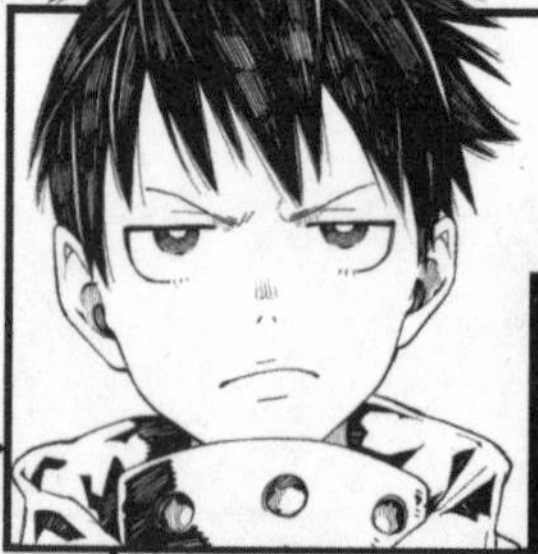

SECOND CLASS FIRE SOLDIER (THIRD GENERATION PYROKINETIC)
SHINRA KUSAKABE
Dreams of becoming a hero who saves people from spontaneous combustion! His weapon is a fiery kick. He wields a special flame called the Adolla Burst. He has no memory of a three-month period in which his personality had apparently been taken over by his doppelganger.

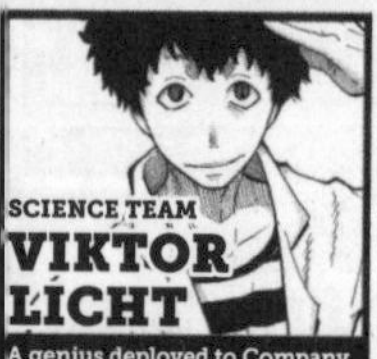

SCIENCE TEAM
VIKTOR LICHT
A genius deployed to Company 8 from Haijima Industries. Has confessed to being a Haijima spy.

A NICE GIRL

LOOKS AWESOME ON THE JOB

A TOUGH BUT WEIRD LADY

HANG IN THERE, ROOKIE!

TERRIFIED

STRICT DISCIPLINARIAN

HAS HIM ON HER MIND

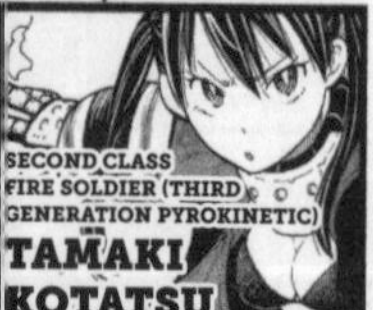

SECOND CLASS FIRE SOLDIER (THIRD GENERATION PYROKINETIC)
TAMAKI KOTATSU
A rookie from Company 1 currently in Company 8's care. She controls nekomata-like flames.

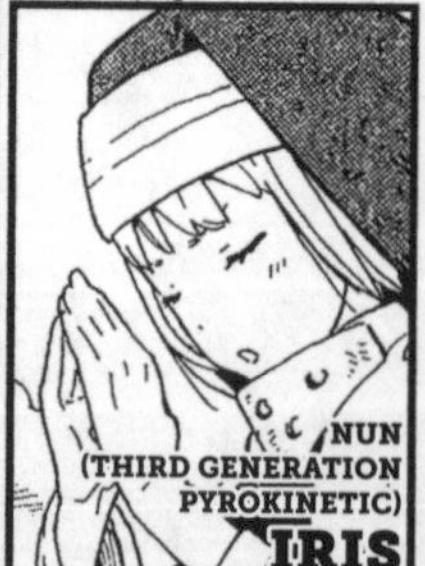

NUN (THIRD GENERATION PYROKINETIC)
IRIS
A sister of the Holy Sol Temple, her prayers are an indispensable part of extinguishing Infernals. Her ignition powers have recently manifested.

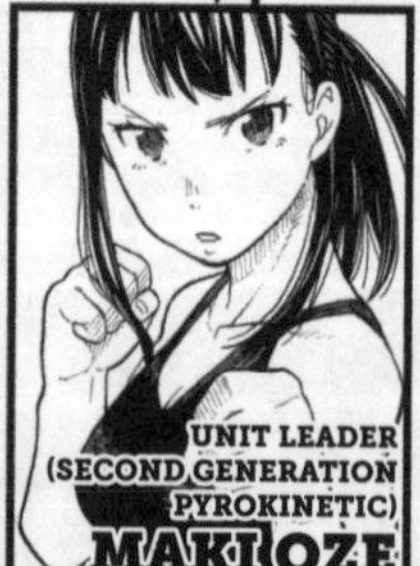

UNIT LEADER (SECOND GENERATION PYROKINETIC)
MAKI OZE
A former member of the military, she is an excellent fighter who controls fire. She's a cool lady, but is mad about love stories, and her beauty is overshadowed by her "head full of flowers and wedding bells."

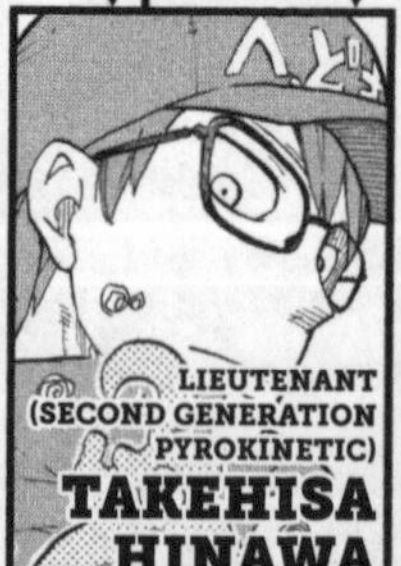

LIEUTENANT (SECOND GENERATION PYROKINETIC)
TAKEHISA HINAWA
A dry, unemotional ex-military man, whose stern discipline is feared among the new recruits. The gun he uses is a cherished memento from his friend who became an Infernal.

THE GIRLS' CLUB

RESPECTS

ASAKUSA HIKESHI THE OLD BOSS

SHINMON HIBACHI

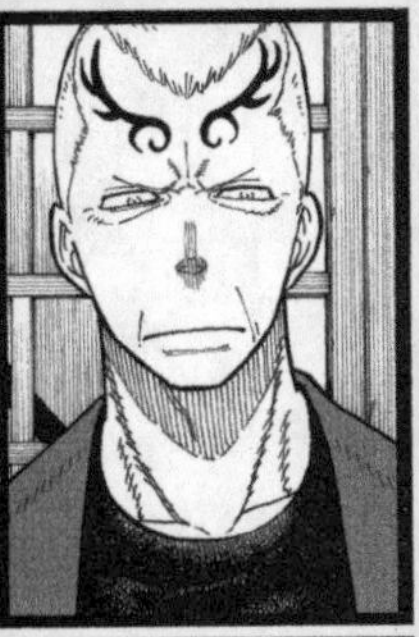

Benimaru's late mentor. He took care of things in Asakusa in the pre-Special Fire Force days and raised Benimaru to be his successor. His doppelganger has appeared and is attacking Asakusa.

HOLY SOL TEMPLE + "EVANGELIST"

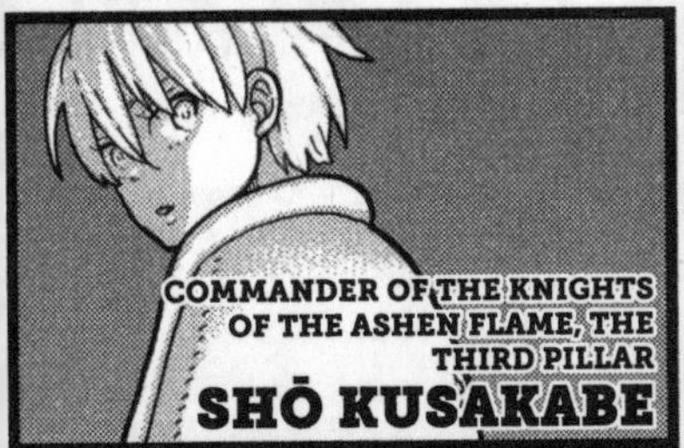

COMMANDER OF THE KNIGHTS OF THE ASHEN FLAME, THE THIRD PILLAR

SHŌ KUSAKABE

Shinra's long-lost brother, the commander of an order of knights that works for the Evangelist. He can use his powers to stop time for all but himself. He was made into a doll for Haumea, but is impelled to leave the Church when he feels his brother's warmth through an Adolla Link.

"GUARDIAN"

ARROW

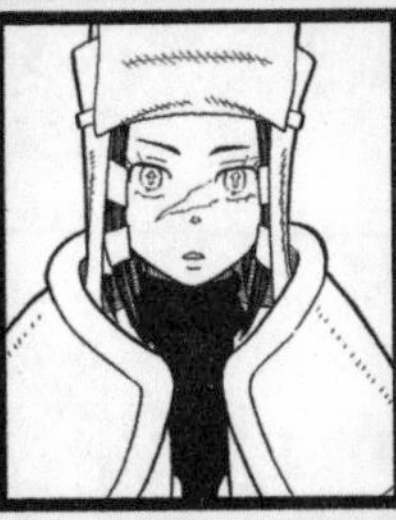

A member of the "White Clad" cult, and Shō's Guardian. Has the power to attack with arrows made of flame. She accompanies Shō when he leaves the Church.

SPECIAL FIRE FORCE COMPANY 7

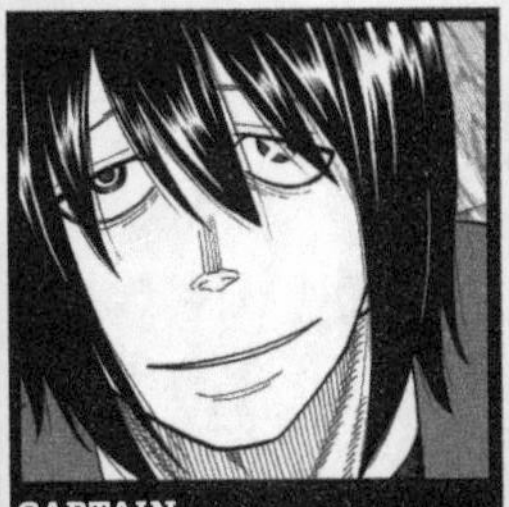

CAPTAIN

SHINMON BENIMARU

A composite fire soldier, with the powers of a second gen and a third gen pyrokinetic. Is haunted by the fact that Hibachi passed on before he could prove his worth to him.

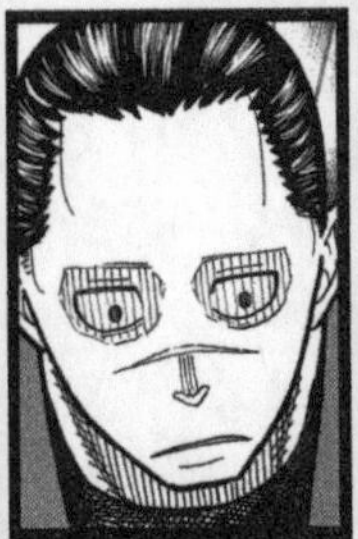

LIEUTENANT

SAGAMIYA KONRO

Has the "holy scar" of one who has experienced an Adolla Link. Refers to Benimaru as Waka.

HAIJIMA INDUSTRIES

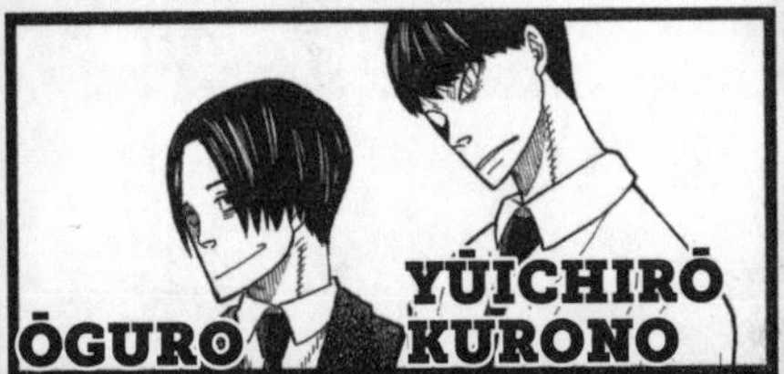

ŌGURO

An elite Haijima executive, who climbed the corporate ladder faster than anyone in history. A horrible human being who nevertheless silences all complaints by continually achieving better-than-perfect results. Non-powered.

YŪICHIRŌ KURONO

The man known as Death, he adores weaklings. Will only take orders from Ōguro and Haijima's CEO, thus forcing Ōguro to accompany him to the field. Third-generation pyrokinetic.

SPECIAL FIRE FORCE COMPANY 2

CAPTAIN

GUSTAV HONDA

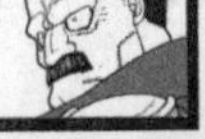

SUMMARY

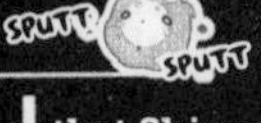
SPUTT
SPUTT

During the battle against the titanic Infernal that appeared in the Pacific Ocean, Shinra makes an Adolla Link that takes him to glimpse the world before the Great Cataclysm. The next thing he knows, three months have passed, and he has no memory of any of them. His friends tell him he was like a different person during that time. Arthur hypothesizes that Shinra had been taken over by his doppelganger. With the Great Cataclysm under way, Infernals are appearing with greater frequency, and pyrokinetic powers are growing stronger. As Company 1 begins to put some Infernals to rest, suddenly a powerful demon Infernal arrives on the scene. Back in Asakusa, Benimaru reacts to its presence...

FIRE FORCE 26
CONTENTS

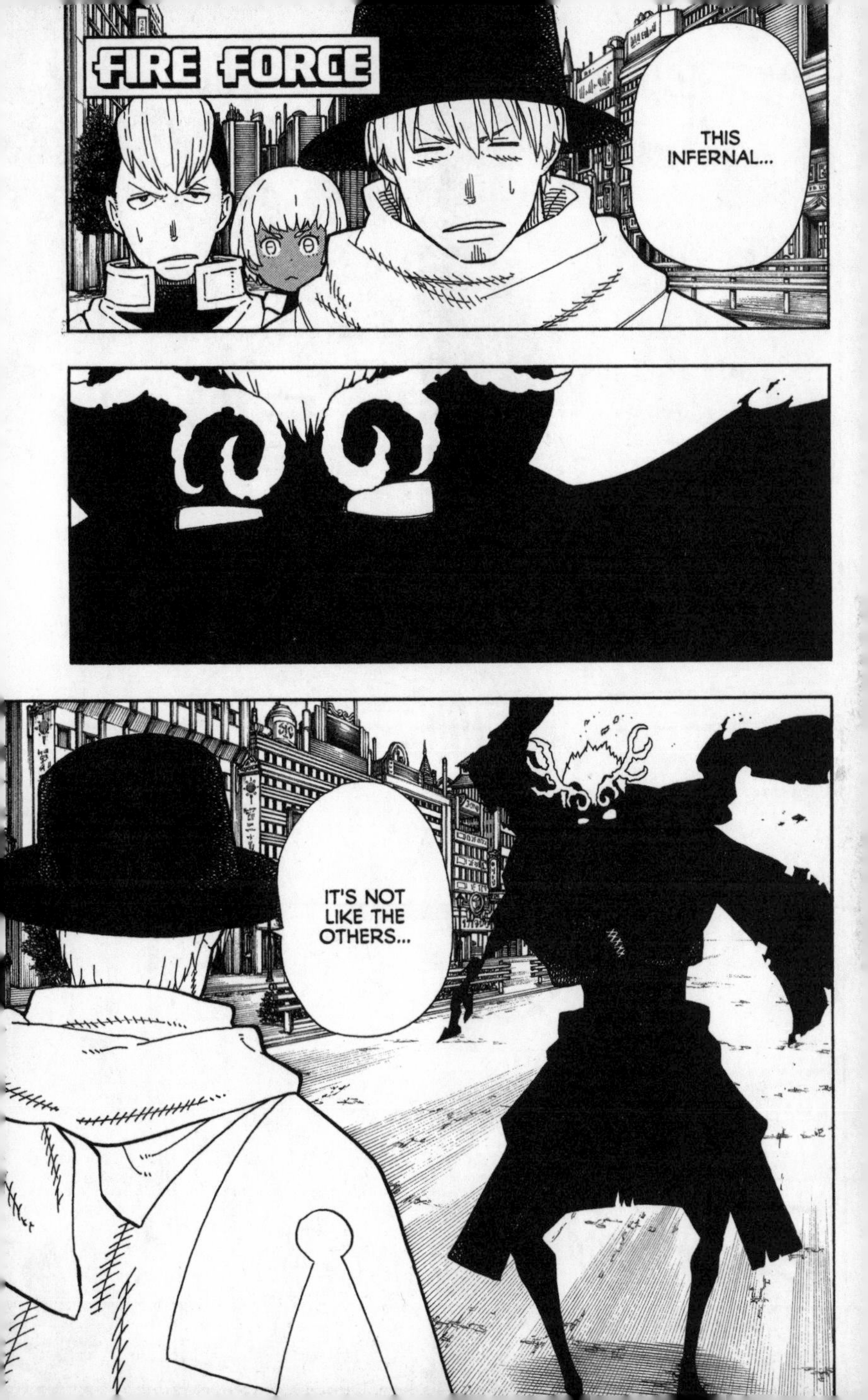
FIRE FORCE
THIS INFERNAL...
IT'S NOT LIKE THE OTHERS...

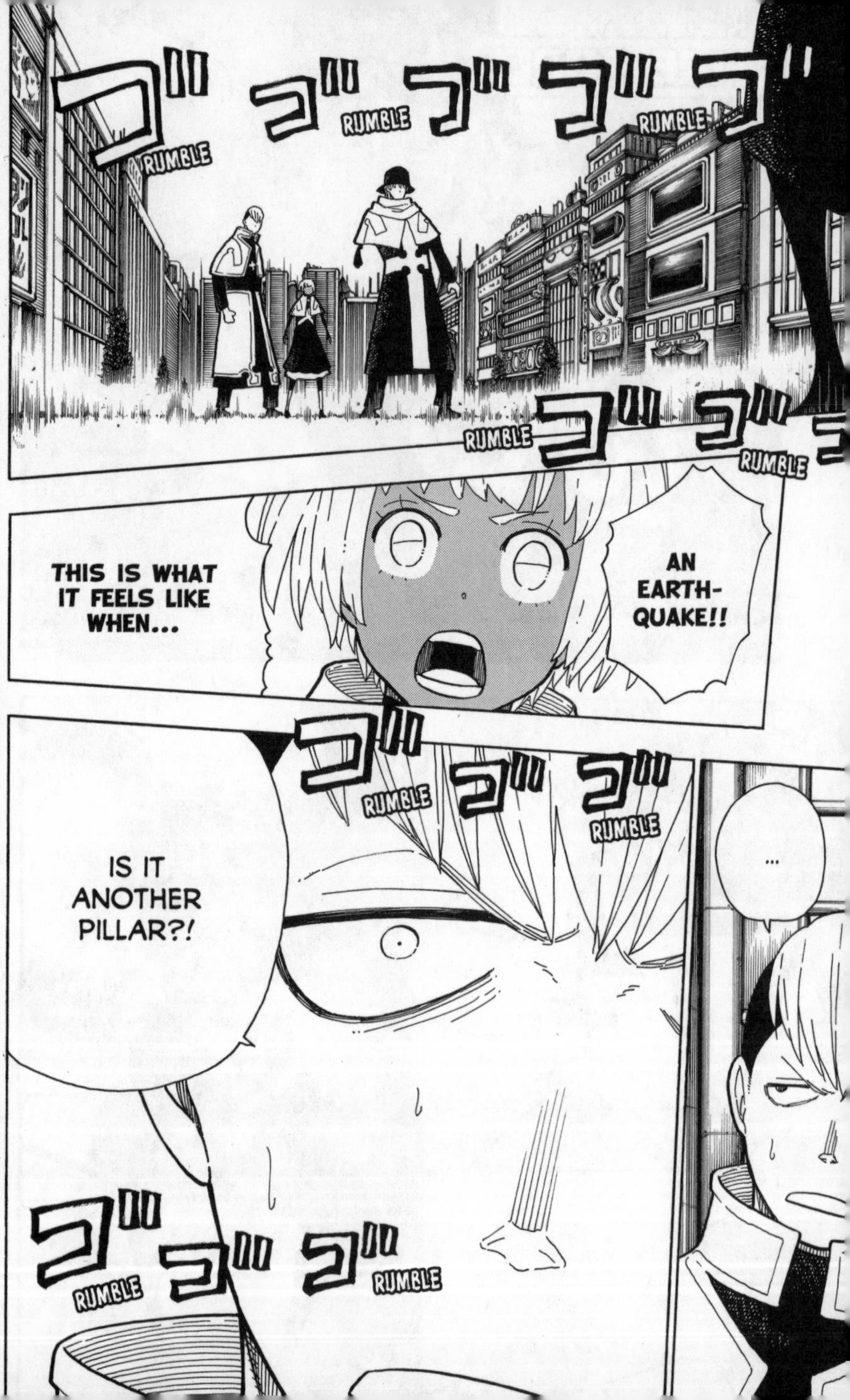
ゴゴゴゴゴ
RUMBLE
RUMBLE
RUMBLE
RUMBLE
RUMBLE
AN EARTH-QUAKE!!
THIS IS WHAT IT FEELS LIKE WHEN...
RUMBLE
RUMBLE
...
IS IT ANOTHER PILLAR?!
RUMBLE
RUMBLE

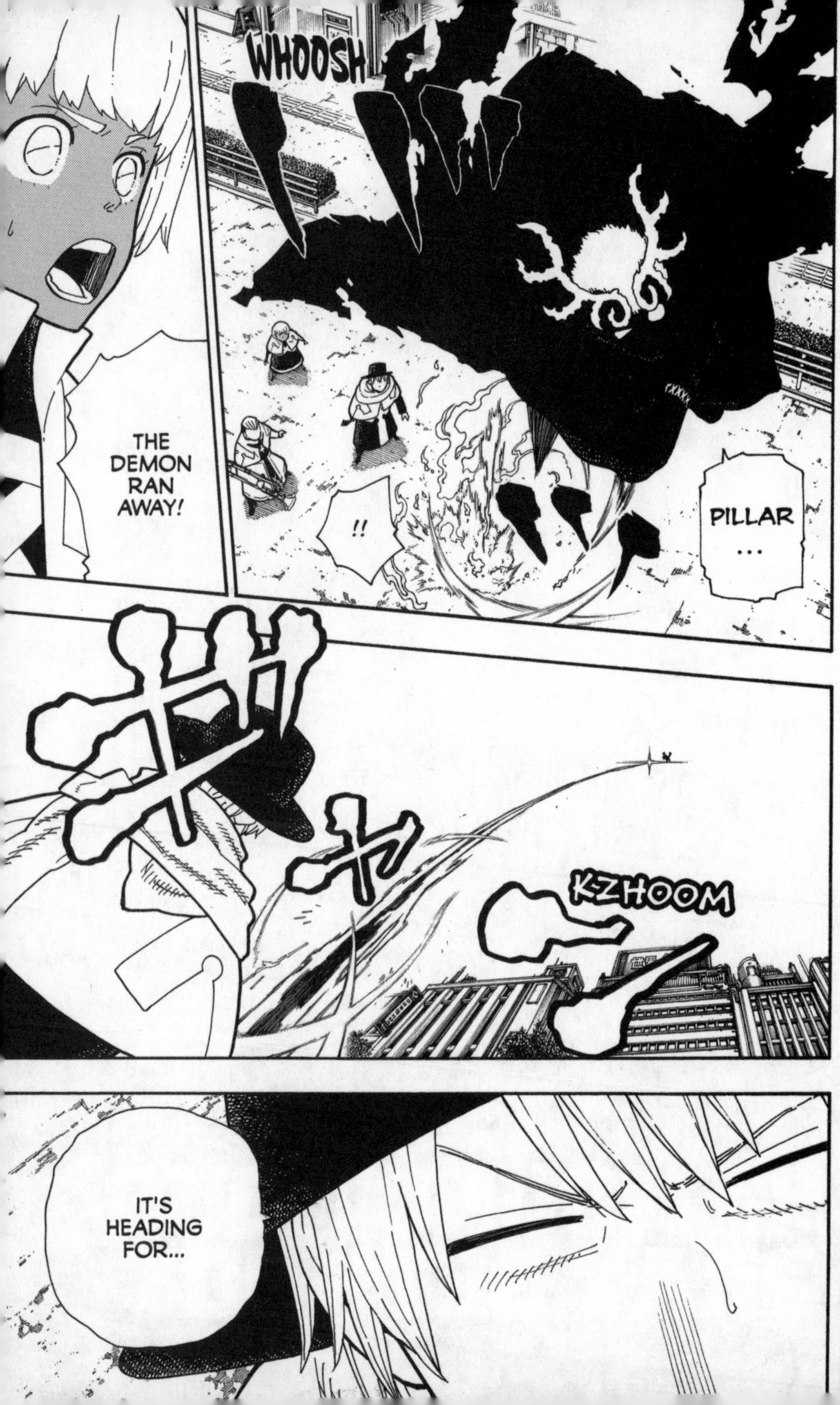
WHOOSH
PILLAR ...
!!
THE DEMON RAN AWAY!
K-ZHOOM
IT'S HEADING FOR...

ASAKUSA.

Sign: Shinjuku Theater

THE RAMBUNCTIOUS BRAT SETS OUT

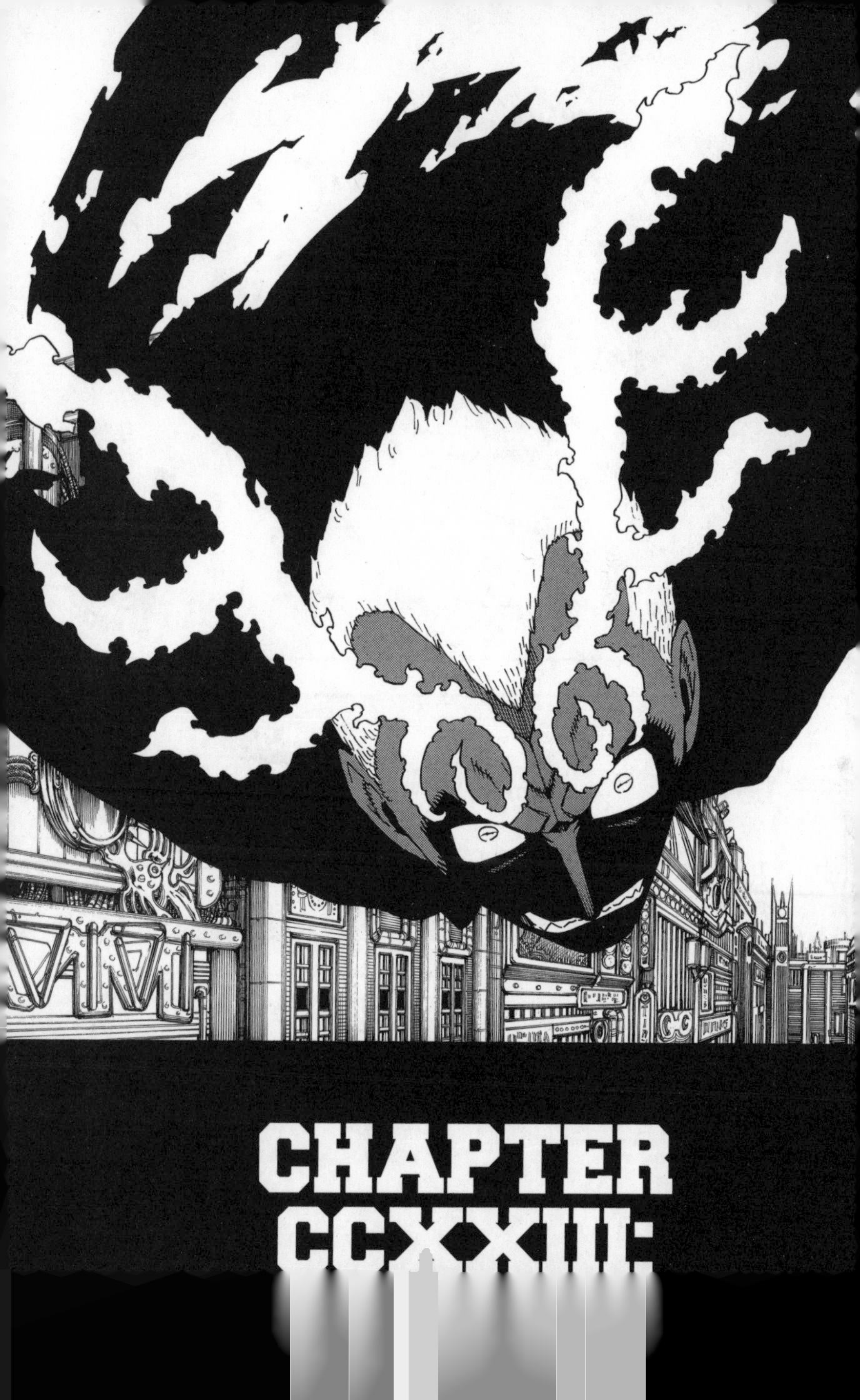

CHAPTER CCXXIII:

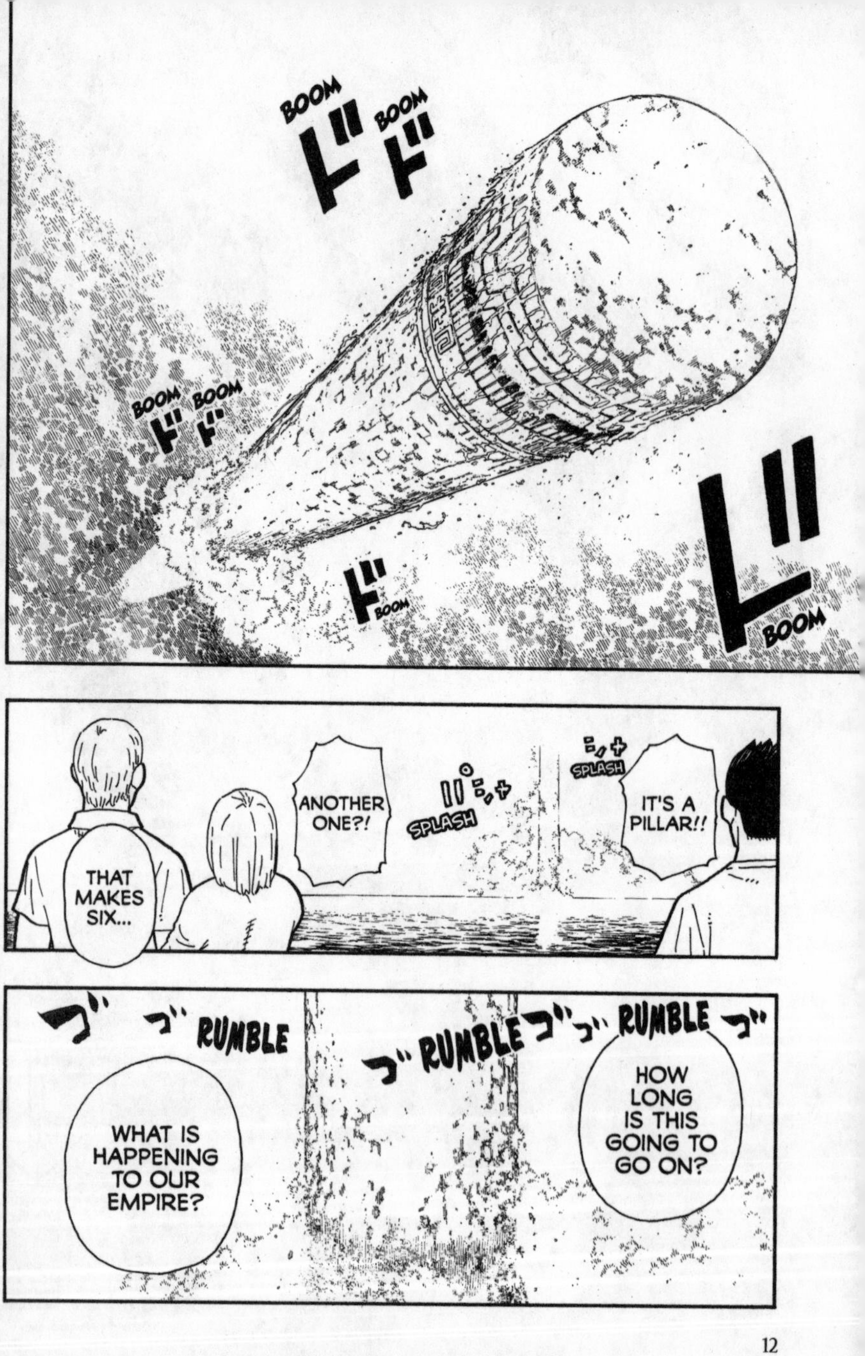
BOOM
BOOM
BOOM
BOOM
BOOM
BOOM
SPLASH
IT'S A PILLAR!!
SPLASH
ANOTHER ONE?!
THAT MAKES SIX...
RUMBLE
RUMBLE
HOW LONG IS THIS GOING TO GO ON?
RUMBLE
WHAT IS HAPPENING TO OUR EMPIRE?

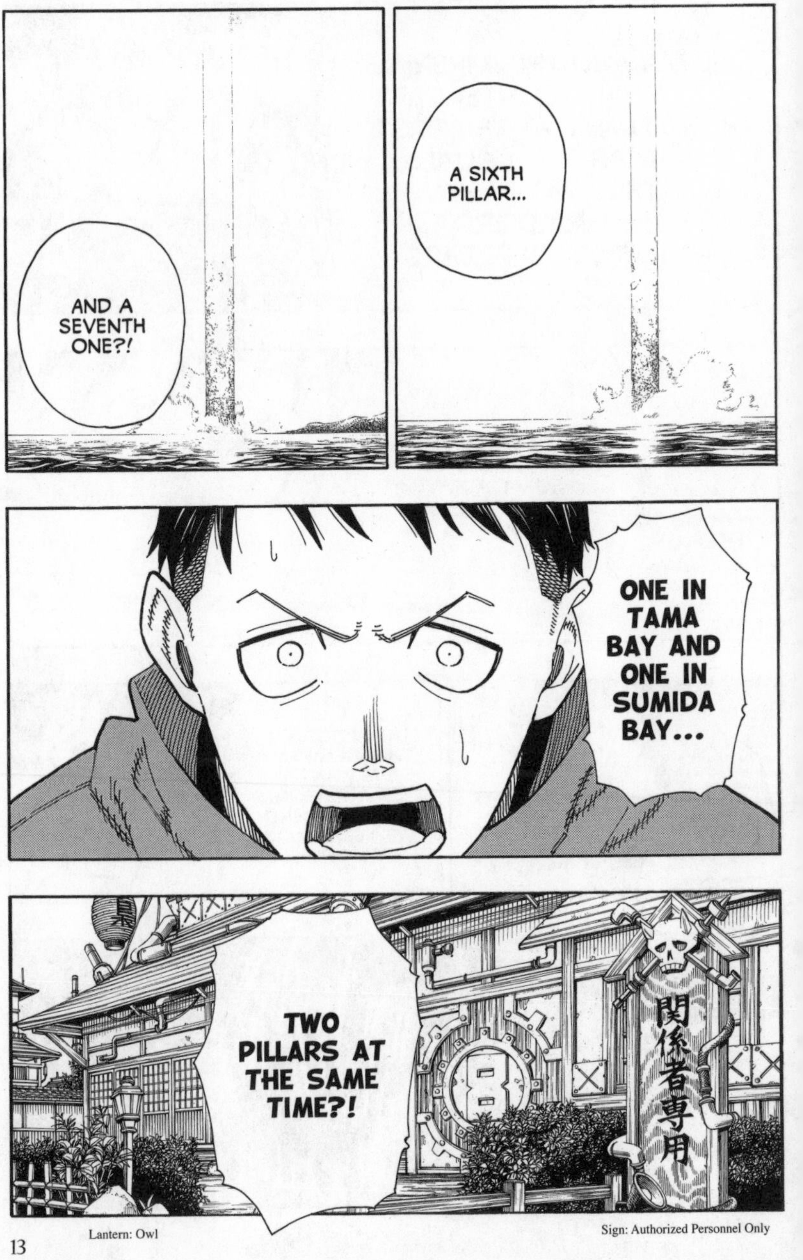
A SIXTH PILLAR...
AND A SEVENTH ONE?!
ONE IN TAMA BAY AND ONE IN SUMIDA BAY...
関係者専用
TWO PILLARS AT THE SAME TIME?!

Lantern: Owl

Sign: Authorized Personnel Only

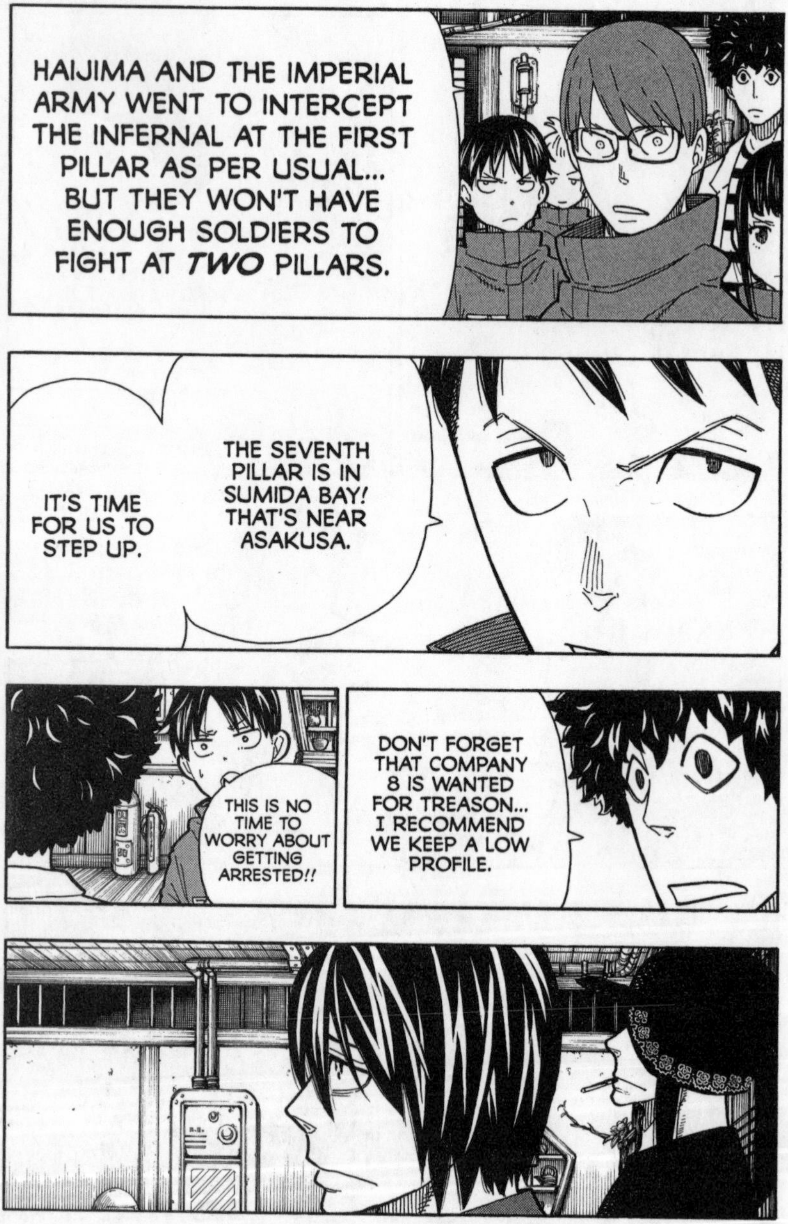
HAIJIMA AND THE IMPERIAL ARMY WENT TO INTERCEPT THE INFERNAL AT THE FIRST PILLAR AS PER USUAL... BUT THEY WON'T HAVE ENOUGH SOLDIERS TO FIGHT AT *TWO* PILLARS.
THE SEVENTH PILLAR IS IN SUMIDA BAY! THAT'S NEAR ASAKUSA.
IT'S TIME FOR US TO STEP UP.
DON'T FORGET THAT COMPANY 8 IS WANTED FOR TREASON... I RECOMMEND WE KEEP A LOW PROFILE.
THIS IS NO TIME TO WORRY ABOUT GETTING ARRESTED!!

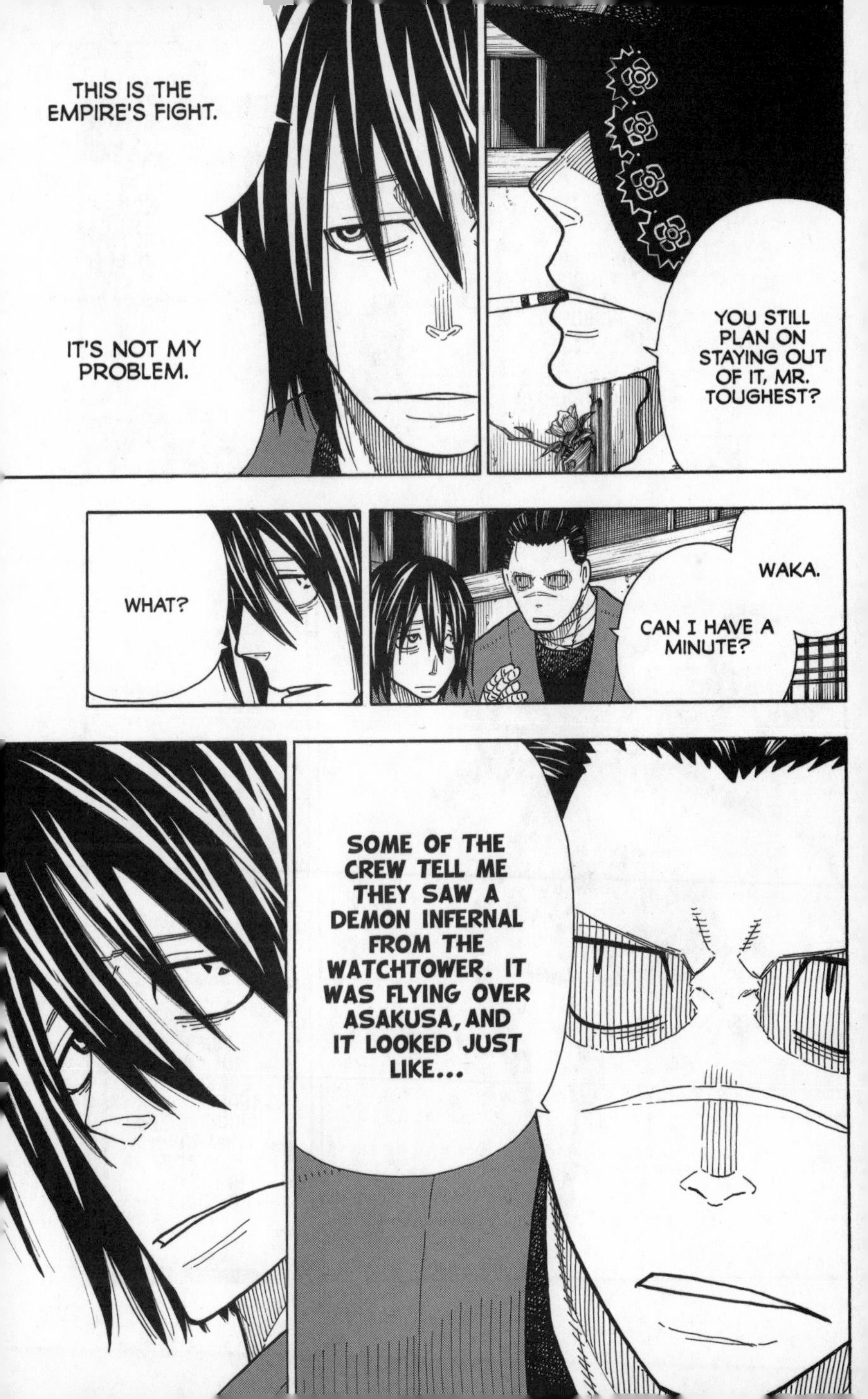
YOU STILL PLAN ON STAYING OUT OF IT, MR. TOUGHEST?
THIS IS THE EMPIRE'S FIGHT.
IT'S NOT MY PROBLEM.
WAKA.
CAN I HAVE A MINUTE?
WHAT?
SOME OF THE CREW TELL ME THEY SAW A DEMON INFERNAL FROM THE WATCHTOWER. IT WAS FLYING OVER ASAKUSA, AND IT LOOKED JUST LIKE...

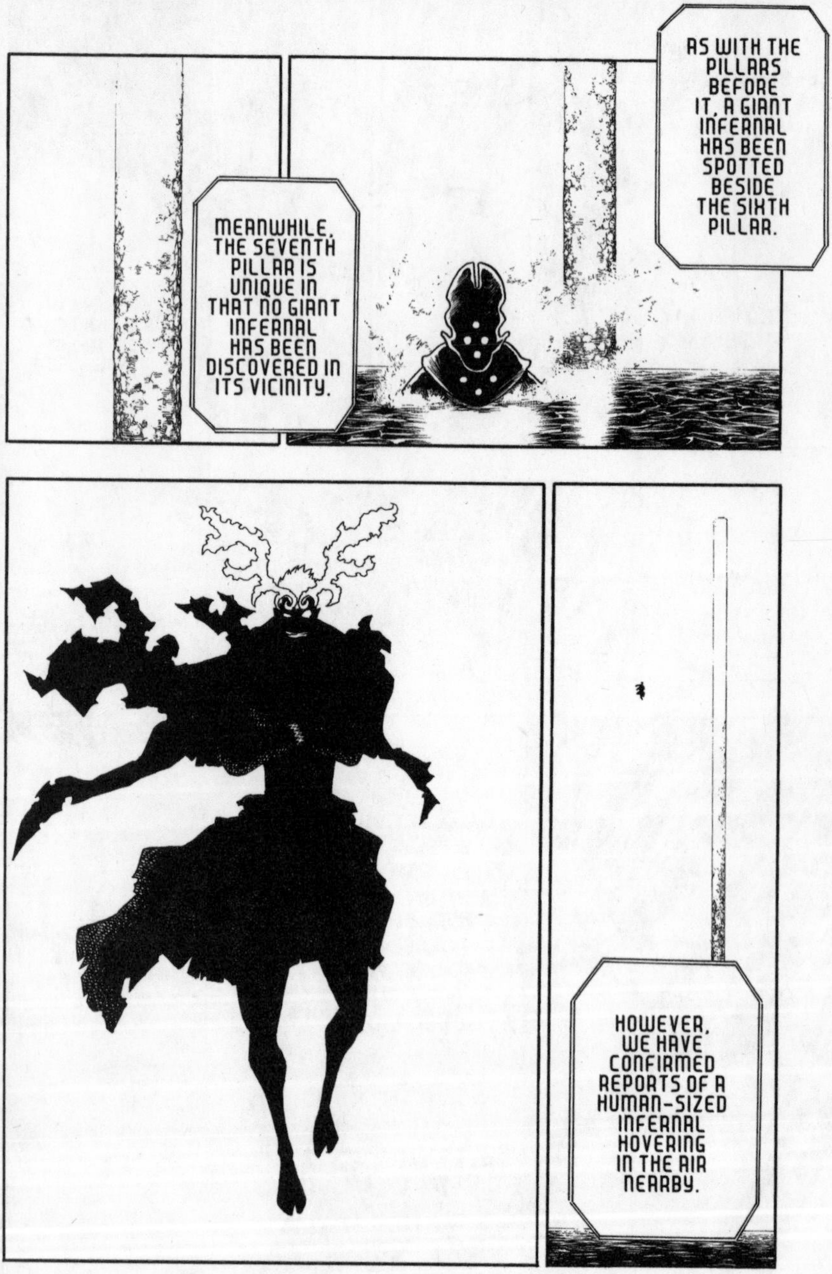
AS WITH THE PILLARS BEFORE IT, A GIANT INFERNAL HAS BEEN SPOTTED BESIDE THE SIXTH PILLAR.
MEANWHILE, THE SEVENTH PILLAR IS UNIQUE IN THAT NO GIANT INFERNAL HAS BEEN DISCOVERED IN ITS VICINITY.
HOWEVER, WE HAVE CONFIRMED REPORTS OF A HUMAN-SIZED INFERNAL HOVERING IN THE AIR NEARBY.

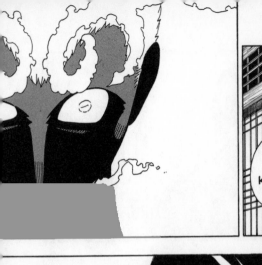

BENI...

...

I KNOW.

THAT'S THE OLD BOSS.

OR IS SOME FOX PLAYING A TRICK ON ME?

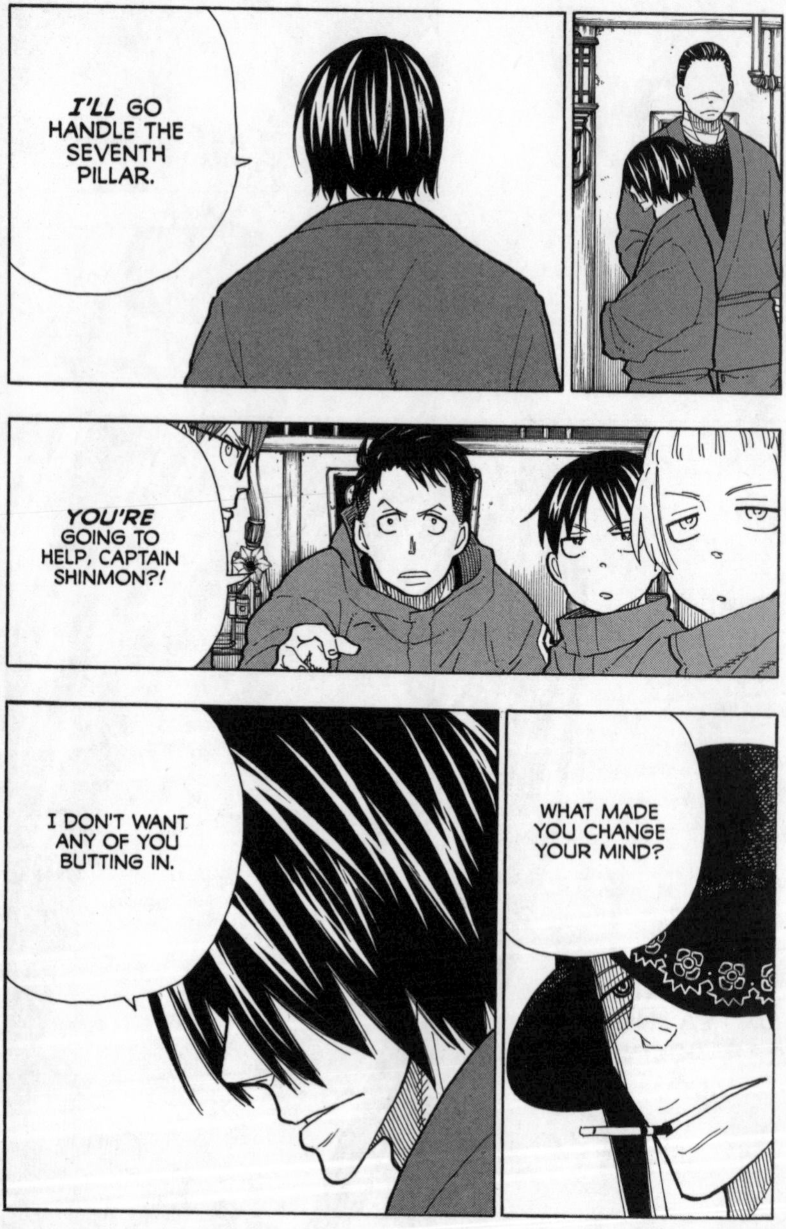
I'LL GO HANDLE THE SEVENTH PILLAR.
YOU'RE GOING TO HELP, CAPTAIN SHINMON?!
WHAT MADE YOU CHANGE YOUR MIND?
I DON'T WANT ANY OF YOU BUTTING IN.

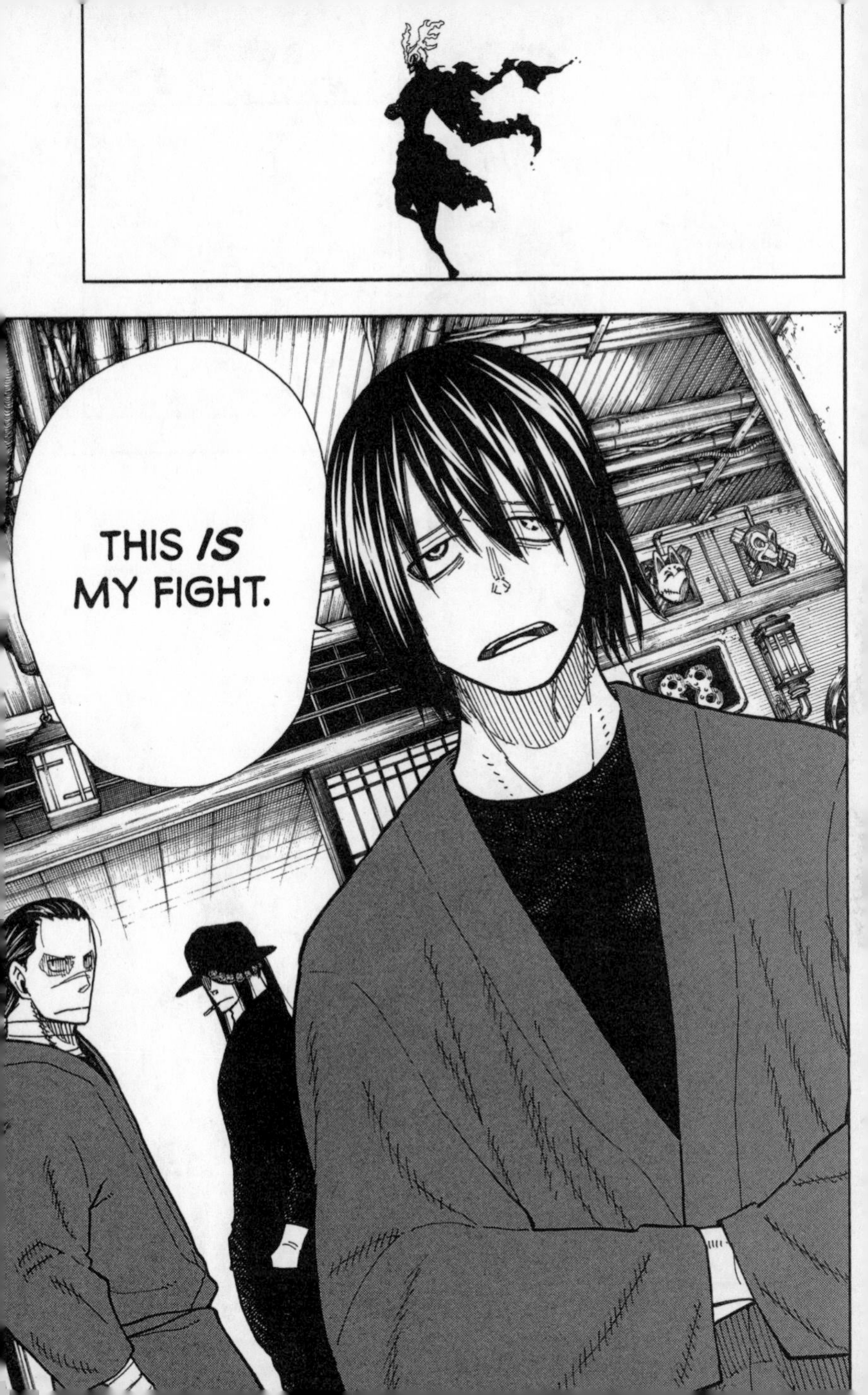
THIS *IS* MY FIGHT.

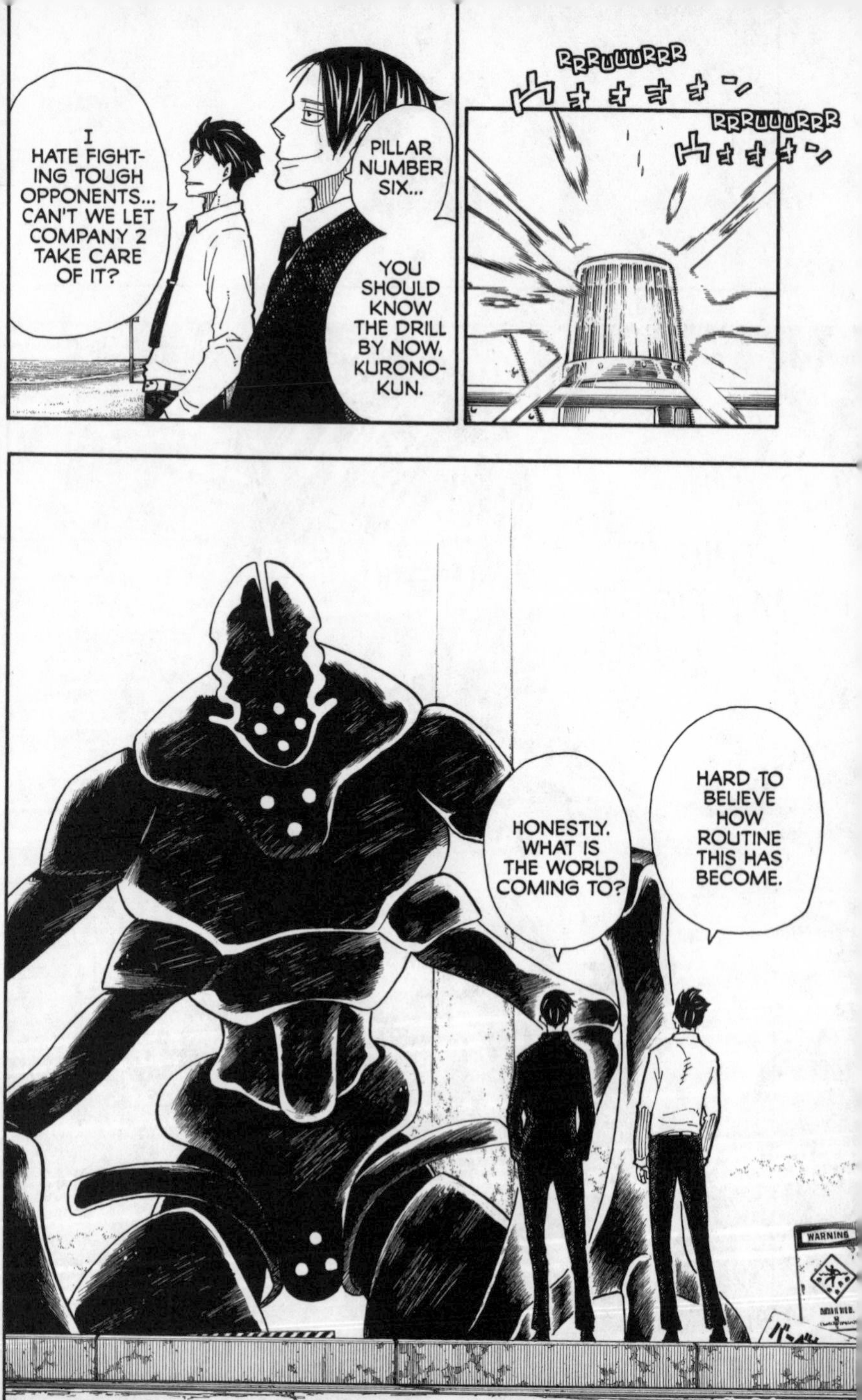
RRRUUUURRR
RRRUUUURRR
PILLAR NUMBER SIX...
I HATE FIGHTING TOUGH OPPONENTS... CAN'T WE LET COMPANY 2 TAKE CARE OF IT?
YOU SHOULD KNOW THE DRILL BY NOW, KURONO-KUN.
HARD TO BELIEVE HOW ROUTINE THIS HAS BECOME.
HONESTLY. WHAT IS THE WORLD COMING TO?
WARNING
Sign: Barbecue

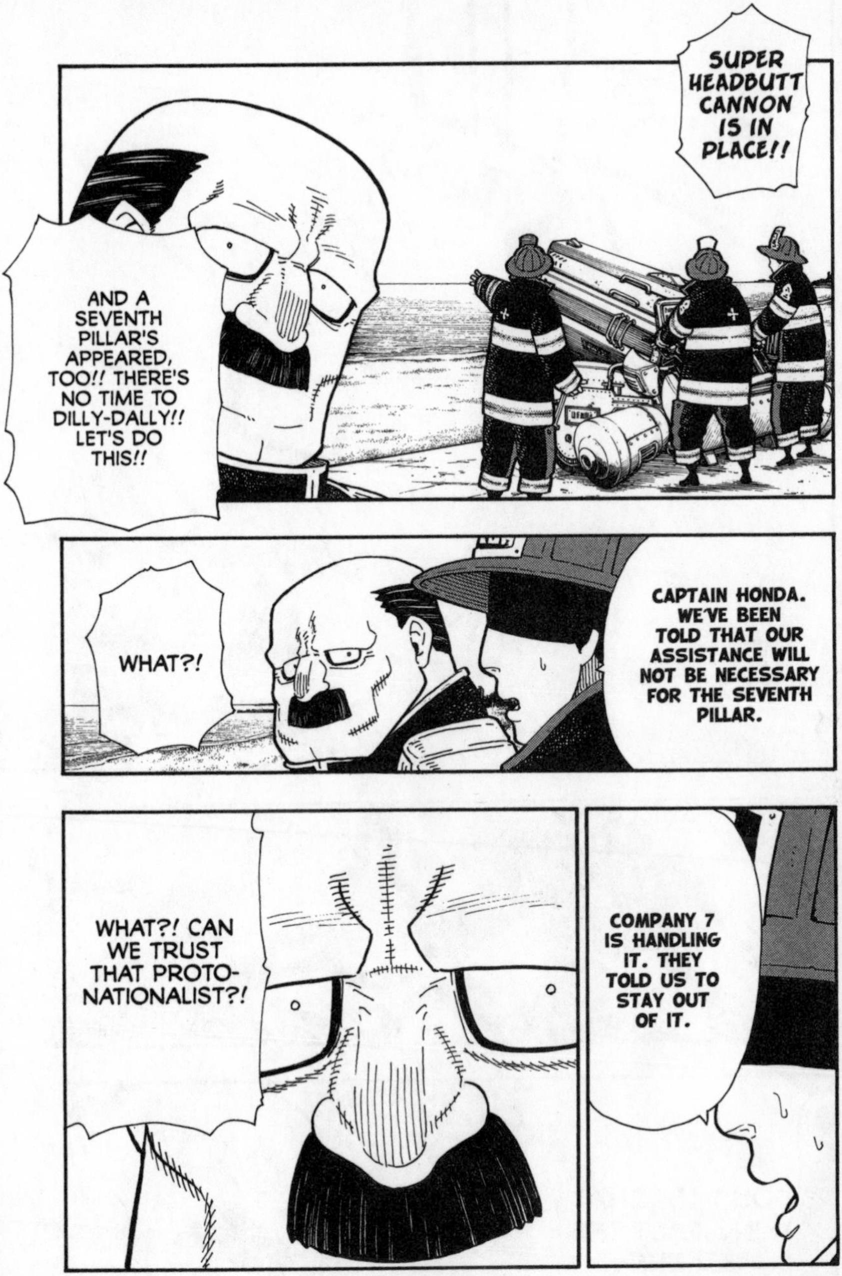
SUPER HEADBUTT CANNON IS IN PLACE!!
AND A SEVENTH PILLAR'S APPEARED, TOO!! THERE'S NO TIME TO DILLY-DALLY!! LET'S DO THIS!!
CAPTAIN HONDA. WE'VE BEEN TOLD THAT OUR ASSISTANCE WILL NOT BE NECESSARY FOR THE SEVENTH PILLAR.
WHAT?!
COMPANY 7 IS HANDLING IT. THEY TOLD US TO STAY OUT OF IT.
WHAT?! CAN WE TRUST THAT PROTO-NATIONALIST?!

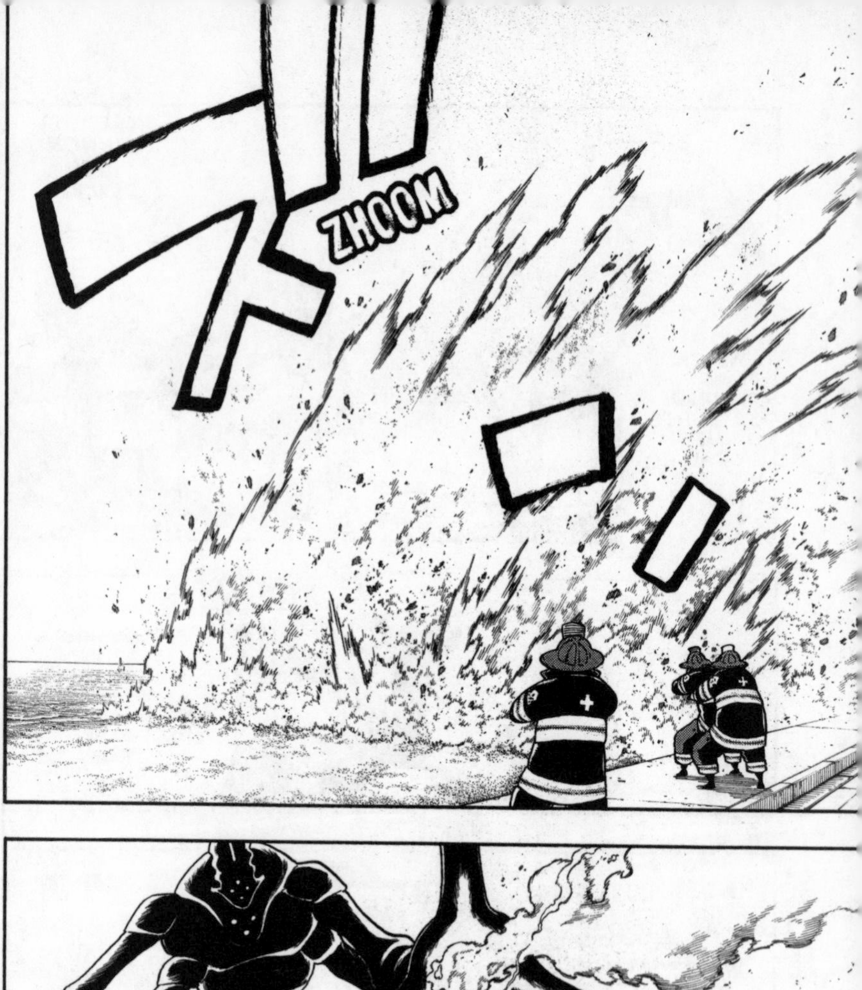
ZHOOM
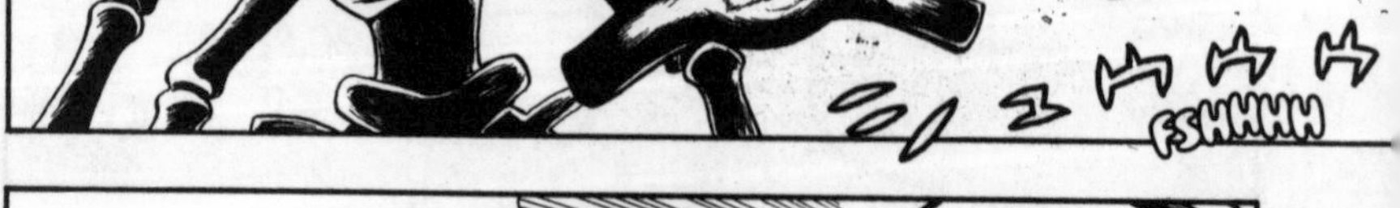
FSHHHH
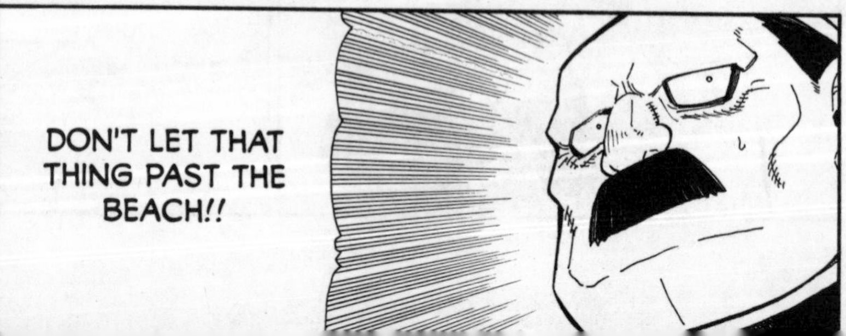
DON'T LET THAT THING PAST THE BEACH!!

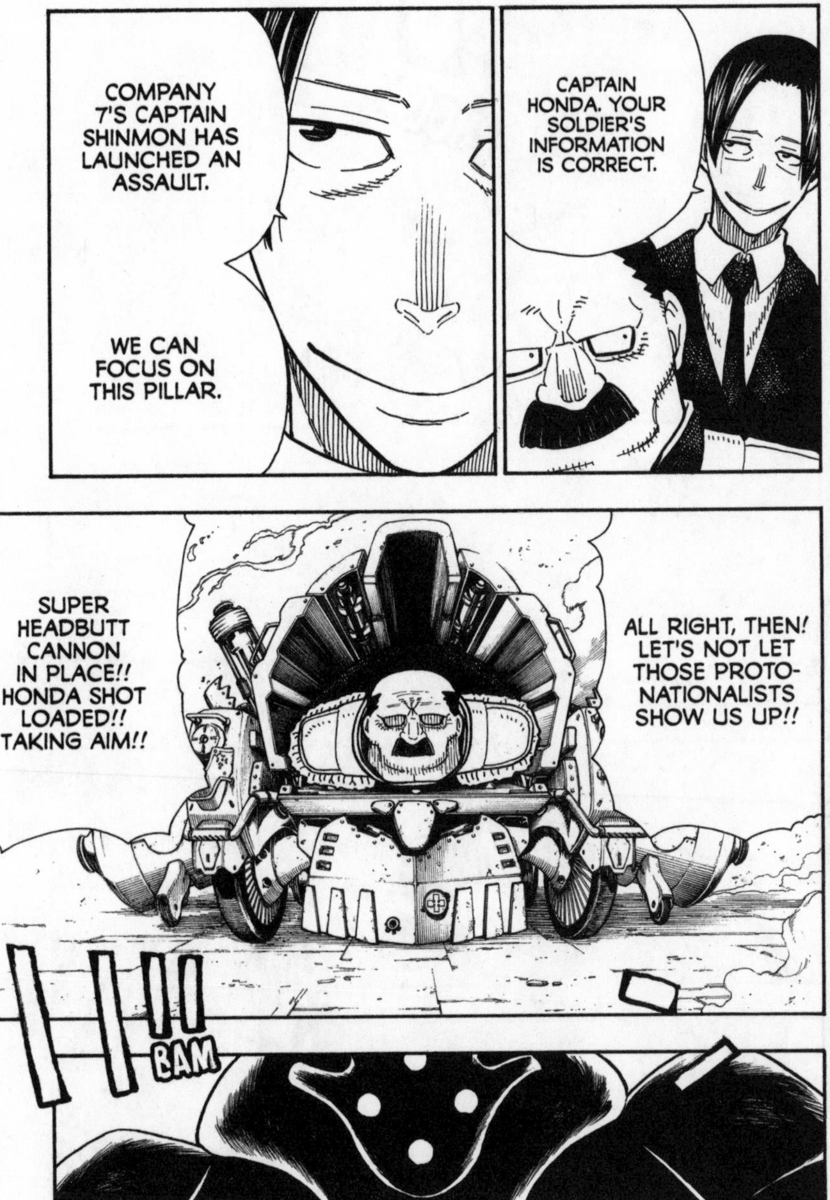
CAPTAIN HONDA. YOUR SOLDIER'S INFORMATION IS CORRECT.
COMPANY 7'S CAPTAIN SHINMON HAS LAUNCHED AN ASSAULT.
WE CAN FOCUS ON THIS PILLAR.
ALL RIGHT, THEN! LET'S NOT LET THOSE PROTO-NATIONALISTS SHOW US UP!!
SUPER HEADBUTT CANNON IN PLACE!! HONDA SHOT LOADED!! TAKING AIM!!
BAM

KA-

ZHOOM

THMP THMP THMP THMP

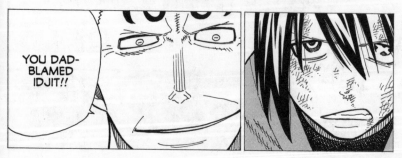
YOU DAD-
BLAMED
IDJIT!!

24

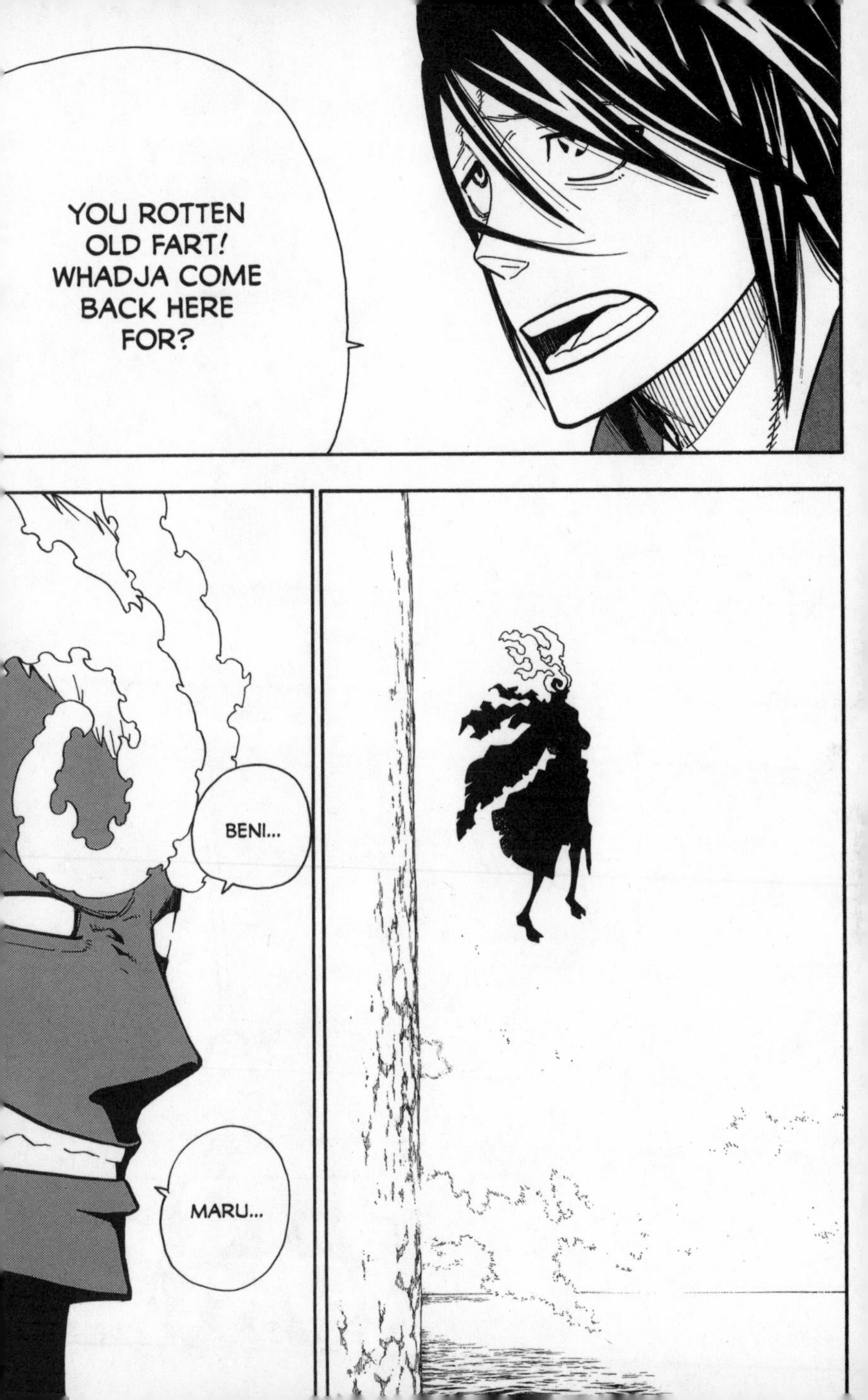

YOU ROTTEN OLD FART! WHADJA COME BACK HERE FOR?
BENI...
MARU...

FIRE FORCE

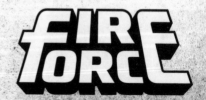

CHAPTER CCXXIV: THE SUN AND THE MOON

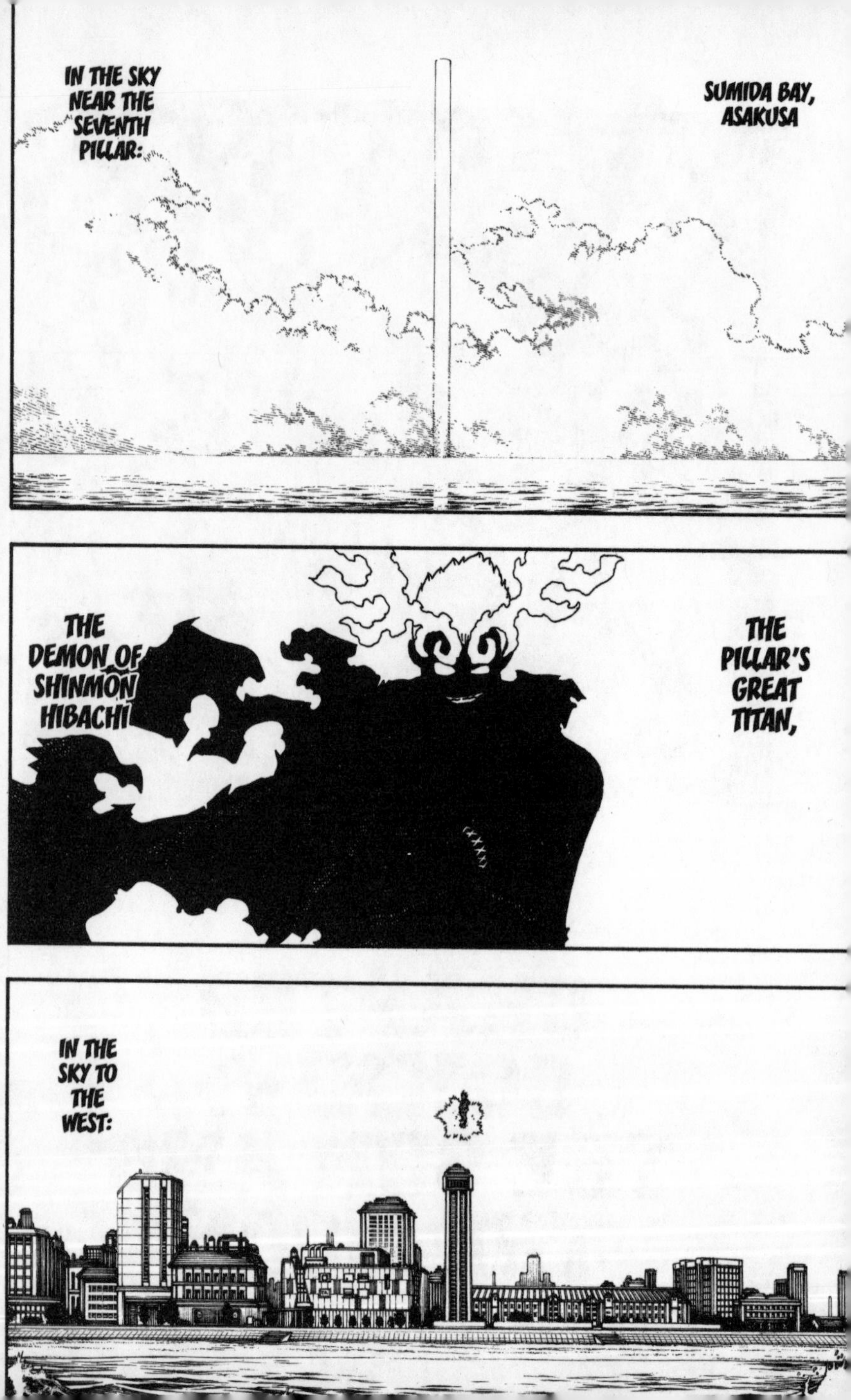
SUMIDA BAY, ASAKUSA
IN THE SKY NEAR THE SEVENTH PILLAR:
THE PILLAR'S GREAT TITAN,
THE DEMON OF SHINMON HIBACHI
IN THE SKY TO THE WEST:

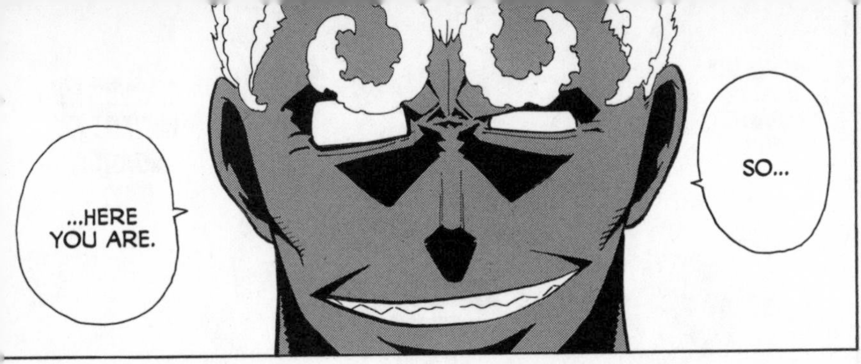
SO...
...HERE YOU ARE.
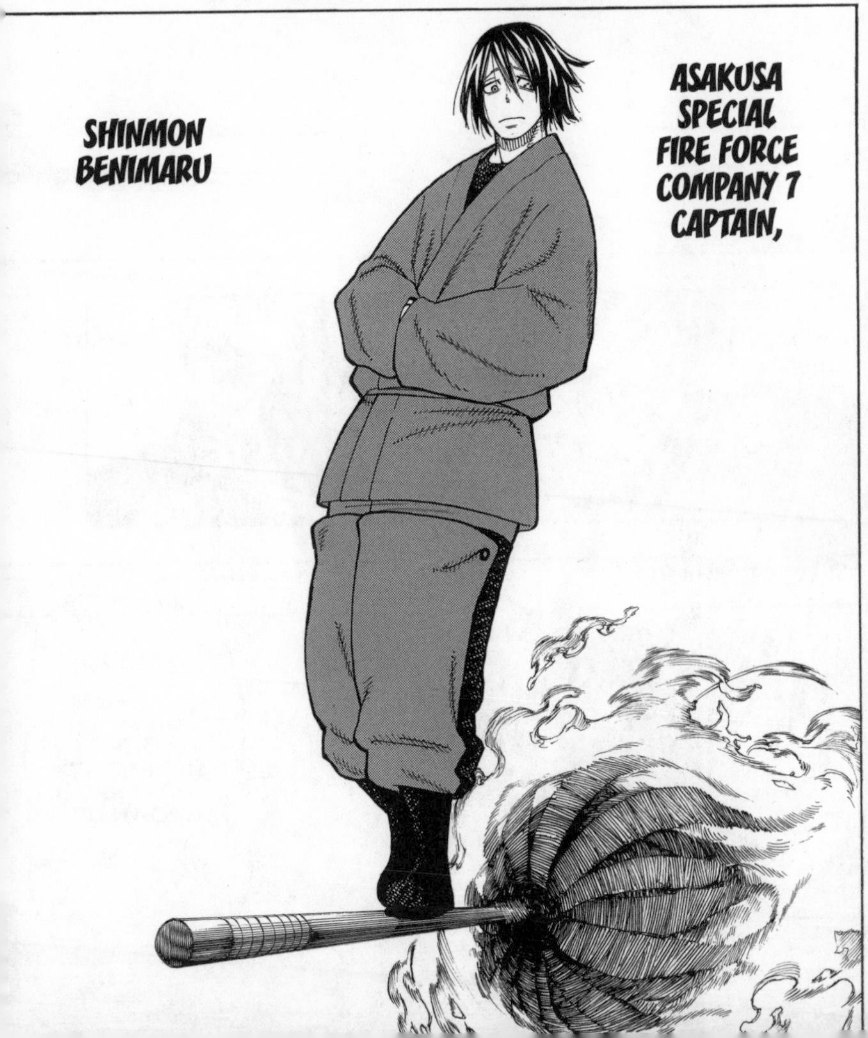
ASAKUSA SPECIAL FIRE FORCE COMPANY 7 CAPTAIN,
SHINMON BENIMARU

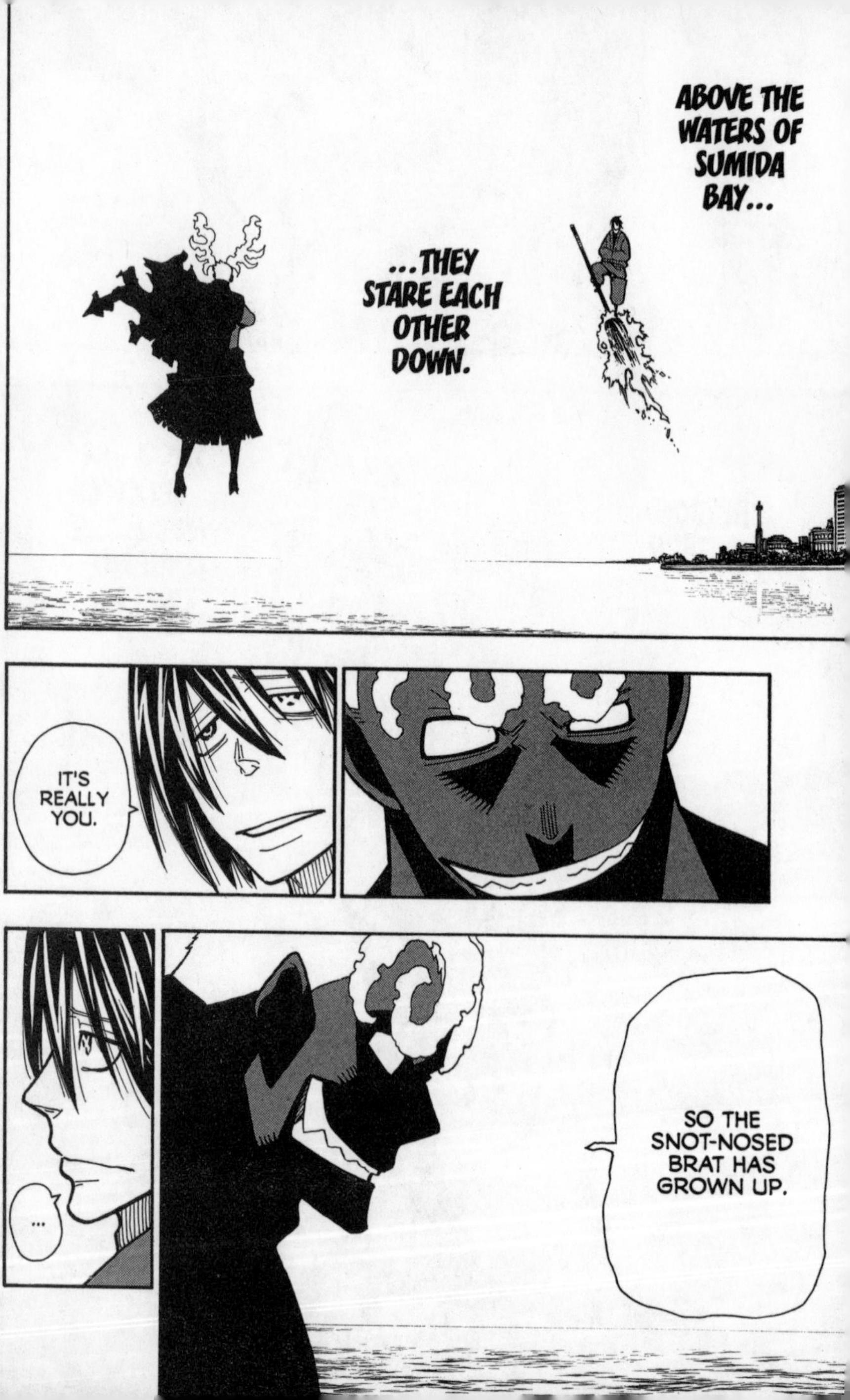
ABOVE THE WATERS OF SUMIDA BAY...
...THEY STARE EACH OTHER DOWN.
IT'S REALLY YOU.
SO THE SNOT-NOSED BRAT HAS GROWN UP.
...

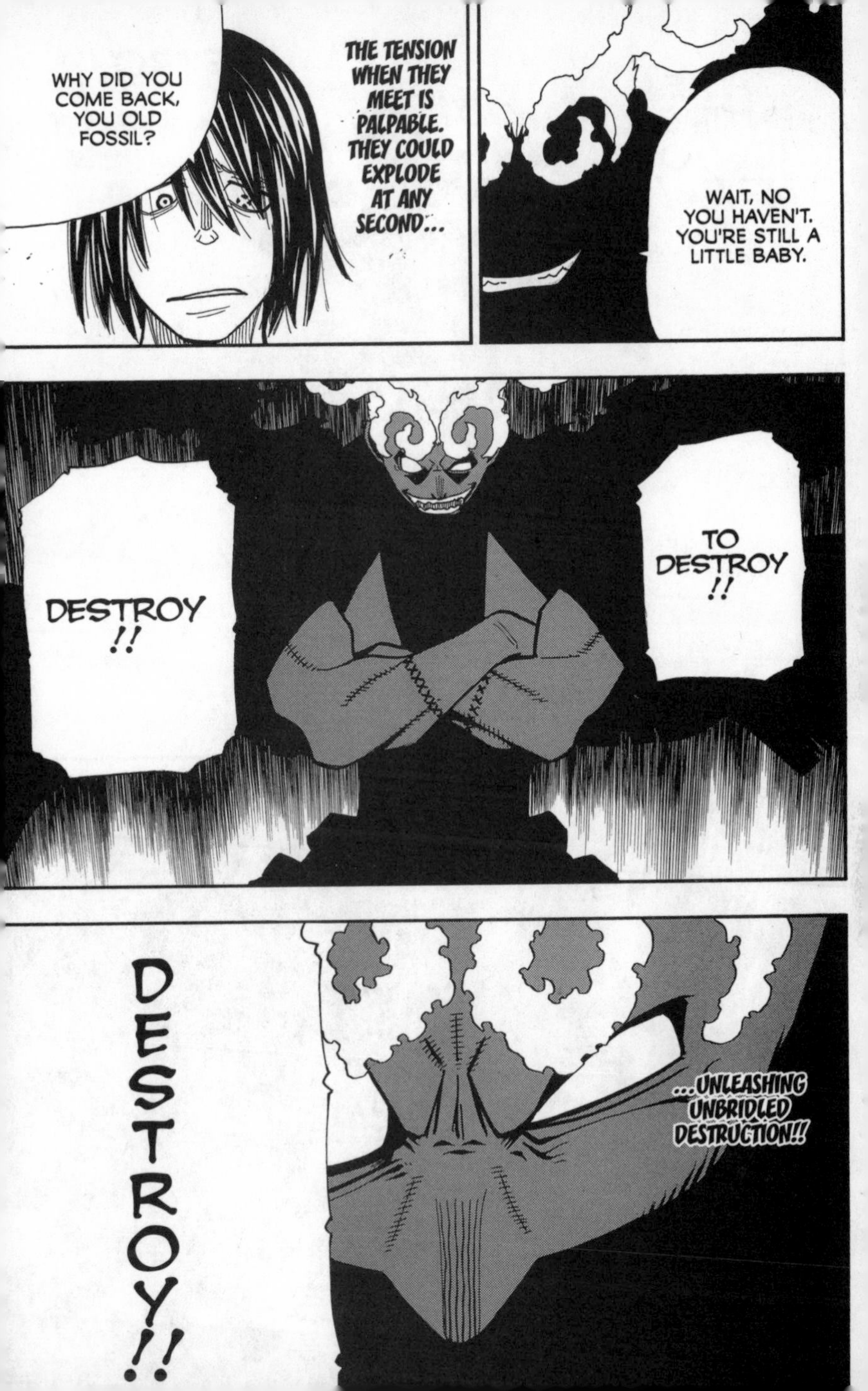
WAIT, NO YOU HAVEN'T. YOU'RE STILL A LITTLE BABY.
THE TENSION WHEN THEY MEET IS PALPABLE. THEY COULD EXPLODE AT ANY SECOND...
WHY DID YOU COME BACK, YOU OLD FOSSIL?
TO DESTROY!!
DESTROY!!
...UNLEASHING UNBRIDLED DESTRUCTION!!
DESTROY!!

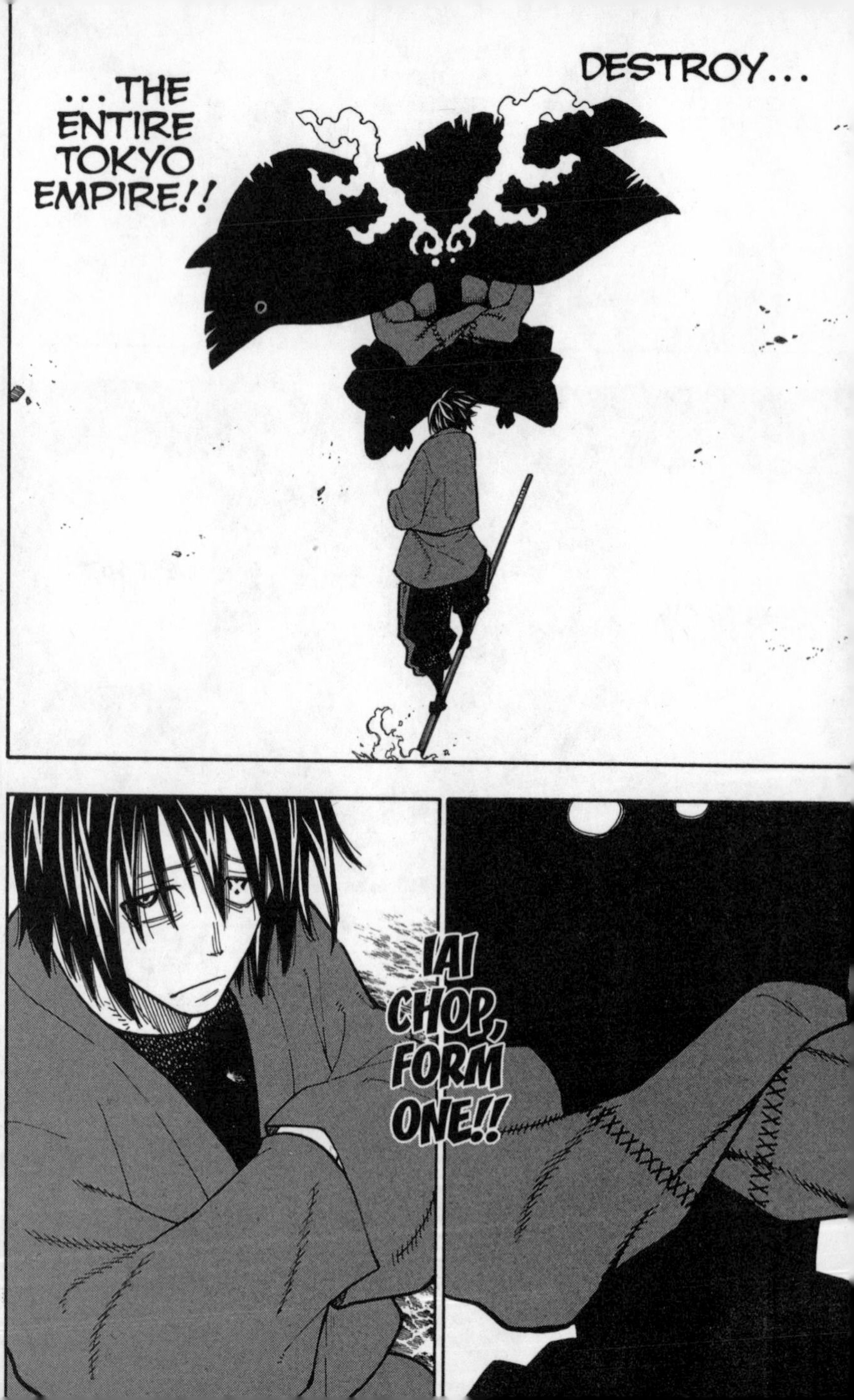
DESTROY...
...THE ENTIRE TOKYO EMPIRE!!
IAI CHOP, FORM ONE!!

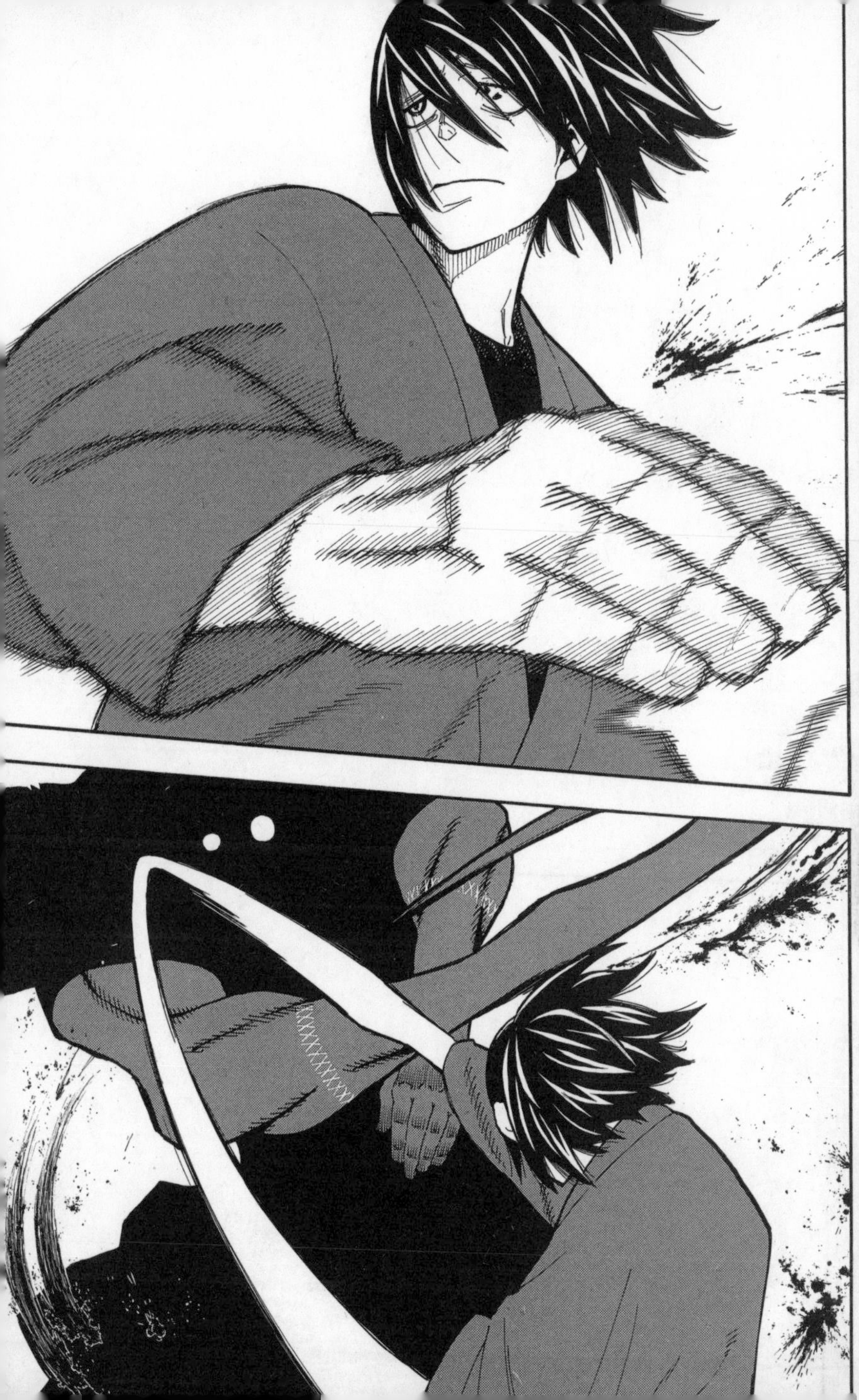

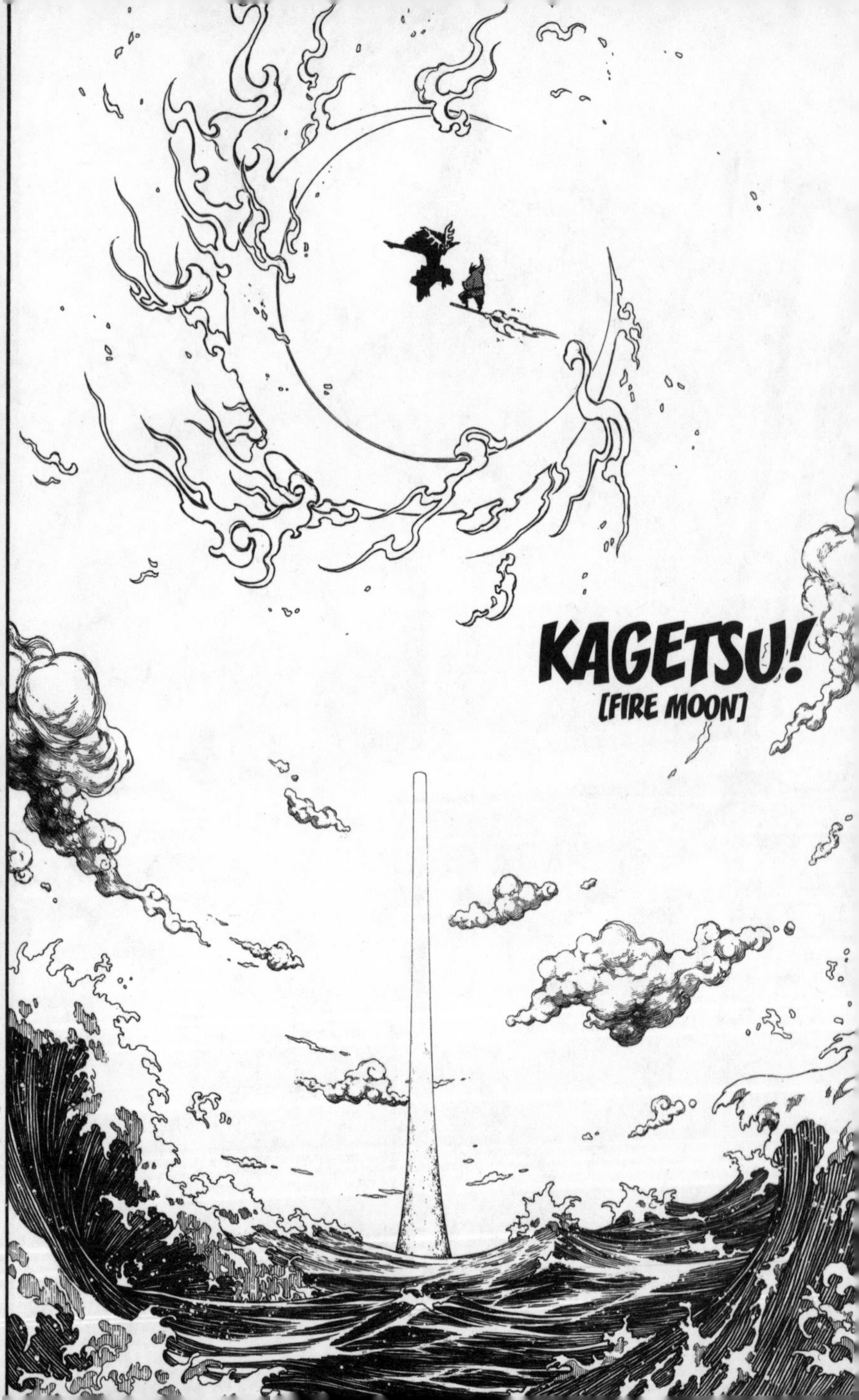
KAGETSU!
[FIRE MOON]

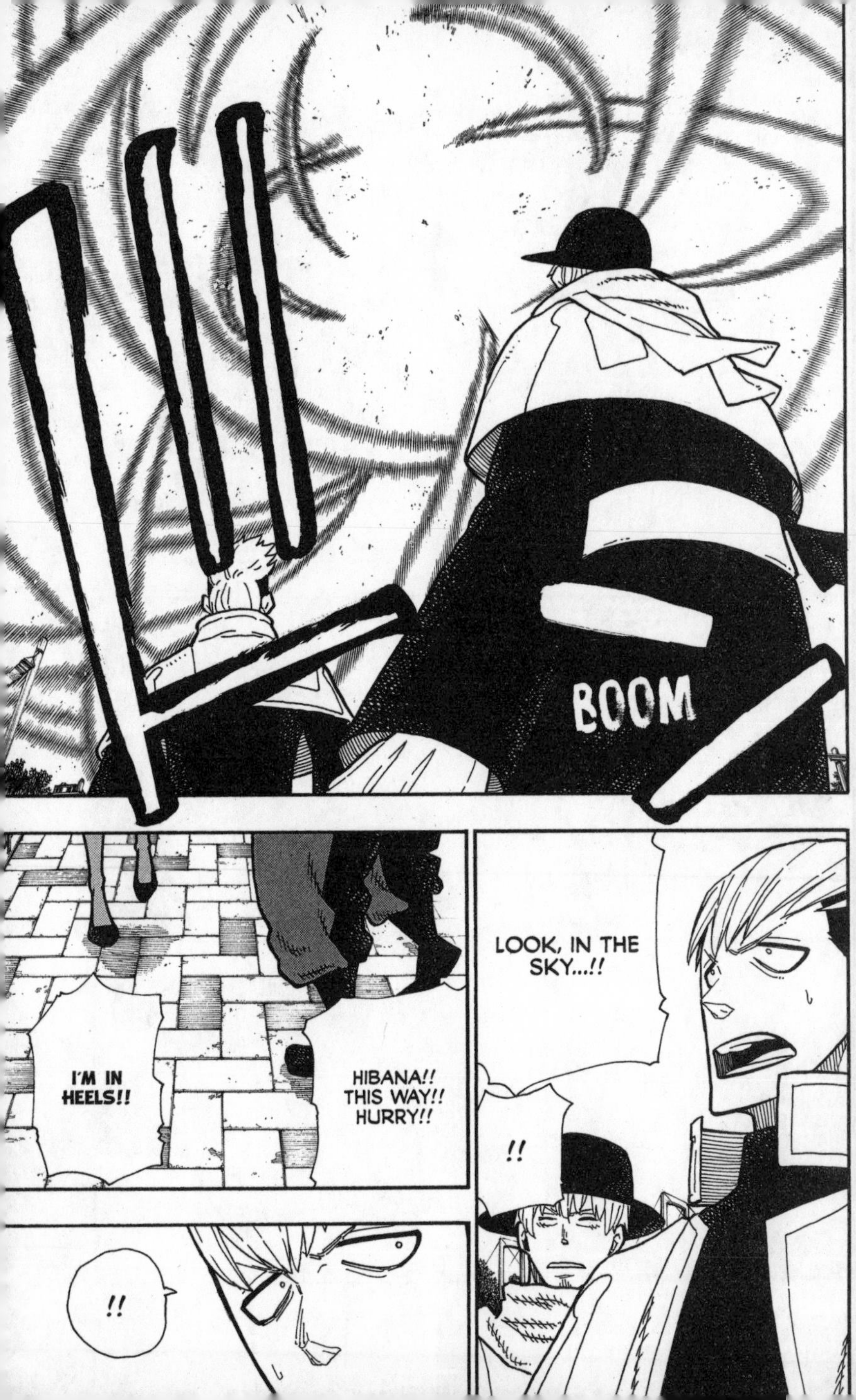
BOOM
LOOK, IN THE SKY...!!
!!
HIBANA!! THIS WAY!! HURRY!!
I'M IN HEELS!!
!!

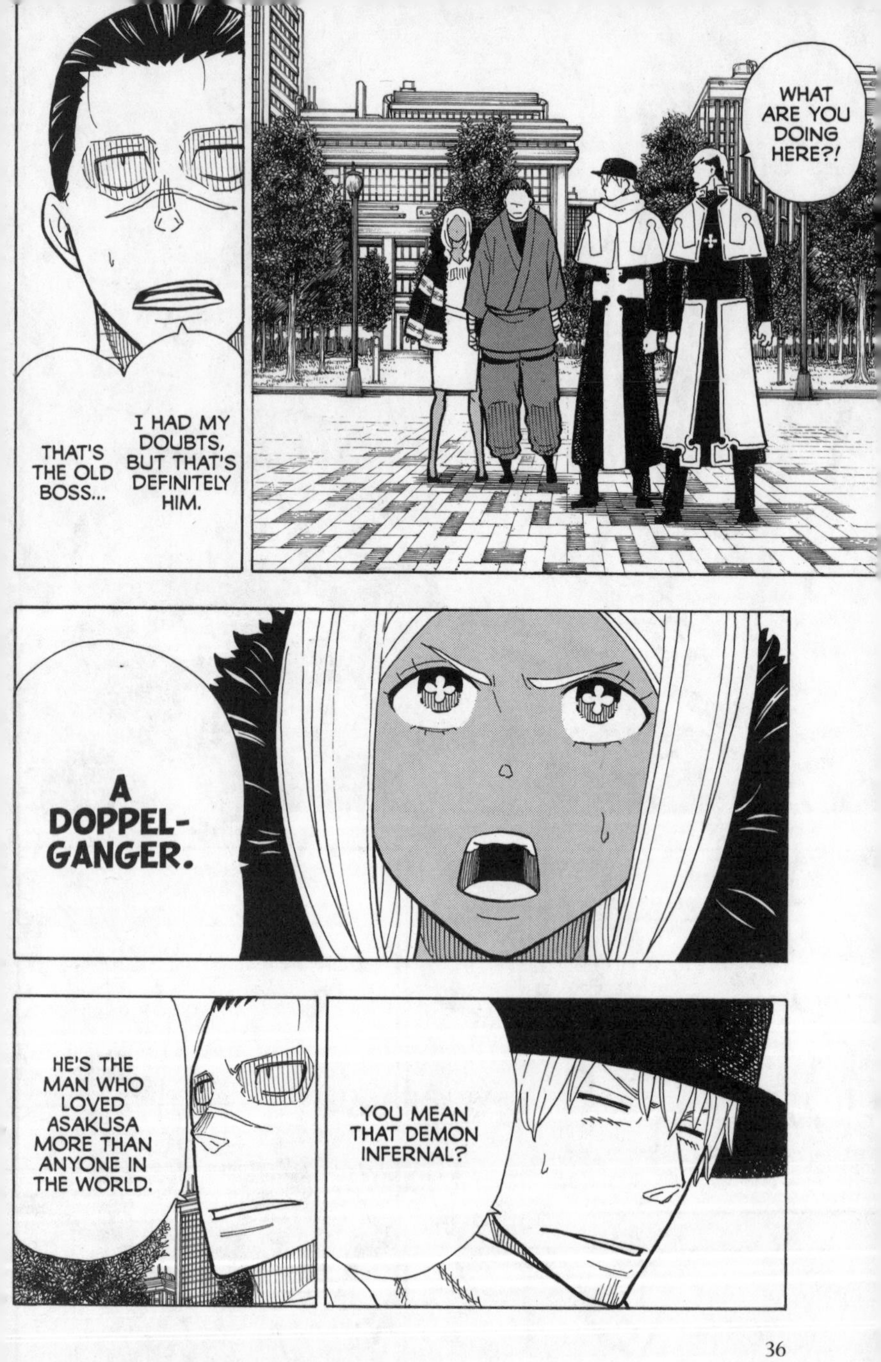
WHAT ARE YOU DOING HERE?!
I HAD MY DOUBTS, BUT THAT'S DEFINITELY HIM.
THAT'S THE OLD BOSS...
A DOPPEL-GANGER.
YOU MEAN THAT DEMON INFERNAL?
HE'S THE MAN WHO LOVED ASAKUSA MORE THAN ANYONE IN THE WORLD.

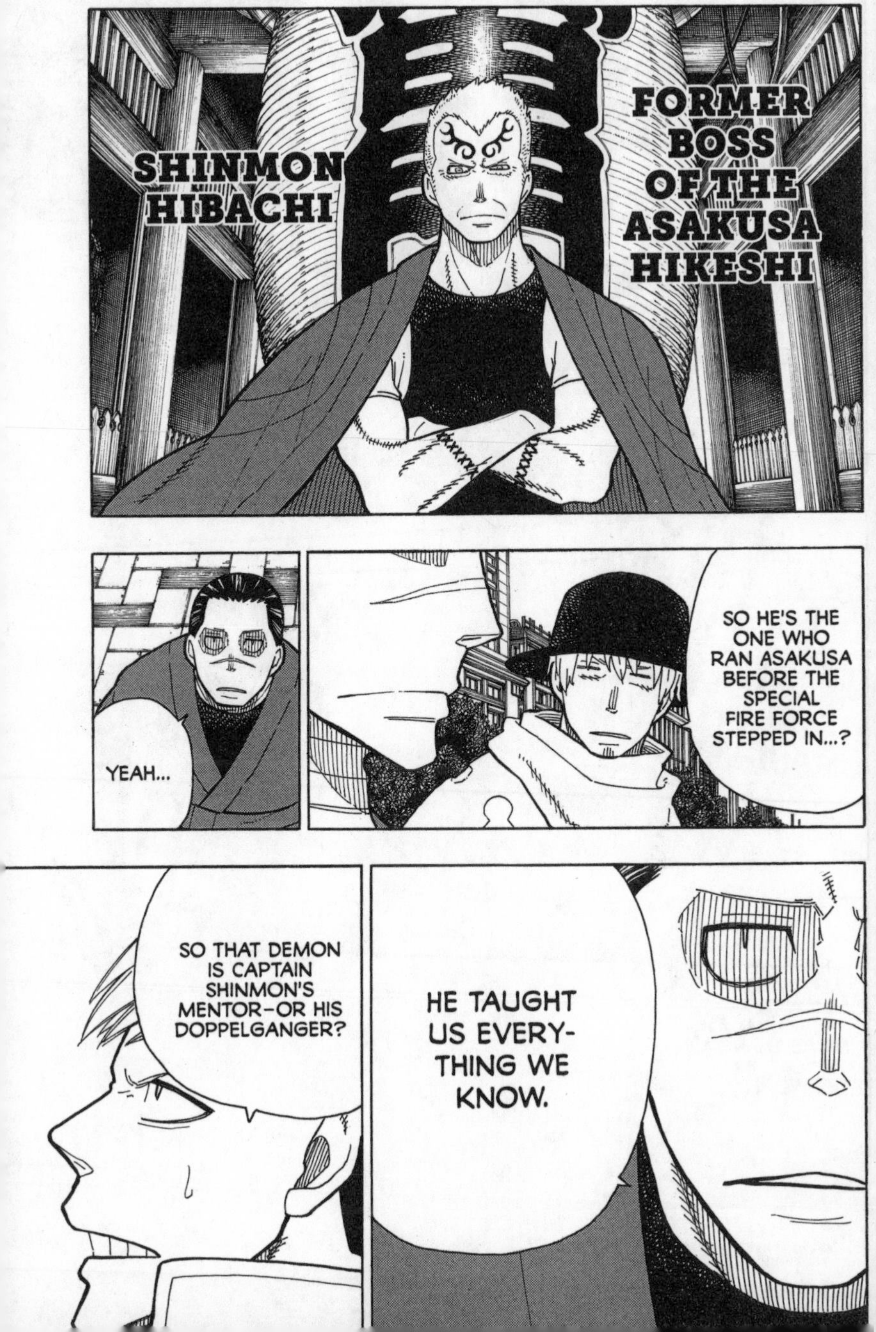
FORMER BOSS OF THE ASAKUSA HIKESHI
SHINMON HIBACHI
SO HE'S THE ONE WHO RAN ASAKUSA BEFORE THE SPECIAL FIRE FORCE STEPPED IN...?
YEAH...
HE TAUGHT US EVERY-THING WE KNOW.
SO THAT DEMON IS CAPTAIN SHINMON'S MENTOR–OR HIS DOPPELGANGER?

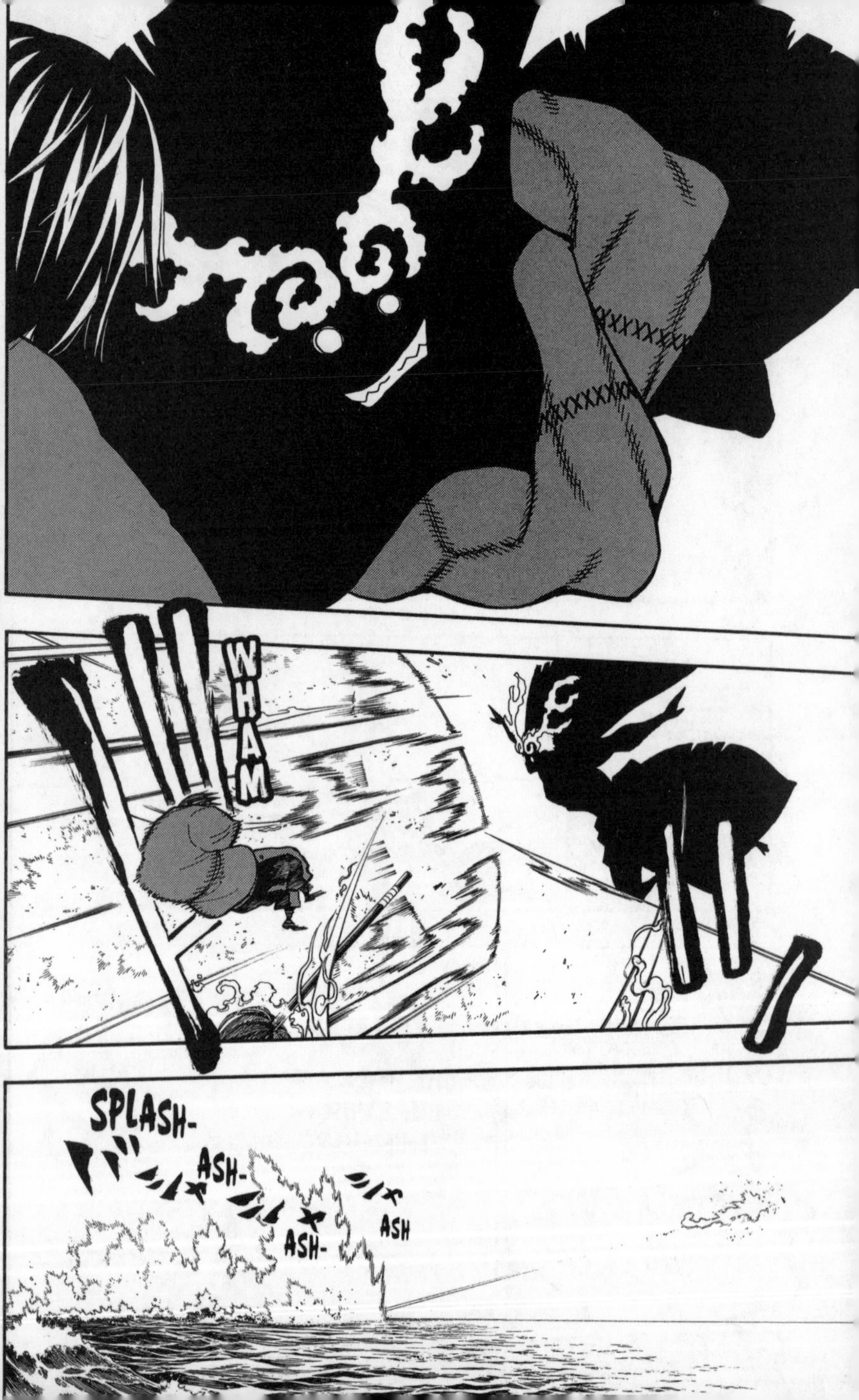
WHAM
SPLASH-
ASH-
ASH-
ASH

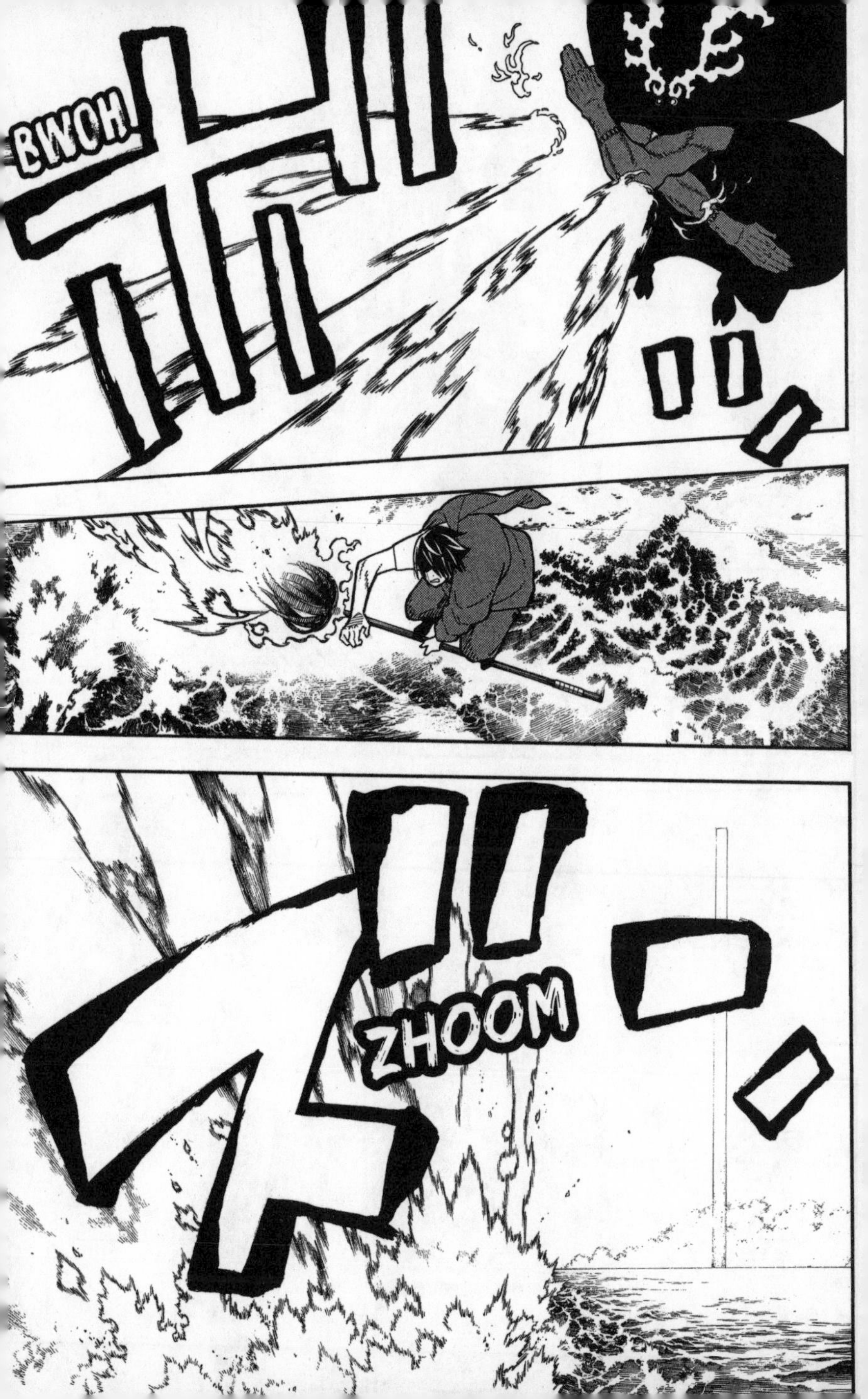
BWOH
ZHOOM

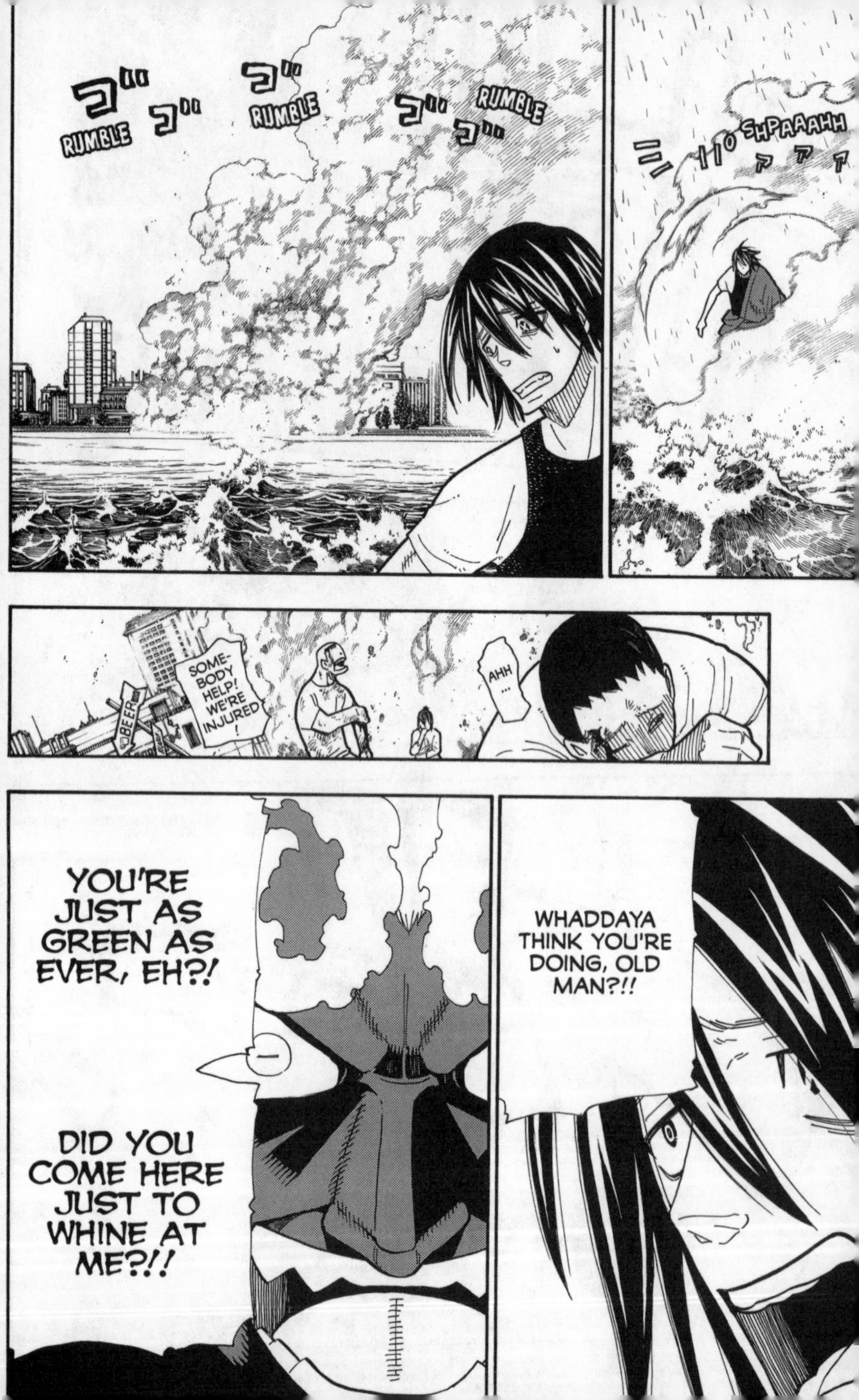
SHPAAAHH
RUMBLE
RUMBLE
RUMBLE
AHH ...
SOME-BODY HELP! WE'RE INJURED!
BEER
WHADDAYA THINK YOU'RE DOING, OLD MAN?!!
YOU'RE JUST AS GREEN AS EVER, EH?!
DID YOU COME HERE JUST TO WHINE AT ME?!!

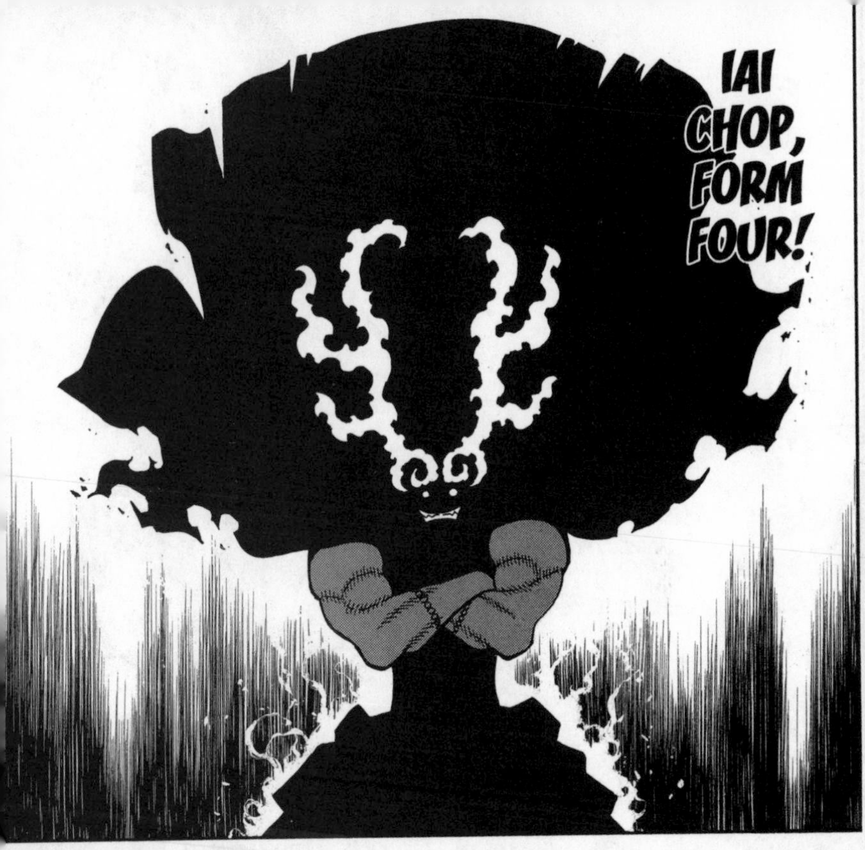
IAI CHOP, FORM FOUR!

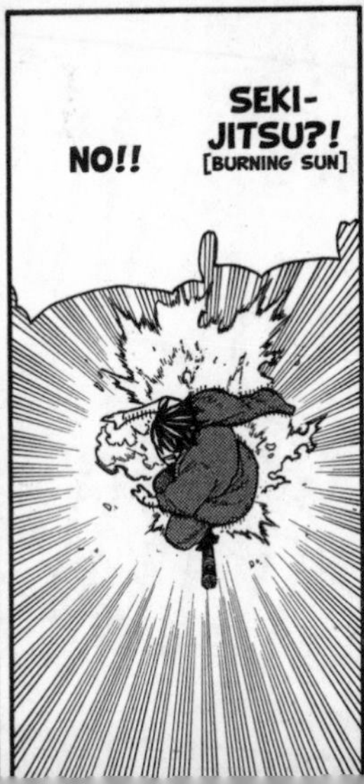
SEKI-JITSU?!
[BURNING SUN]
NO!!

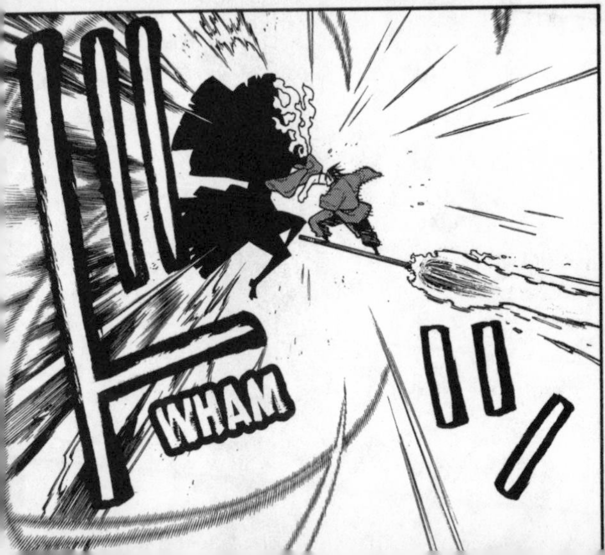
WHAM

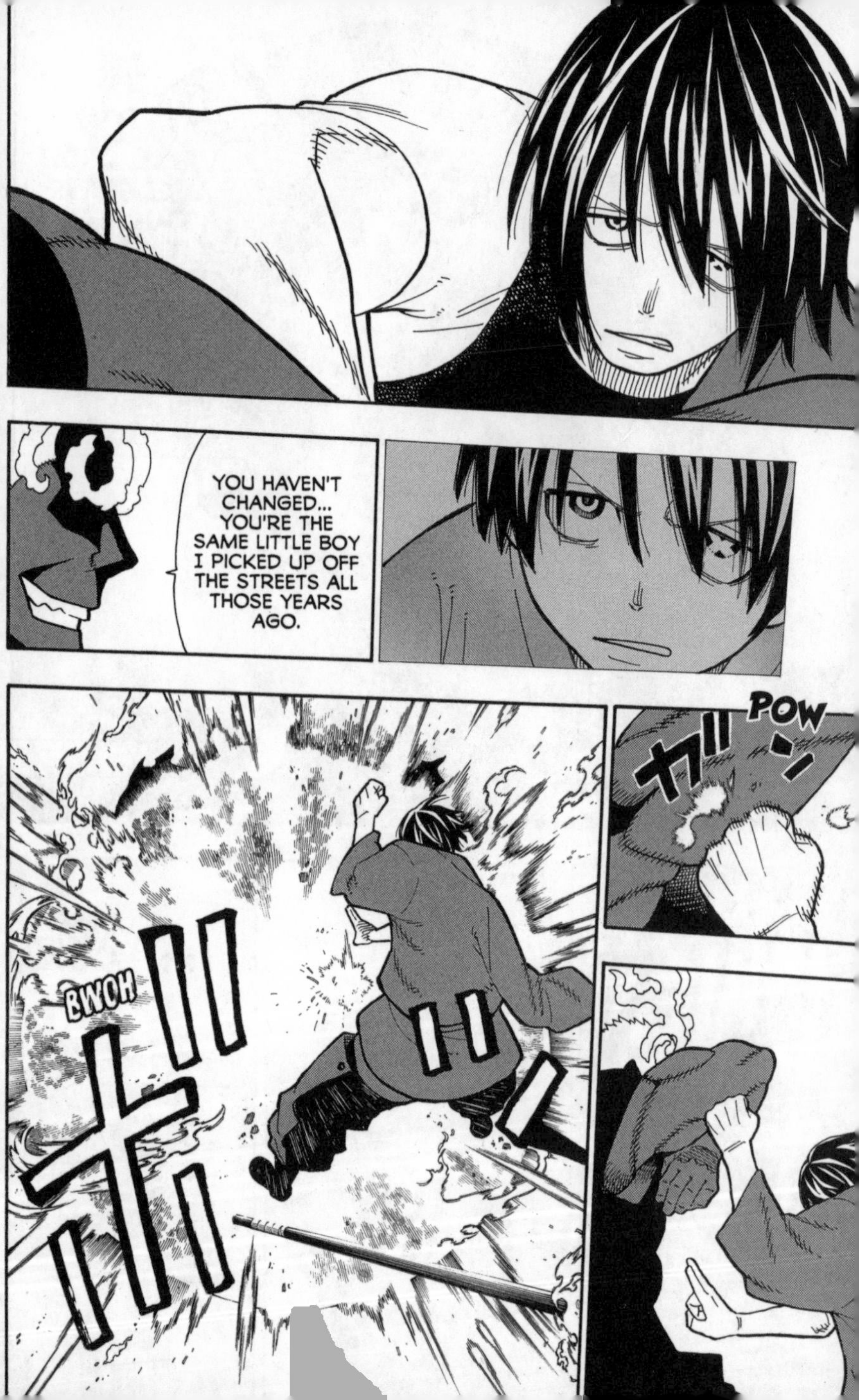
YOU HAVEN'T CHANGED... YOU'RE THE SAME LITTLE BOY I PICKED UP OFF THE STREETS ALL THOSE YEARS AGO.
POW
BWOH

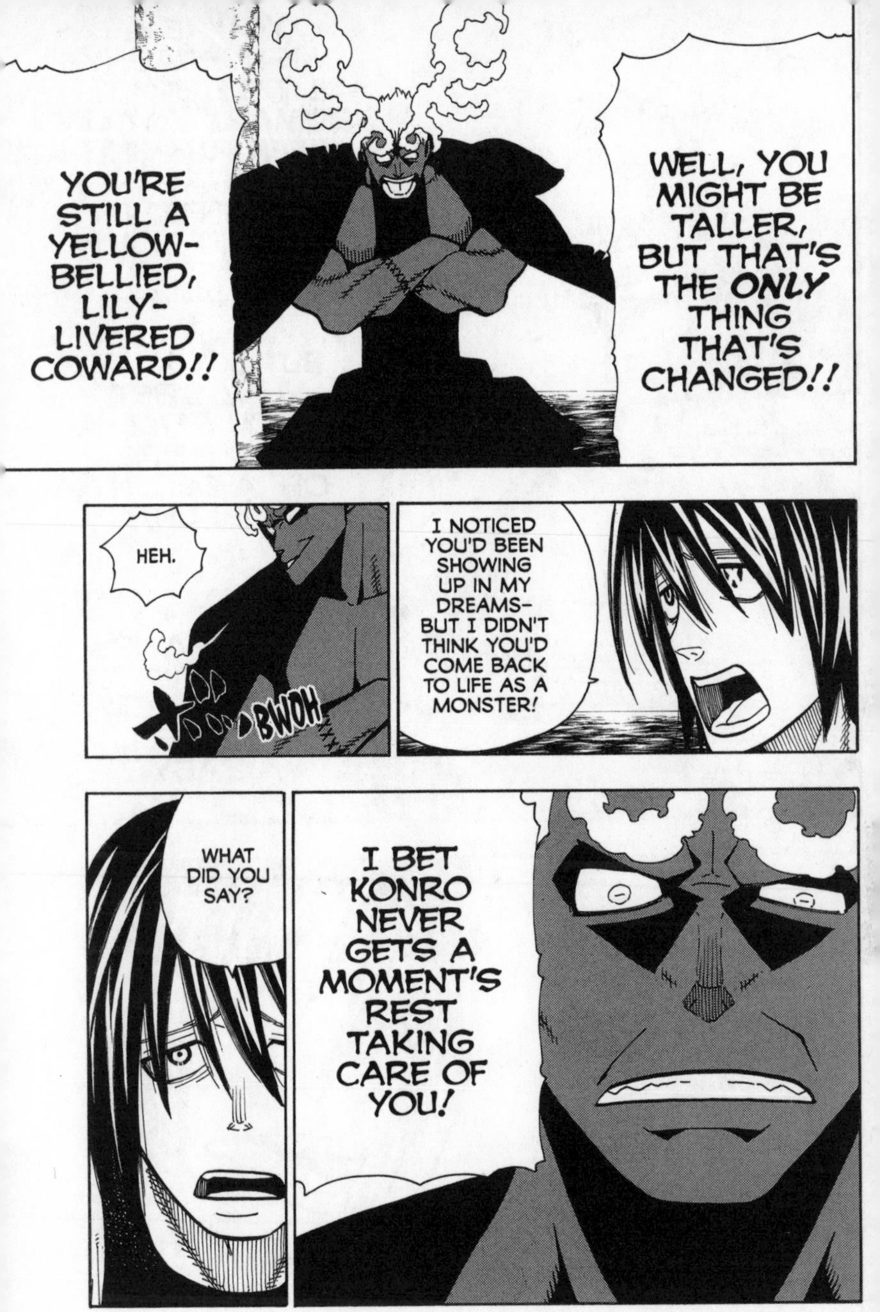
WELL, YOU MIGHT BE TALLER, BUT THAT'S THE ONLY THING THAT'S CHANGED!!
YOU'RE STILL A YELLOW-BELLIED, LILY-LIVERED COWARD!!
I NOTICED YOU'D BEEN SHOWING UP IN MY DREAMS– BUT I DIDN'T THINK YOU'D COME BACK TO LIFE AS A MONSTER!
HEH.
BWOH
I BET KONRO NEVER GETS A MOMENT'S REST TAKING CARE OF YOU!
WHAT DID YOU SAY?

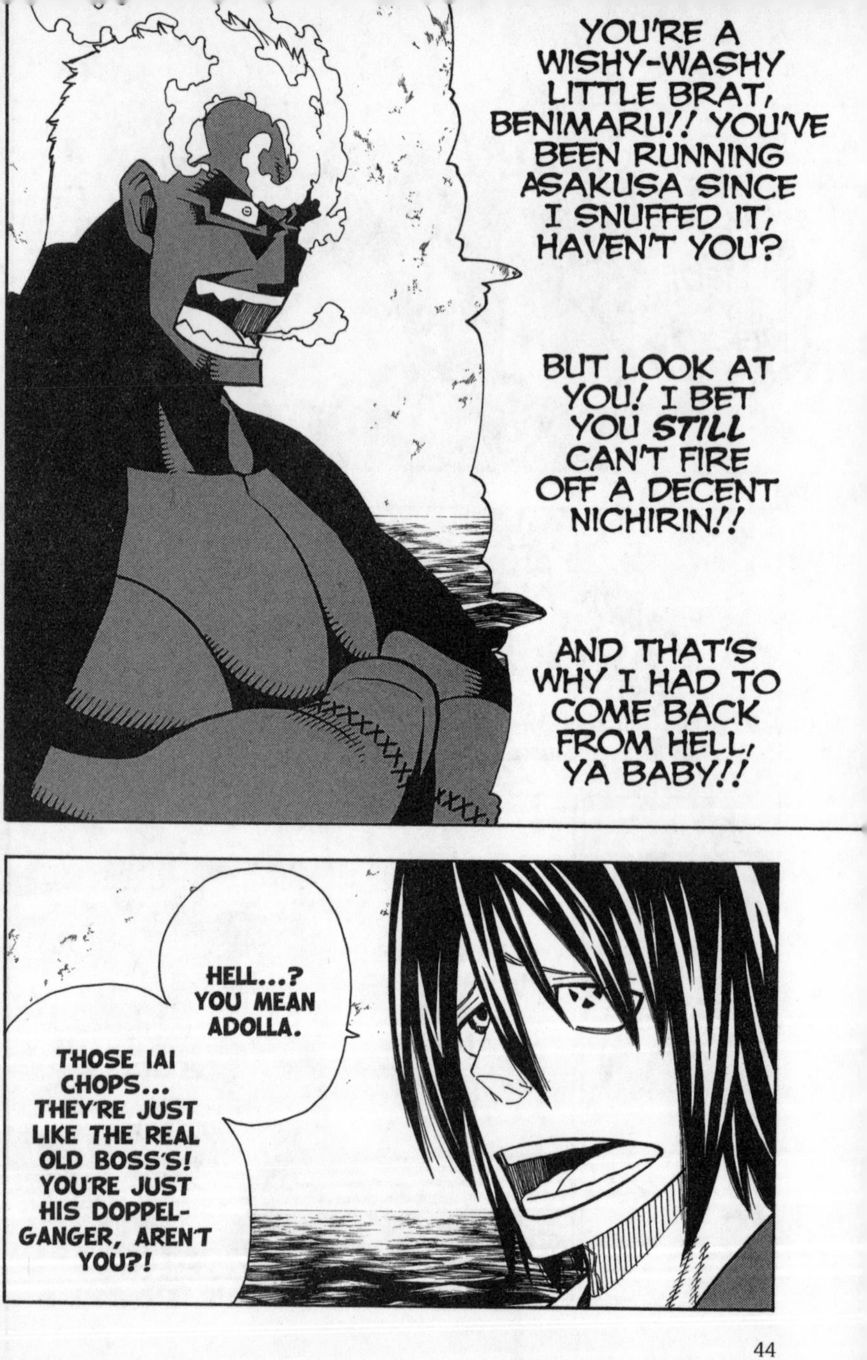
YOU'RE A WISHY-WASHY LITTLE BRAT, BENIMARU!! YOU'VE BEEN RUNNING ASAKUSA SINCE I SNUFFED IT, HAVEN'T YOU?
BUT LOOK AT YOU! I BET YOU *STILL* CAN'T FIRE OFF A DECENT NICHIRIN!!
AND THAT'S WHY I HAD TO COME BACK FROM HELL, YA BABY!!
HELL...? YOU MEAN ADOLLA.
THOSE IAI CHOPS... THEY'RE JUST LIKE THE REAL OLD BOSS'S! YOU'RE JUST HIS DOPPEL-GANGER, AREN'T YOU?!

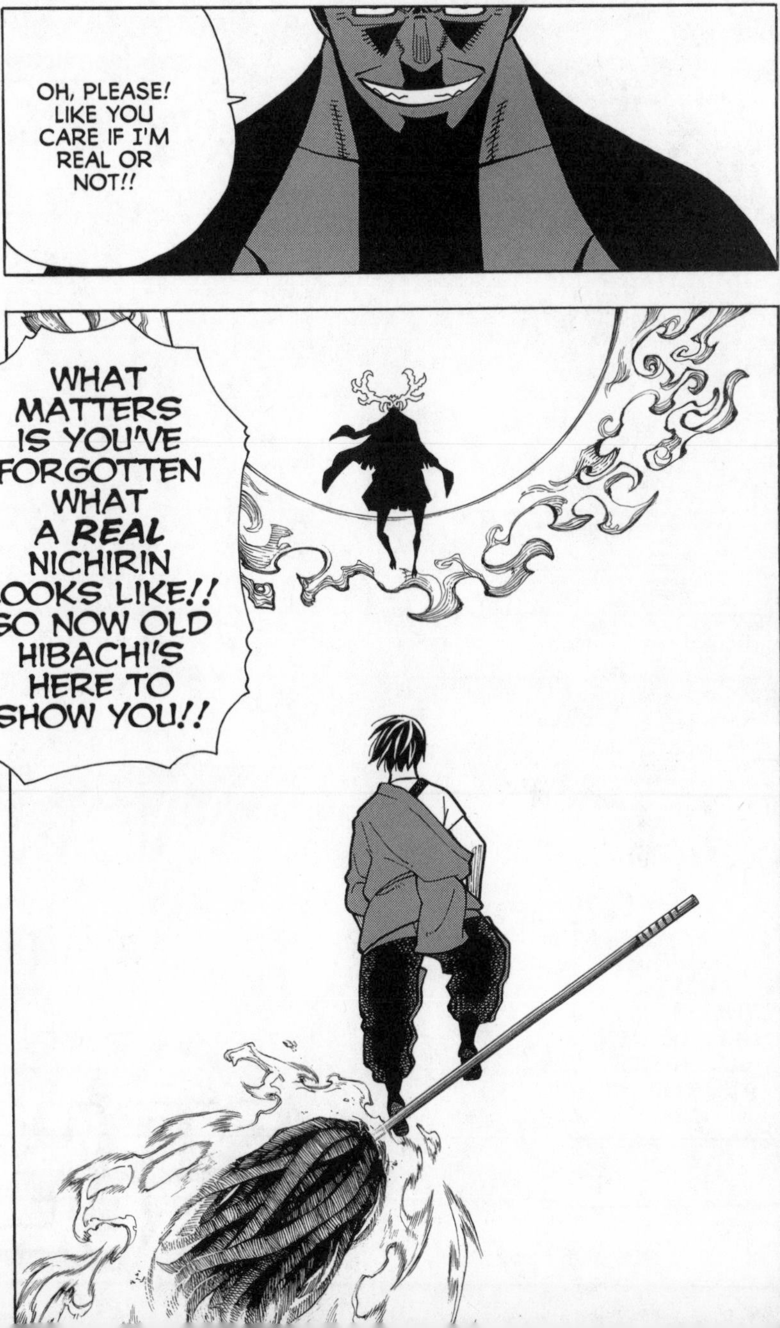
OH, PLEASE! LIKE YOU CARE IF I'M REAL OR NOT!!
WHAT MATTERS IS YOU'VE FORGOTTEN WHAT A *REAL* NICHIRIN LOOKS LIKE!! SO NOW OLD HIBACHI'S HERE TO SHOW YOU!!

FIRE FORCE

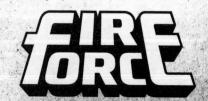

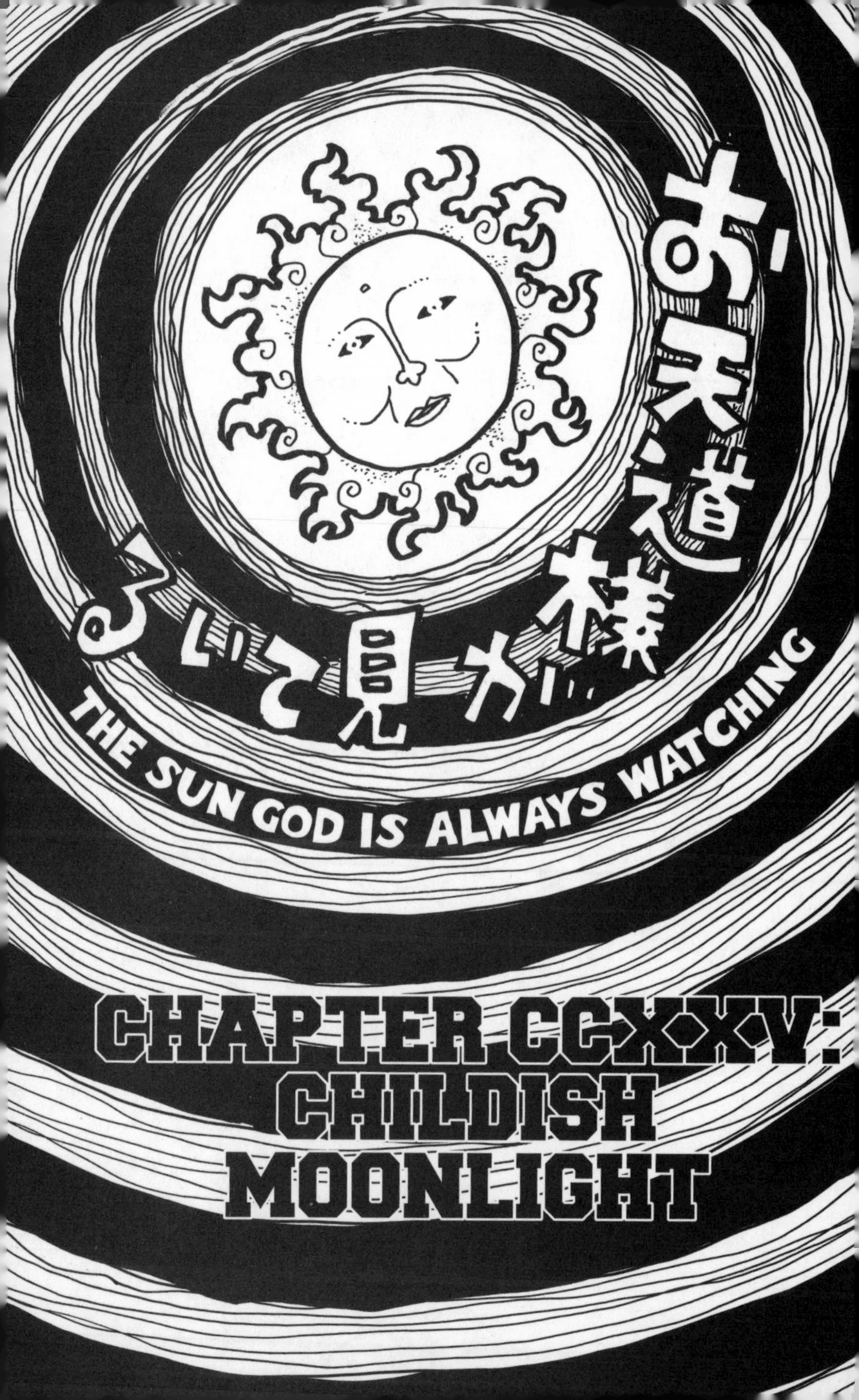
お天道様が見ている
THE SUN GOD IS ALWAYS WATCHING

CHAPTER CCXXV: CHILDISH MOONLIGHT

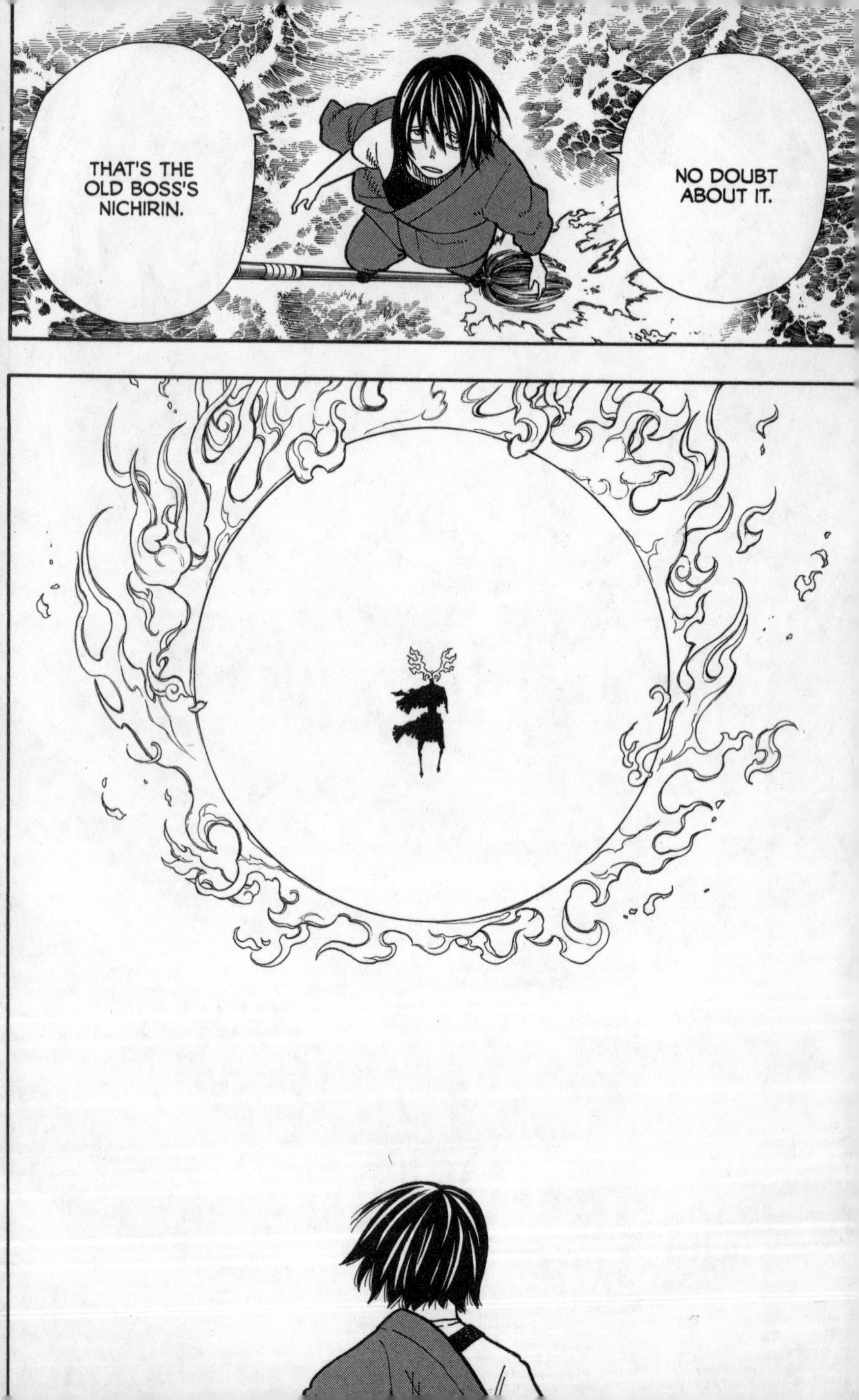
NO DOUBT ABOUT IT.
THAT'S THE OLD BOSS'S NICHIRIN.

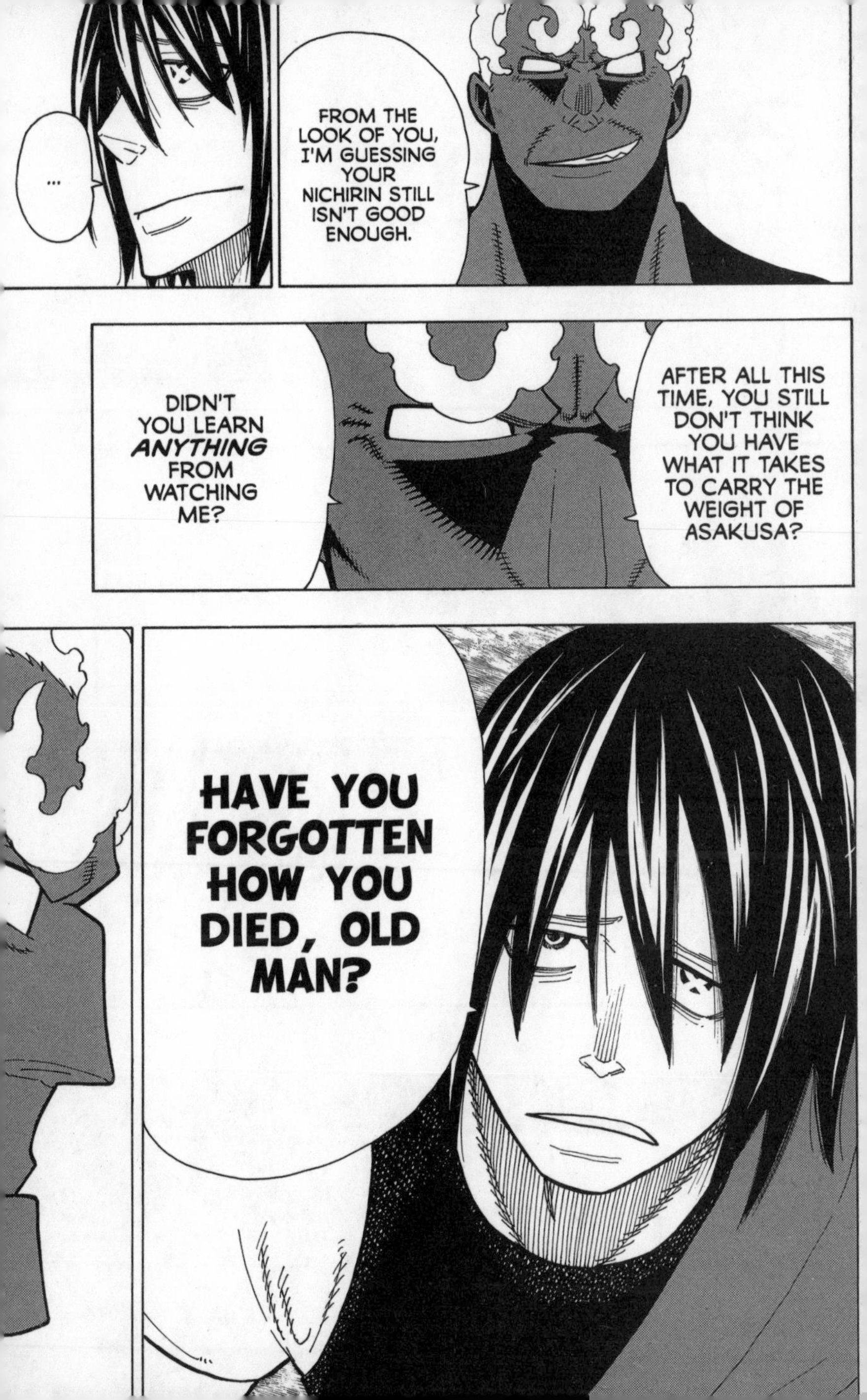
FROM THE LOOK OF YOU, I'M GUESSING YOUR NICHIRIN STILL ISN'T GOOD ENOUGH.
...
AFTER ALL THIS TIME, YOU STILL DON'T THINK YOU HAVE WHAT IT TAKES TO CARRY THE WEIGHT OF ASAKUSA?
DIDN'T YOU LEARN *ANYTHING* FROM WATCHING ME?
HAVE YOU FORGOTTEN HOW YOU DIED, OLD MAN?

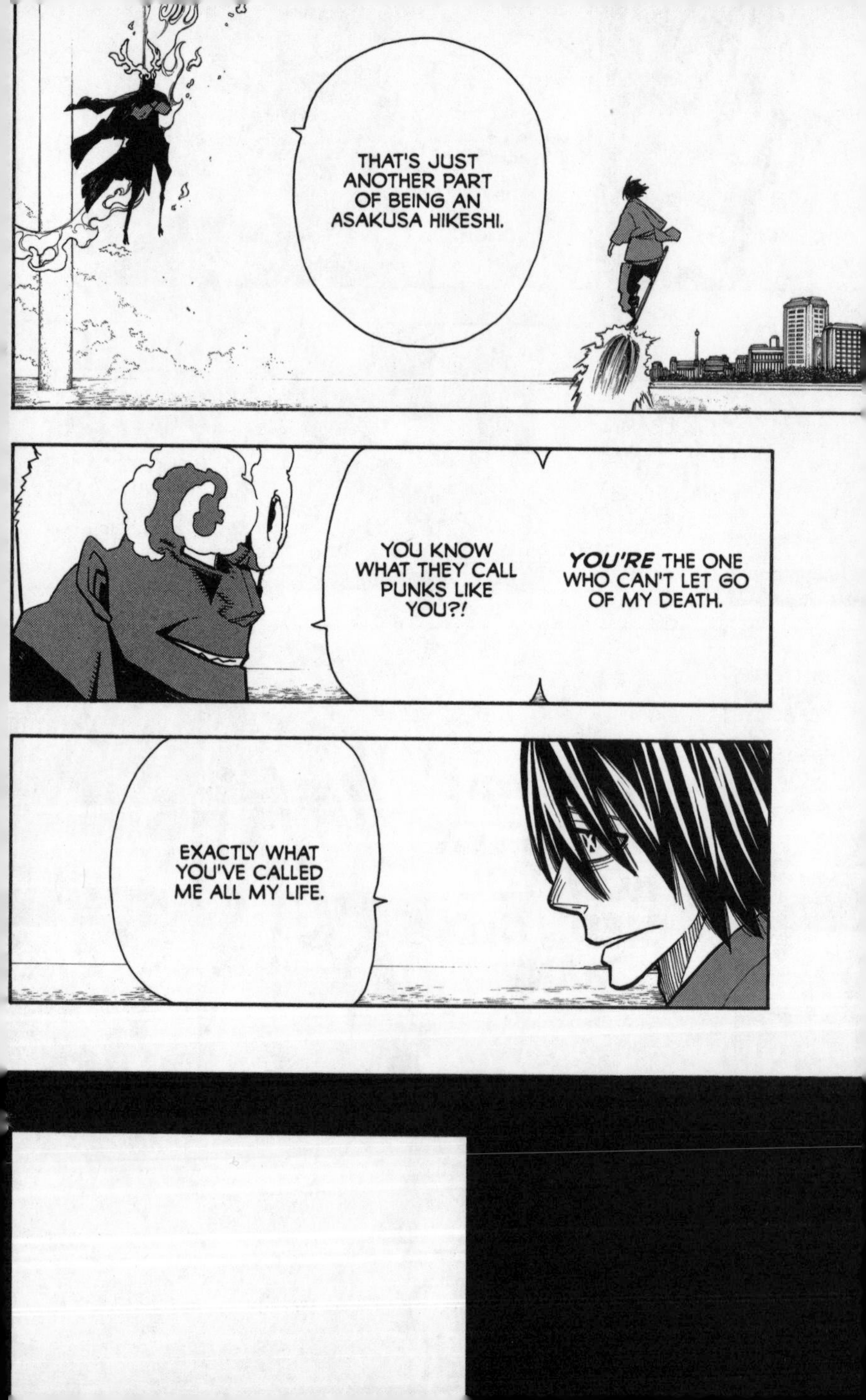
THAT'S JUST ANOTHER PART OF BEING AN ASAKUSA HIKESHI.
YOU'RE THE ONE WHO CAN'T LET GO OF MY DEATH.
YOU KNOW WHAT THEY CALL PUNKS LIKE YOU?!
EXACTLY WHAT YOU'VE CALLED ME ALL MY LIFE.

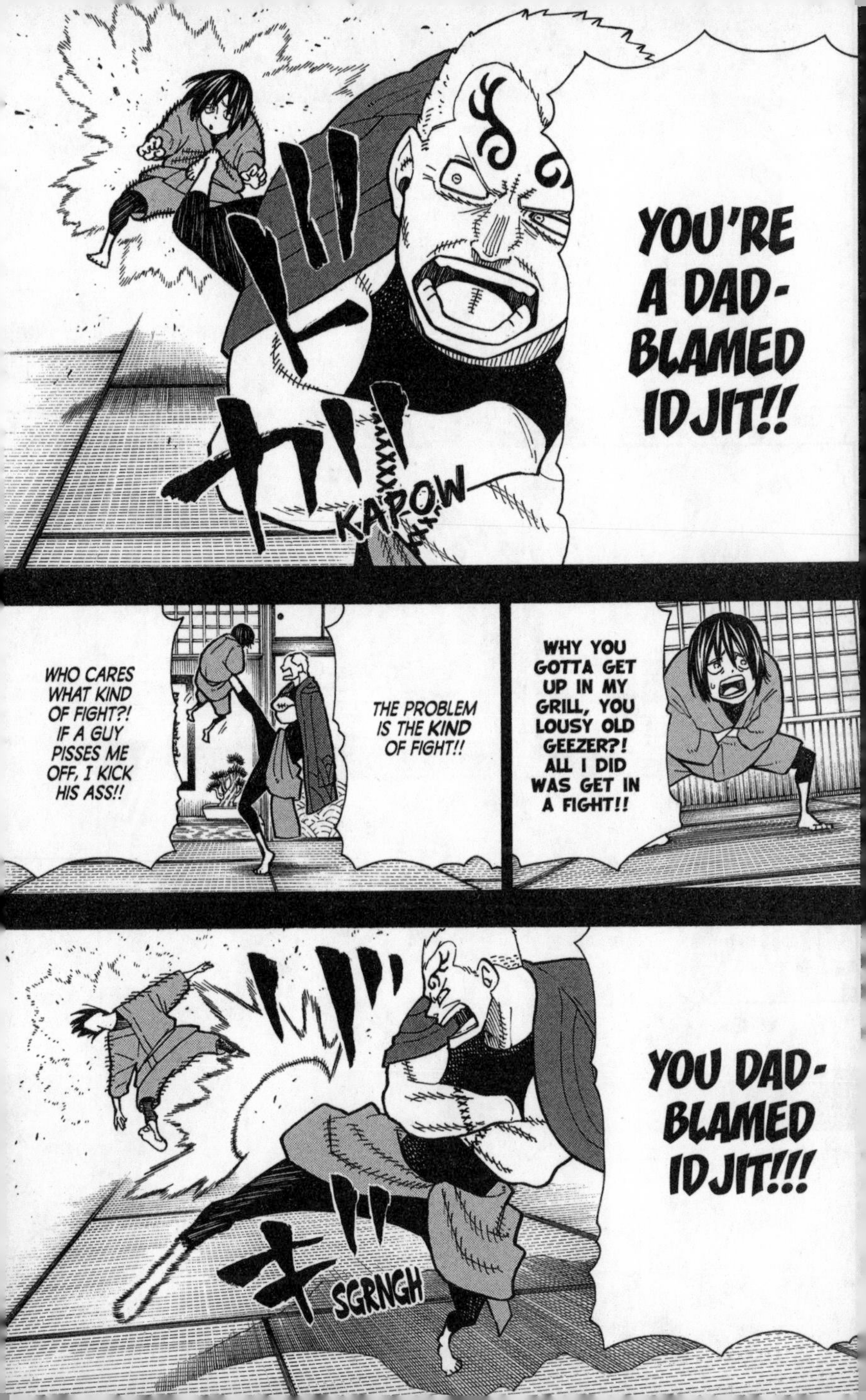
YOU'RE A DAD-BLAMED IDJIT!!
KAPOW
WHY YOU GOTTA GET UP IN MY GRILL, YOU LOUSY OLD GEEZER?! ALL I DID WAS GET IN A FIGHT!!
THE PROBLEM IS THE KIND OF FIGHT!!
WHO CARES WHAT KIND OF FIGHT?! IF A GUY PISSES ME OFF, I KICK HIS ASS!!
YOU DAD-BLAMED IDJIT!!!
SGRNGH

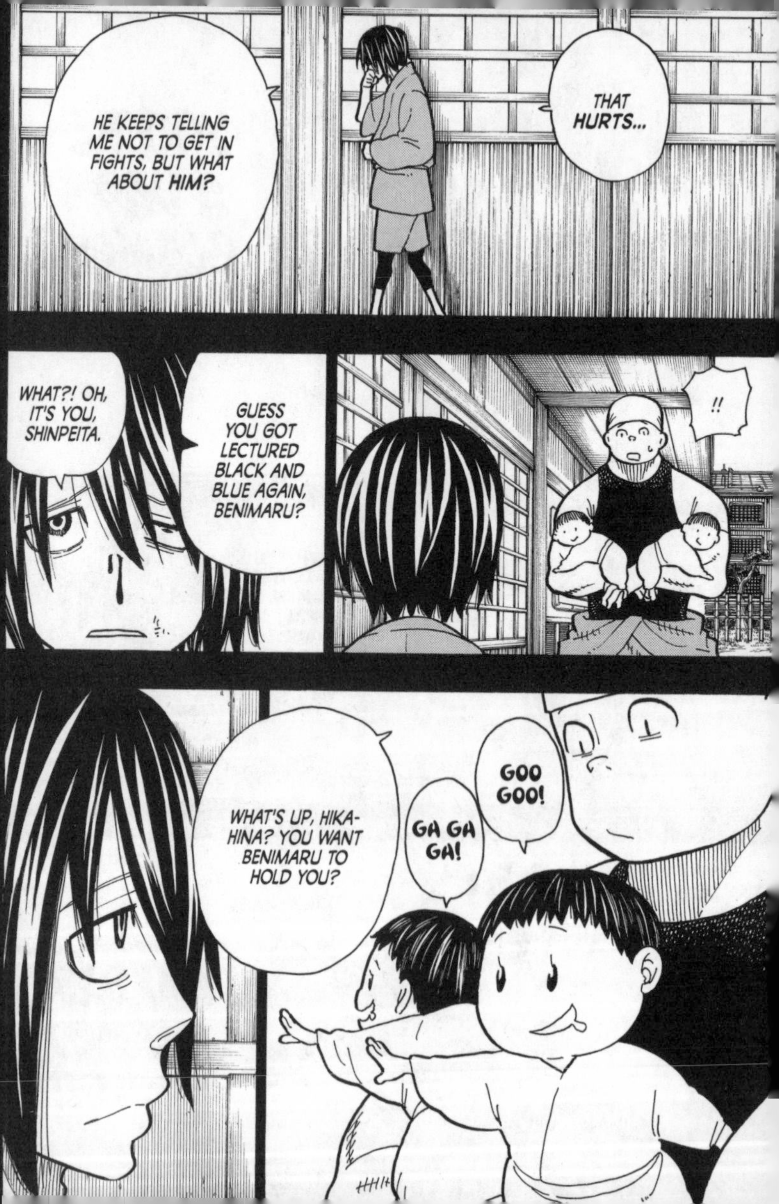
THAT HURTS...
HE KEEPS TELLING ME NOT TO GET IN FIGHTS, BUT WHAT ABOUT HIM?
!!
GUESS YOU GOT LECTURED BLACK AND BLUE AGAIN, BENIMARU?
WHAT?! OH, IT'S YOU, SHINPEITA.
GOO GOO!
GA GA GA!
WHAT'S UP, HIKA-HINA? YOU WANT BENIMARU TO HOLD YOU?

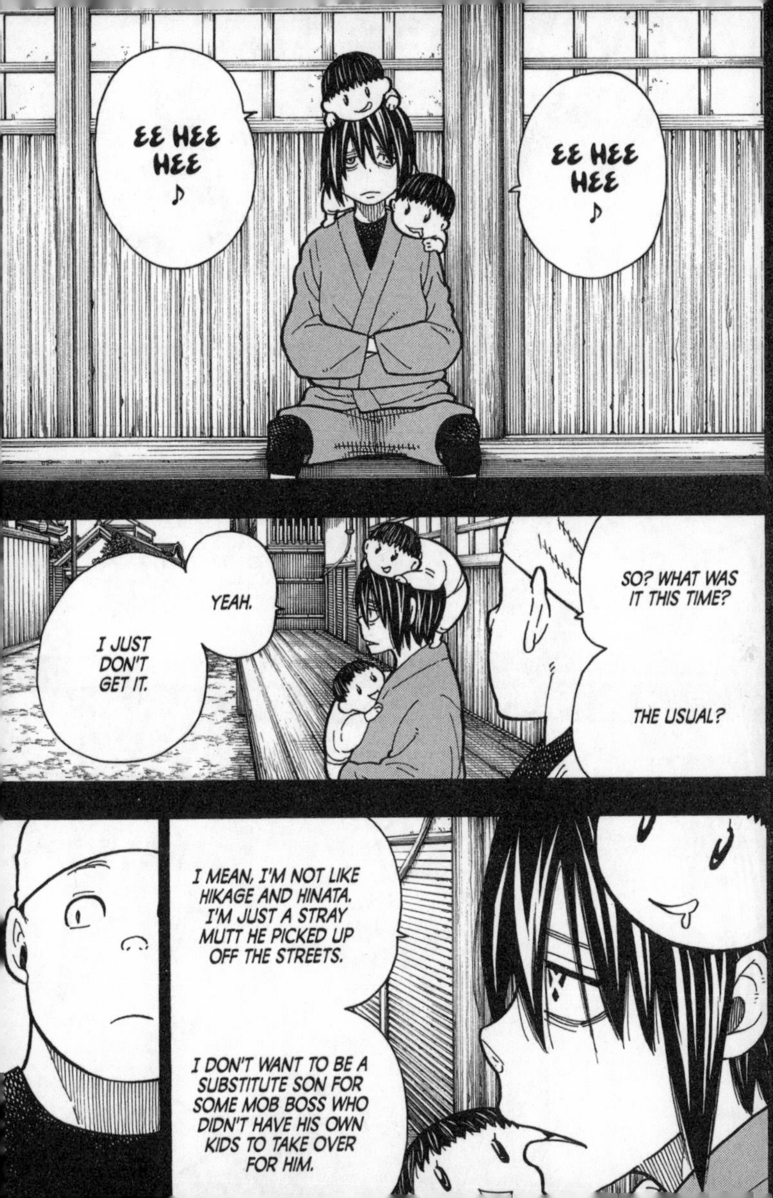
EE HEE HEE ♪
EE HEE HEE ♪
SO? WHAT WAS IT THIS TIME?
THE USUAL?
YEAH.
I JUST DON'T GET IT.
I MEAN, I'M NOT LIKE HIKAGE AND HINATA. I'M JUST A STRAY MUTT HE PICKED UP OFF THE STREETS.
I DON'T WANT TO BE A SUBSTITUTE SON FOR SOME MOB BOSS WHO DIDN'T HAVE HIS OWN KIDS TO TAKE OVER FOR HIM.

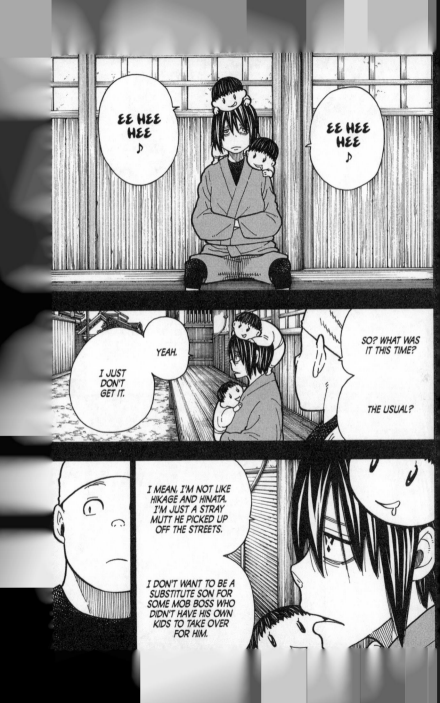

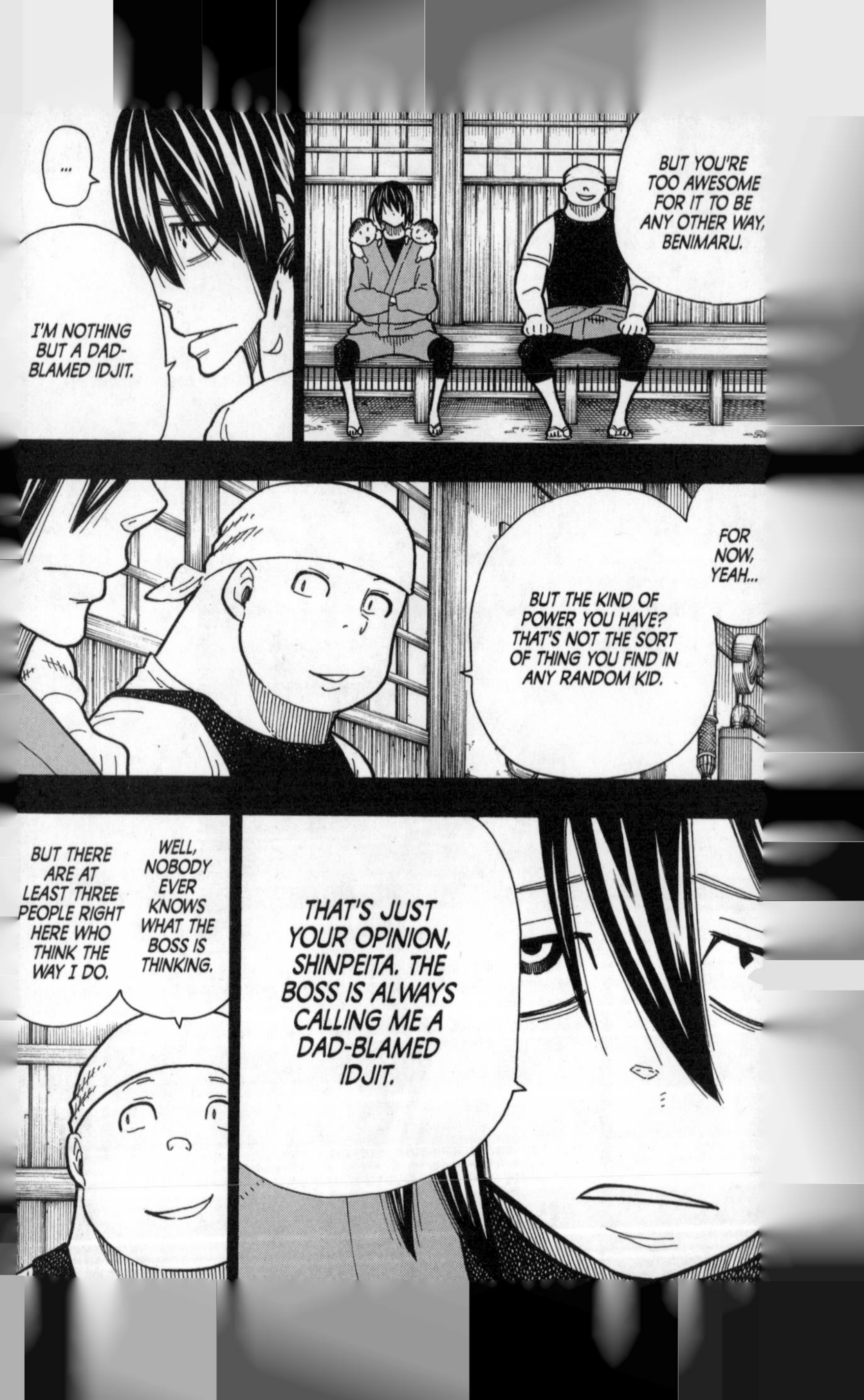
BUT YOU'RE TOO AWESOME FOR IT TO BE ANY OTHER WAY, BENIMARU.
...
I'M NOTHING BUT A DAD-BLAMED IDJIT.
FOR NOW, YEAH...
BUT THE KIND OF POWER YOU HAVE? THAT'S NOT THE SORT OF THING YOU FIND IN ANY RANDOM KID.
THAT'S JUST YOUR OPINION, SHINPEITA. THE BOSS IS ALWAYS CALLING ME A DAD-BLAMED IDJIT.
WELL, NOBODY EVER KNOWS WHAT THE BOSS IS THINKING.
BUT THERE ARE AT LEAST THREE PEOPLE RIGHT HERE WHO THINK THE WAY I DO.

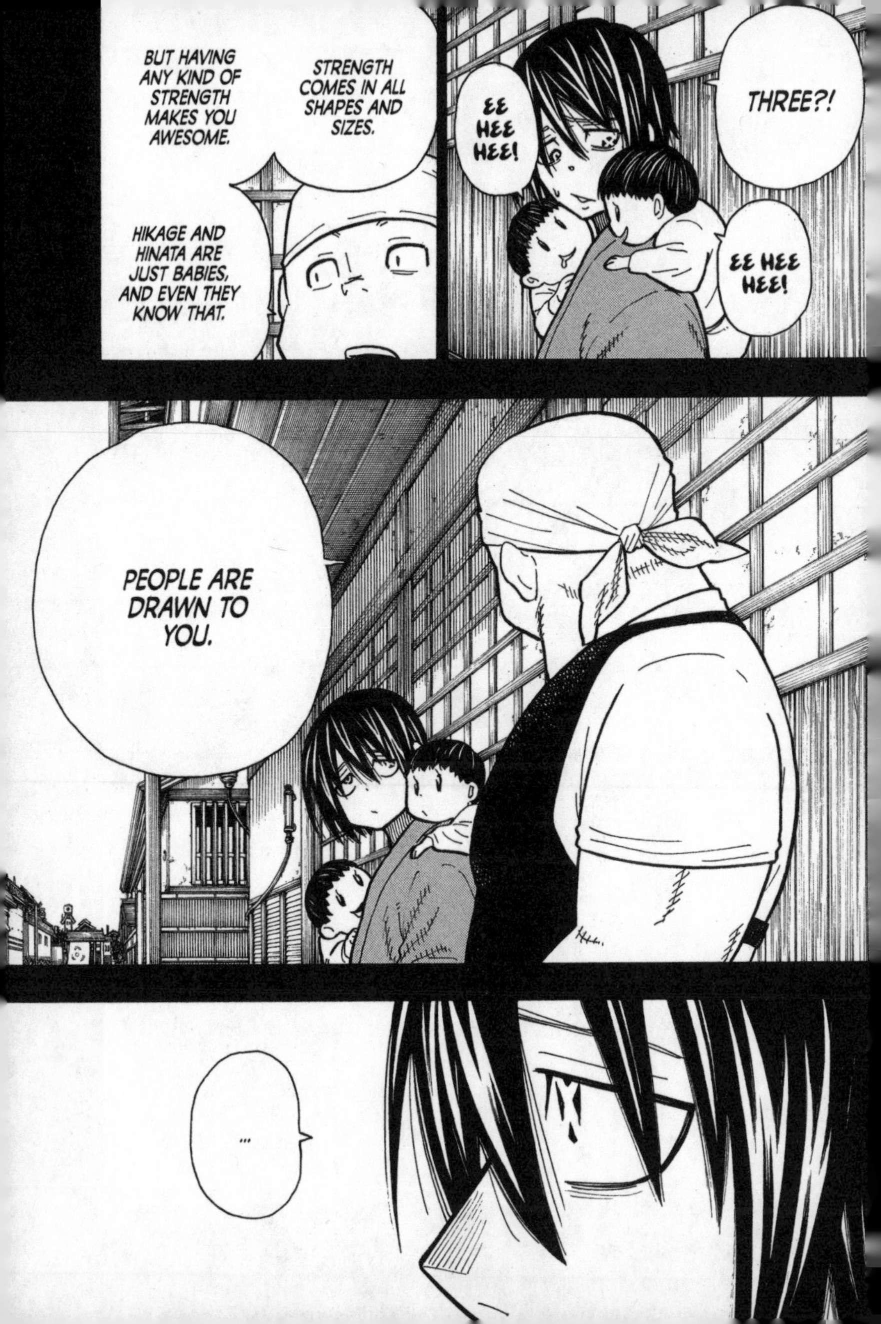
THREE?!
EE HEE HEE!
EE HEE HEE!
STRENGTH COMES IN ALL SHAPES AND SIZES.
BUT HAVING ANY KIND OF STRENGTH MAKES YOU AWESOME.
HIKAGE AND HINATA ARE JUST BABIES, AND EVEN THEY KNOW THAT.
PEOPLE ARE DRAWN TO YOU.
...

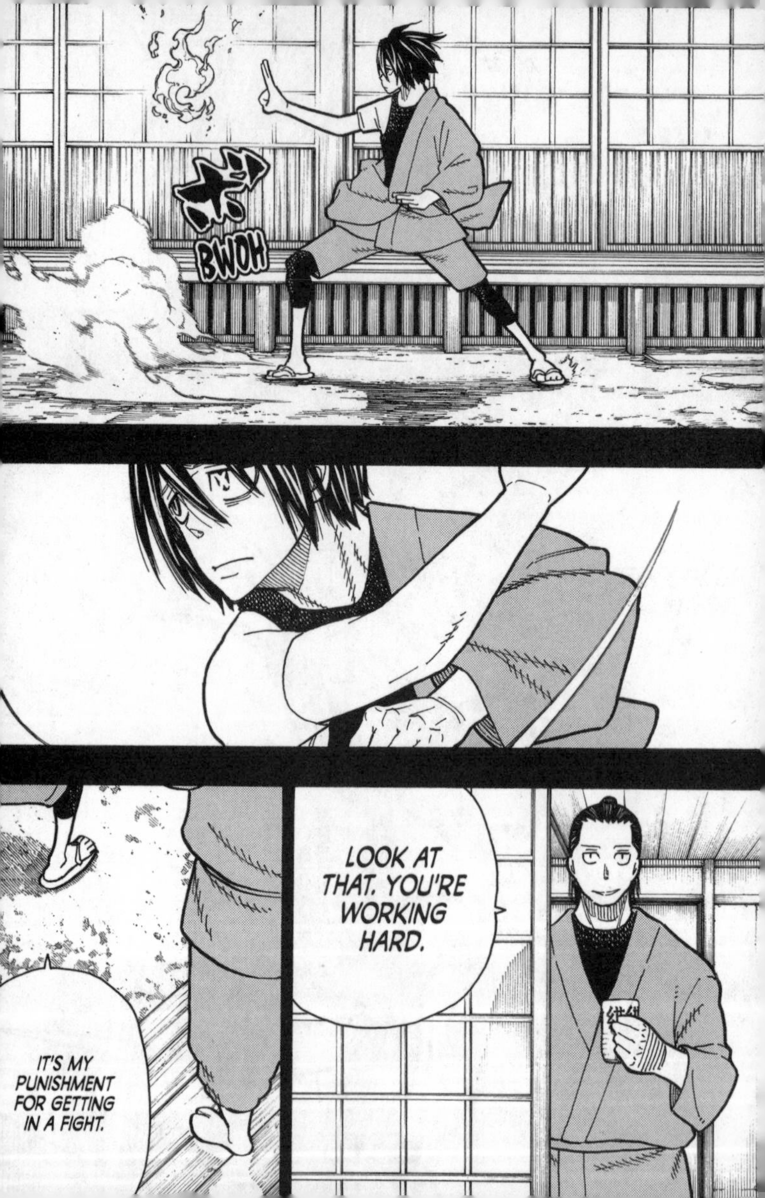
BWOH
LOOK AT THAT. YOU'RE WORKING HARD.
IT'S MY PUNISHMENT FOR GETTING IN A FIGHT.

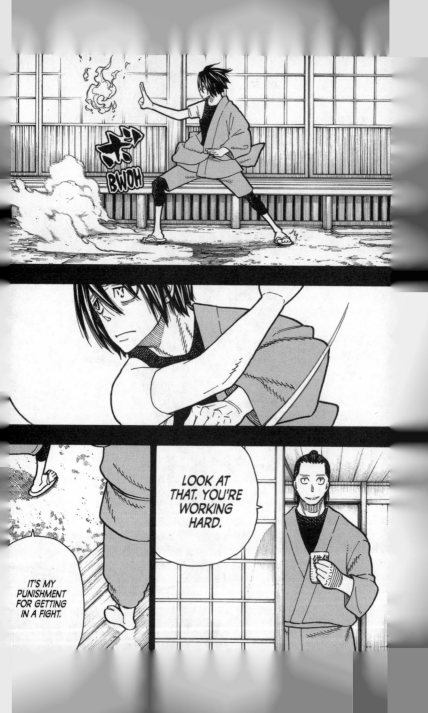

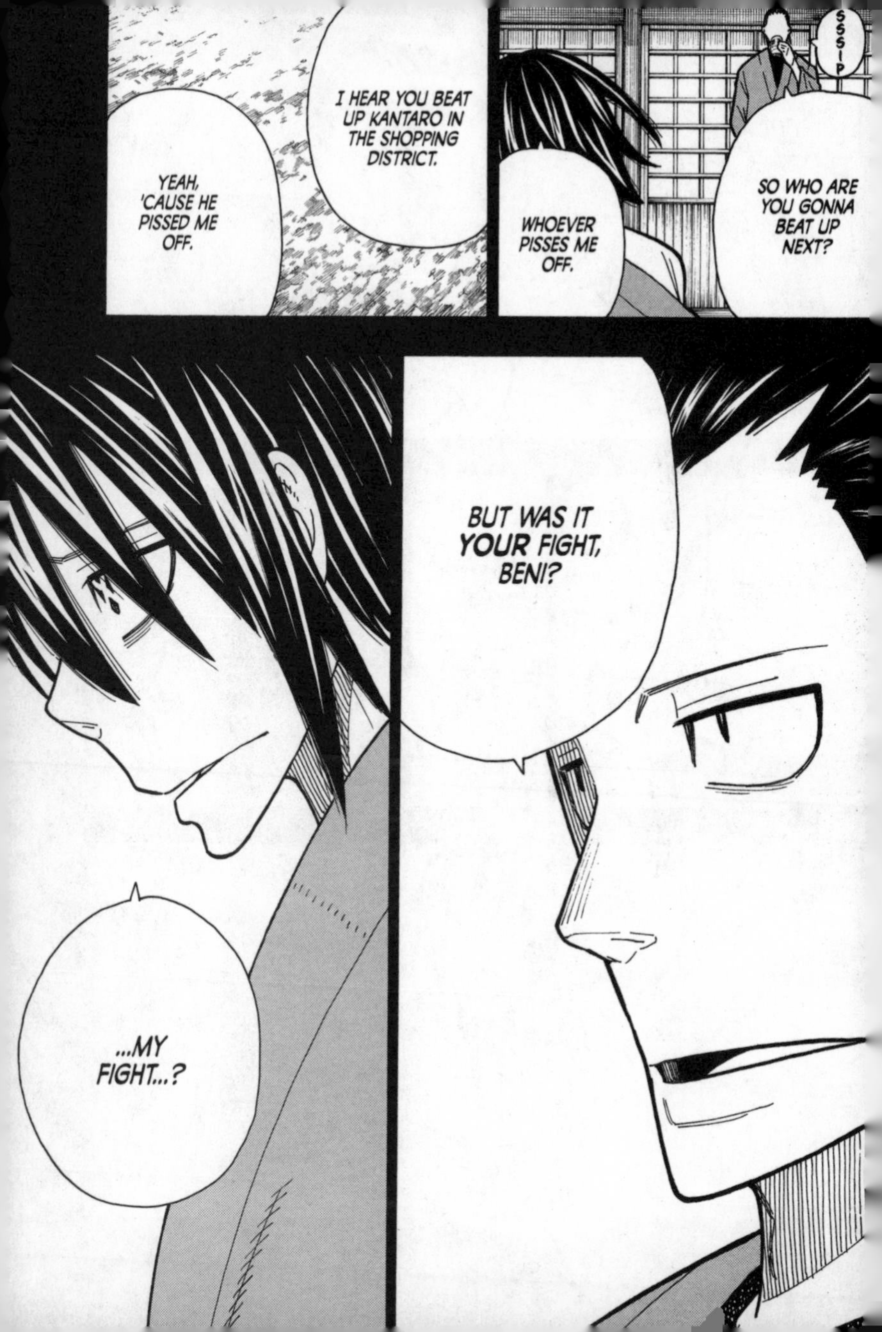
SSSIP
SO WHO ARE YOU GONNA BEAT UP NEXT?
WHOEVER PISSES ME OFF.
I HEAR YOU BEAT UP KANTARO IN THE SHOPPING DISTRICT.
YEAH, 'CAUSE HE PISSED ME OFF.
BUT WAS IT YOUR FIGHT, BENI?
...MY FIGHT...?

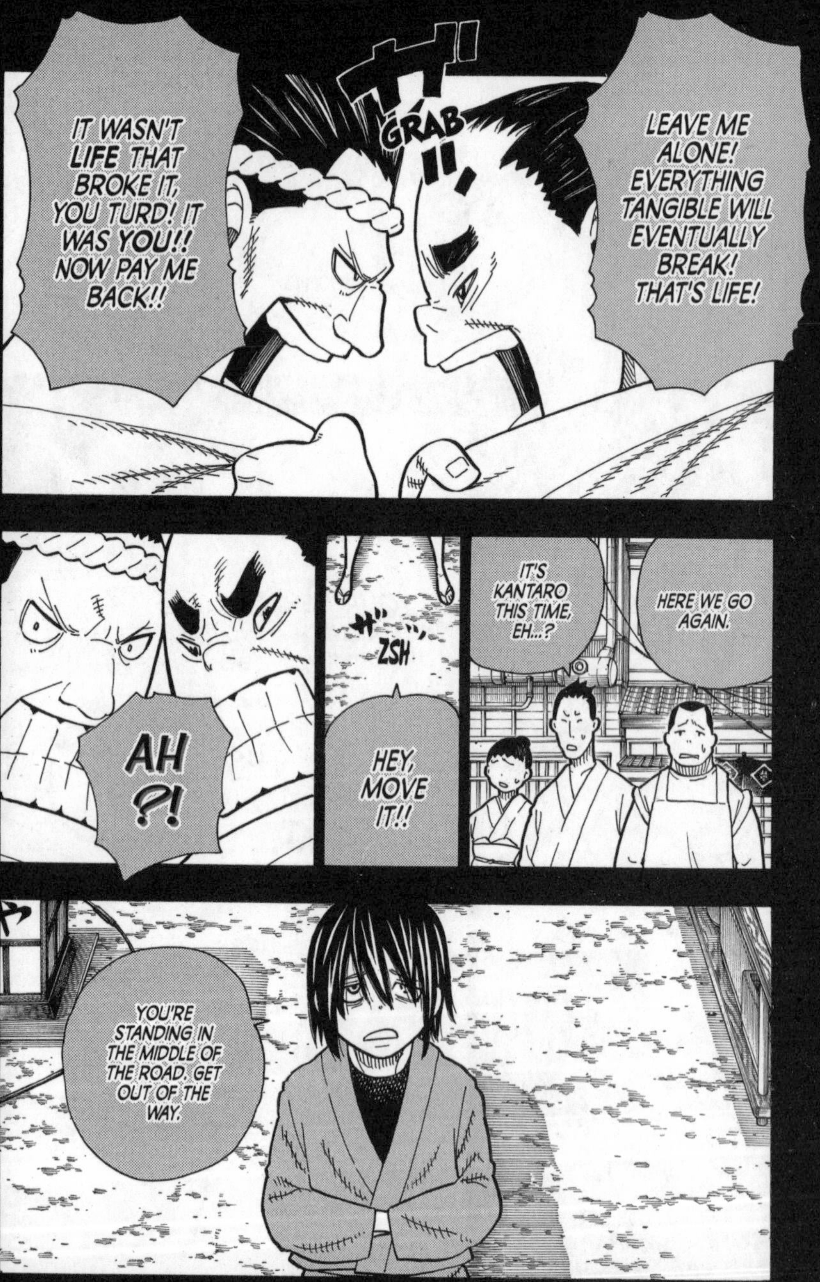
LEAVE ME ALONE! EVERYTHING TANGIBLE WILL EVENTUALLY BREAK! THAT'S LIFE!
GRAB
IT WASN'T LIFE THAT BROKE IT, YOU TURD! IT WAS YOU!! NOW PAY ME BACK!!
HERE WE GO AGAIN.
IT'S KANTARO THIS TIME, EH...?
ZSH
HEY, MOVE IT!!
AH ?!
YOU'RE STANDING IN THE MIDDLE OF THE ROAD. GET OUT OF THE WAY.

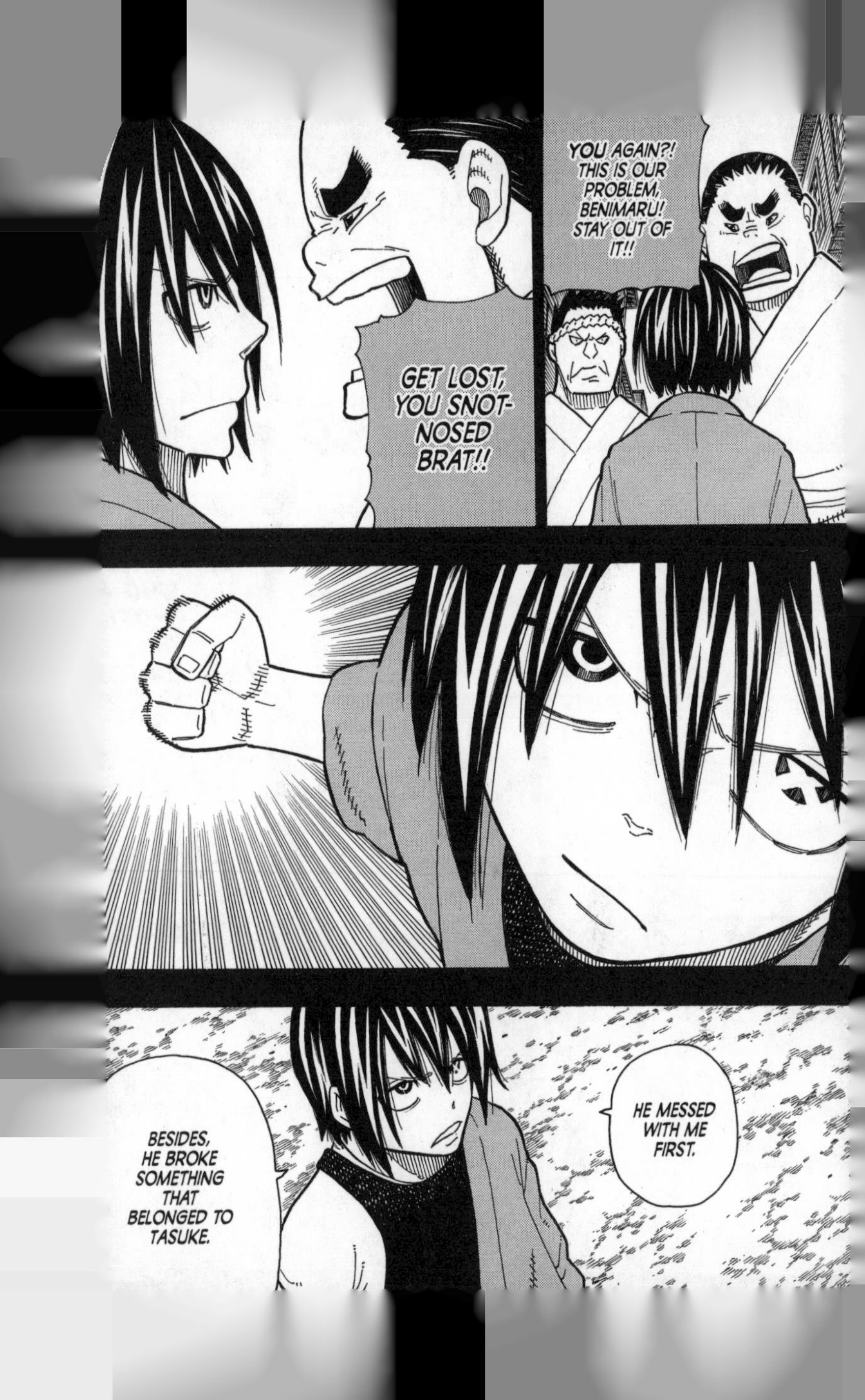
YOU AGAIN?! THIS IS OUR PROBLEM, BENIMARU! STAY OUT OF IT!!
GET LOST, YOU SNOT-NOSED BRAT!!
HE MESSED WITH ME FIRST.
BESIDES, HE BROKE SOMETHING THAT BELONGED TO TASUKE.

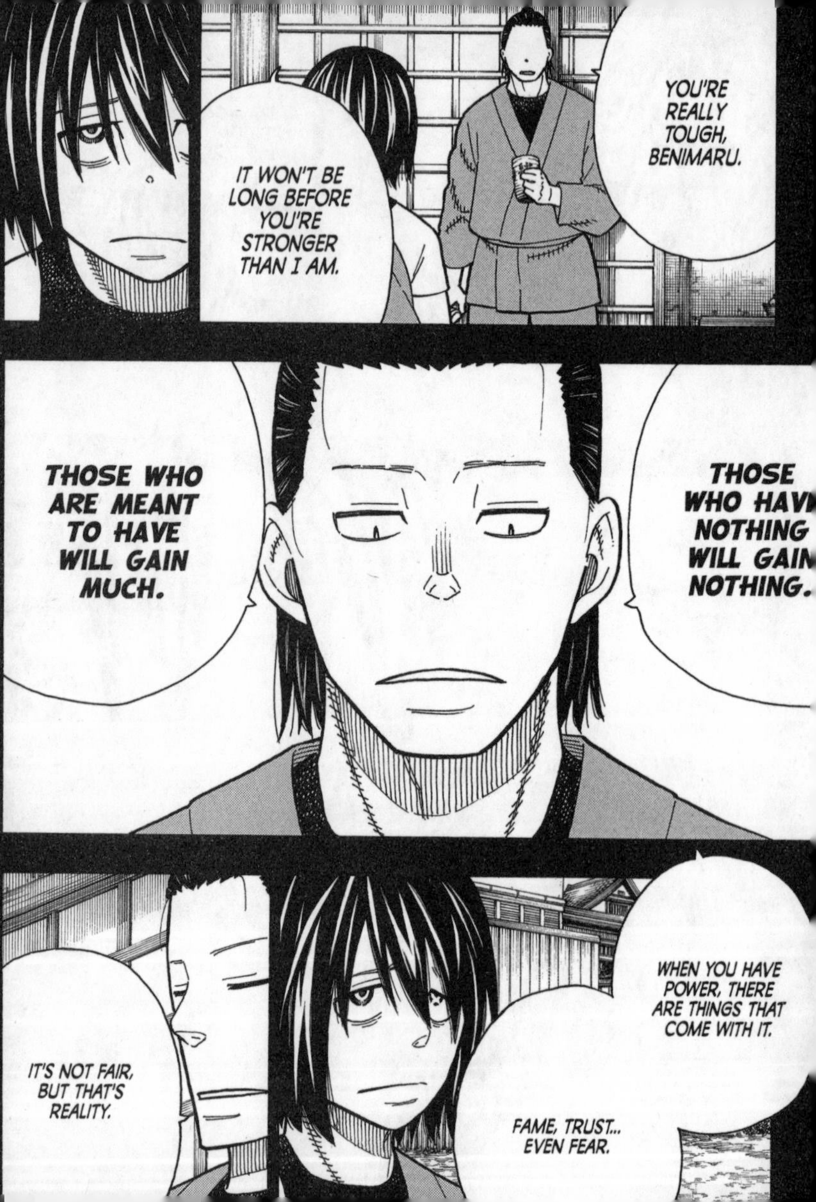
YOU'RE REALLY TOUGH, BENIMARU.
IT WON'T BE LONG BEFORE YOU'RE STRONGER THAN I AM.
THOSE WHO HAV NOTHING WILL GAIN NOTHING.
THOSE WHO ARE MEANT TO HAVE WILL GAIN MUCH.
WHEN YOU HAVE POWER, THERE ARE THINGS THAT COME WITH IT.
FAME, TRUST... EVEN FEAR.
IT'S NOT FAIR, BUT THAT'S REALITY.

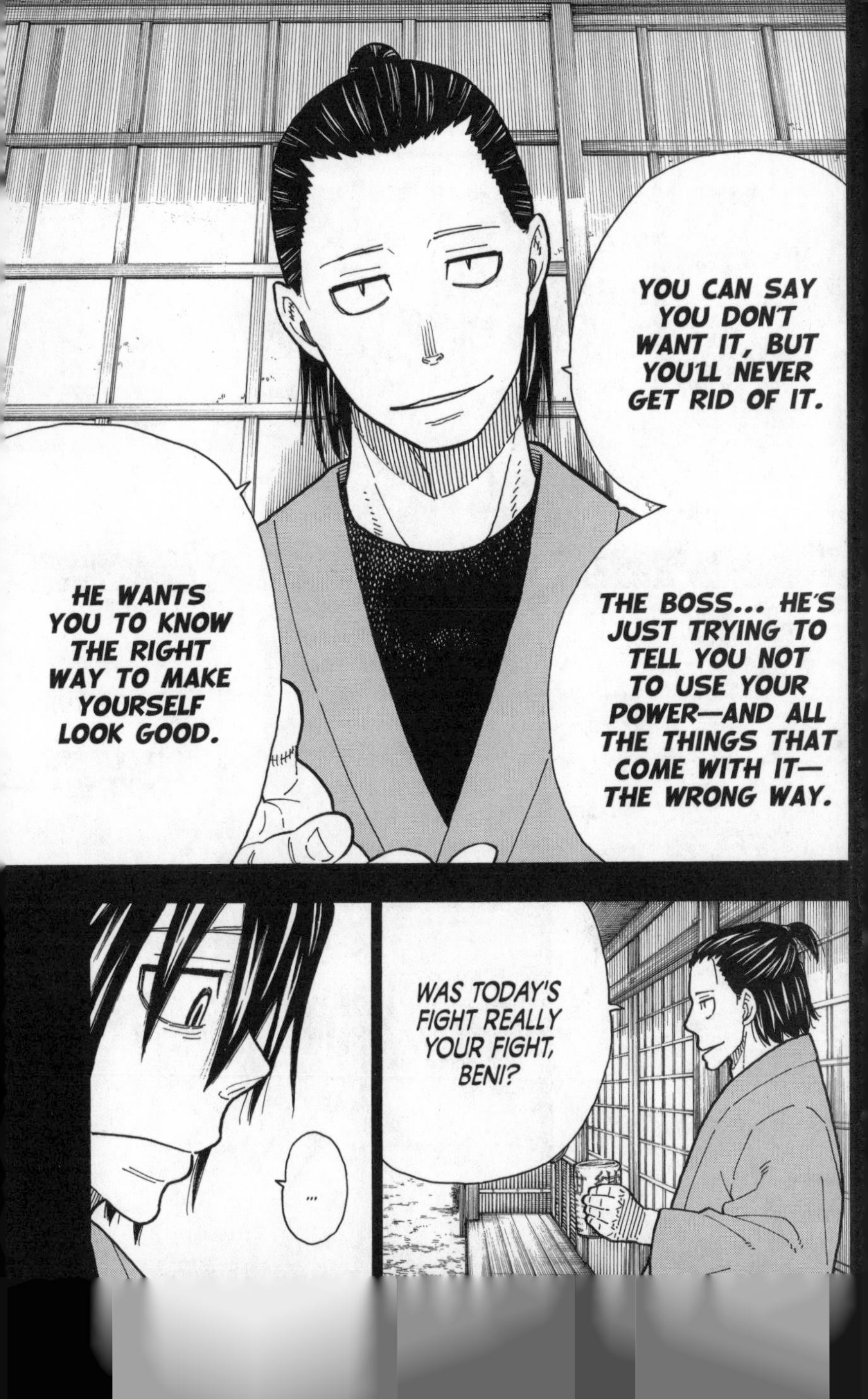
YOU CAN SAY YOU DON'T WANT IT, BUT YOU'LL NEVER GET RID OF IT.
THE BOSS... HE'S JUST TRYING TO TELL YOU NOT TO USE YOUR POWER—AND ALL THE THINGS THAT COME WITH IT—THE WRONG WAY.
HE WANTS YOU TO KNOW THE RIGHT WAY TO MAKE YOURSELF LOOK GOOD.
WAS TODAY'S FIGHT REALLY YOUR FIGHT, BENI?
...

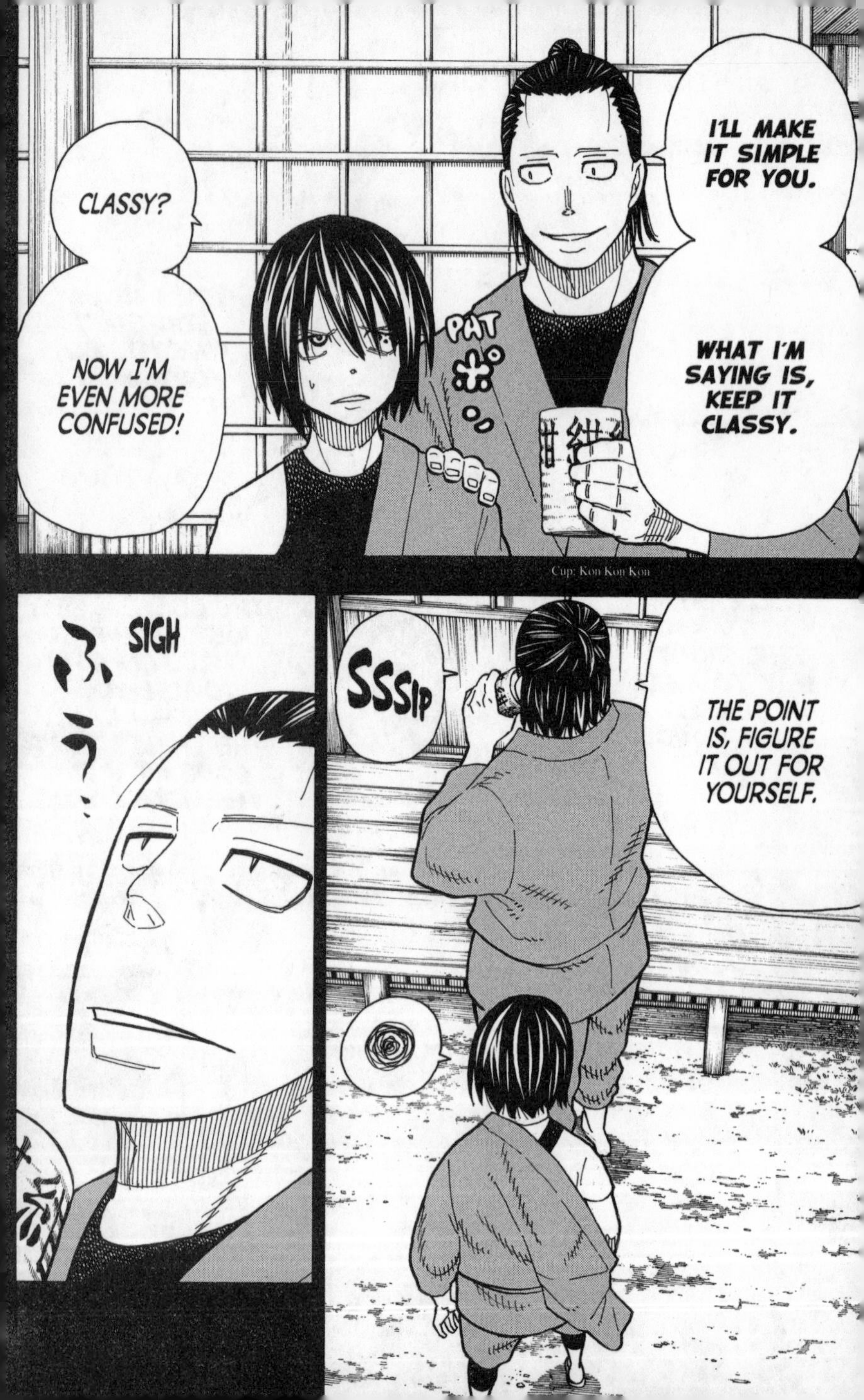
I'LL MAKE IT SIMPLE FOR YOU.
WHAT I'M SAYING IS, KEEP IT CLASSY.
PAT
CLASSY?
NOW I'M EVEN MORE CONFUSED!
Cup: Kon Kon Kon
THE POINT IS, FIGURE IT OUT FOR YOURSELF.
SSSIP
SIGH
ふう…

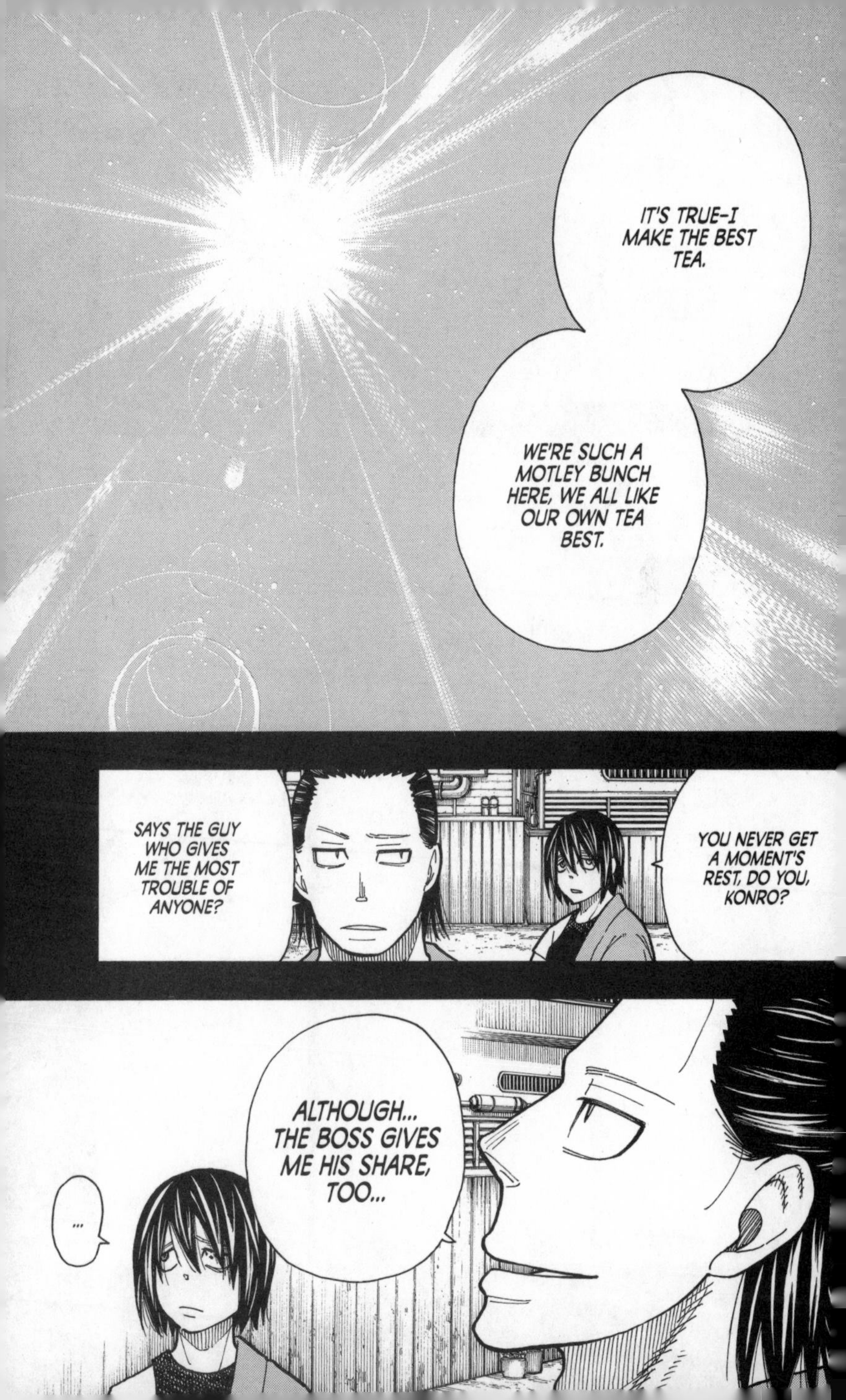
IT'S TRUE–I MAKE THE BEST TEA.
WE'RE SUCH A MOTLEY BUNCH HERE, WE ALL LIKE OUR OWN TEA BEST.
YOU NEVER GET A MOMENT'S REST, DO YOU, KONRO?
SAYS THE GUY WHO GIVES ME THE MOST TROUBLE OF ANYONE?
ALTHOUGH... THE BOSS GIVES ME HIS SHARE, TOO...
...

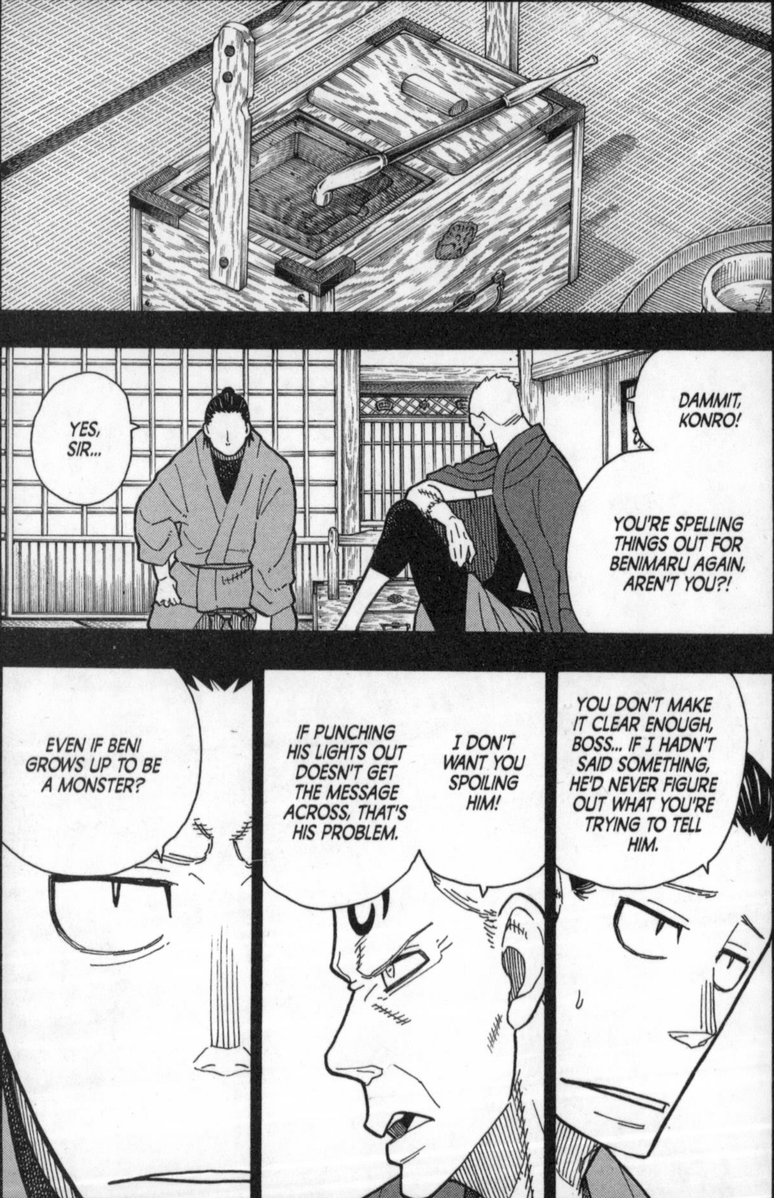
DAMMIT, KONRO!
YOU'RE SPELLING THINGS OUT FOR BENIMARU AGAIN, AREN'T YOU?!
YES, SIR...
YOU DON'T MAKE IT CLEAR ENOUGH, BOSS... IF I HADN'T SAID SOMETHING, HE'D NEVER FIGURE OUT WHAT YOU'RE TRYING TO TELL HIM.
I DON'T WANT YOU SPOILING HIM!
IF PUNCHING HIS LIGHTS OUT DOESN'T GET THE MESSAGE ACROSS, THAT'S HIS PROBLEM.
EVEN IF BENI GROWS UP TO BE A MONSTER?

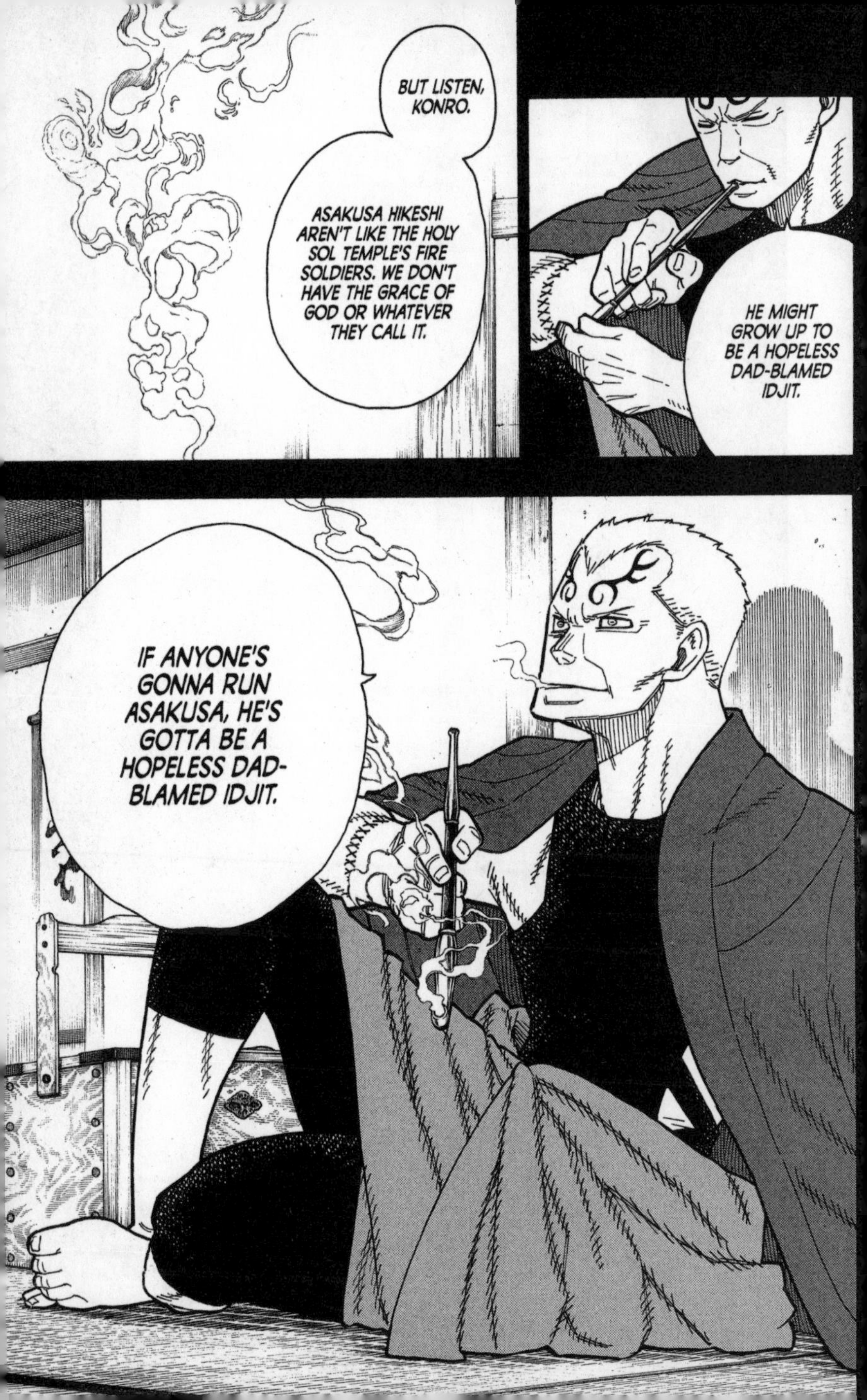
HE MIGHT GROW UP TO BE A HOPELESS DAD-BLAMED IDJIT.
BUT LISTEN, KONRO.
ASAKUSA HIKESHI AREN'T LIKE THE HOLY SOL TEMPLE'S FIRE SOLDIERS. WE DON'T HAVE THE GRACE OF GOD OR WHATEVER THEY CALL IT.
IF ANYONE'S GONNA RUN ASAKUSA, HE'S GOTTA BE A HOPELESS DAD-BLAMED IDJIT.

FIRE
FORCE

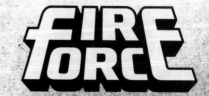

CHAPTER CCXXVI: THE BURDEN BEARER'S FATE

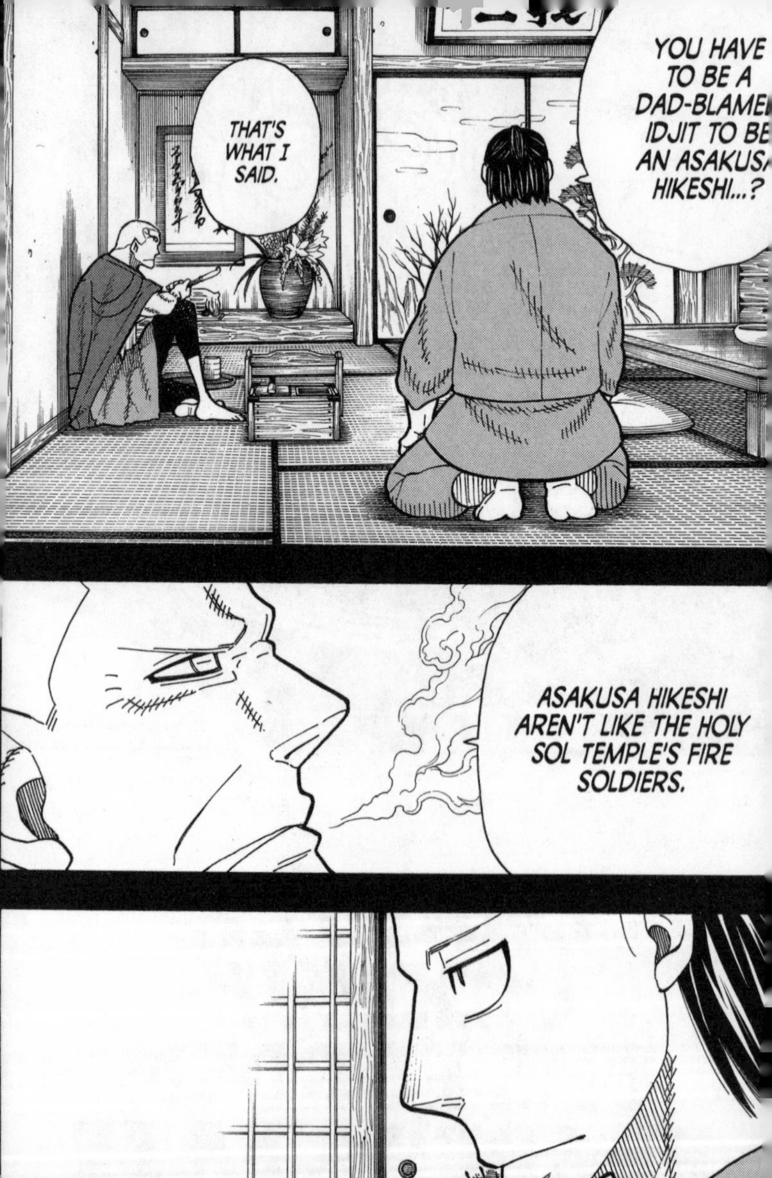
YOU HAVE TO BE A DAD-BLAMED IDJIT TO BE AN ASAKUSA HIKESHI...?
THAT'S WHAT I SAID.
ASAKUSA HIKESHI AREN'T LIKE THE HOLY SOL TEMPLE'S FIRE SOLDIERS.

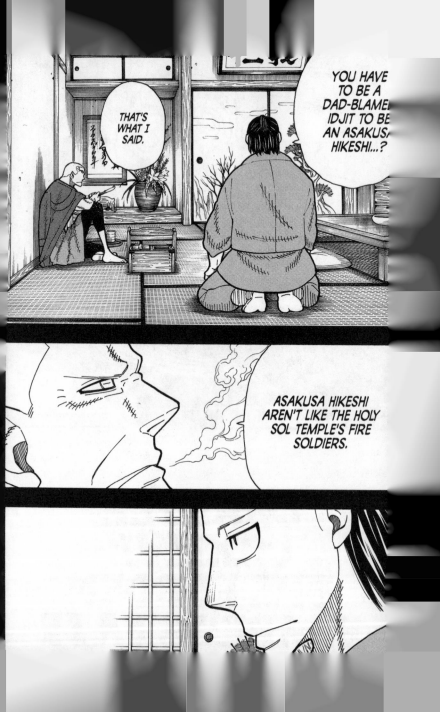

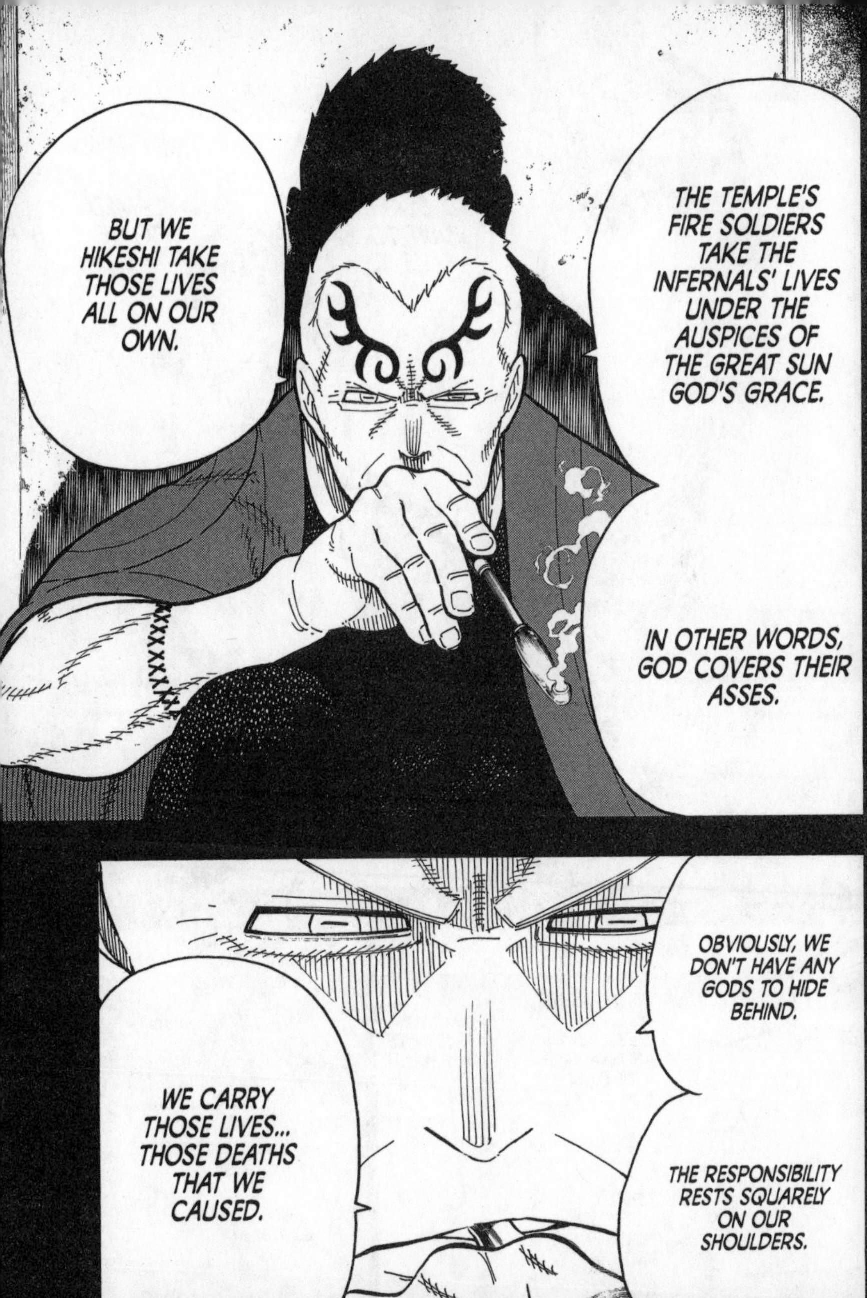
THE TEMPLE'S FIRE SOLDIERS TAKE THE INFERNALS' LIVES UNDER THE AUSPICES OF THE GREAT SUN GOD'S GRACE.
IN OTHER WORDS, GOD COVERS THEIR ASSES.
BUT WE HIKESHI TAKE THOSE LIVES ALL ON OUR OWN.
OBVIOUSLY, WE DON'T HAVE ANY GODS TO HIDE BEHIND.
THE RESPONSIBILITY RESTS SQUARELY ON OUR SHOULDERS.
WE CARRY THOSE LIVES... THOSE DEATHS THAT WE CAUSED.

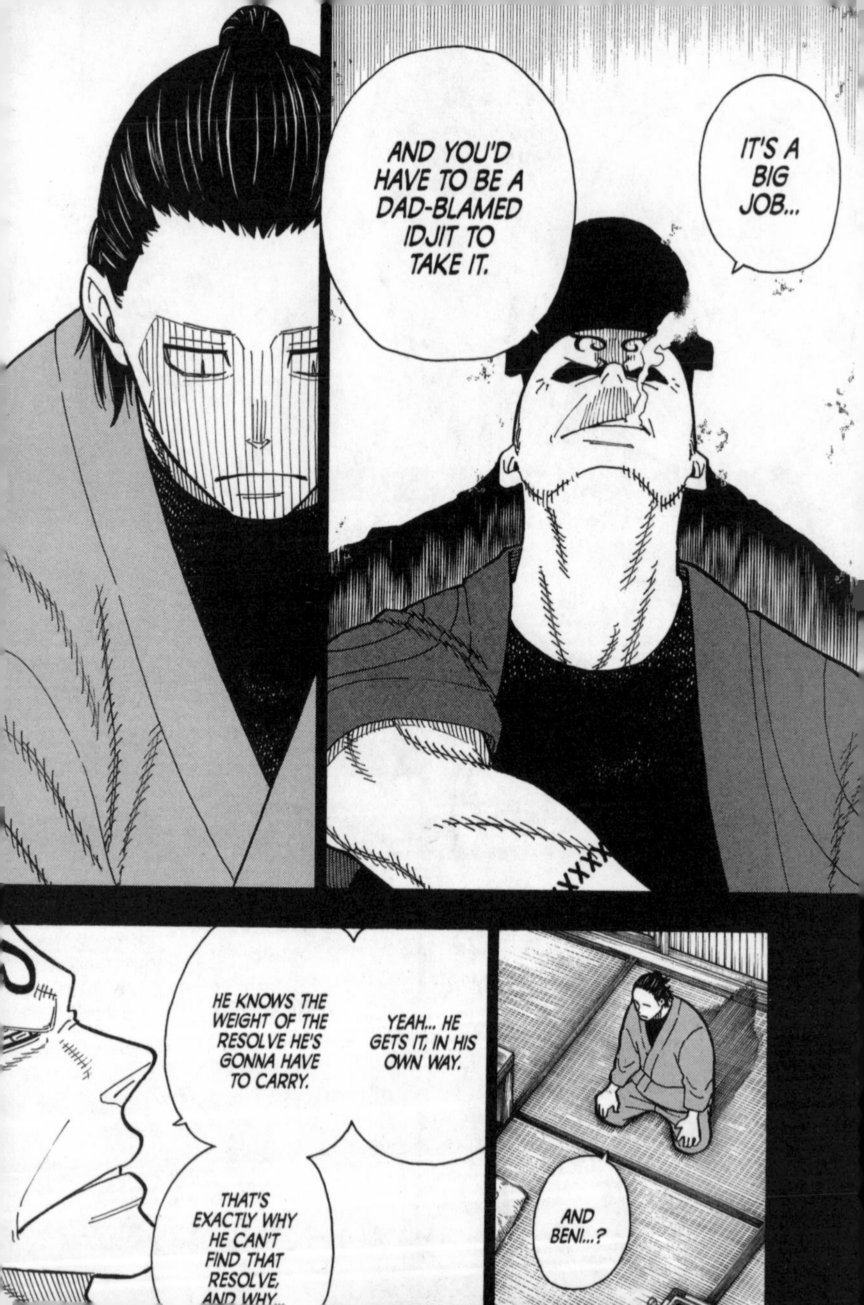

IT'S A BIG JOB...
AND YOU'D HAVE TO BE A DAD-BLAMED IDJIT TO TAKE IT.
AND BENI...?
YEAH... HE GETS IT, IN HIS OWN WAY.
HE KNOWS THE WEIGHT OF THE RESOLVE HE'S GONNA HAVE TO CARRY.
THAT'S EXACTLY WHY HE CAN'T FIND THAT RESOLVE, AND WHY...

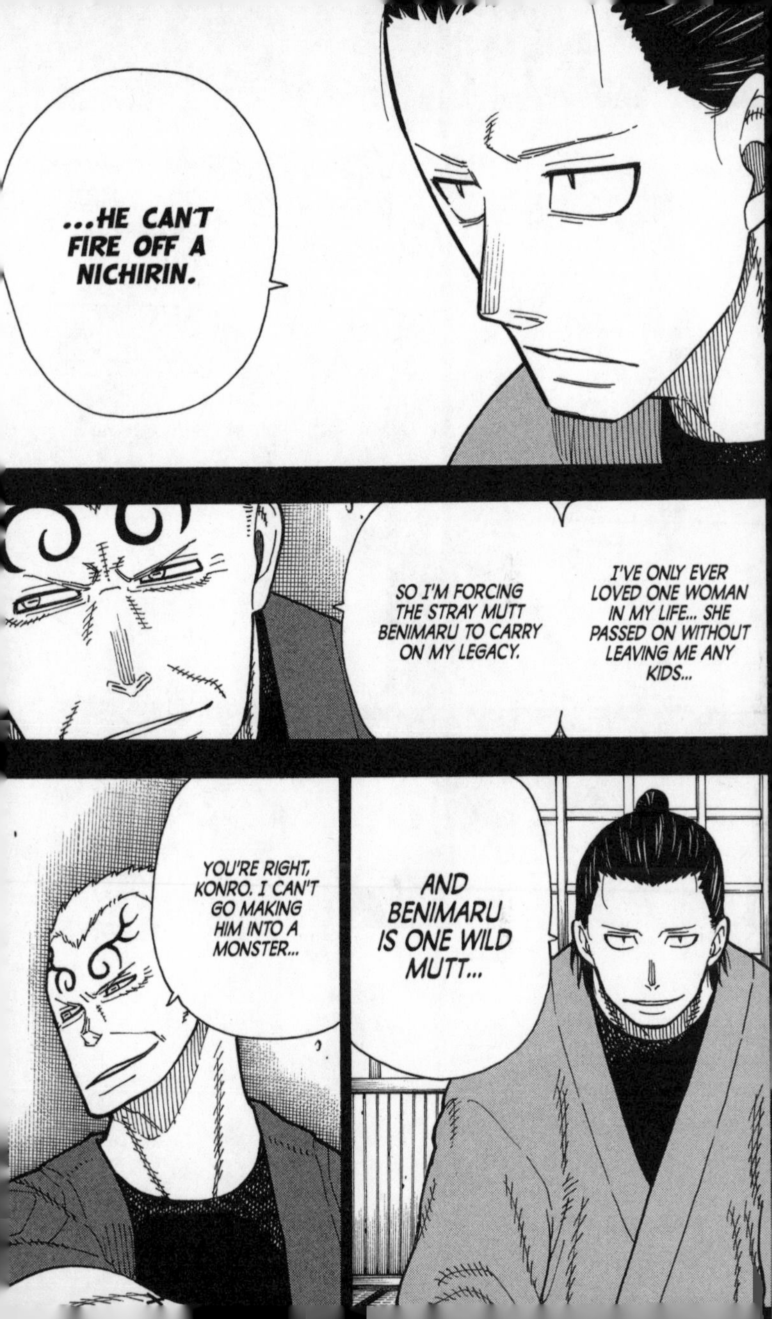
...HE CAN'T FIRE OFF A NICHIRIN.
I'VE ONLY EVER LOVED ONE WOMAN IN MY LIFE... SHE PASSED ON WITHOUT LEAVING ME ANY KIDS...
SO I'M FORCING THE STRAY MUTT BENIMARU TO CARRY ON MY LEGACY.
AND BENIMARU IS ONE WILD MUTT...
YOU'RE RIGHT, KONRO. I CAN'T GO MAKING HIM INTO A MONSTER...

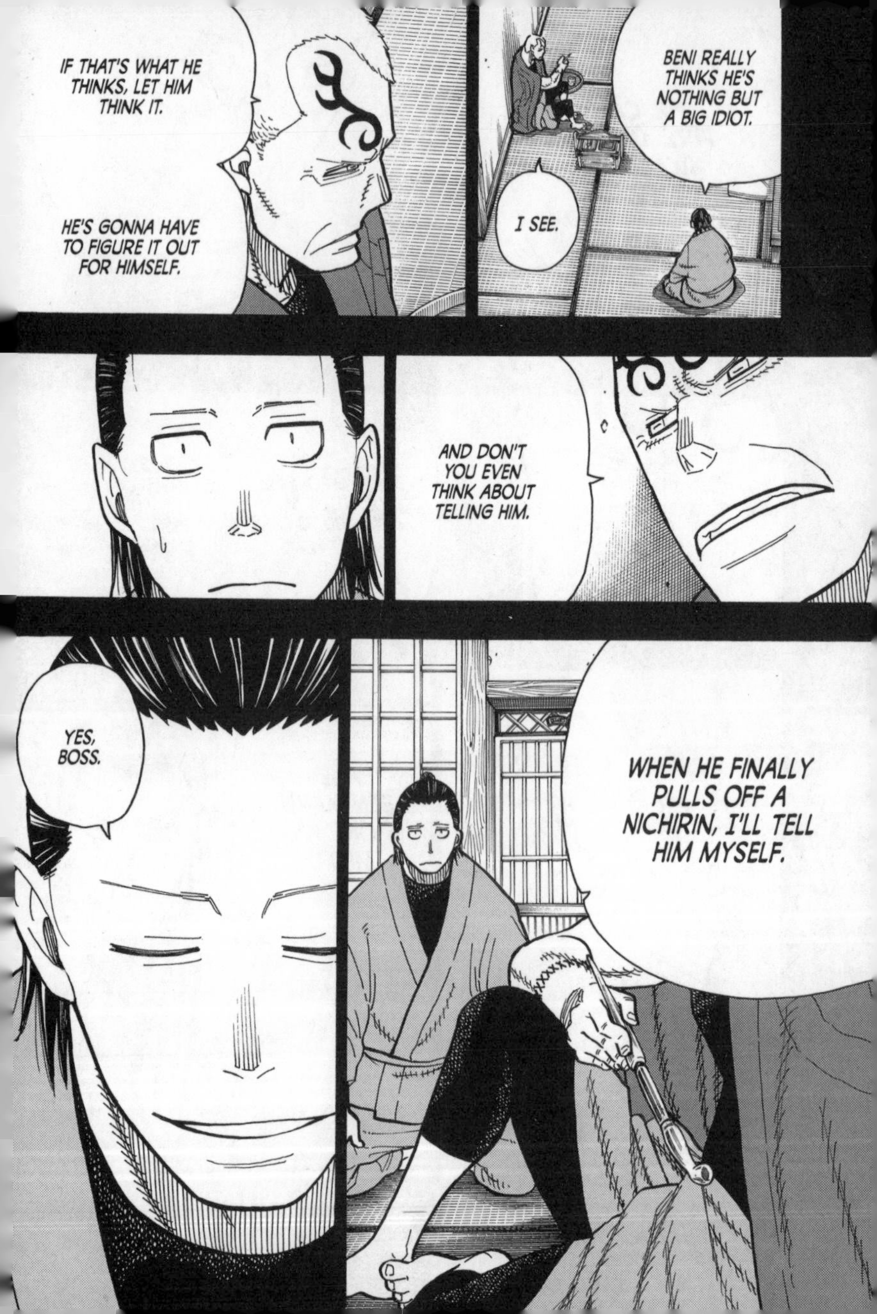
BENI REALLY THINKS HE'S NOTHING BUT A BIG IDIOT.
I SEE.
IF THAT'S WHAT HE THINKS, LET HIM THINK IT.
HE'S GONNA HAVE TO FIGURE IT OUT FOR HIMSELF.
AND DON'T YOU EVEN THINK ABOUT TELLING HIM.
WHEN HE FINALLY PULLS OFF A NICHIRIN, I'LL TELL HIM MYSELF.
YES, BOSS.

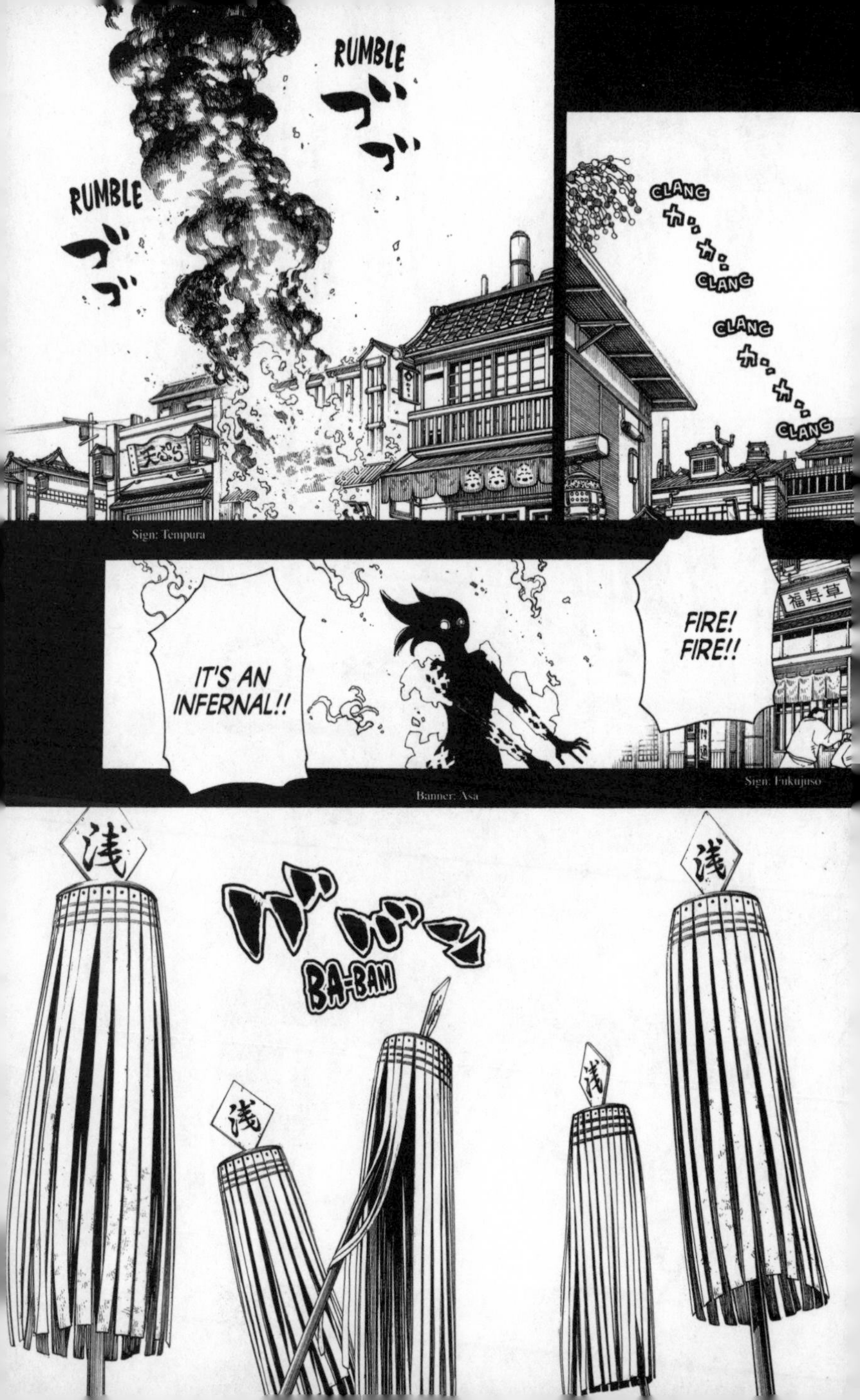
CLANG
CLANG
CLANG
CLANG
RUMBLE
RUMBLE
Sign: Tempura
FIRE! FIRE!!
IT'S AN INFERNAL!!
Sign: Fukujuso
Banner: Asa
BA-BAM

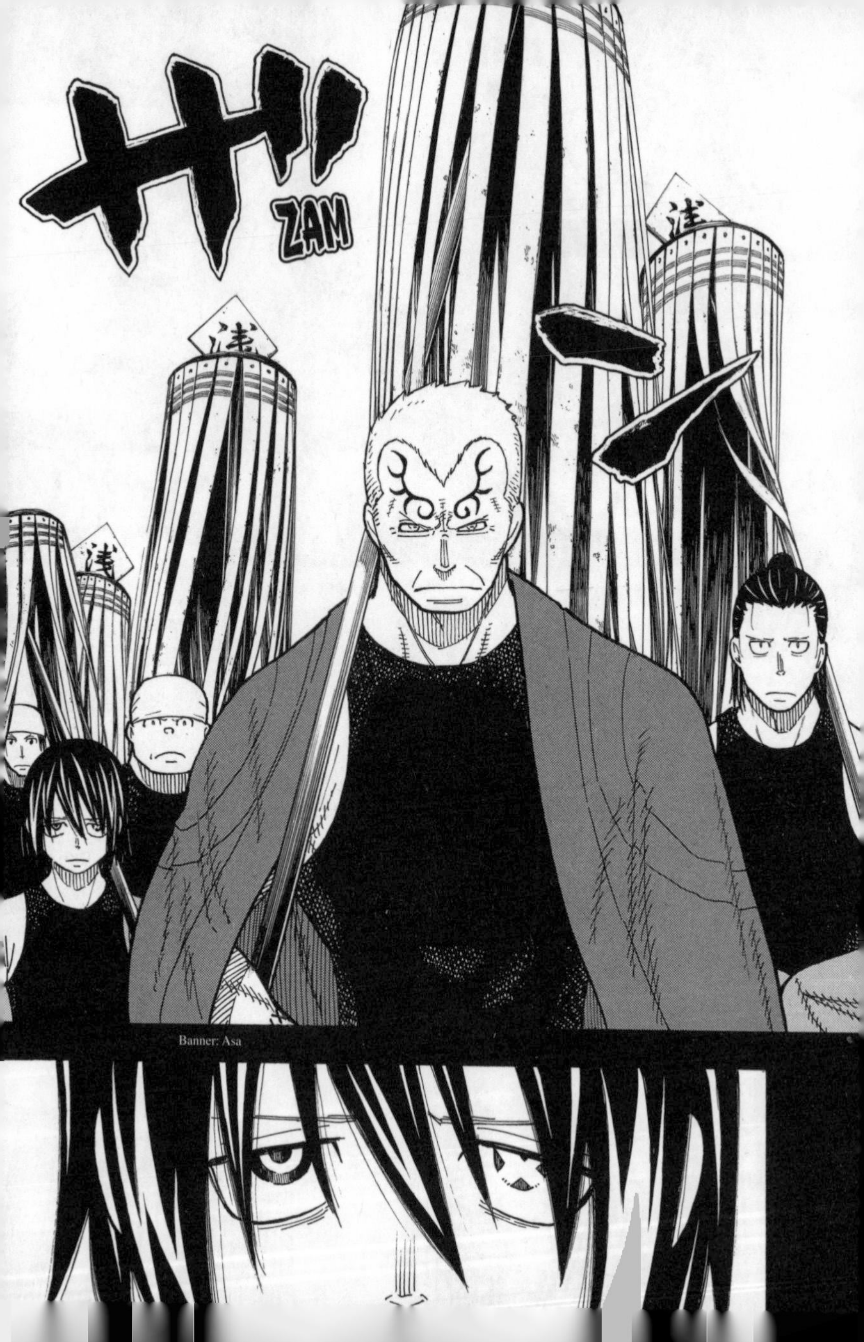
ZAM
浅
Banner: Asa

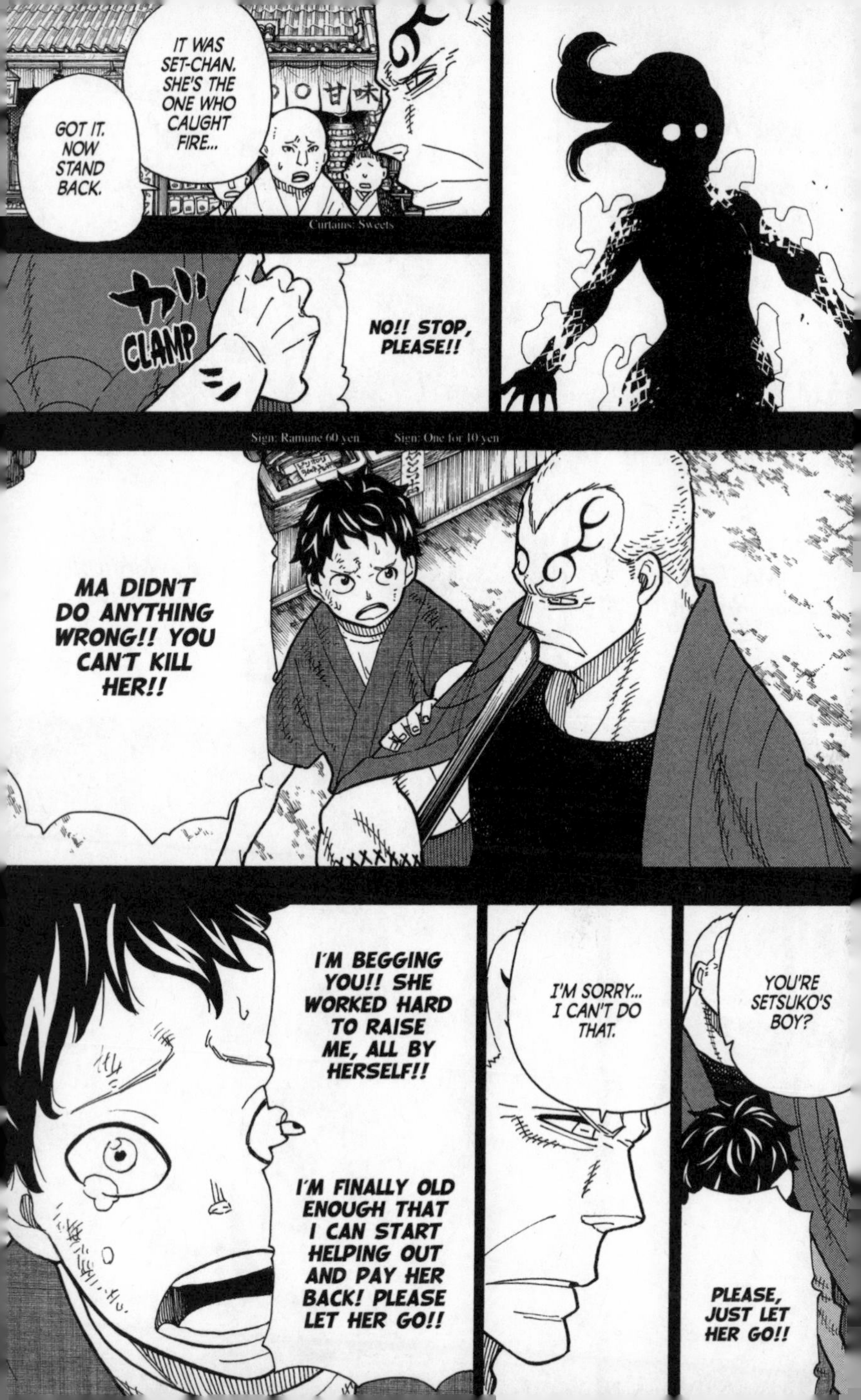
IT WAS SET-CHAN. SHE'S THE ONE WHO CAUGHT FIRE...
GOT IT. NOW STAND BACK.
Curtains: Sweets
NO!! STOP, PLEASE!!
CLAMP
Sign: Ramune 60 yen
Sign: One for 10 yen
MA DIDN'T DO ANYTHING WRONG!! YOU CAN'T KILL HER!!
YOU'RE SETSUKO'S BOY?
PLEASE, JUST LET HER GO!!
I'M SORRY... I CAN'T DO THAT.
I'M BEGGING YOU!! SHE WORKED HARD TO RAISE ME, ALL BY HERSELF!!
I'M FINALLY OLD ENOUGH THAT I CAN START HELPING OUT AND PAY HER BACK! PLEASE LET HER GO!!

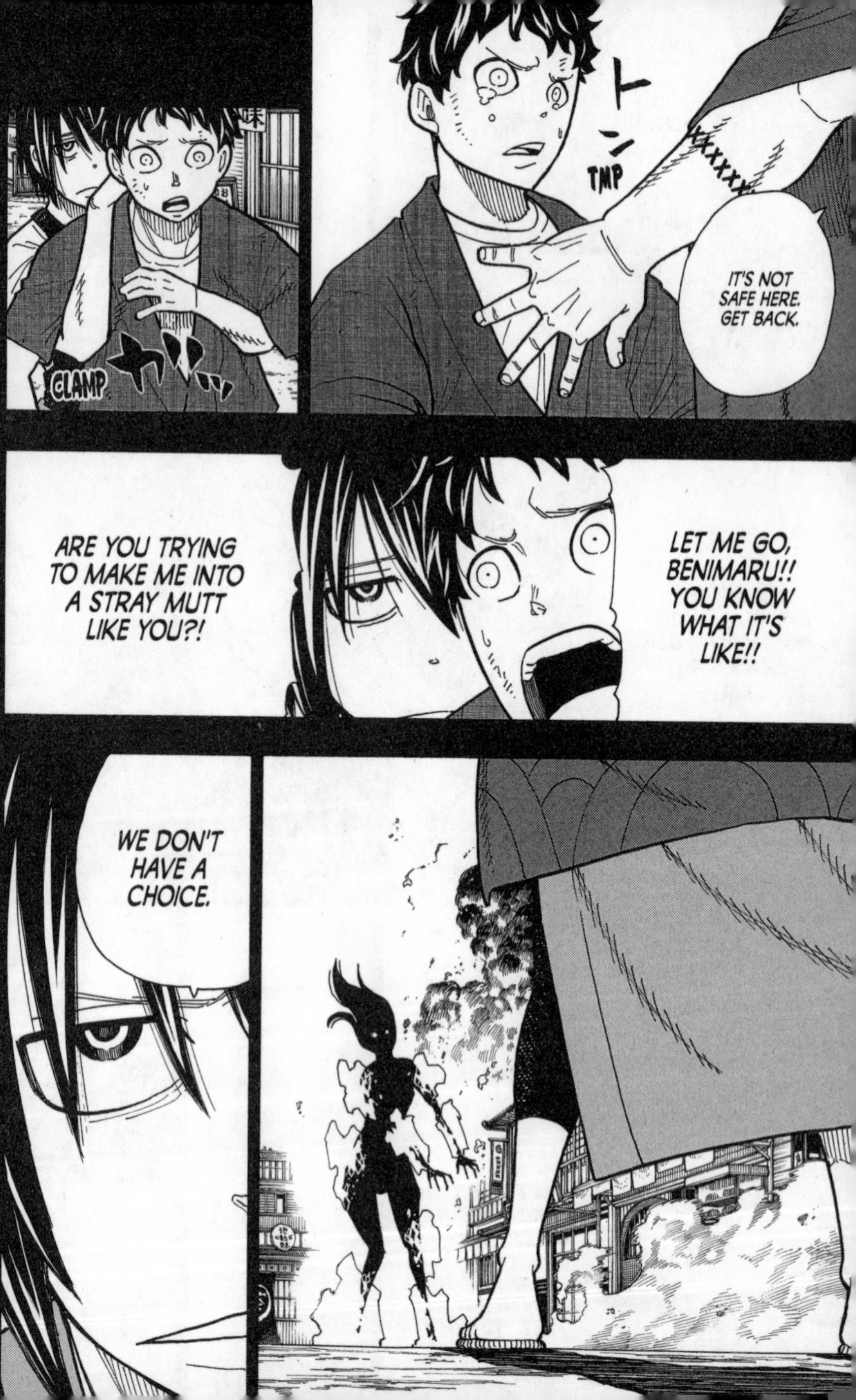

TMP
IT'S NOT SAFE HERE. GET BACK.
CLAMP
LET ME GO, BENIMARU!! YOU KNOW WHAT IT'S LIKE!!
ARE YOU TRYING TO MAKE ME INTO A STRAY MUTT LIKE YOU?!
WE DON'T HAVE A CHOICE.

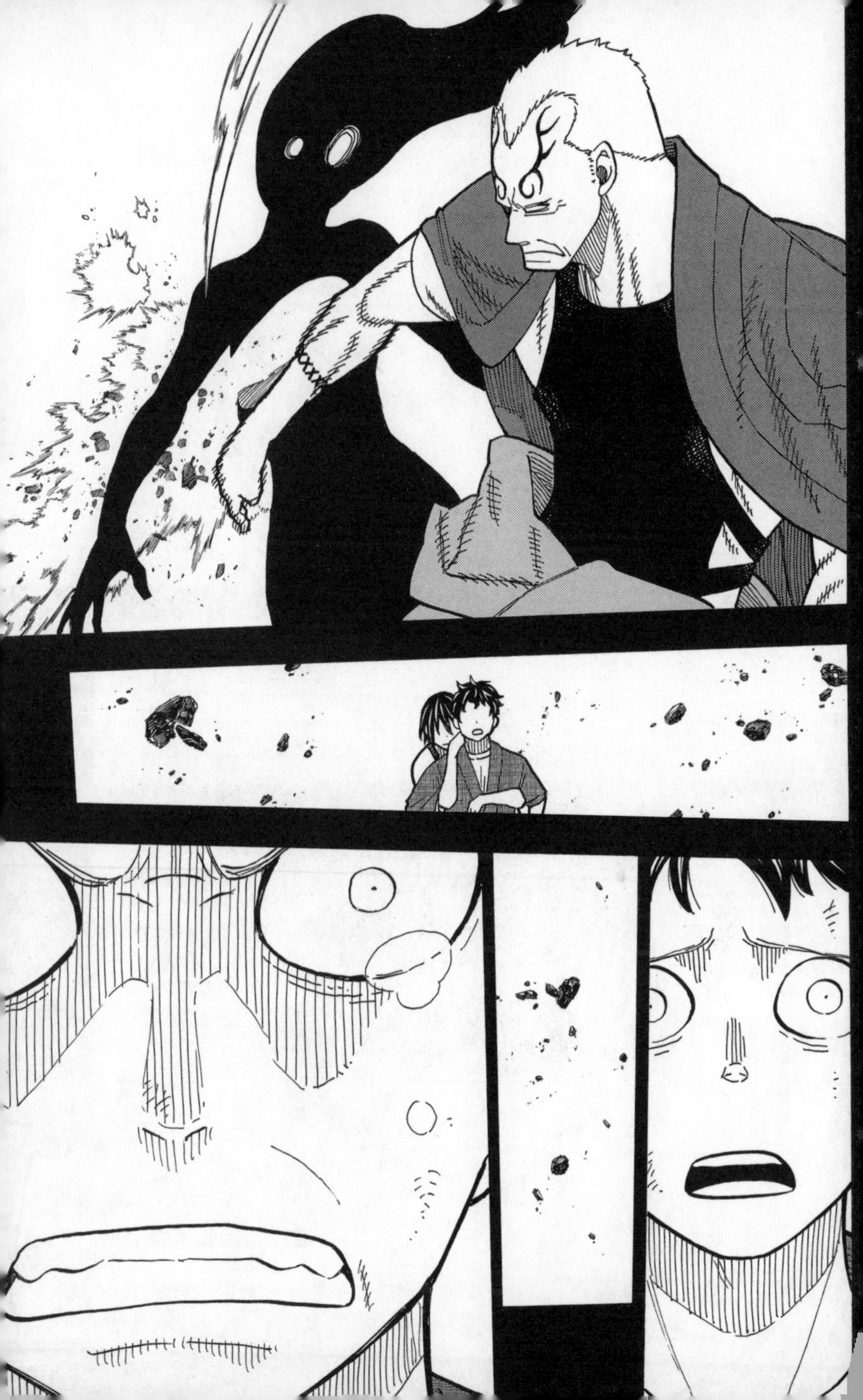

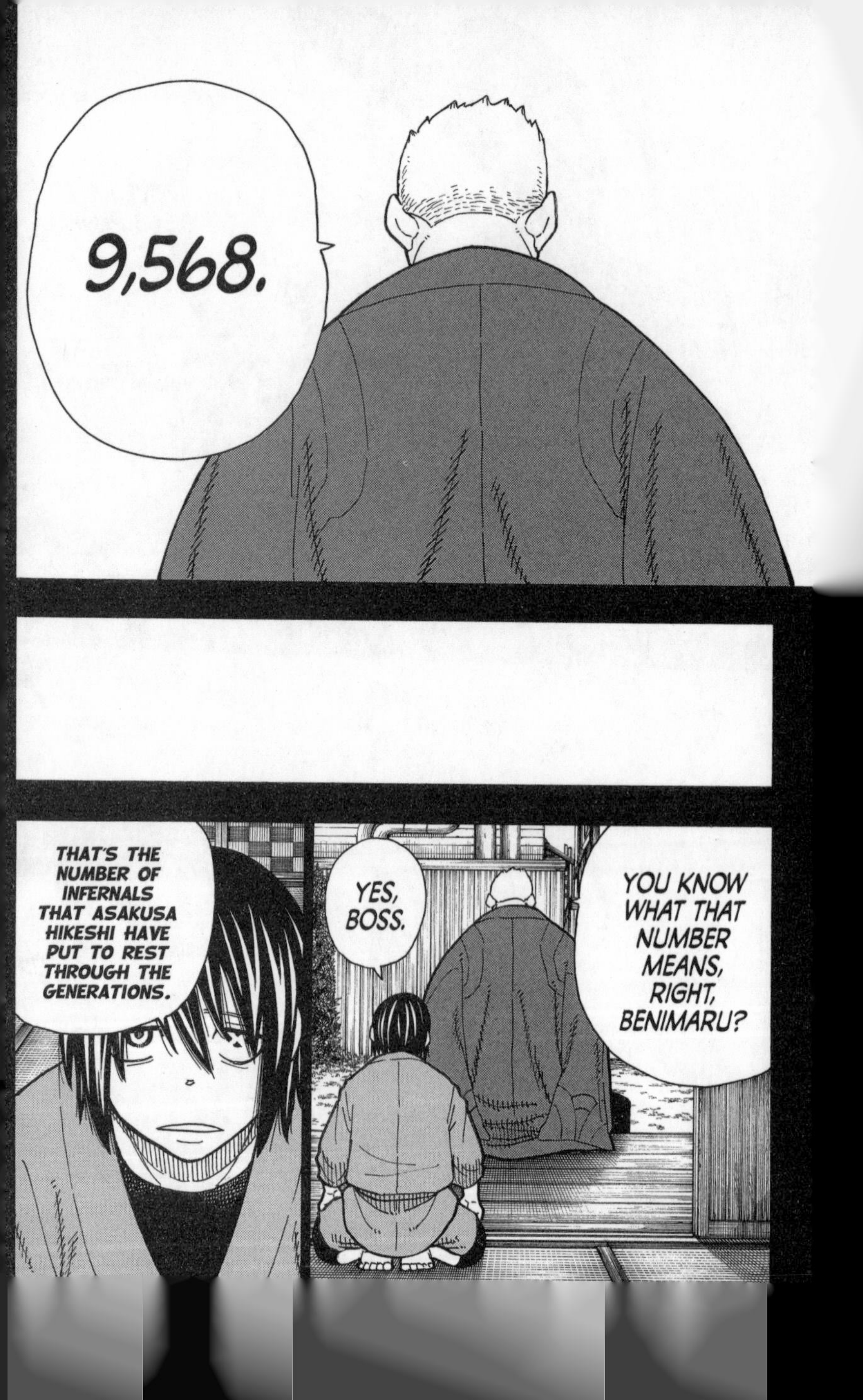
9,568.
YOU KNOW WHAT THAT NUMBER MEANS, RIGHT, BENIMARU?
YES, BOSS.
THAT'S THE NUMBER OF INFERNALS THAT ASAKUSA HIKESHI HAVE PUT TO REST THROUGH THE GENERATIONS.

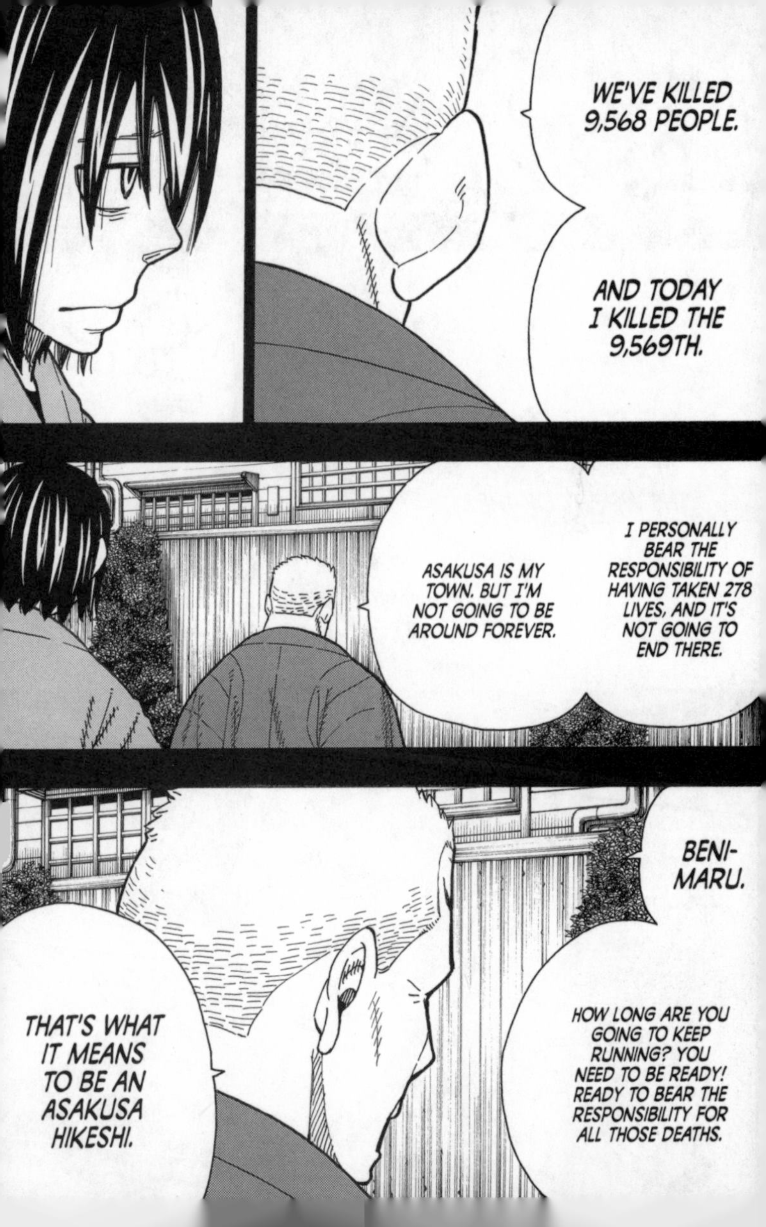
WE'VE KILLED 9,568 PEOPLE.
AND TODAY I KILLED THE 9,569TH.
I PERSONALLY BEAR THE RESPONSIBILITY OF HAVING TAKEN 278 LIVES, AND IT'S NOT GOING TO END THERE.
ASAKUSA IS MY TOWN. BUT I'M NOT GOING TO BE AROUND FOREVER.
BENI-MARU.
HOW LONG ARE YOU GOING TO KEEP RUNNING? YOU NEED TO BE READY! READY TO BEAR THE RESPONSIBILITY FOR ALL THOSE DEATHS.
THAT'S WHAT IT MEANS TO BE AN ASAKUSA HIKESHI.

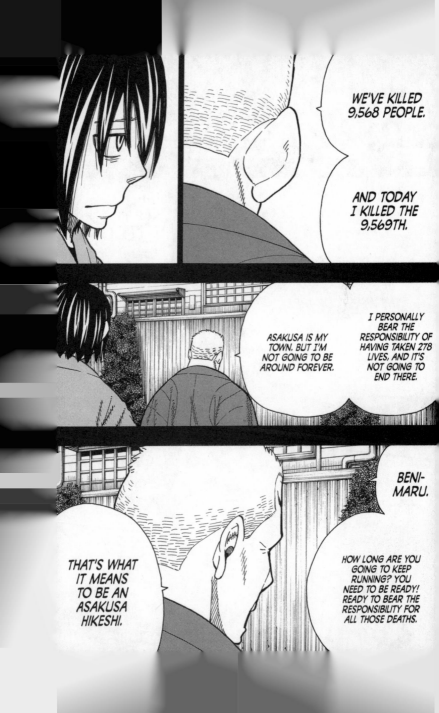

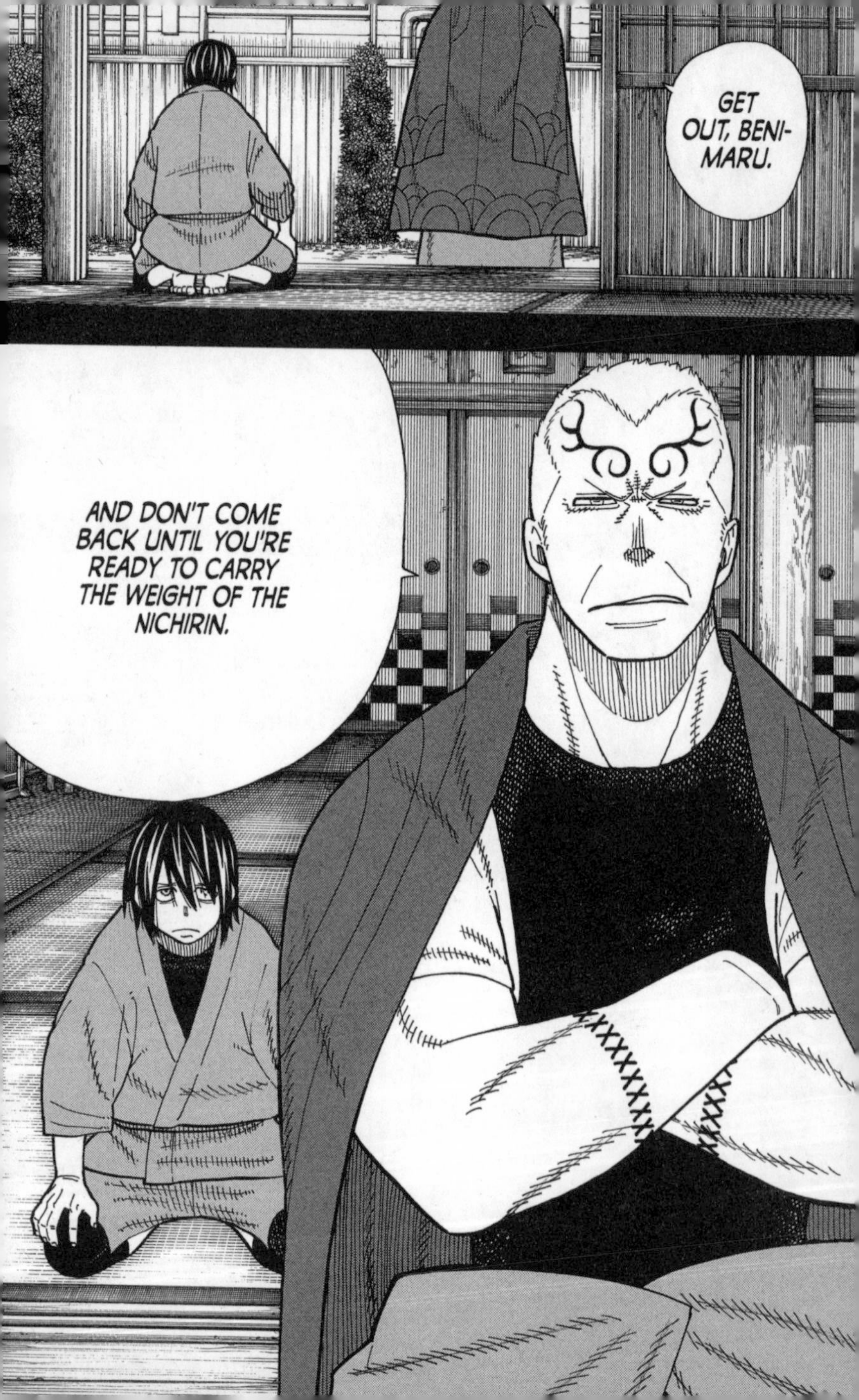
GET OUT, BENI-MARU.
AND DON'T COME BACK UNTIL YOU'RE READY TO CARRY THE WEIGHT OF THE NICHIRIN.

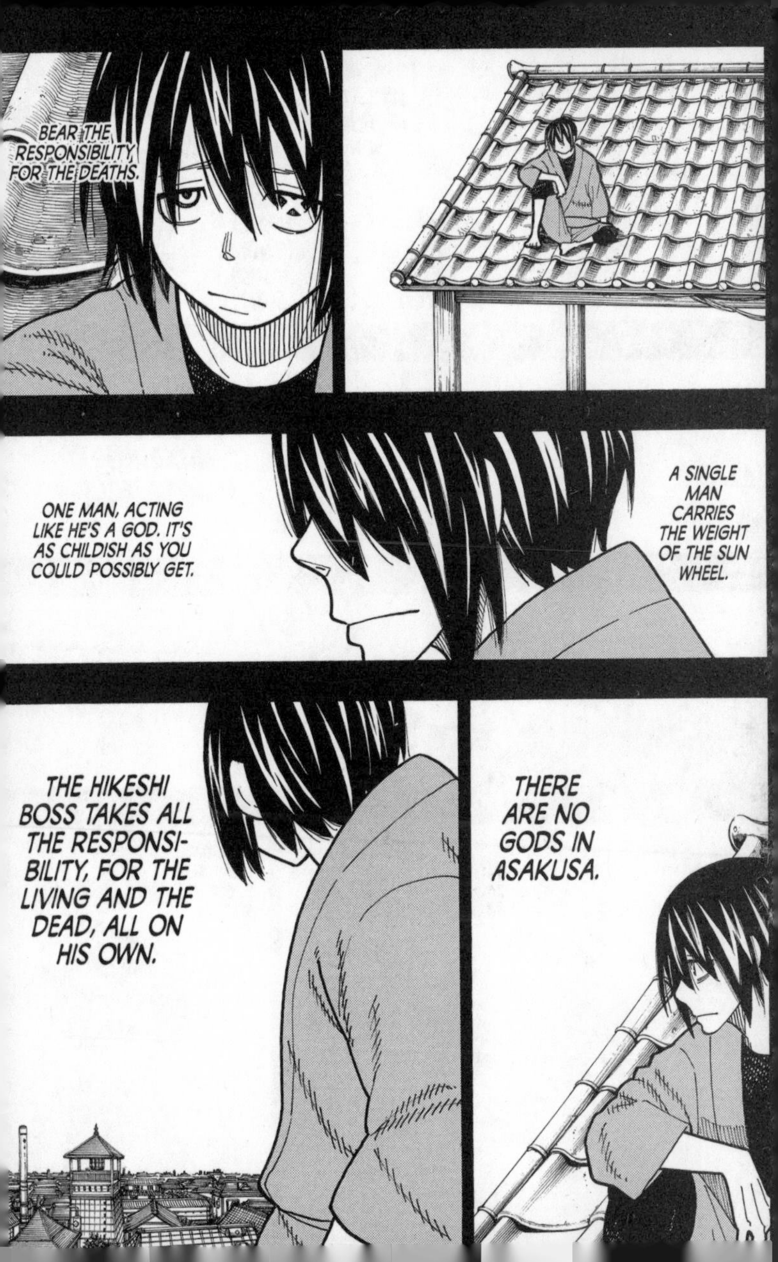
BEAR THE RESPONSIBILITY FOR THE DEATHS.
A SINGLE MAN CARRIES THE WEIGHT OF THE SUN WHEEL.
ONE MAN, ACTING LIKE HE'S A GOD. IT'S AS CHILDISH AS YOU COULD POSSIBLY GET.
THERE ARE NO GODS IN ASAKUSA.
THE HIKESHI BOSS TAKES ALL THE RESPONSI-BILITY, FOR THE LIVING AND THE DEAD, ALL ON HIS OWN.

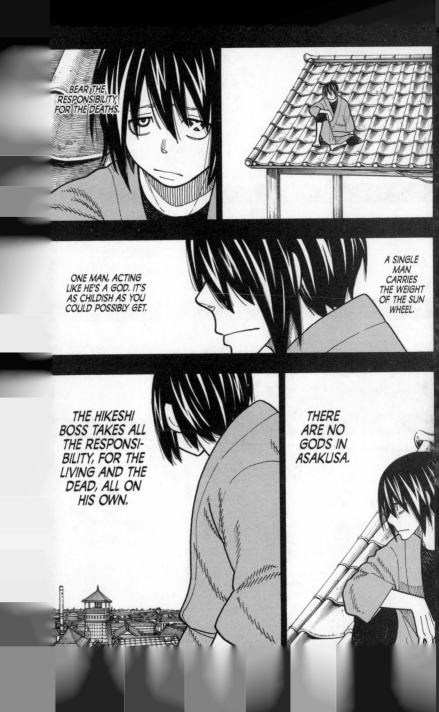

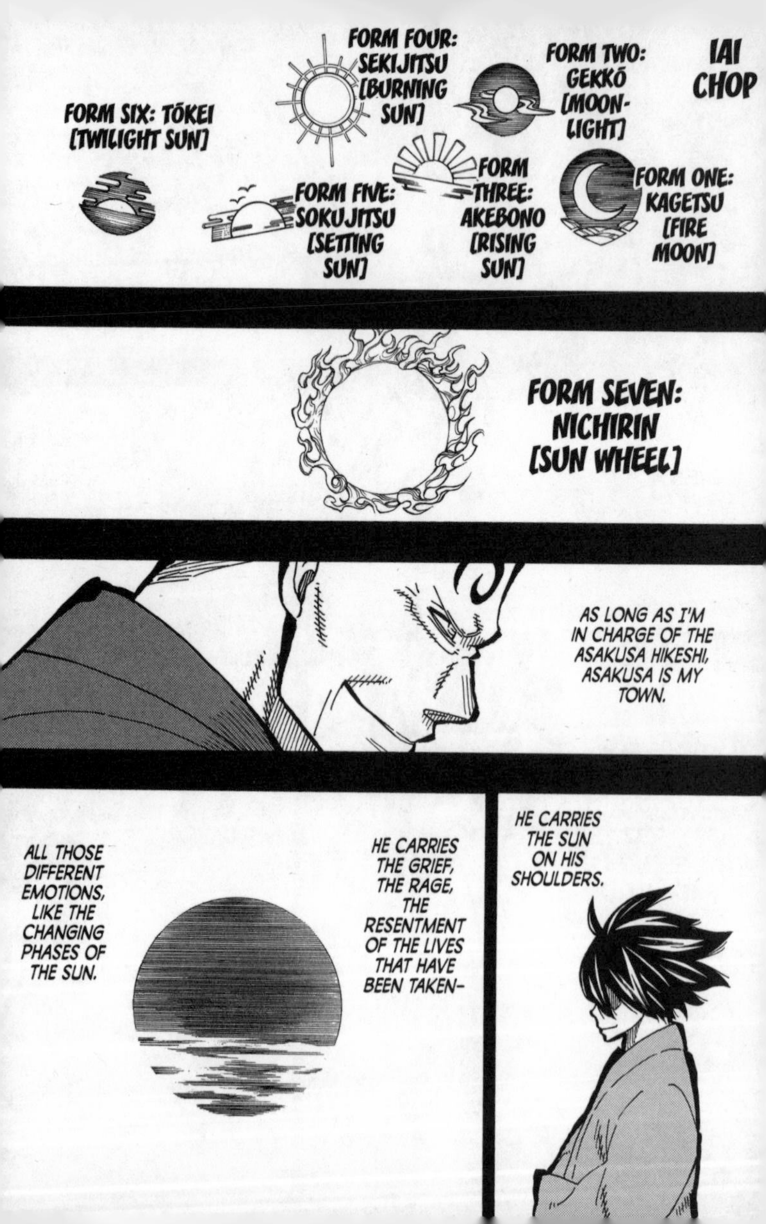
IAI CHOP
FORM ONE: KAGETSU [FIRE MOON]
FORM TWO: GEKKŌ [MOON-LIGHT]
FORM THREE: AKEBONO [RISING SUN]
FORM FOUR: SEKIJITSU [BURNING SUN]
FORM FIVE: SOKUJITSU [SETTING SUN]
FORM SIX: TŌKEI [TWILIGHT SUN]
FORM SEVEN: NICHIRIN [SUN WHEEL]
AS LONG AS I'M IN CHARGE OF THE ASAKUSA HIKESHI, ASAKUSA IS MY TOWN.
HE CARRIES THE SUN ON HIS SHOULDERS.
HE CARRIES THE GRIEF, THE RAGE, THE RESENTMENT OF THE LIVES THAT HAVE BEEN TAKEN-
ALL THOSE DIFFERENT EMOTIONS, LIKE THE CHANGING PHASES OF THE SUN.

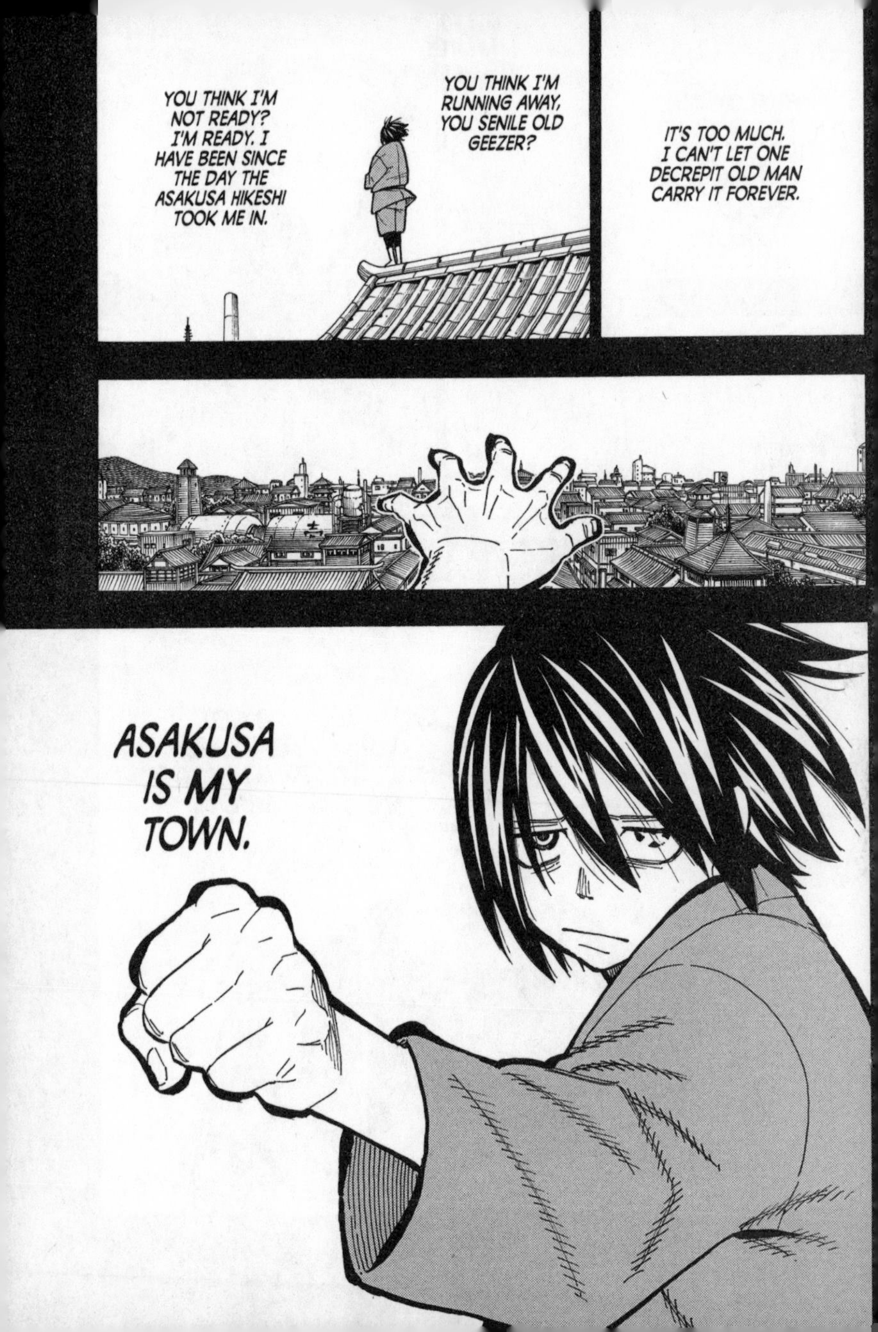
IT'S TOO MUCH. I CAN'T LET ONE DECREPIT OLD MAN CARRY IT FOREVER.
YOU THINK I'M RUNNING AWAY, YOU SENILE OLD GEEZER?
YOU THINK I'M NOT READY? I'M READY. I HAVE BEEN SINCE THE DAY THE ASAKUSA HIKESHI TOOK ME IN.
ASAKUSA IS MY TOWN.

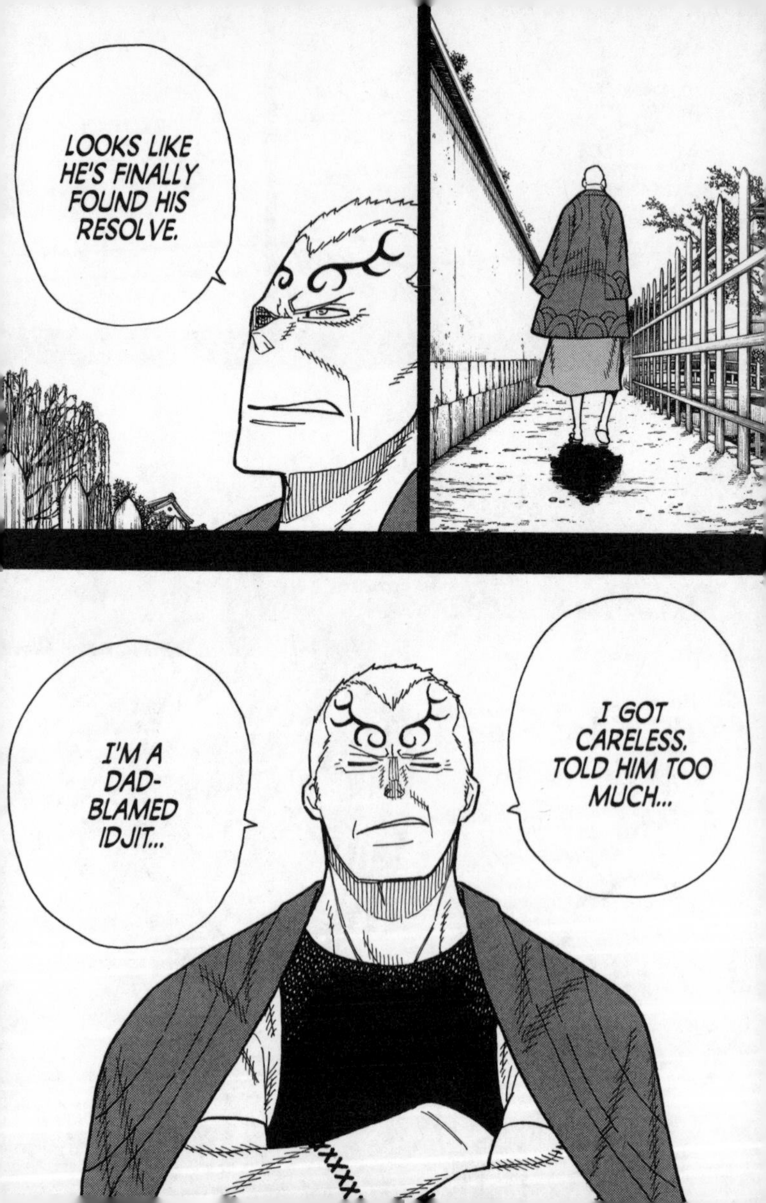
LOOKS LIKE HE'S FINALLY FOUND HIS RESOLVE.
I GOT CARELESS. TOLD HIM TOO MUCH...
I'M A DAD-BLAMED IDJIT...

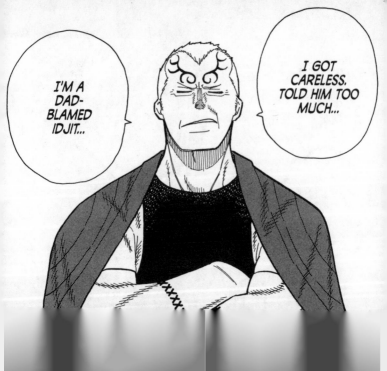

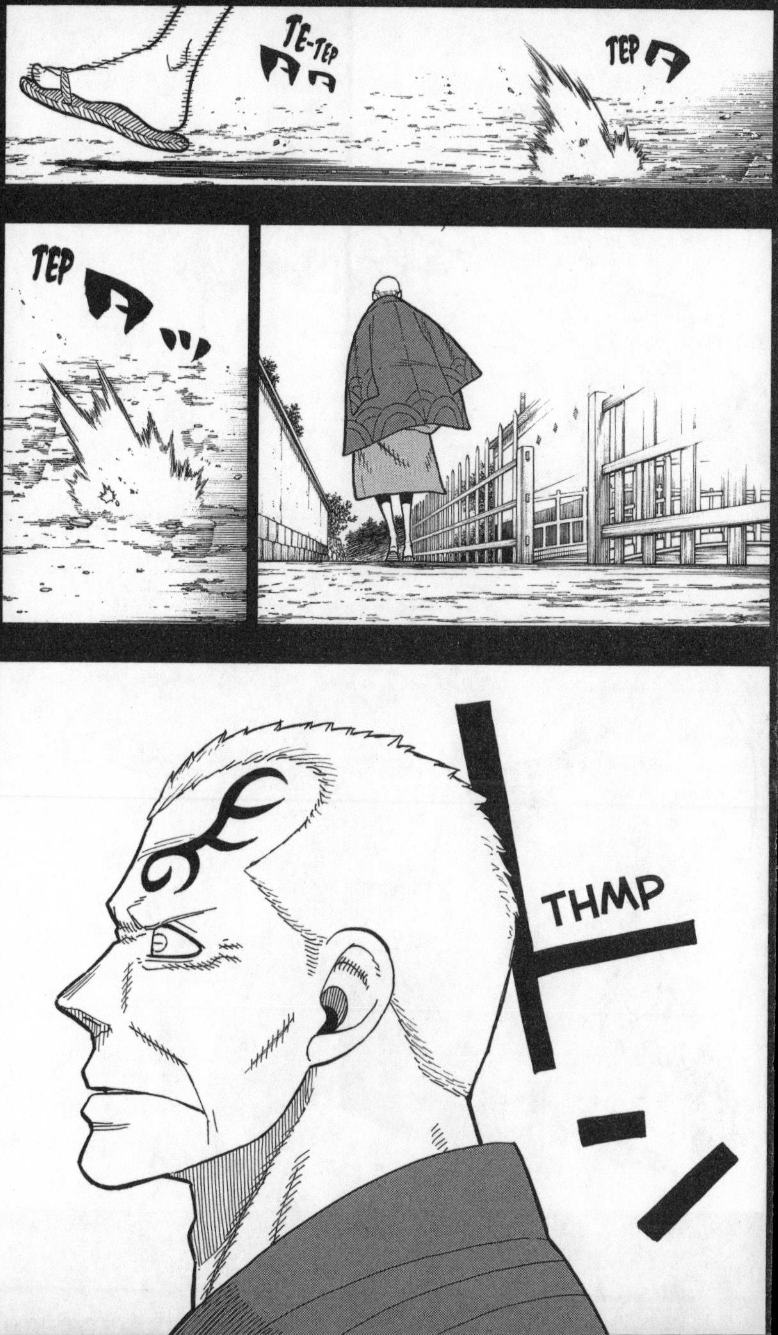
TEP
TE-TEP
TEP
THMP

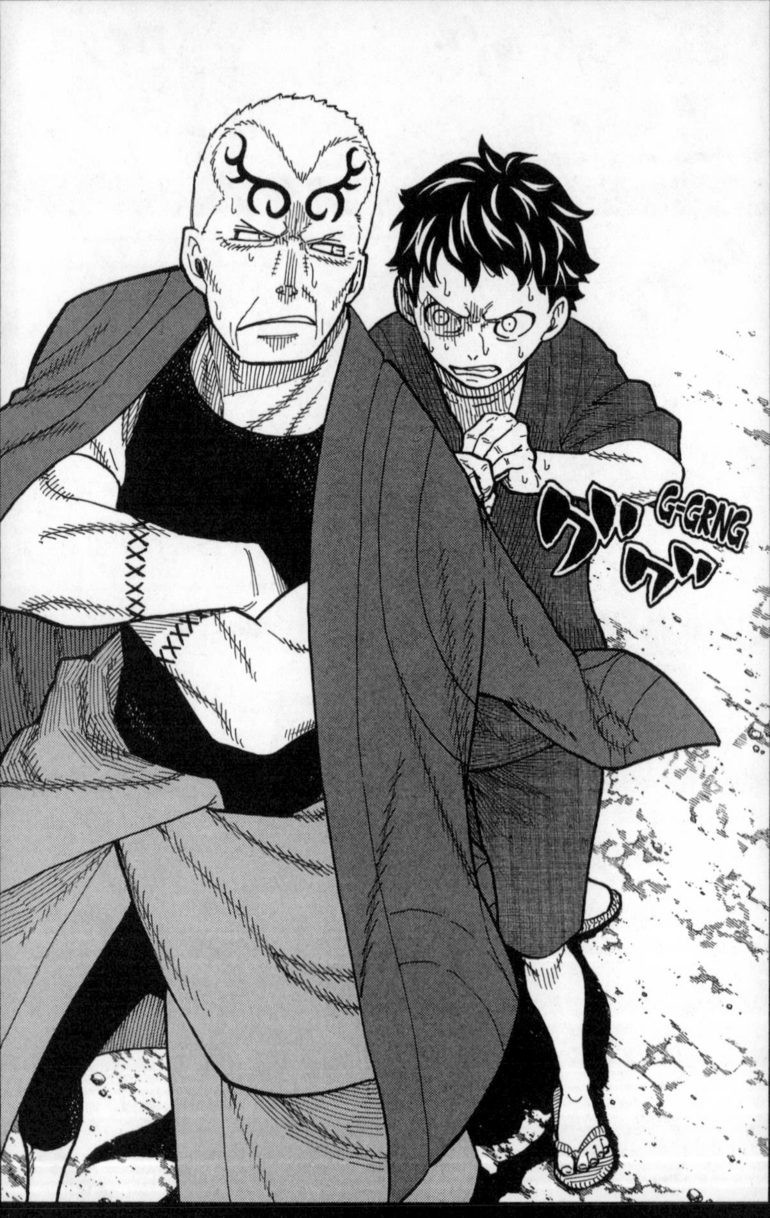
G-GRNG

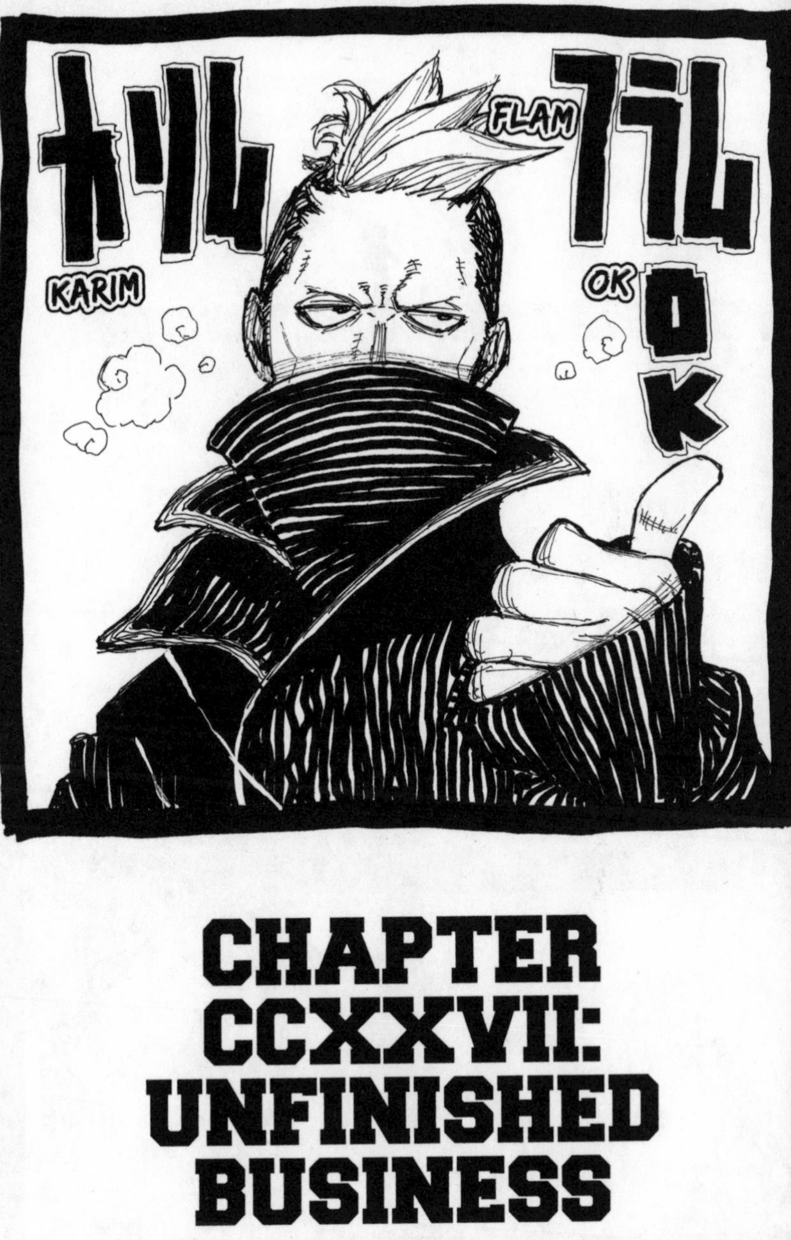
カリム
KARIM
FLAM
フラム
OK
OK

CHAPTER CCXXVII: UNFINISHED BUSINESS

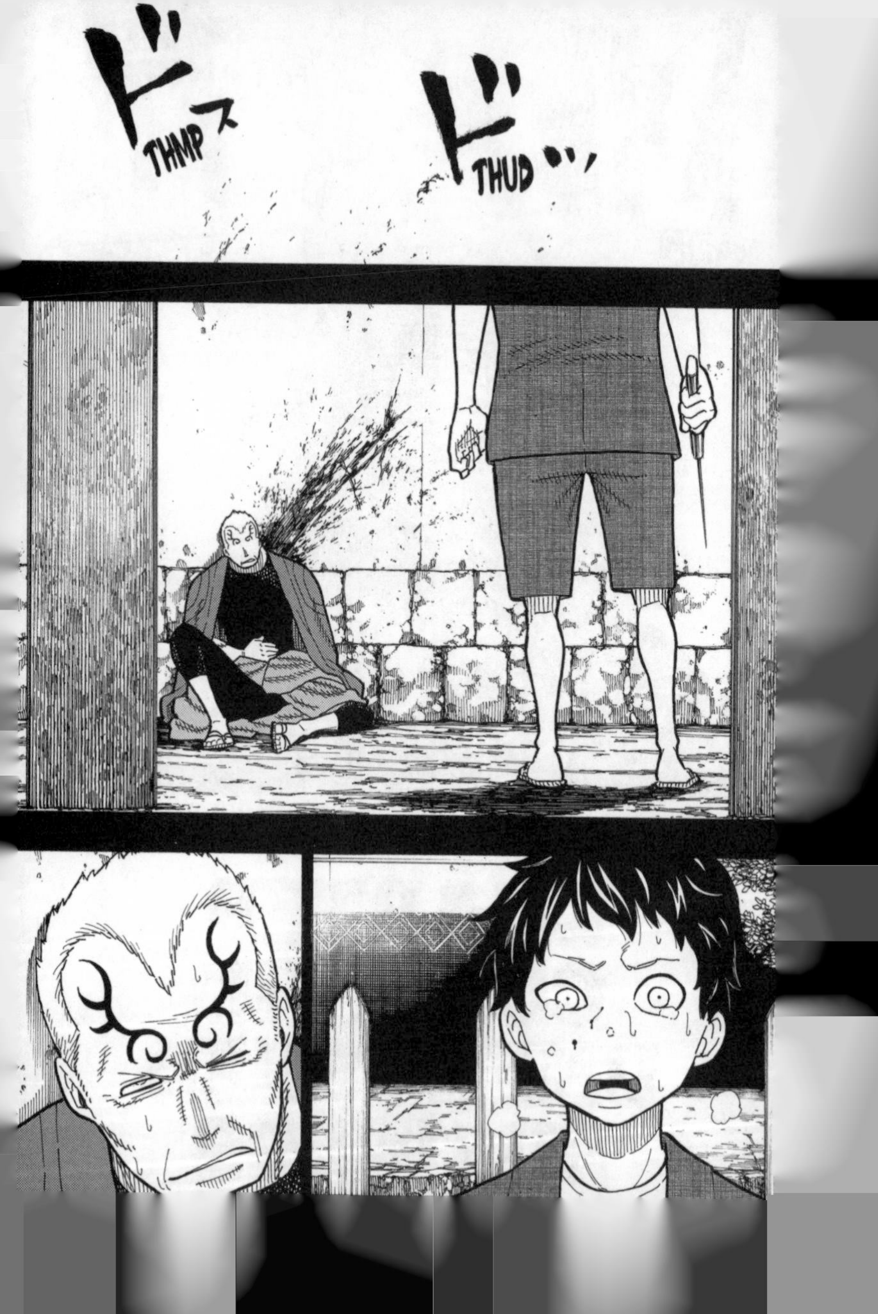
ド…
THUD
ドス
THMP

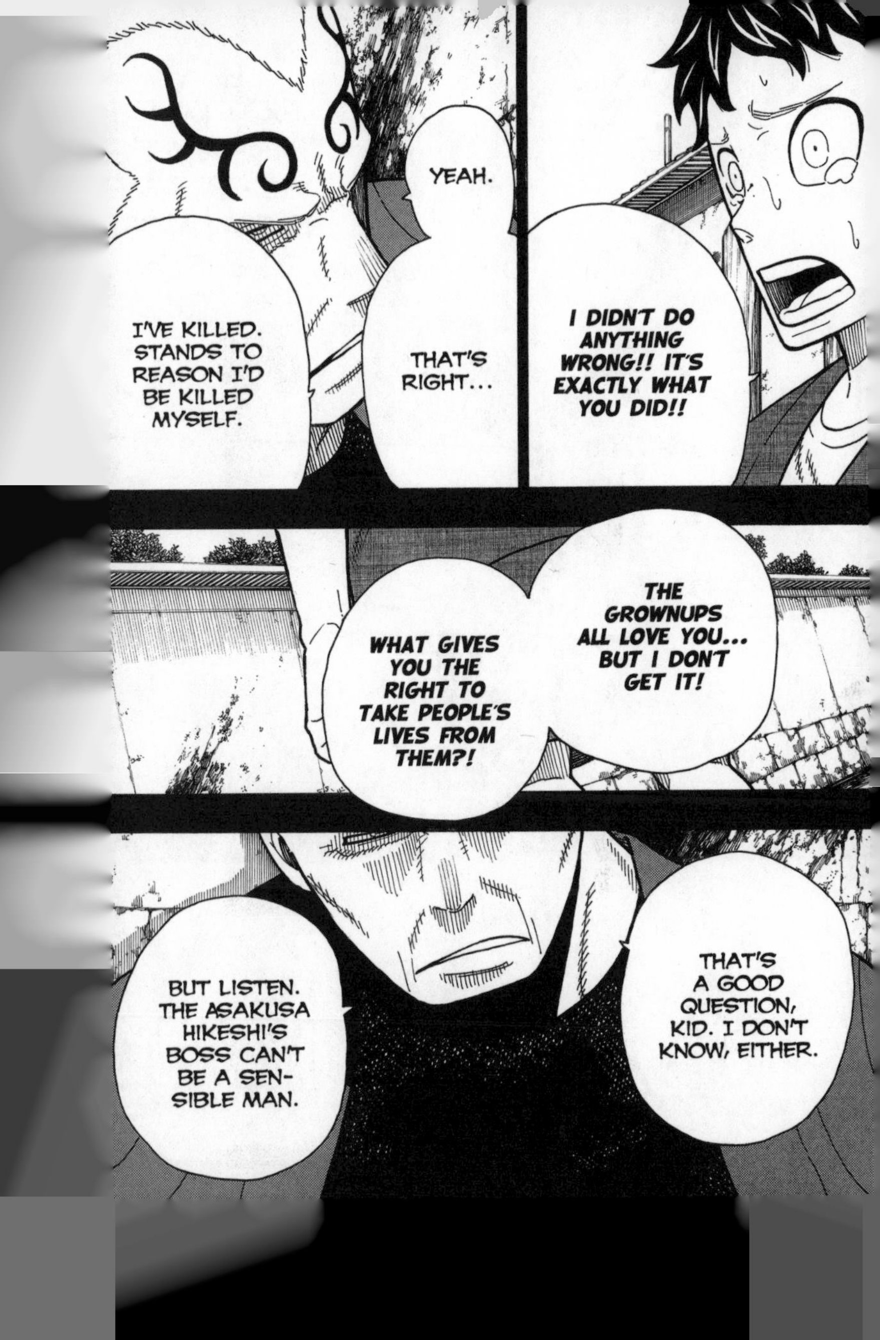
I DIDN'T DO ANYTHING WRONG!! IT'S EXACTLY WHAT YOU DID!!
YEAH.
THAT'S RIGHT...
I'VE KILLED. STANDS TO REASON I'D BE KILLED MYSELF.
THE GROWNUPS ALL LOVE YOU... BUT I DON'T GET IT!
WHAT GIVES YOU THE RIGHT TO TAKE PEOPLE'S LIVES FROM THEM?!
THAT'S A GOOD QUESTION, KID. I DON'T KNOW, EITHER.
BUT LISTEN. THE ASAKUSA HIKESHI'S BOSS CAN'T BE A SEN-SIBLE MAN.

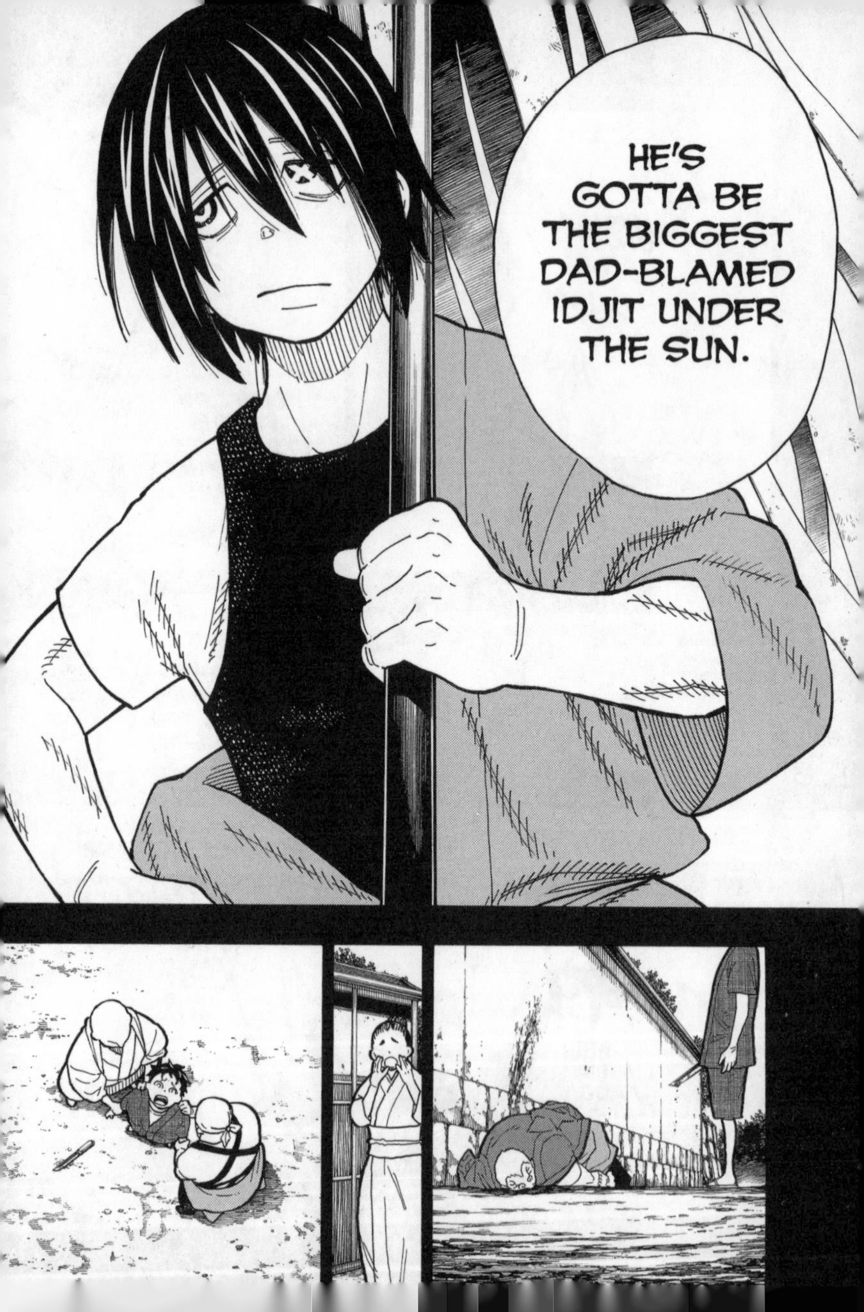
HE'S GOTTA BE THE BIGGEST DAD-BLAMED IDJIT UNDER THE SUN.

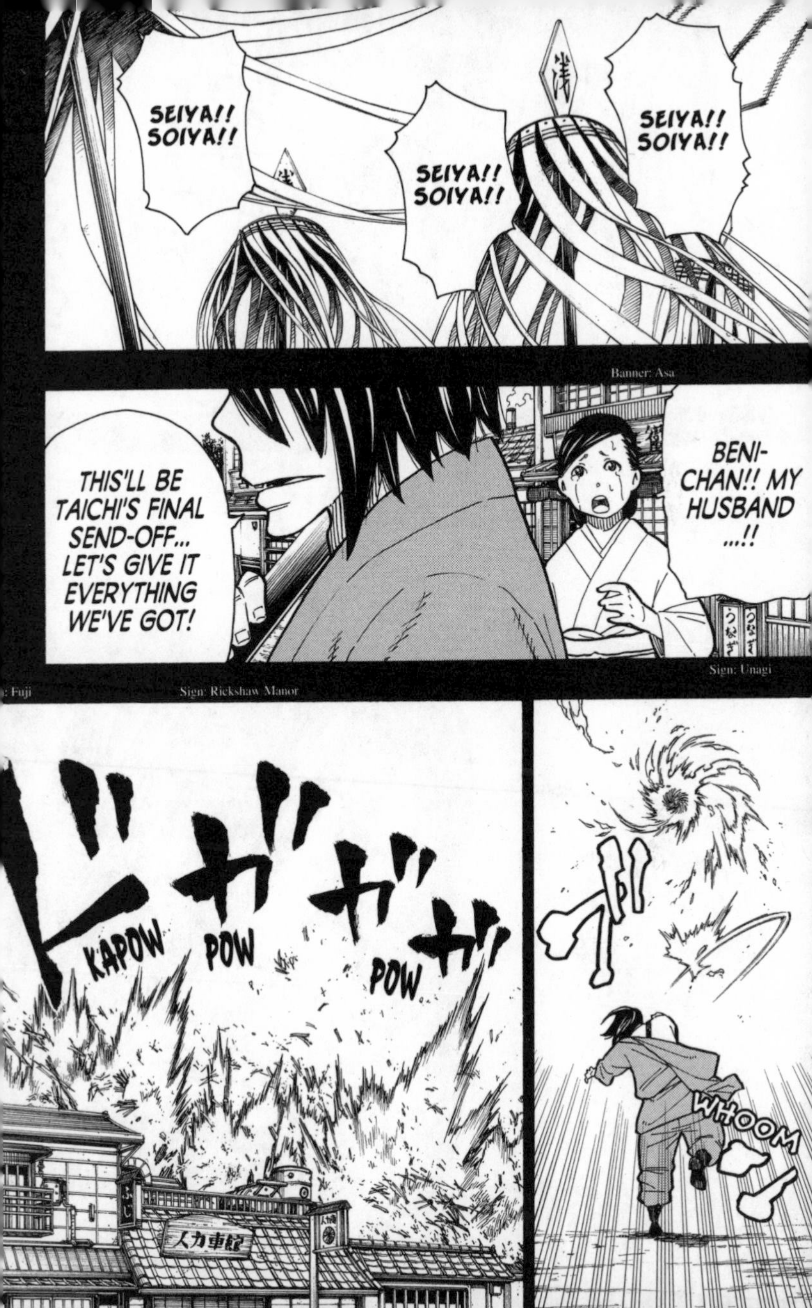
SEIYA!! SOIYA!!
SEIYA!! SOIYA!!
SEIYA!! SOIYA!!
Banner: Asa
BENI-CHAN!! MY HUSBAND ...!!
THIS'LL BE TAICHI'S FINAL SEND-OFF... LET'S GIVE IT EVERYTHING WE'VE GOT!
Sign: Unagi
Sign: Rickshaw Manor
: Fuji
WHOOM
KAPOW
POW
POW

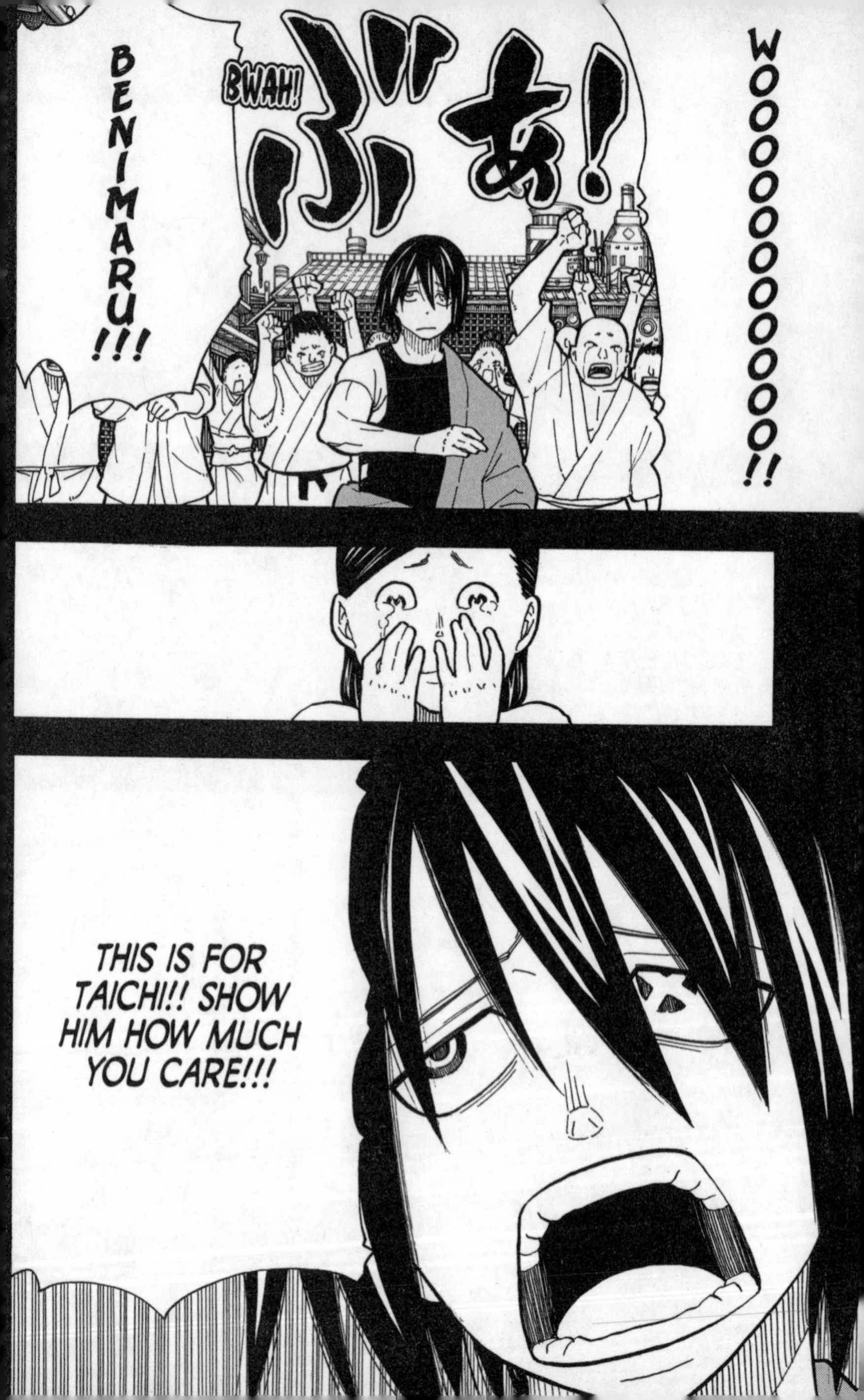
WOOOOOOOOOOO!!
BWAH!
ぶあ!
BENIMARU!!!
THIS IS FOR TAICHI!! SHOW HIM HOW MUCH YOU CARE!!!

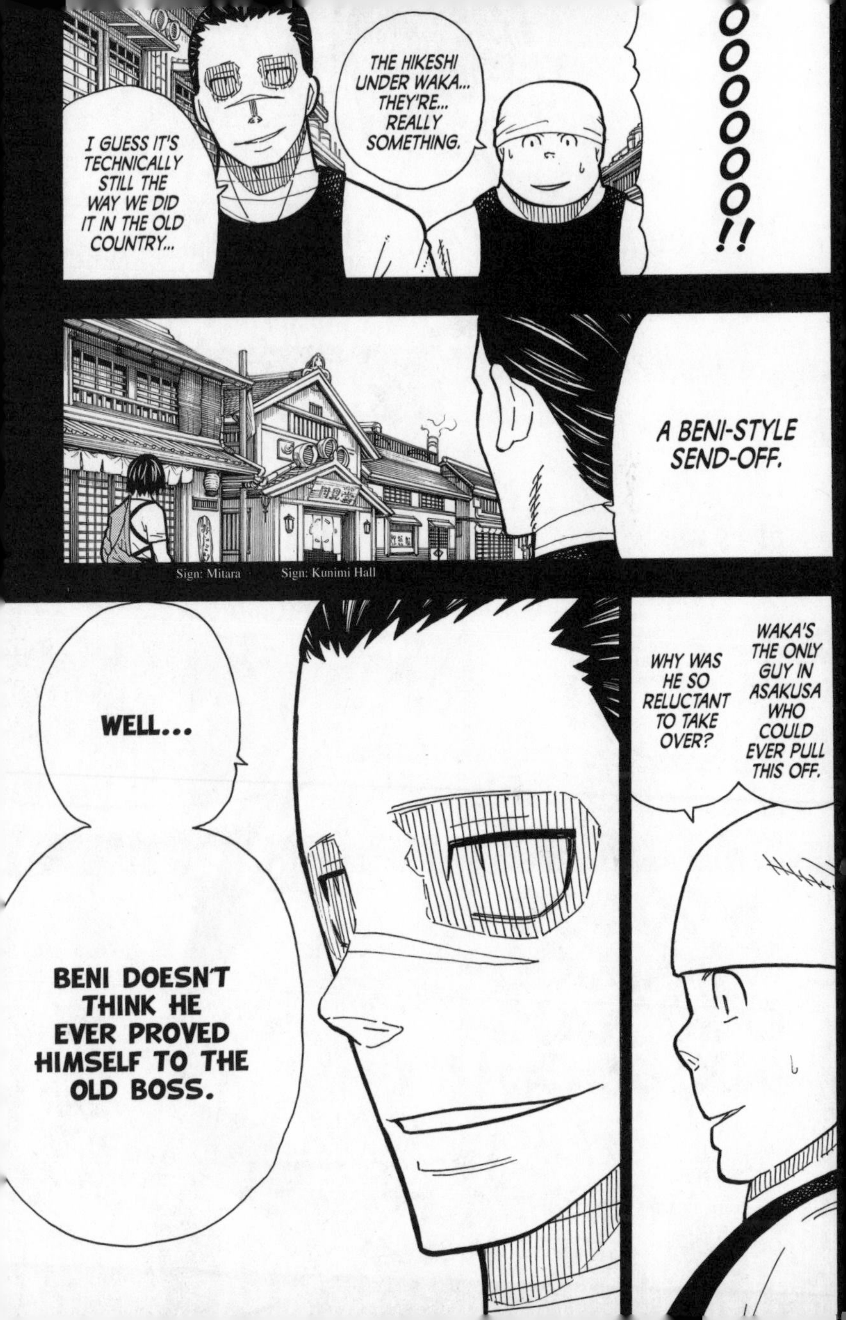
OOOOOOO!!
THE HIKESHI UNDER WAKA... THEY'RE... REALLY SOMETHING.
I GUESS IT'S TECHNICALLY STILL THE WAY WE DID IT IN THE OLD COUNTRY...
A BENI-STYLE SEND-OFF.
WAKA'S THE ONLY GUY IN ASAKUSA WHO COULD EVER PULL THIS OFF.
WHY WAS HE SO RELUCTANT TO TAKE OVER?
WELL...
BENI DOESN'T THINK HE EVER PROVED HIMSELF TO THE OLD BOSS.
Sign: Mitara Sign: Kunimi Hall

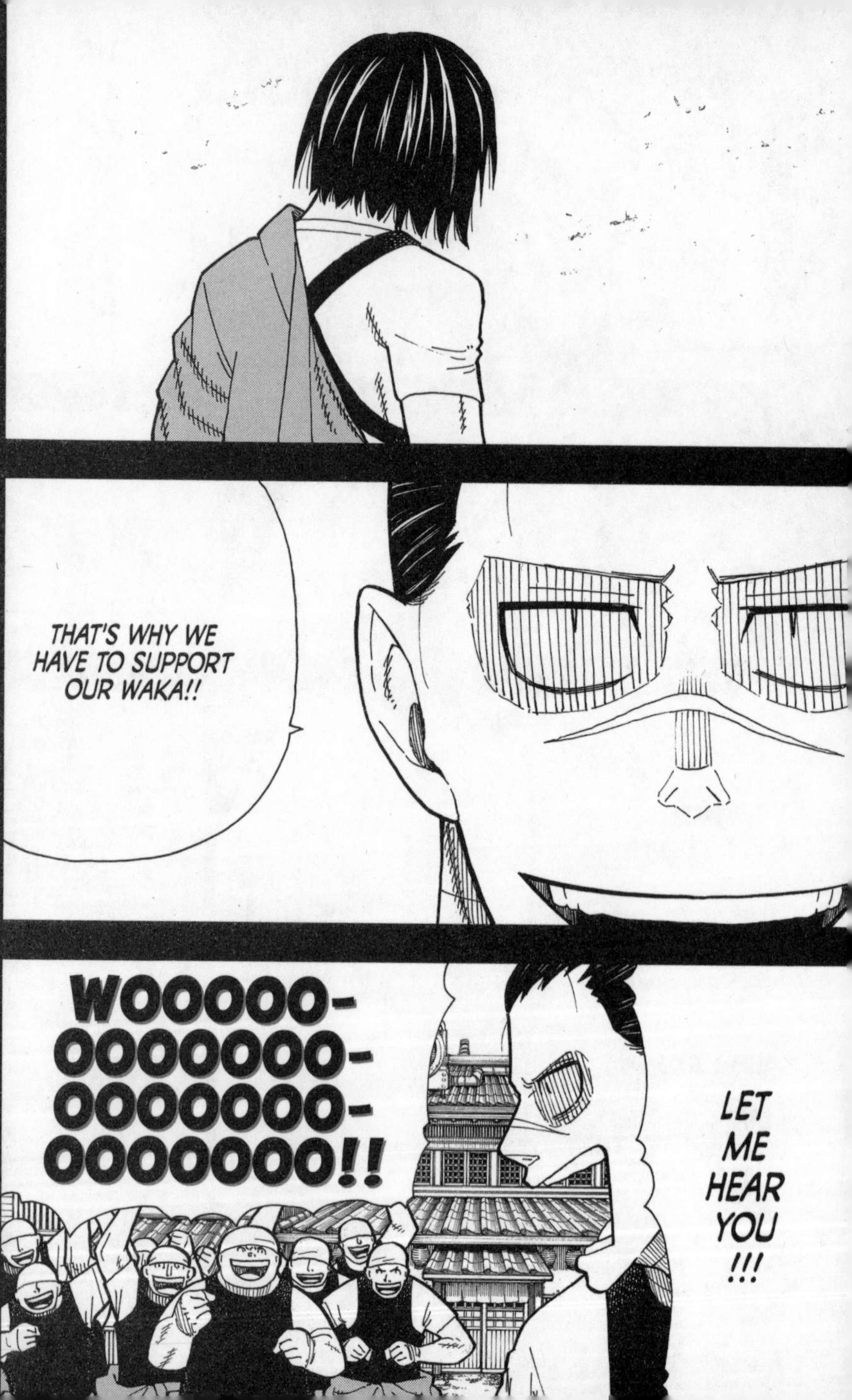
THAT'S WHY WE HAVE TO SUPPORT OUR WAKA!!
LET ME HEAR YOU !!!
WOOOOO-OOOOOOO-OOOOOOO-OOOOOOO!!

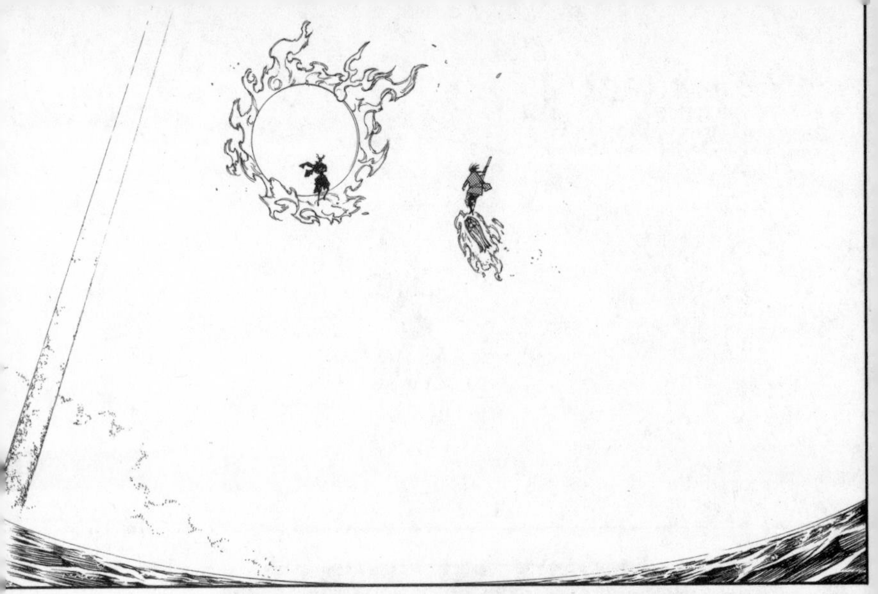

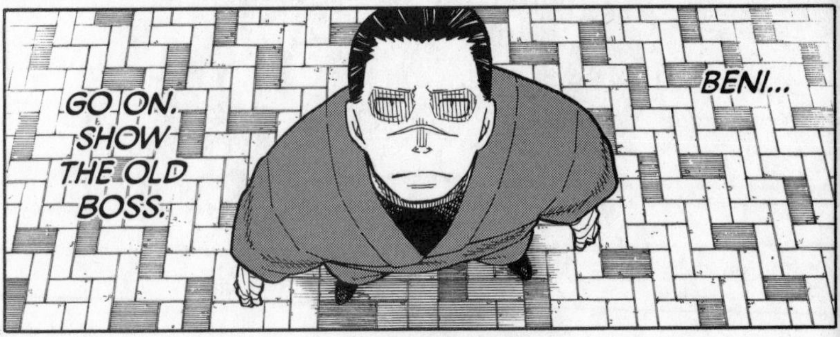
BENI...
GO ON. SHOW THE OLD BOSS.

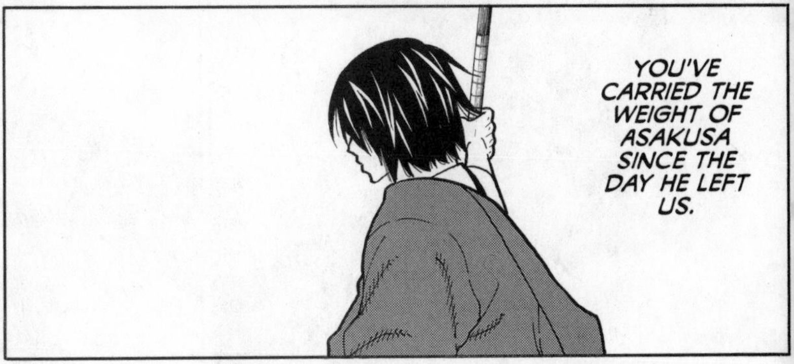
YOU'VE CARRIED THE WEIGHT OF ASAKUSA SINCE THE DAY HE LEFT US.

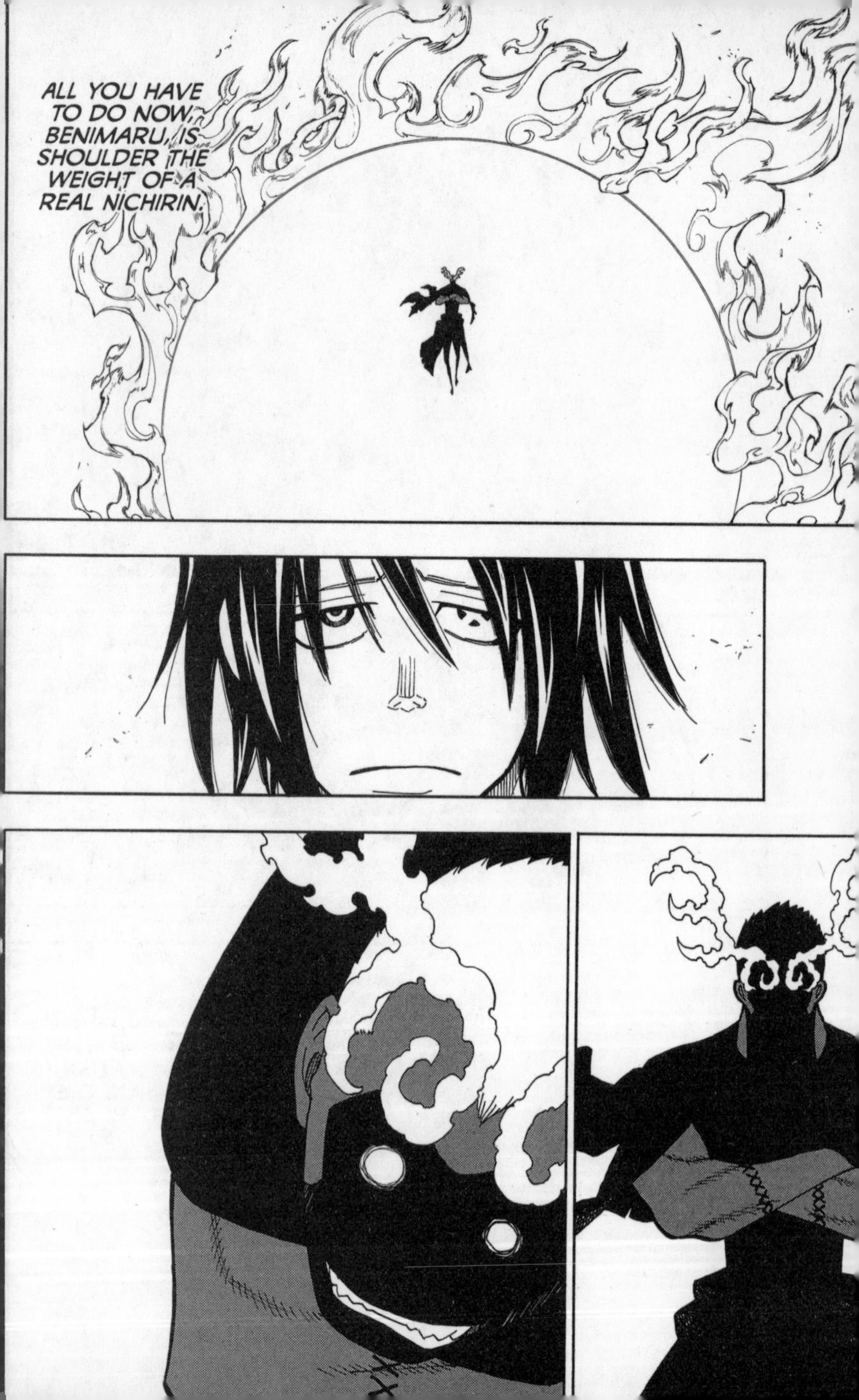
ALL YOU HAVE TO DO NOW, BENIMARU, IS SHOULDER THE WEIGHT OF A REAL NICHIRIN.

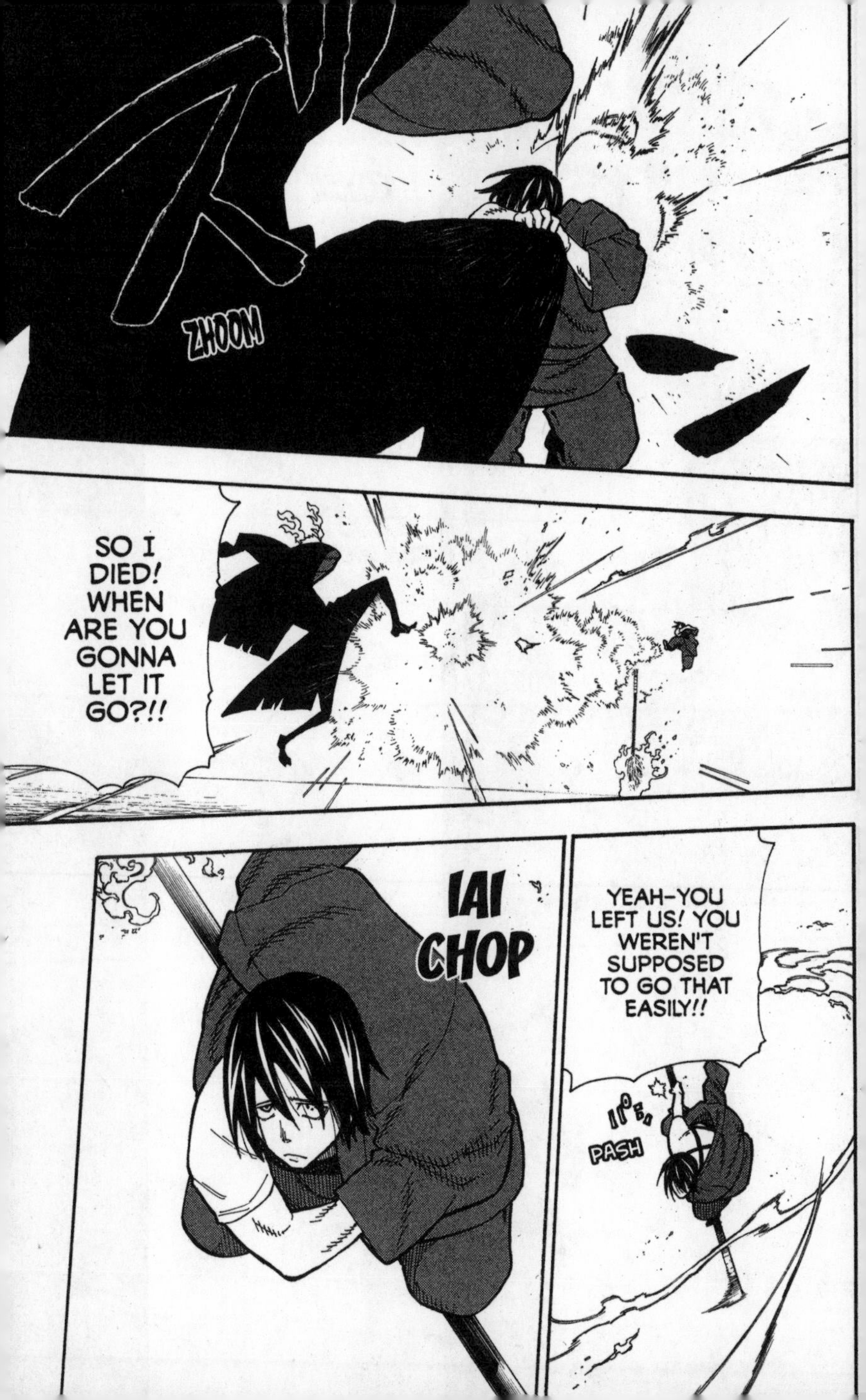
ZHOOM
SO I DIED! WHEN ARE YOU GONNA LET IT GO?!!
YEAH–YOU LEFT US! YOU WEREN'T SUPPOSED TO GO THAT EASILY!!
PASH
IAI CHOP

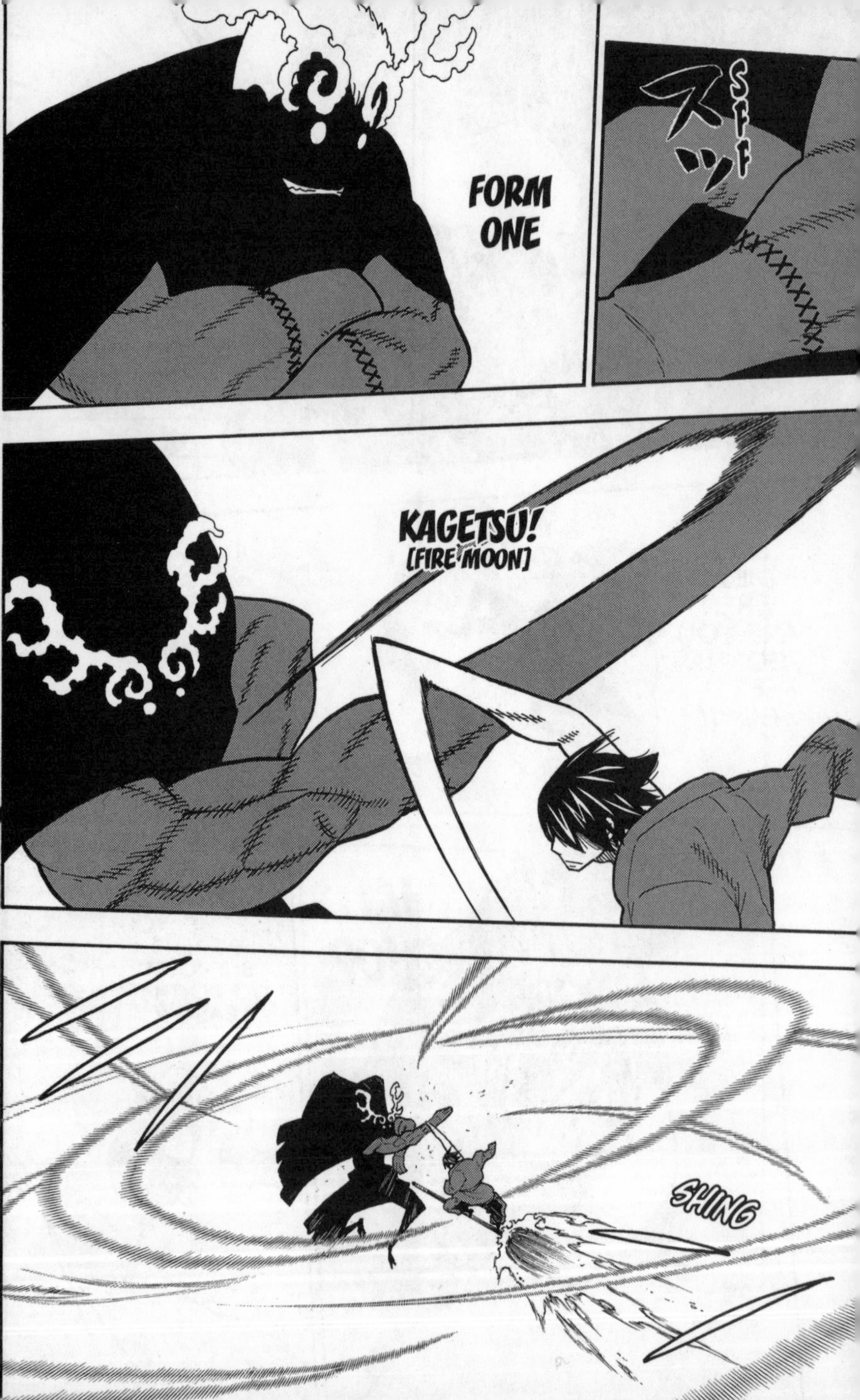
SFF
スッ
FORM ONE
KAGETSU!
[FIRE MOON]
SHING

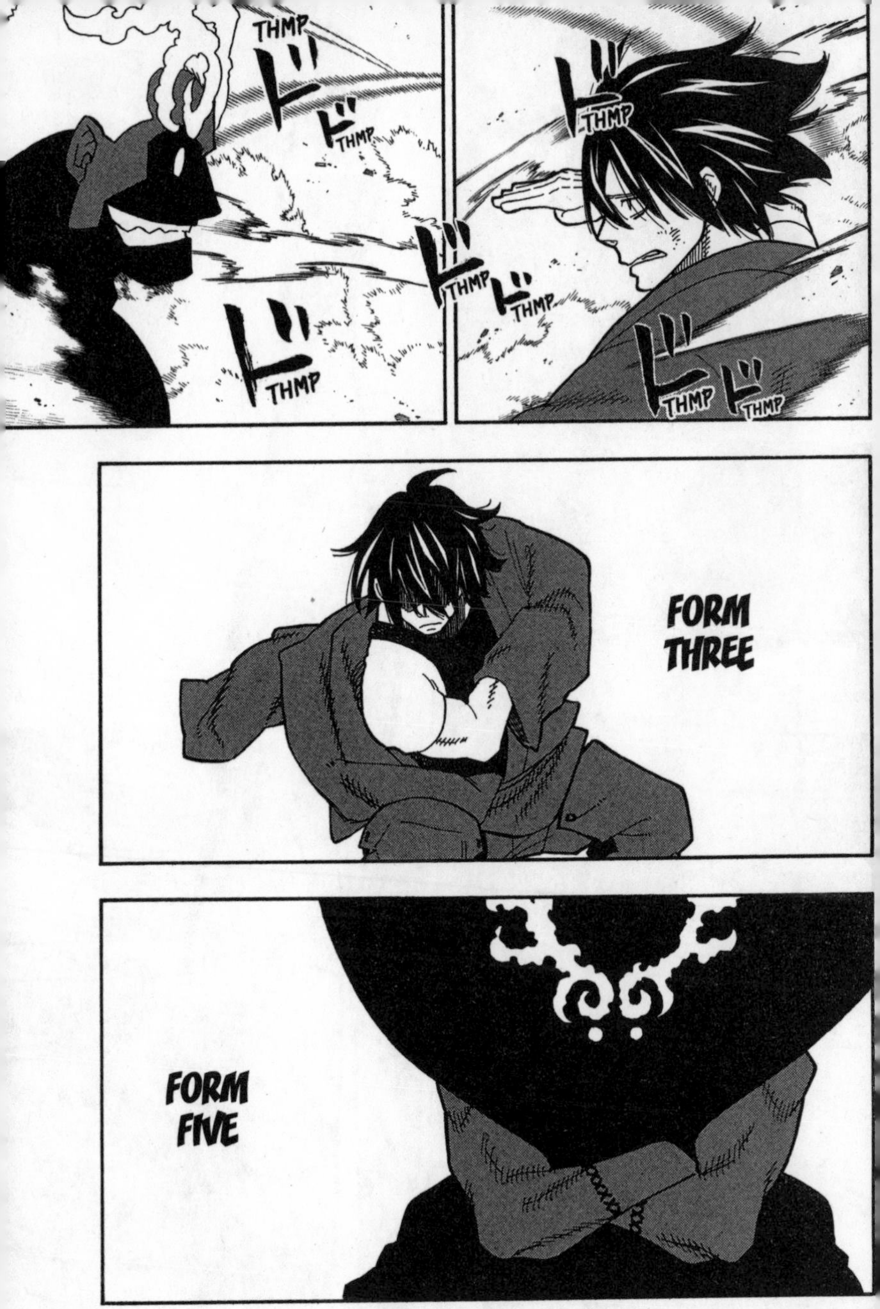

ド THMP
ド THMP
ド THMP
ド THMP
ド THMP
THMP
ド
ド THMP
ド THMP
FORM THREE
FORM FIVE

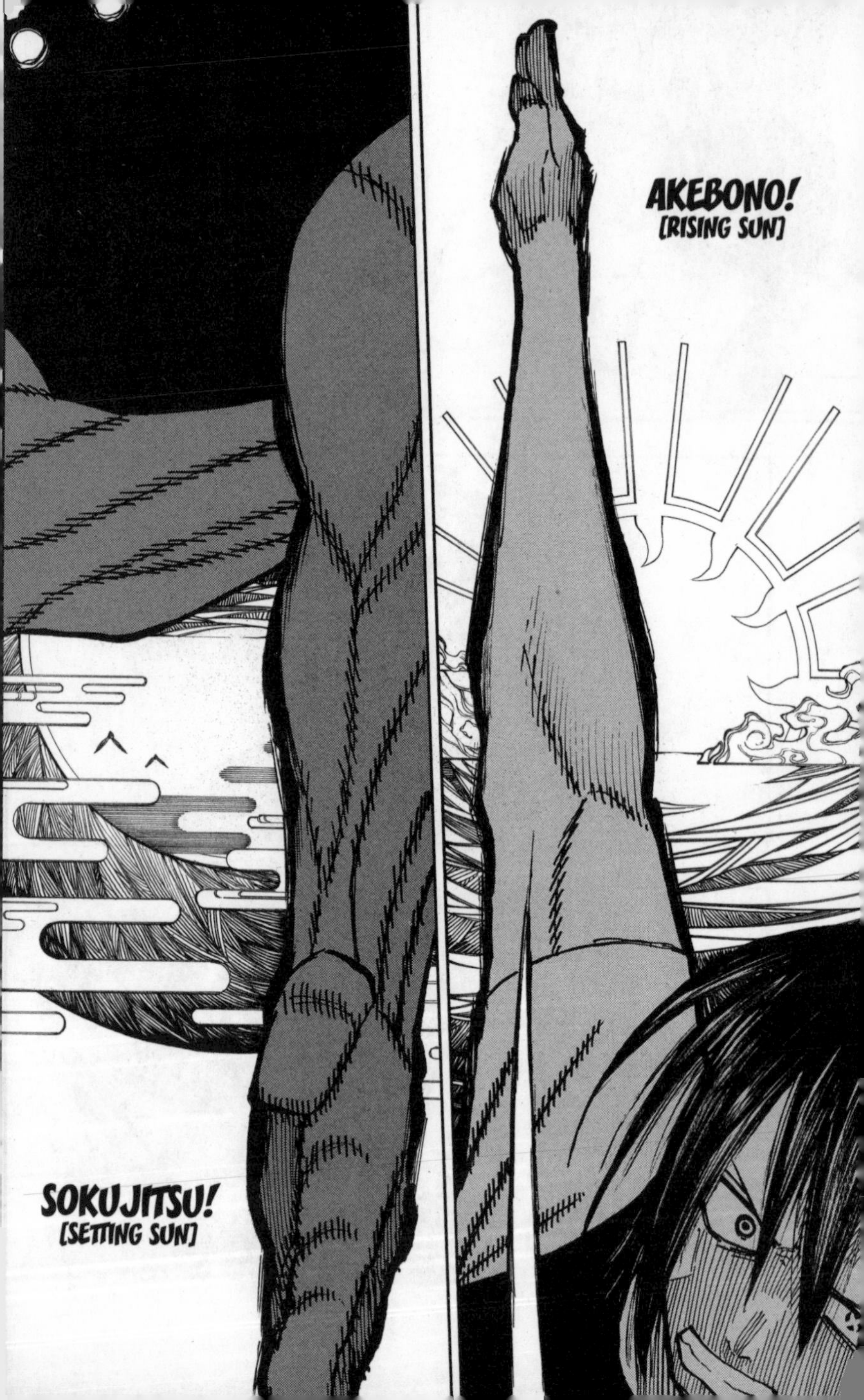
AKEBONO!
[RISING SUN]
SOKUJITSU!
[SETTING SUN]

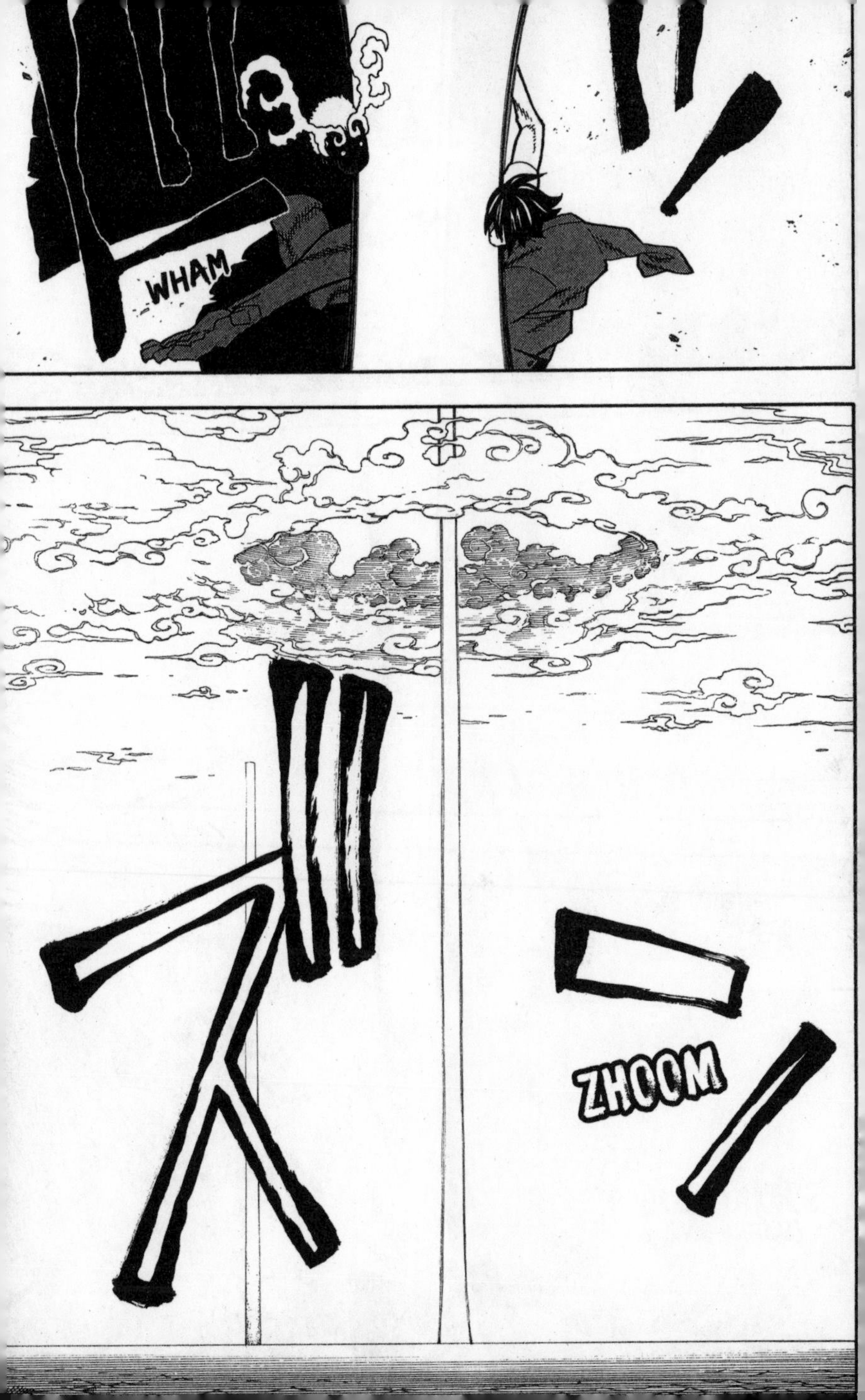
WHAM
ZHOOM

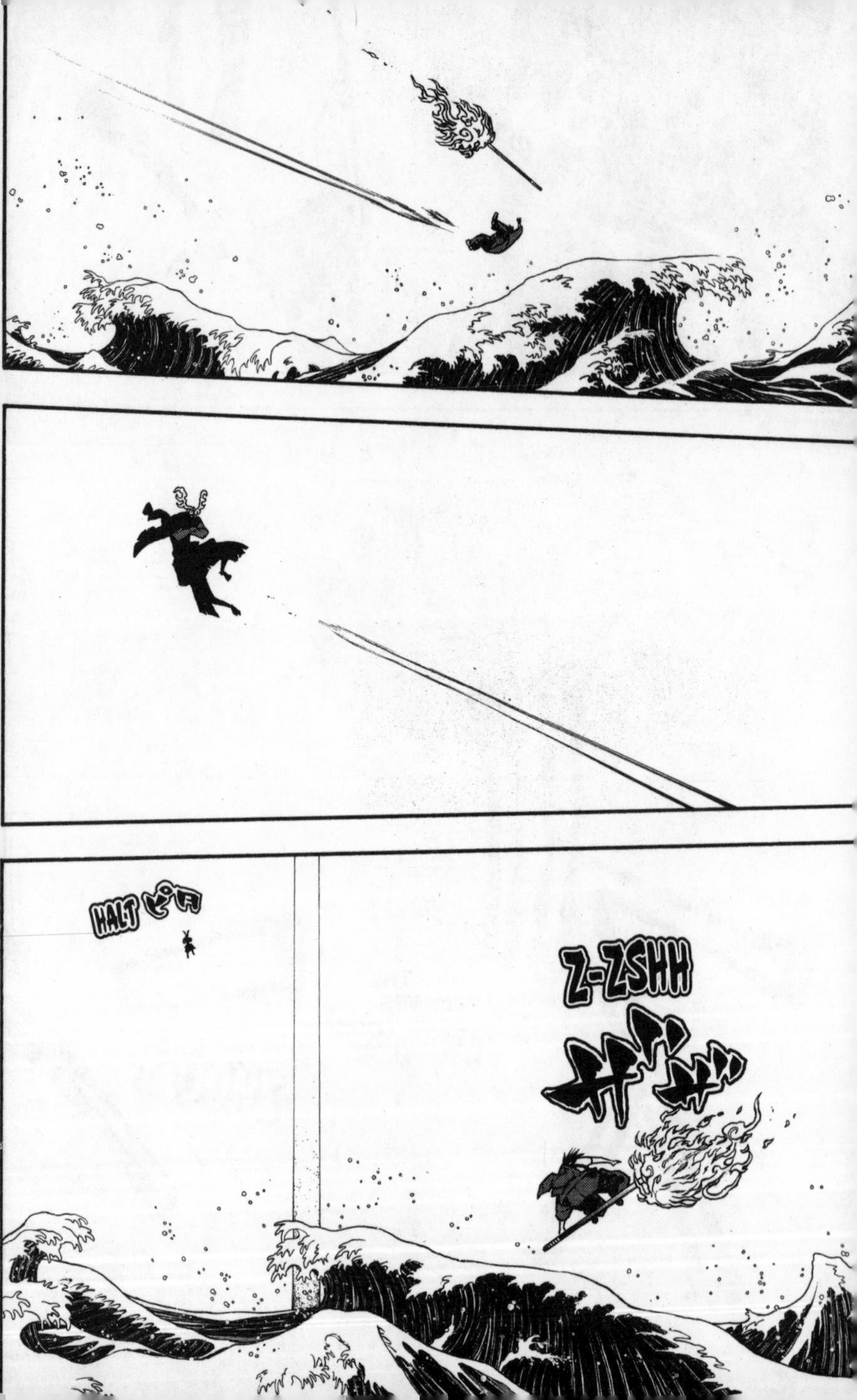
Z-ZSHH
HALT

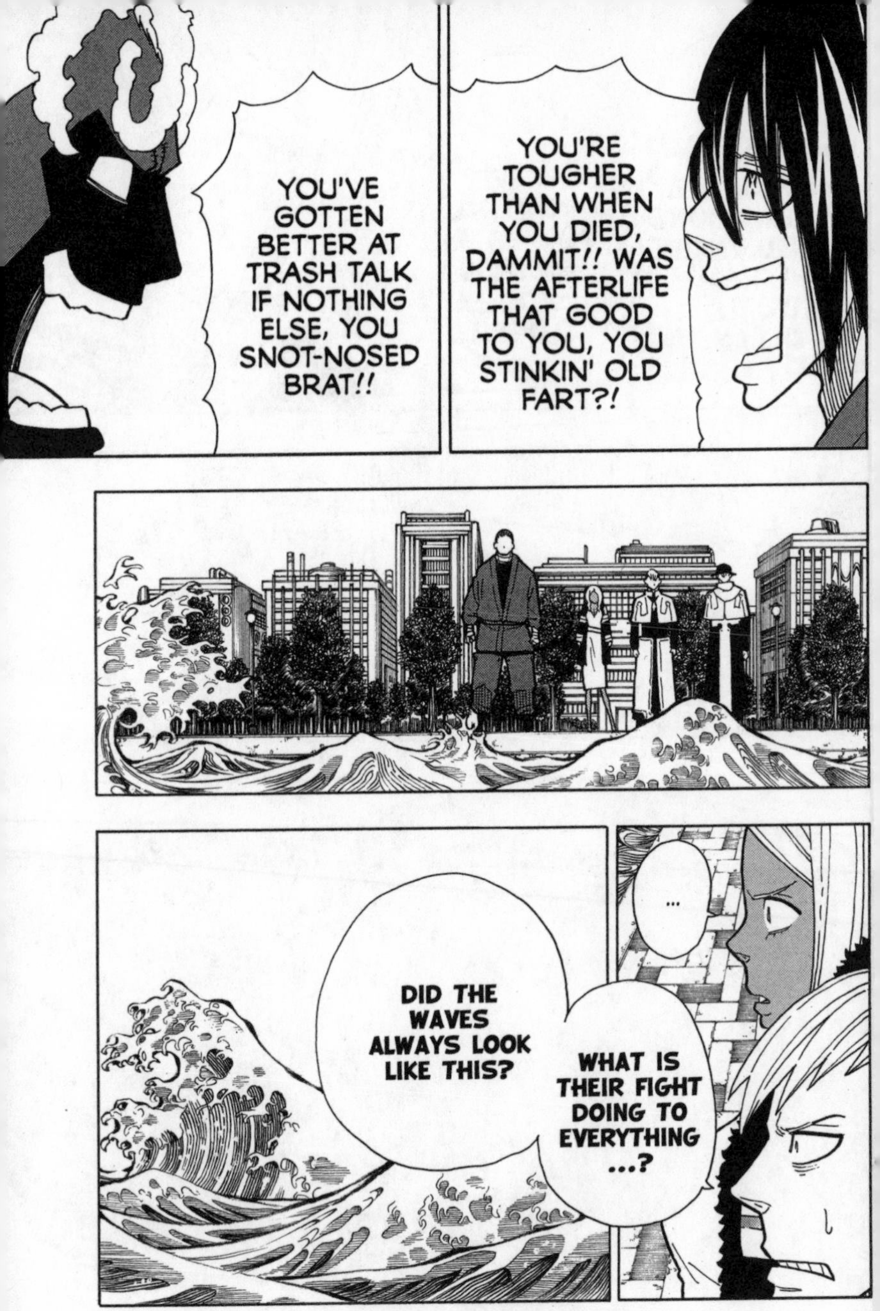

YOU'RE TOUGHER THAN WHEN YOU DIED, DAMMIT!! WAS THE AFTERLIFE THAT GOOD TO YOU, YOU STINKIN' OLD FART?!
YOU'VE GOTTEN BETTER AT TRASH TALK IF NOTHING ELSE, YOU SNOT-NOSED BRAT!!
...
WHAT IS THEIR FIGHT DOING TO EVERYTHING ...?
DID THE WAVES ALWAYS LOOK LIKE THIS?

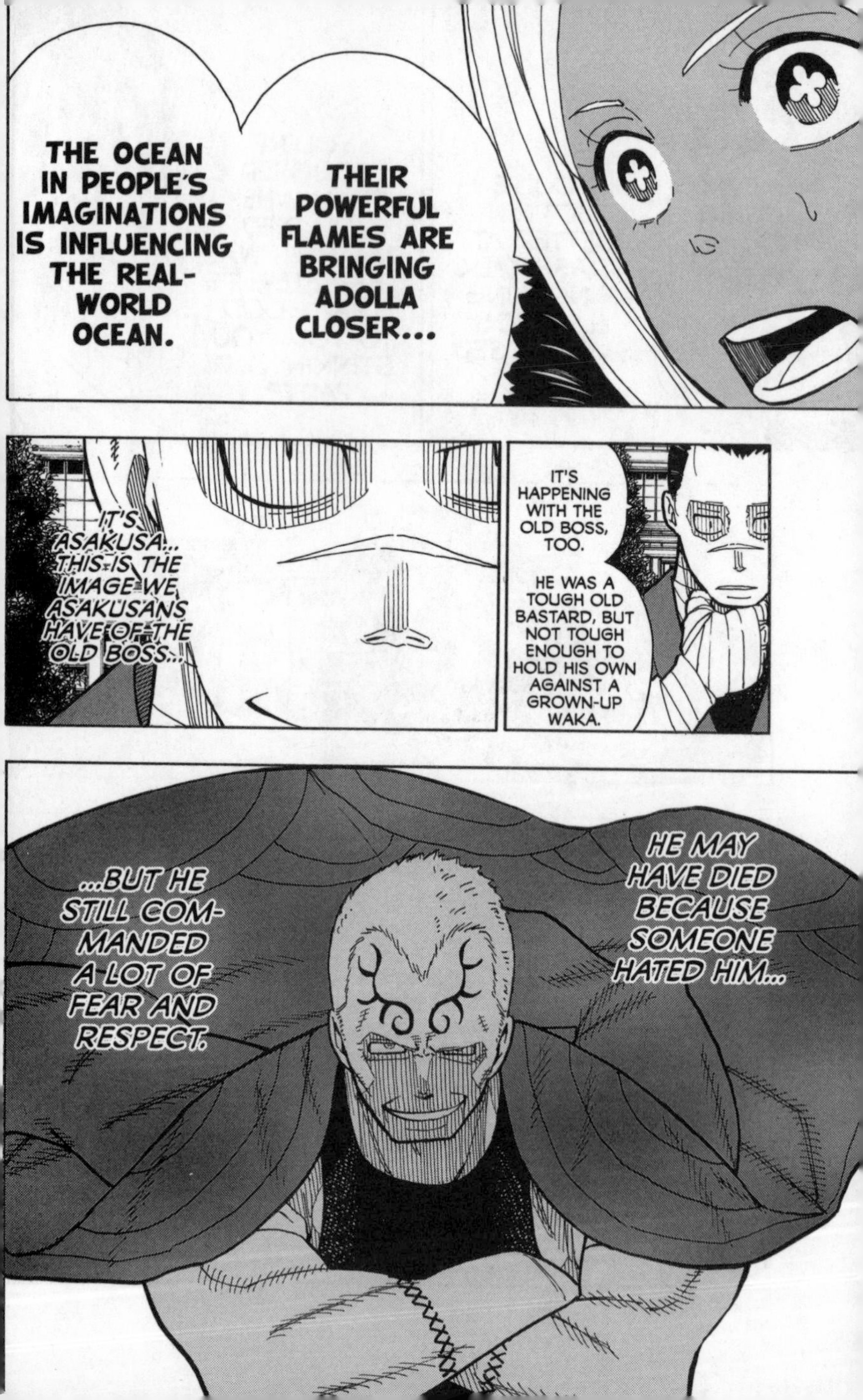
THEIR POWERFUL FLAMES ARE BRINGING ADOLLA CLOSER...
THE OCEAN IN PEOPLE'S IMAGINATIONS IS INFLUENCING THE REAL-WORLD OCEAN.
IT'S HAPPENING WITH THE OLD BOSS, TOO.
HE WAS A TOUGH OLD BASTARD, BUT NOT TOUGH ENOUGH TO HOLD HIS OWN AGAINST A GROWN-UP WAKA.
IT'S ASAKUSA... THIS IS THE IMAGE WE ASAKUSANS HAVE OF THE OLD BOSS...
HE MAY HAVE DIED BECAUSE SOMEONE HATED HIM...
...BUT HE STILL COM-MANDED A LOT OF FEAR AND RESPECT.

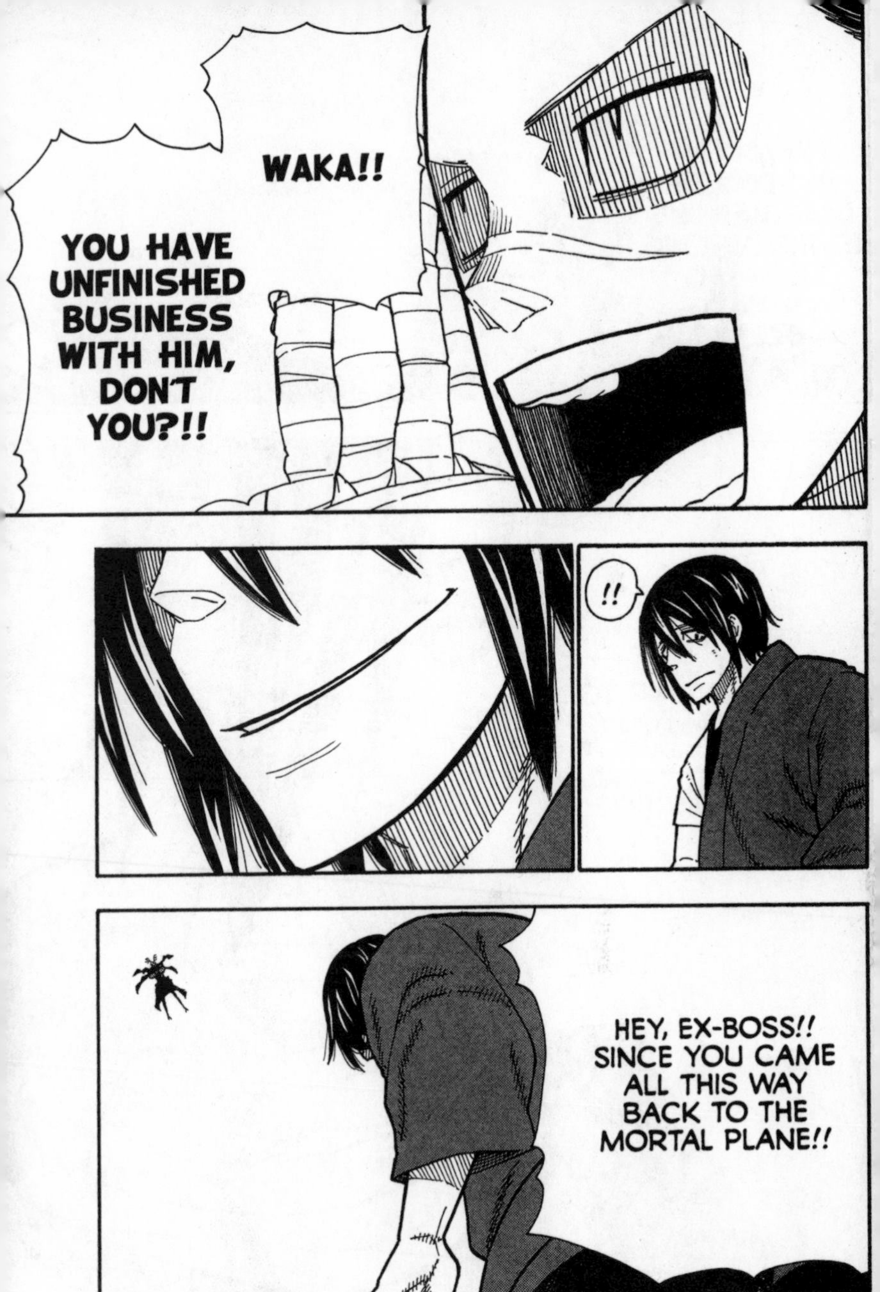
WAKA!!
YOU HAVE UNFINISHED BUSINESS WITH HIM, DON'T YOU?!!
!!
HEY, EX-BOSS!! SINCE YOU CAME ALL THIS WAY BACK TO THE MORTAL PLANE!!

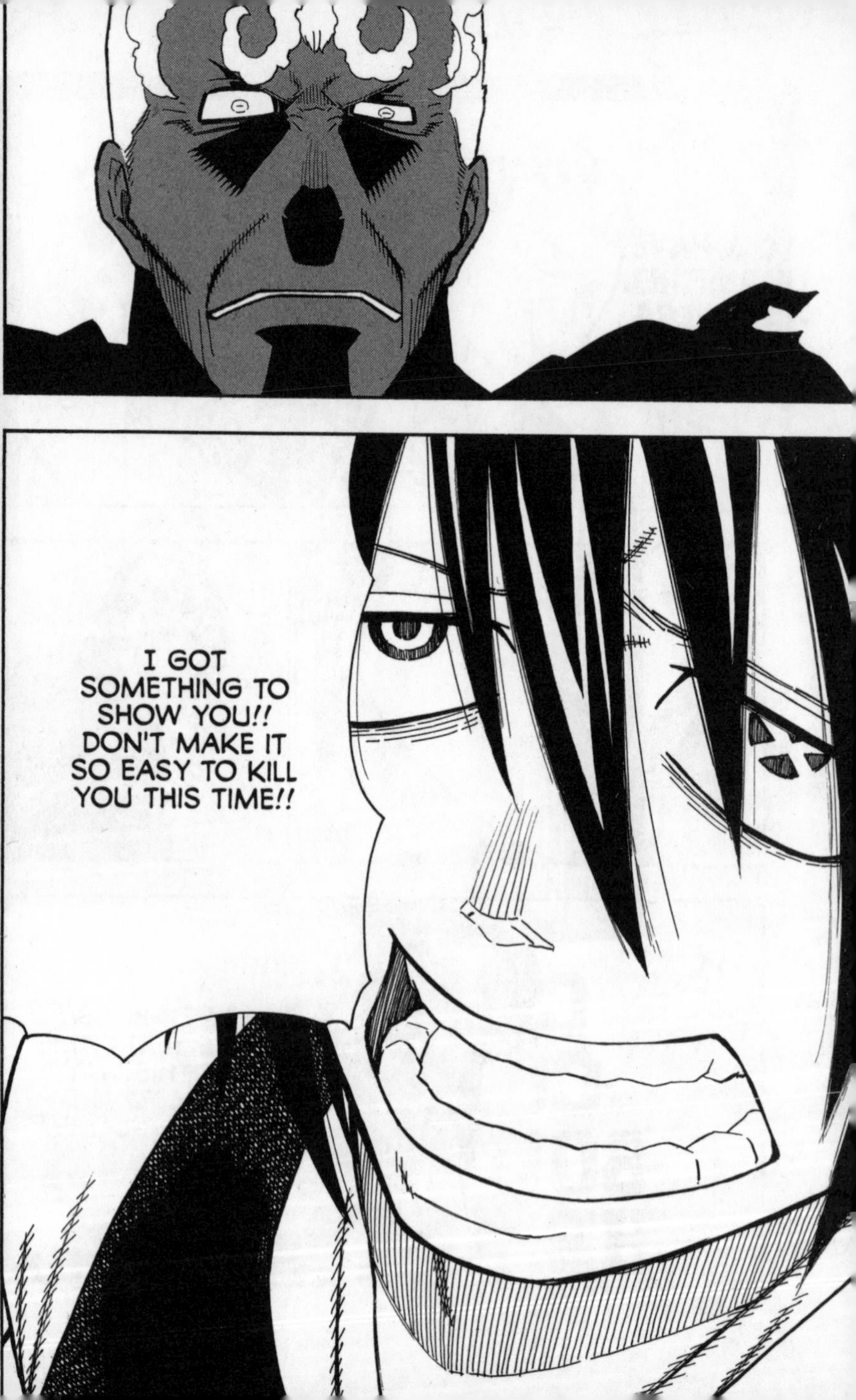
I GOT SOMETHING TO SHOW YOU!! DON'T MAKE IT SO EASY TO KILL YOU THIS TIME!!

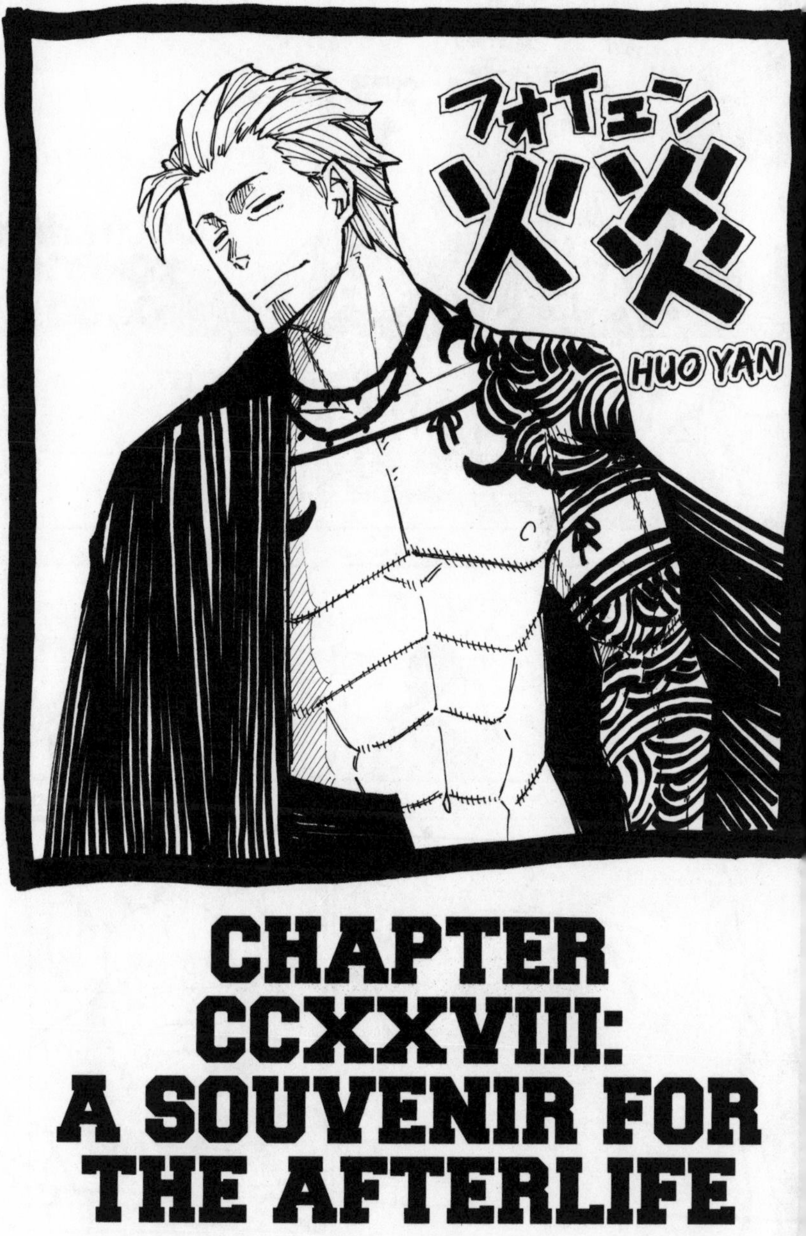
フオイェン
火炎
HUO YAN

CHAPTER CCXXVIII: A SOUVENIR FOR THE AFTERLIFE

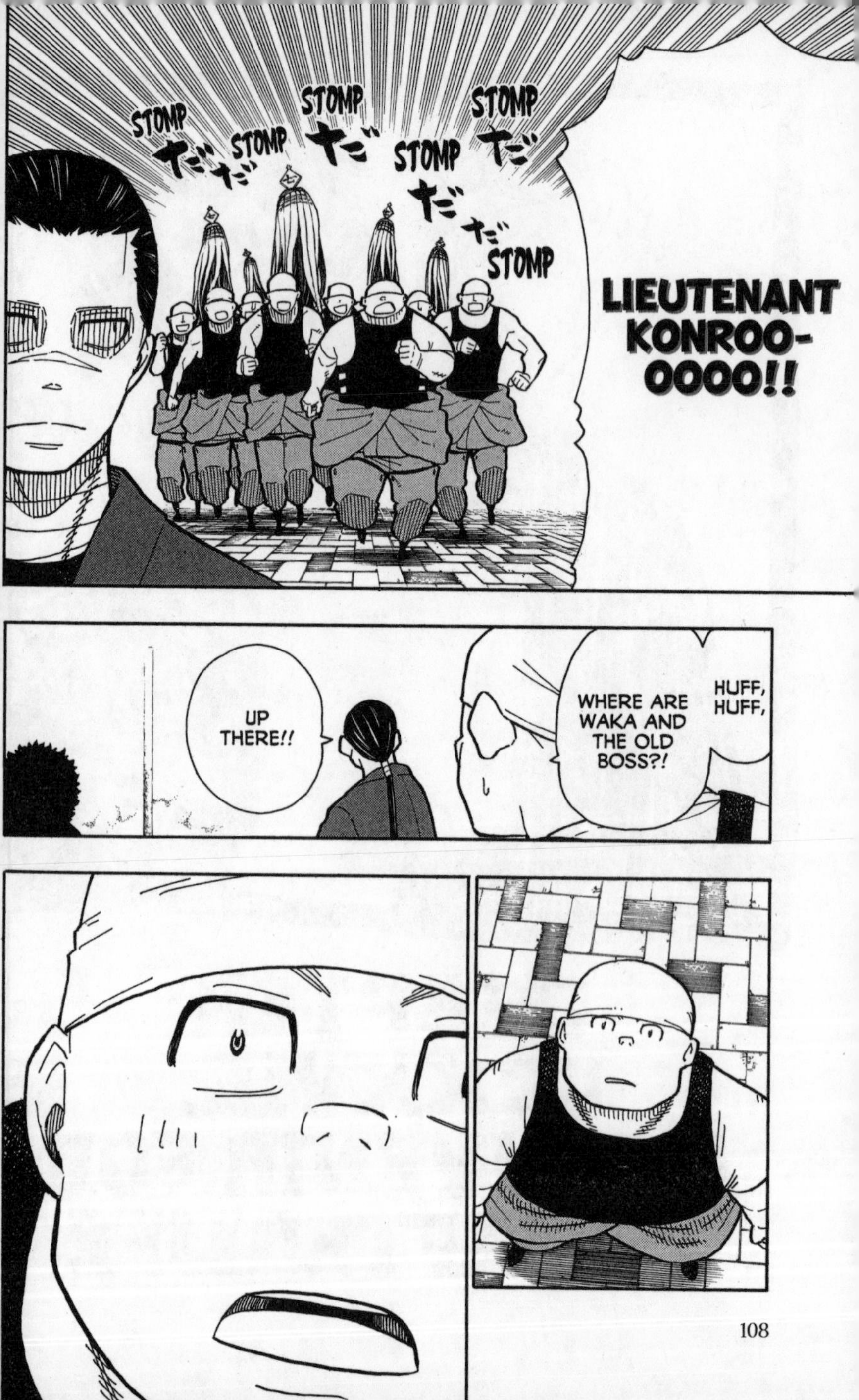

LIEUTENANT KONROO-OOOO!!
STOMP
STOMP
STOMP
STOMP
STOMP
STOMP
HUFF, HUFF,
WHERE ARE WAKA AND THE OLD BOSS?!
UP THERE!!

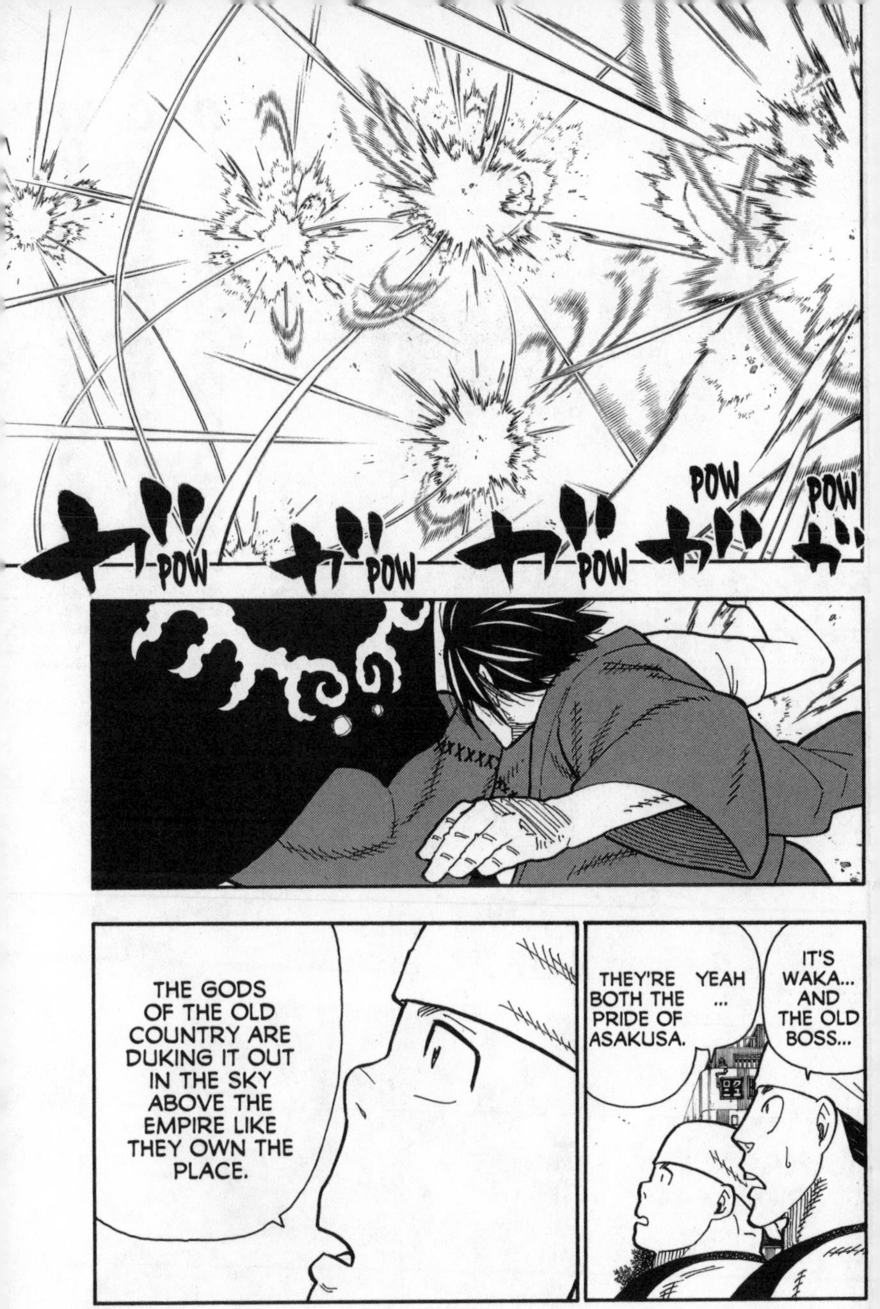
POW
POW
POW
POW
POW
IT'S WAKA... AND THE OLD BOSS...
YEAH ...
THEY'RE BOTH THE PRIDE OF ASAKUSA.
THE GODS OF THE OLD COUNTRY ARE DUKING IT OUT IN THE SKY ABOVE THE EMPIRE LIKE THEY OWN THE PLACE.

Sign: Olq, Inu

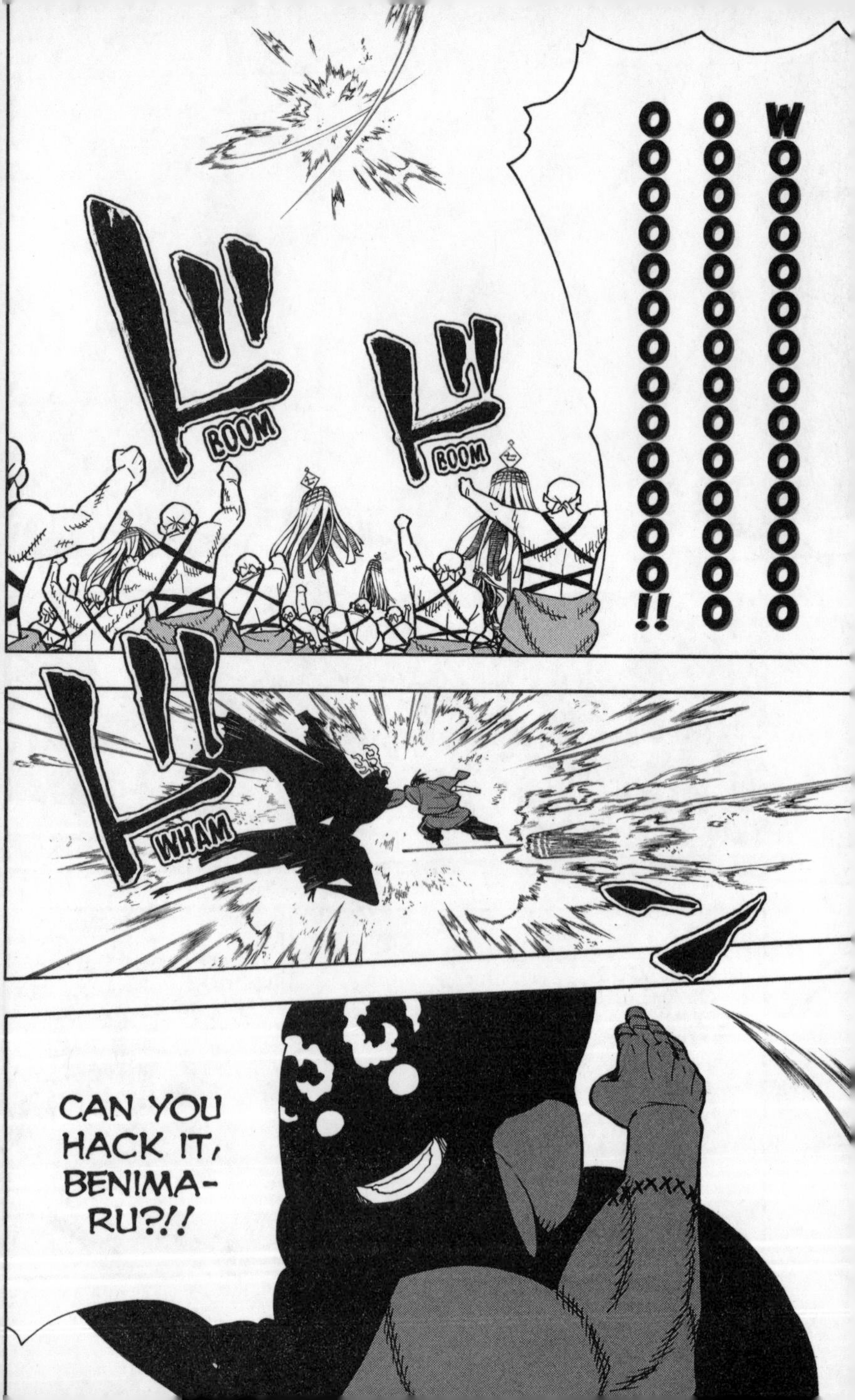

WOOOOOOOOOOOOOOOOOOOOOOOOOOOOOOOOOOOOOOOOOOOOOO!!
BOOM
BOOM
WHAM
CAN YOU HACK IT, BENIMA-RU?!!

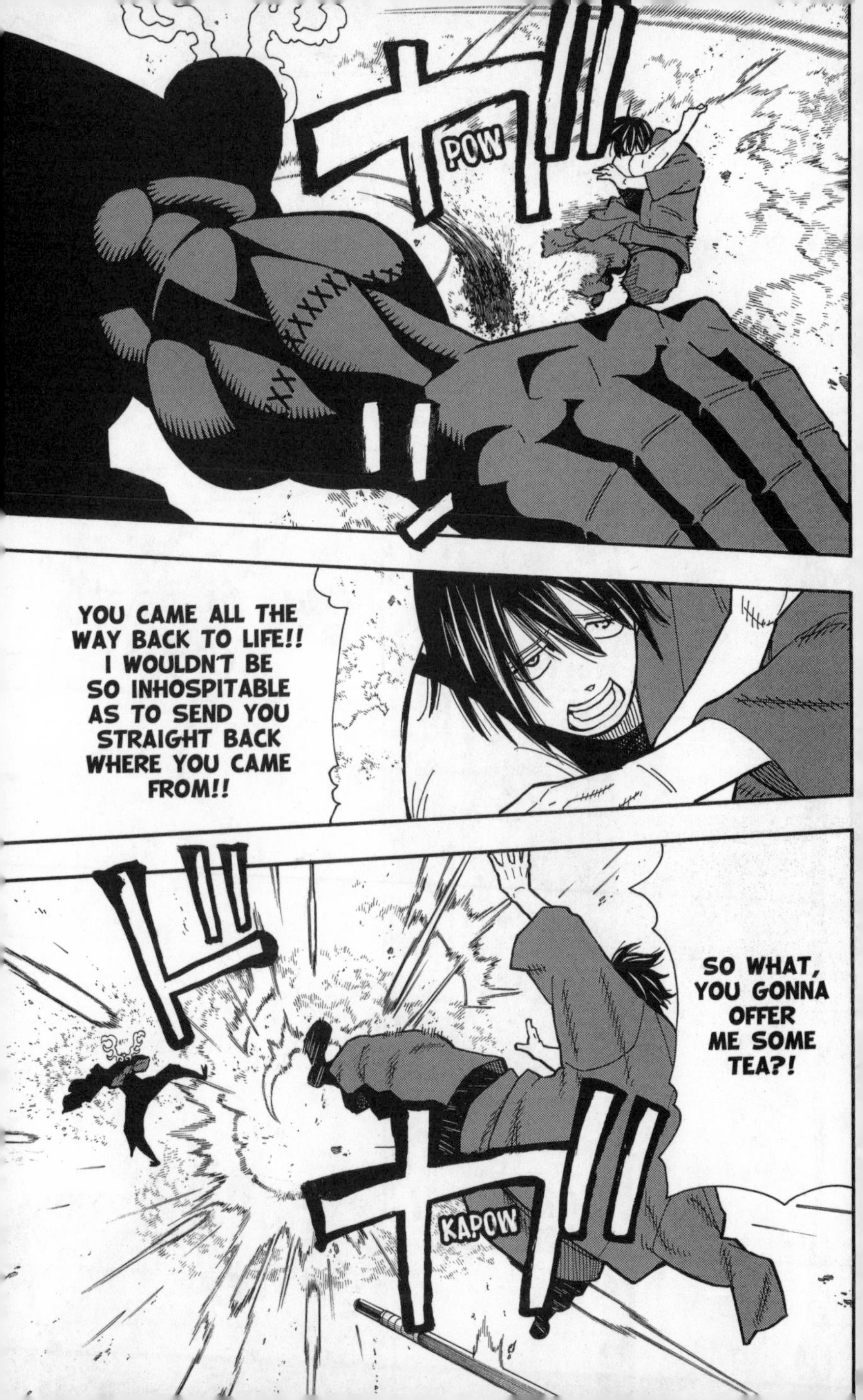
POW
YOU CAME ALL THE WAY BACK TO LIFE!! I WOULDN'T BE SO INHOSPITABLE AS TO SEND YOU STRAIGHT BACK WHERE YOU CAME FROM!!
SO WHAT, YOU GONNA OFFER ME SOME TEA?!
KAPOW

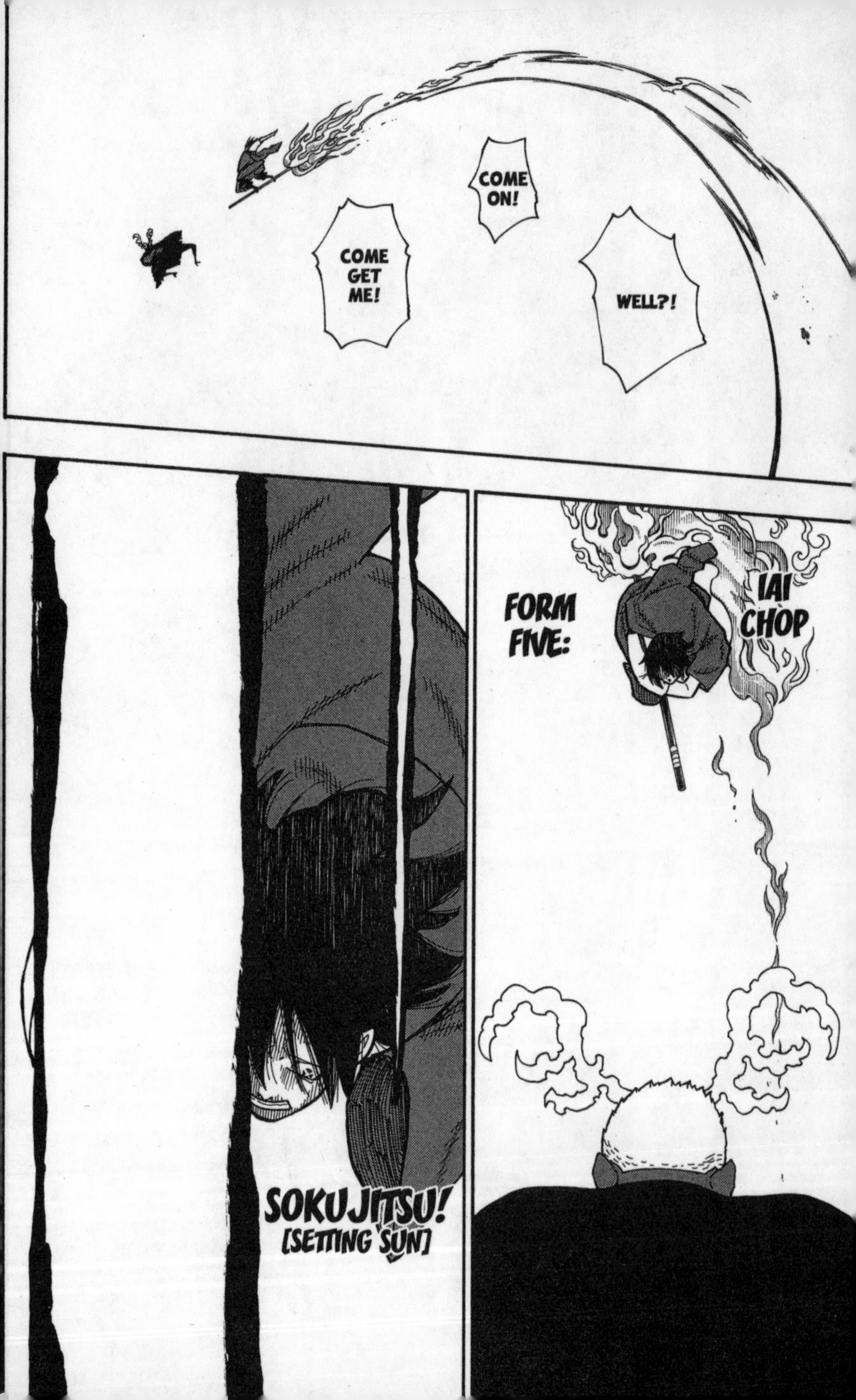
WELL?!
COME ON!
COME GET ME!
FORM FIVE:
IAI CHOP
SOKUJITSU!
[SETTING SUN]

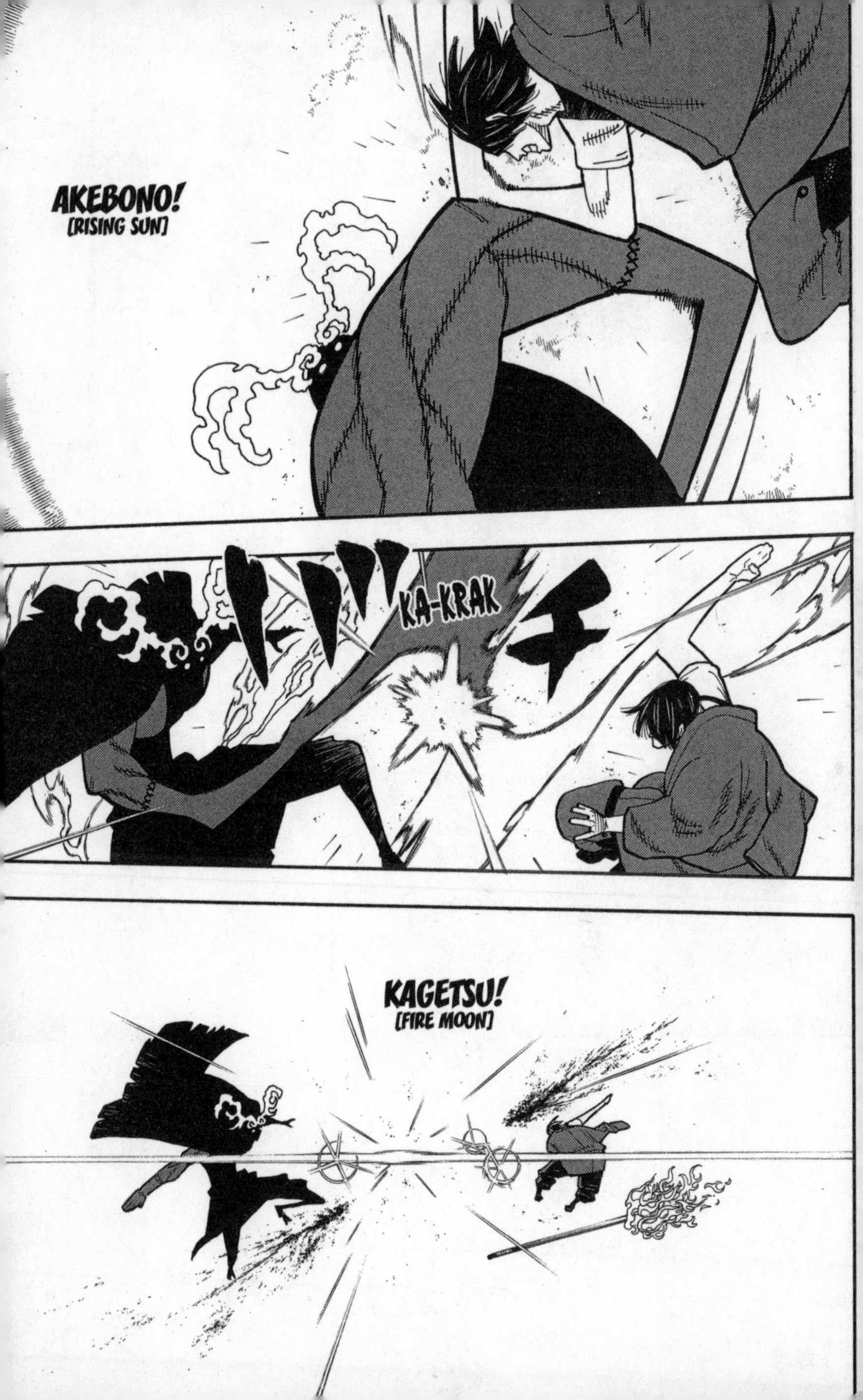
AKEBONO!
[RISING SUN]
KA-KRAK
KAGETSU!
[FIRE MOON]

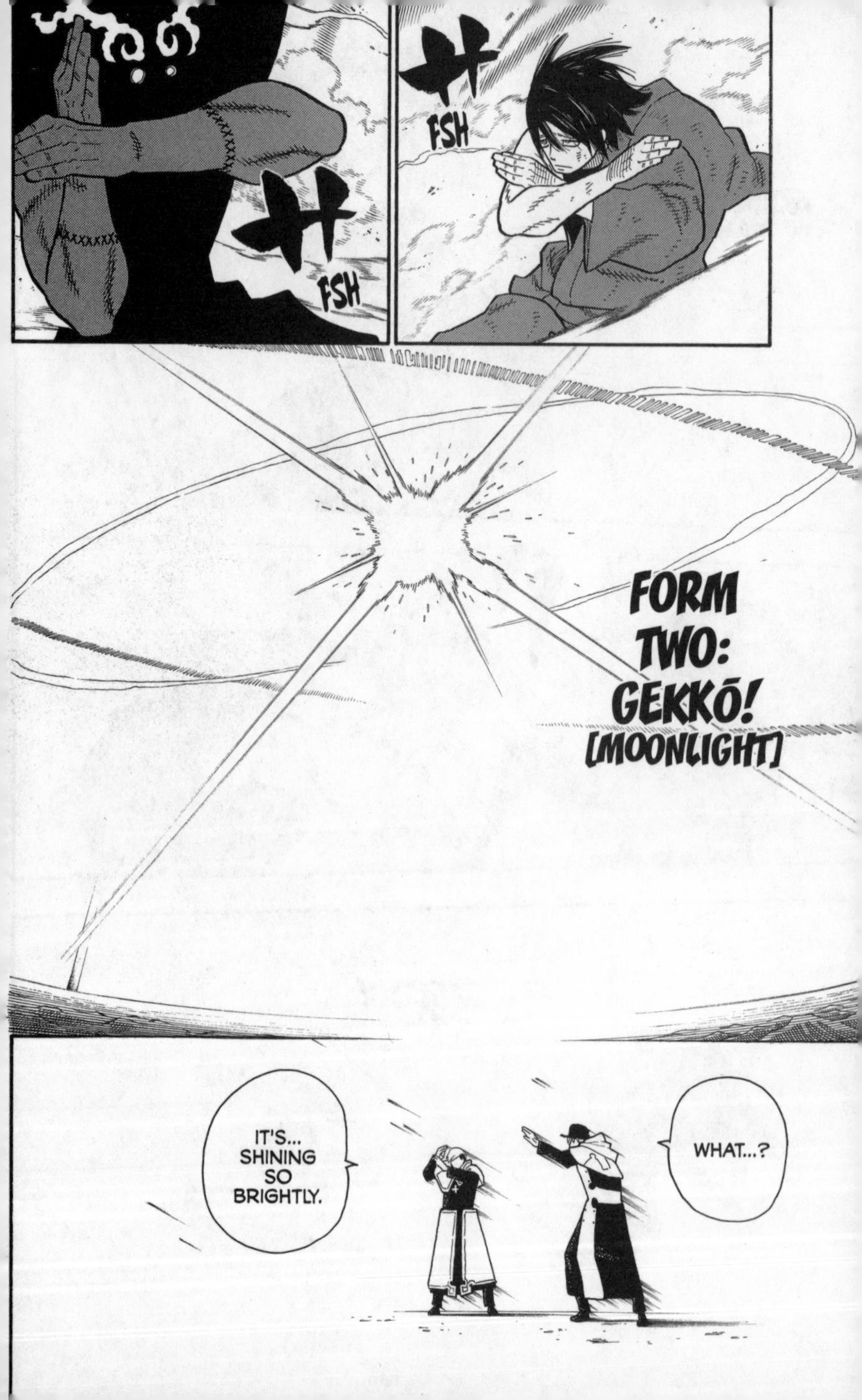
FSH
FSH
FORM TWO: GEKKŌ! [MOONLIGHT]
WHAT...?
IT'S... SHINING SO BRIGHTLY.

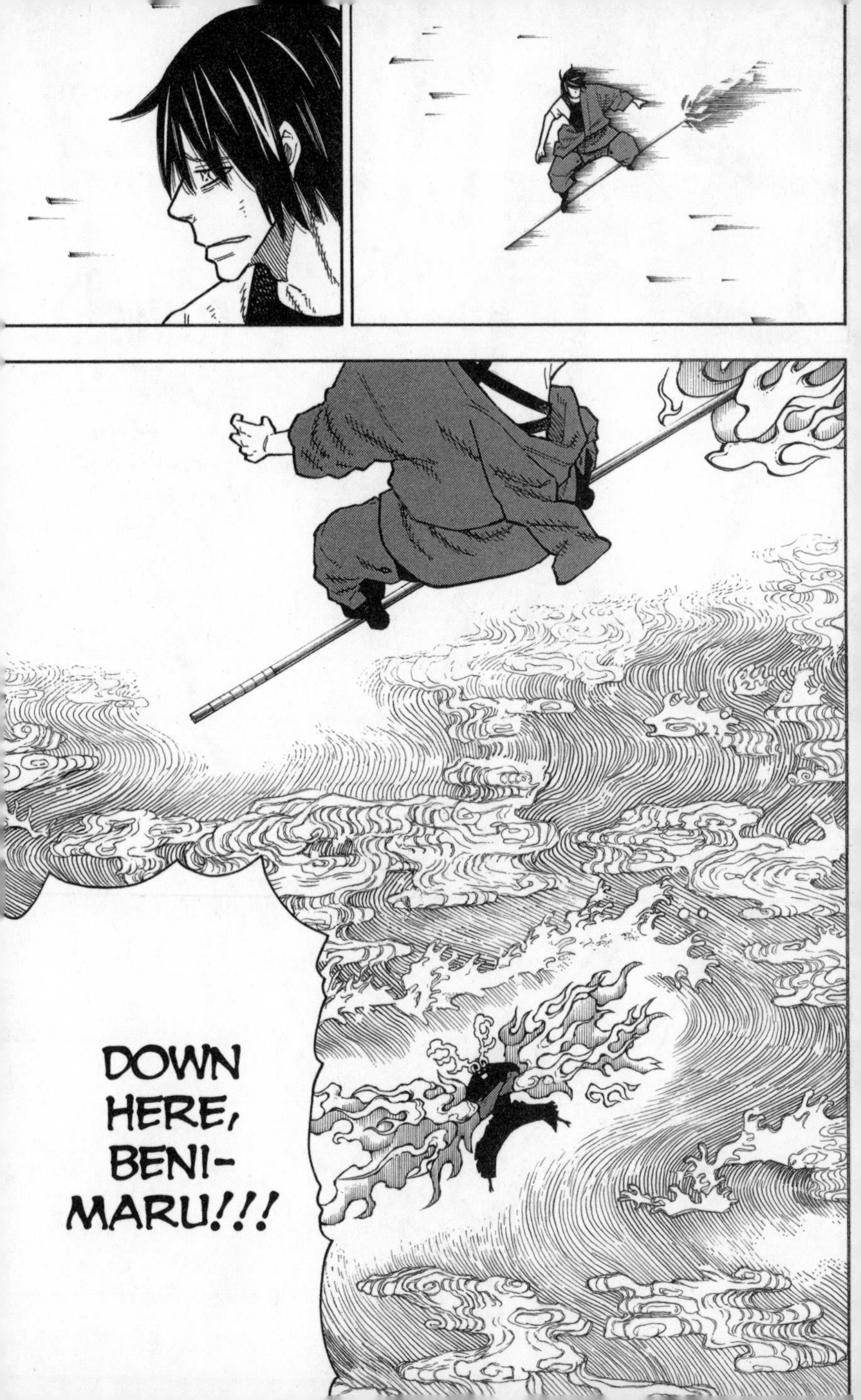
DOWN HERE, BENI-MARU!!!

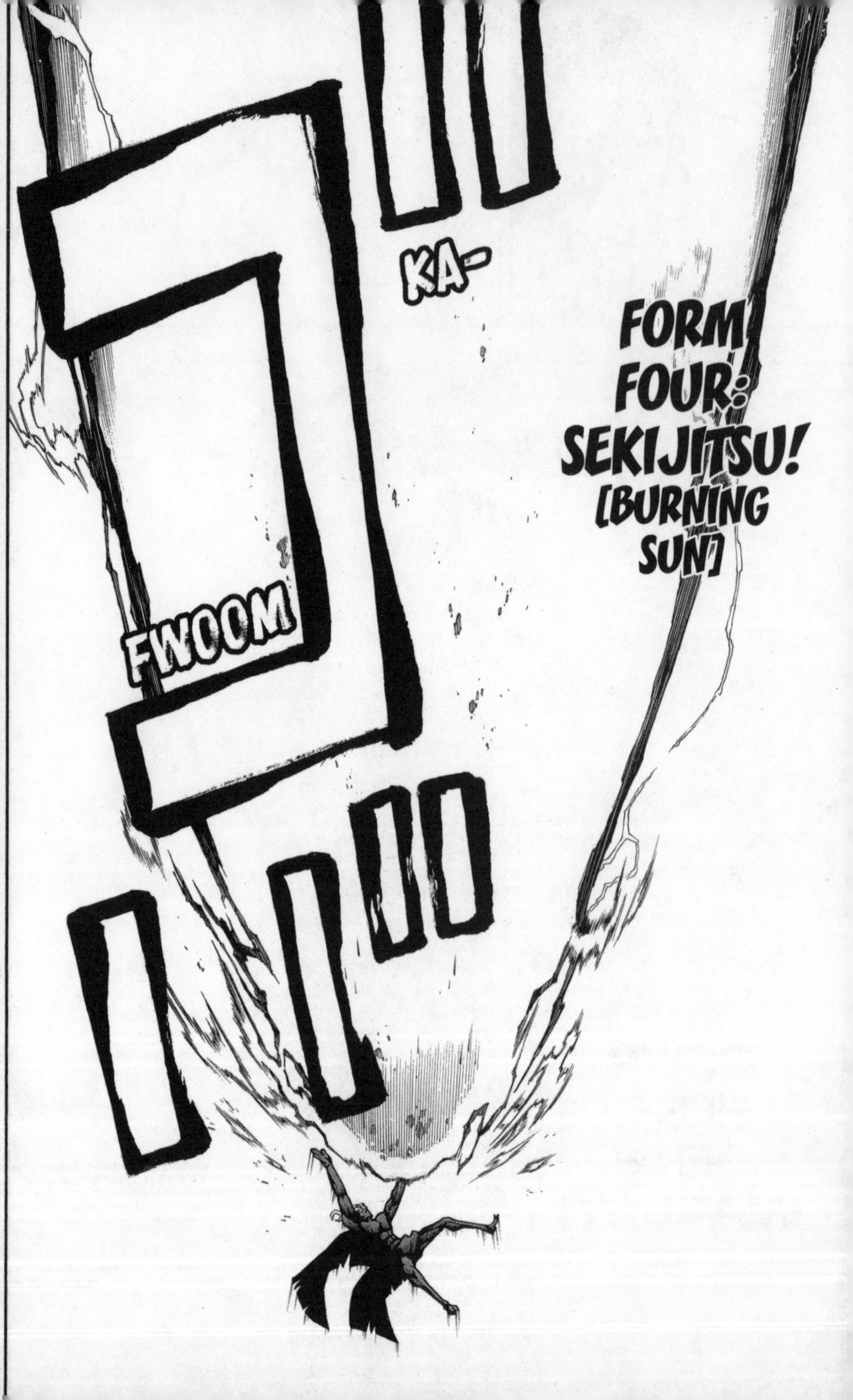
FORM FOUR: SEKIJITSU! [BURNING SUN]
KA-
FWOOM

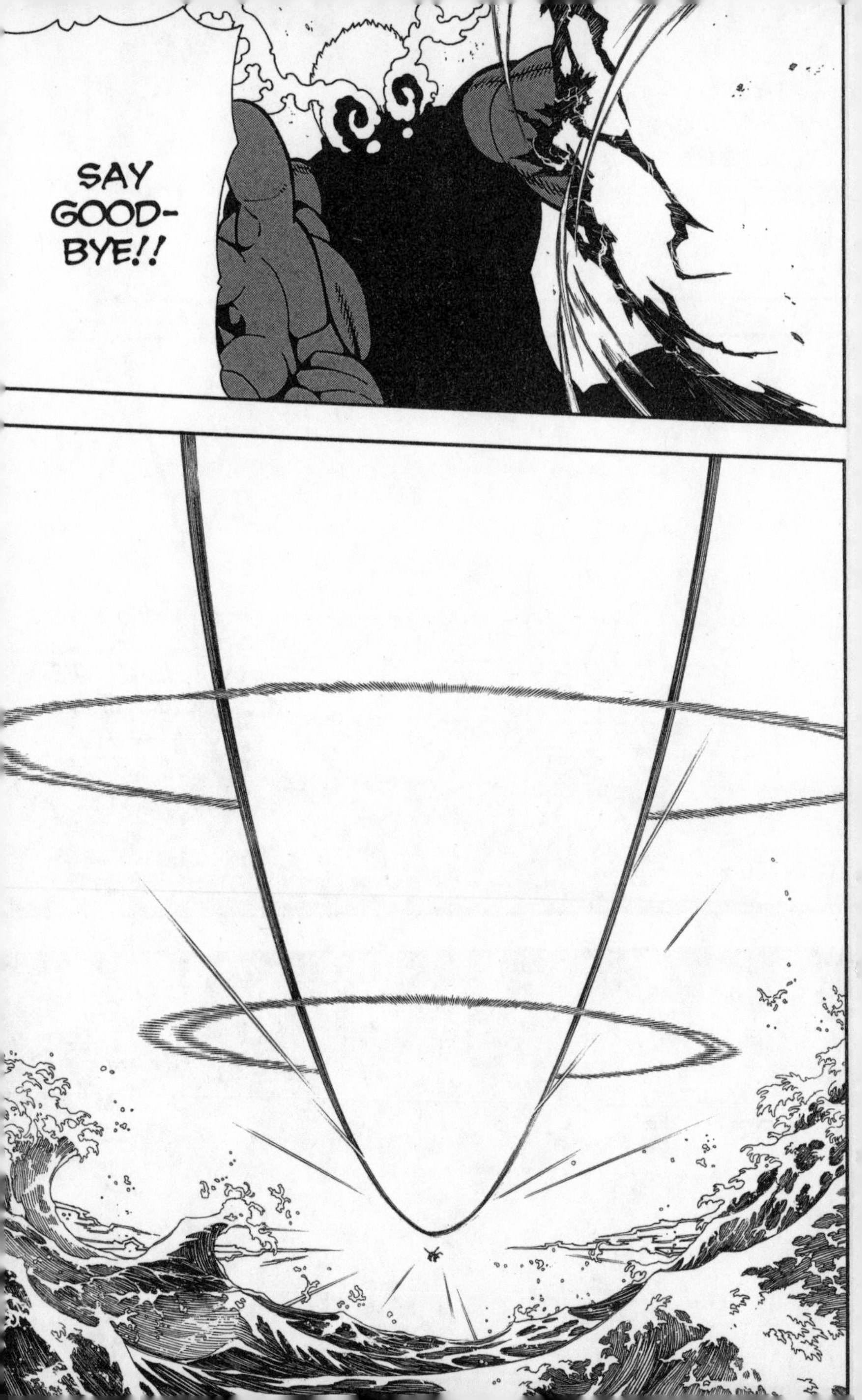
SAY GOOD-BYE!!

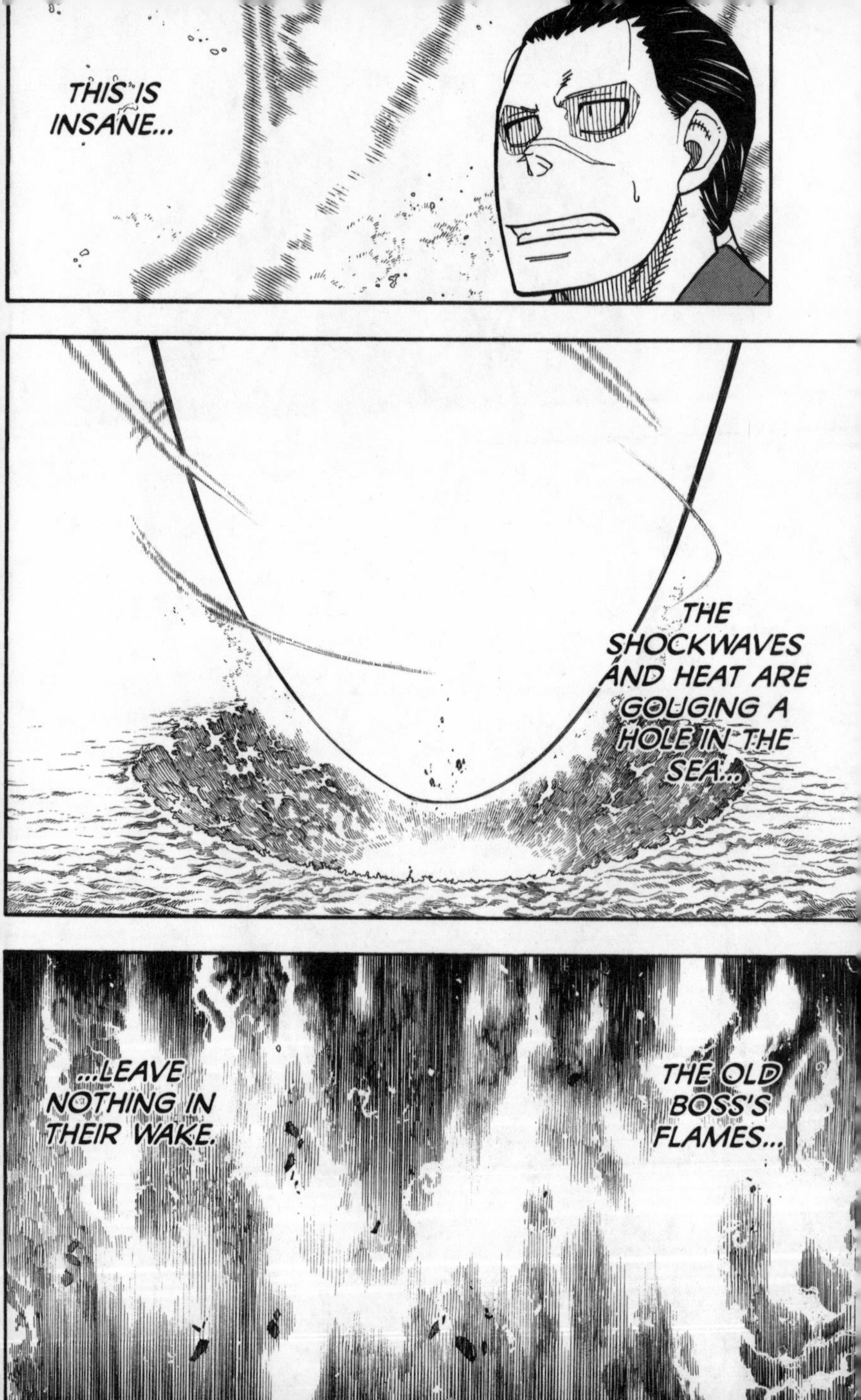
THIS IS INSANE...
THE SHOCKWAVES AND HEAT ARE GOUGING A HOLE IN THE SEA...
THE OLD BOSS'S FLAMES...
...LEAVE NOTHING IN THEIR WAKE.

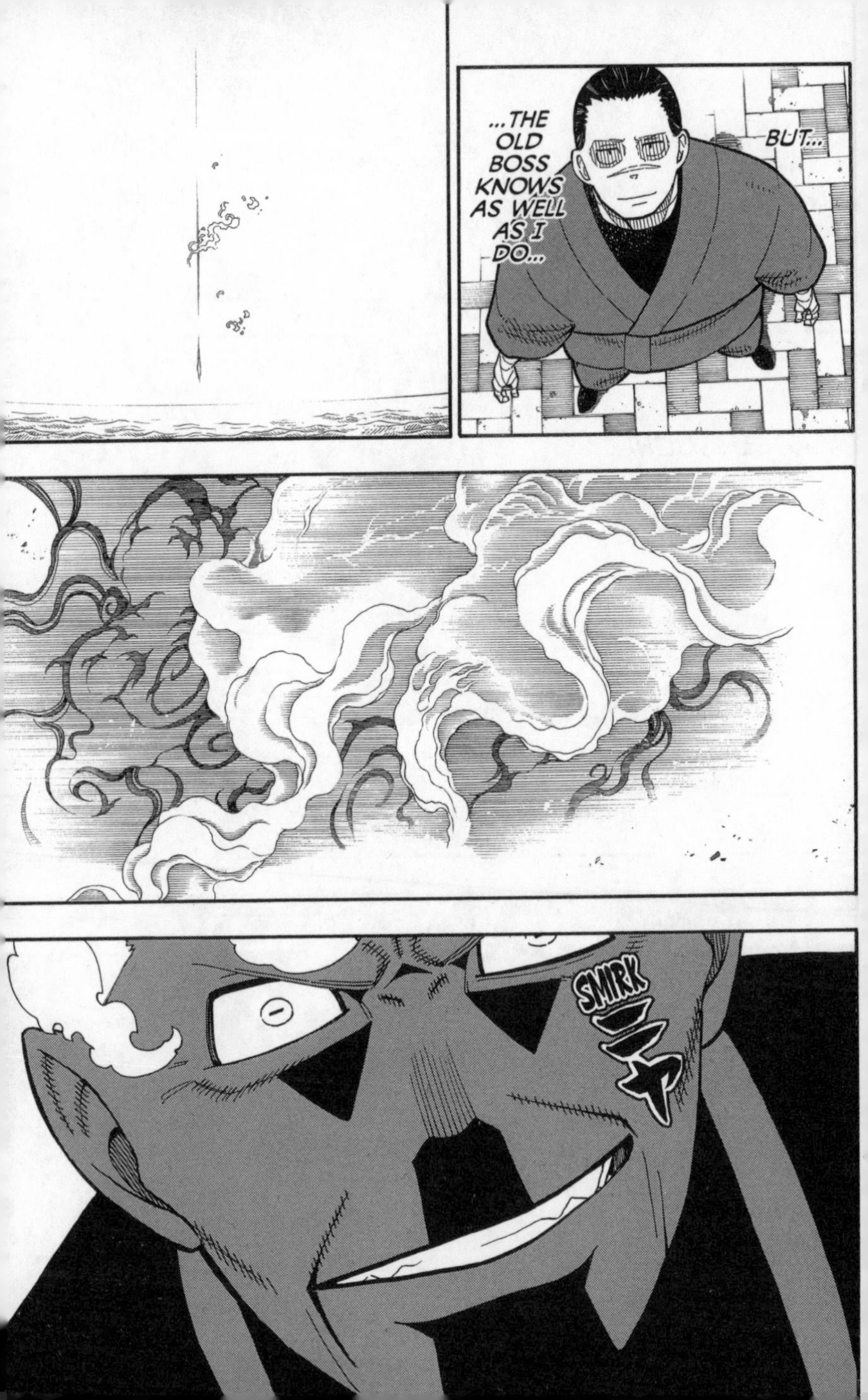
BUT...
...THE OLD BOSS KNOWS AS WELL AS I DO...
SMIRK

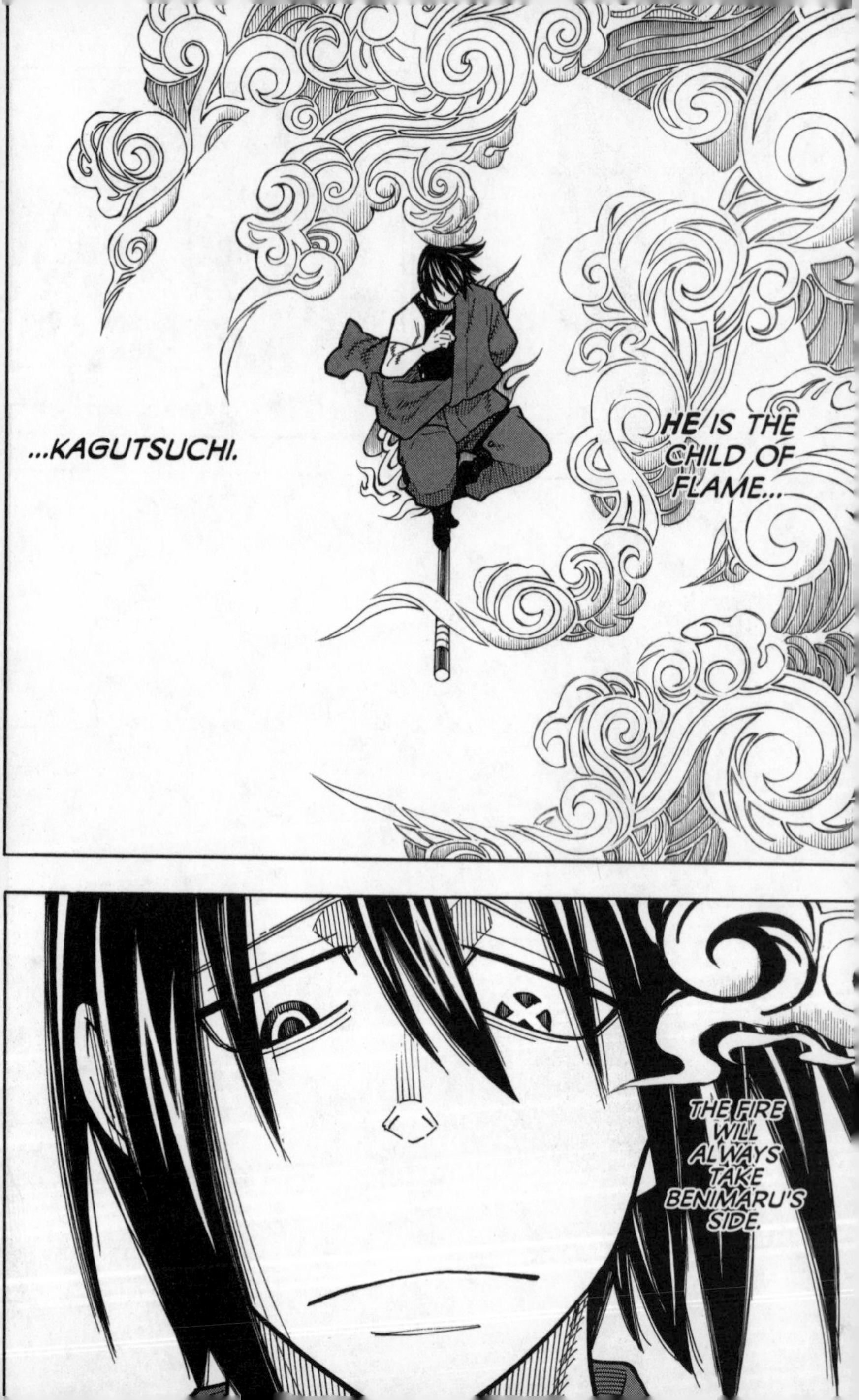
HE IS THE CHILD OF FLAME...
...KAGUTSUCHI.
THE FIRE WILL ALWAYS TAKE BENIMARU'S SIDE.

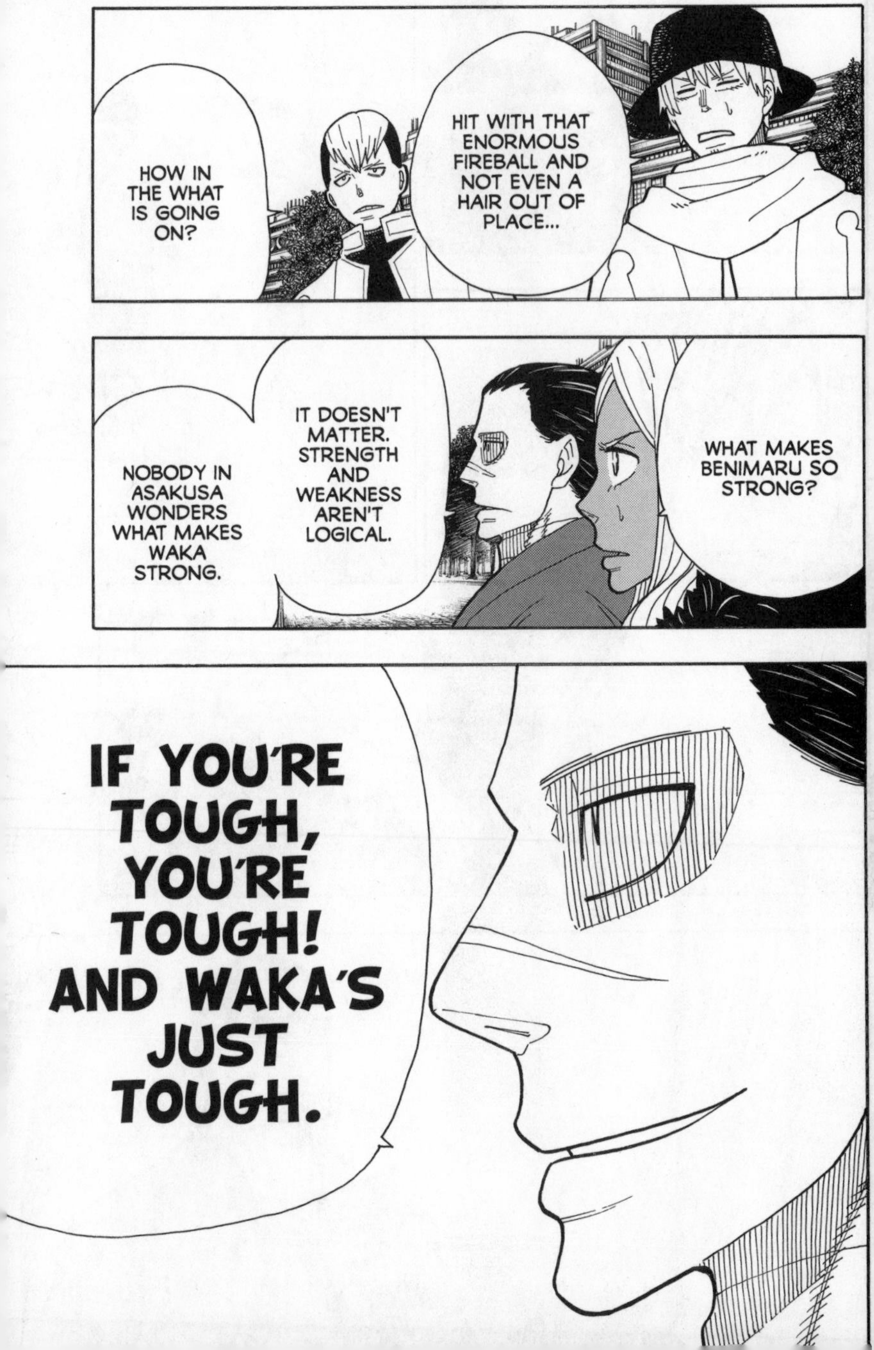
HIT WITH THAT ENORMOUS FIREBALL AND NOT EVEN A HAIR OUT OF PLACE...
HOW IN THE WHAT IS GOING ON?
WHAT MAKES BENIMARU SO STRONG?
IT DOESN'T MATTER. STRENGTH AND WEAKNESS AREN'T LOGICAL.
NOBODY IN ASAKUSA WONDERS WHAT MAKES WAKA STRONG.
IF YOU'RE TOUGH, YOU'RE TOUGH! AND WAKA'S JUST TOUGH.

YOU'RE THE SAME MONSTER YOU EVER WERE.

THERE'S SOMETHING I REALLY NEED TO SAY TO YOU!

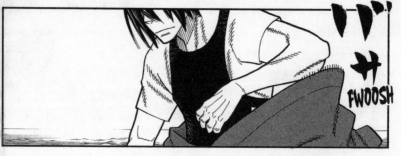

FWOOSH

!!

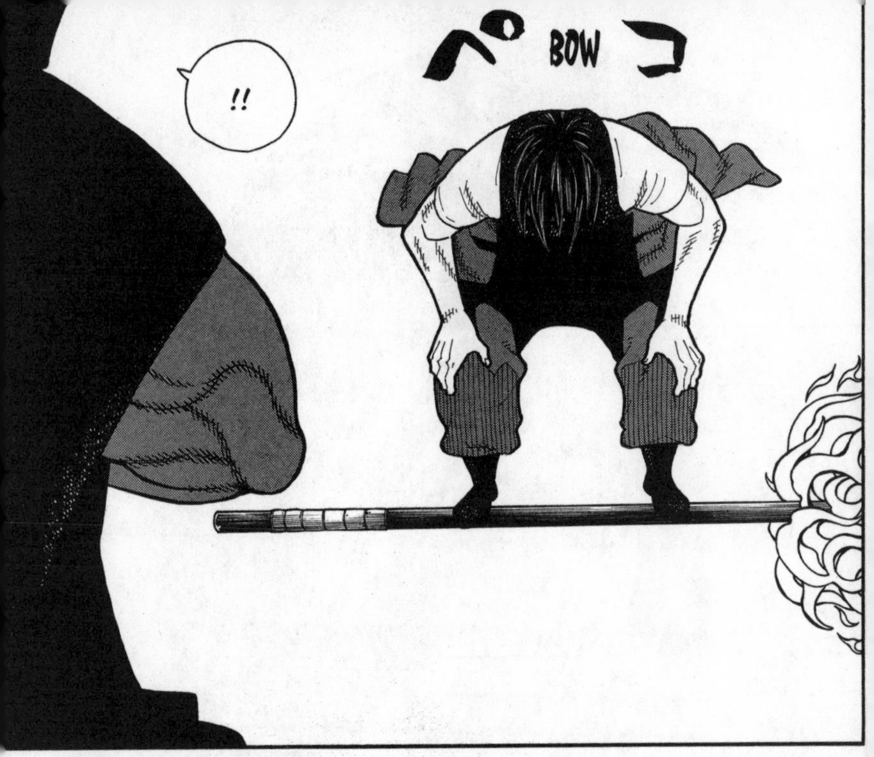
ペ BOW コ
!!

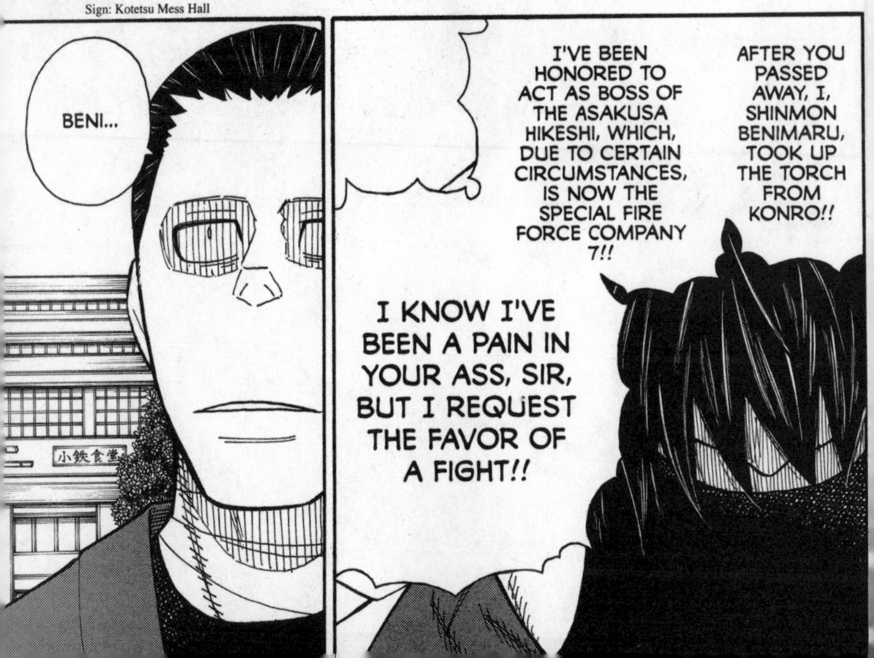
AFTER YOU PASSED AWAY, I, SHINMON BENIMARU, TOOK UP THE TORCH FROM KONRO!!
I'VE BEEN HONORED TO ACT AS BOSS OF THE ASAKUSA HIKESHI, WHICH, DUE TO CERTAIN CIRCUMSTANCES, IS NOW THE SPECIAL FIRE FORCE COMPANY 7!!
I KNOW I'VE BEEN A PAIN IN YOUR ASS, SIR, BUT I REQUEST THE FAVOR OF A FIGHT!!
BENI...
小鉄食堂
Sign: Kotetsu Mess Hall

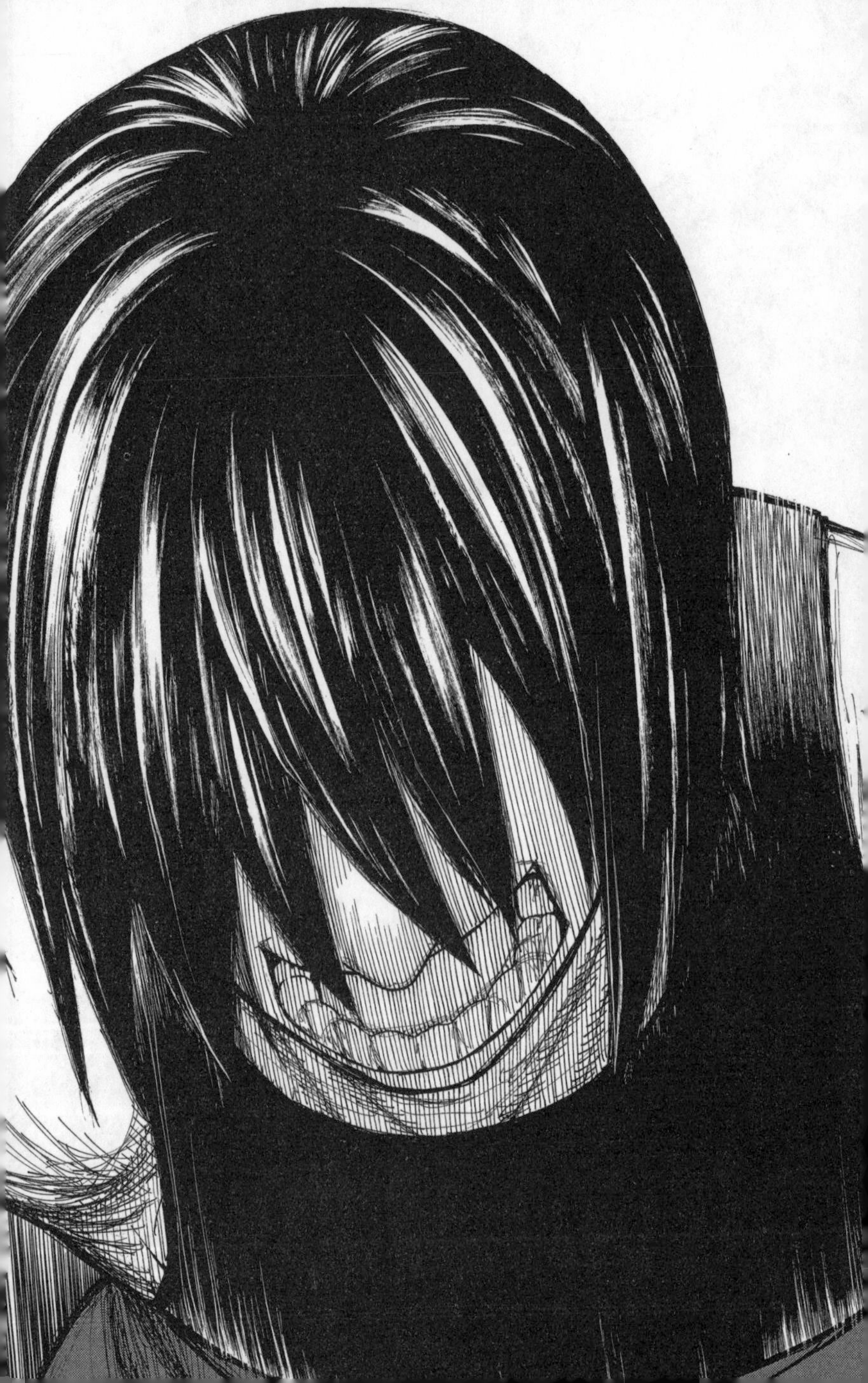

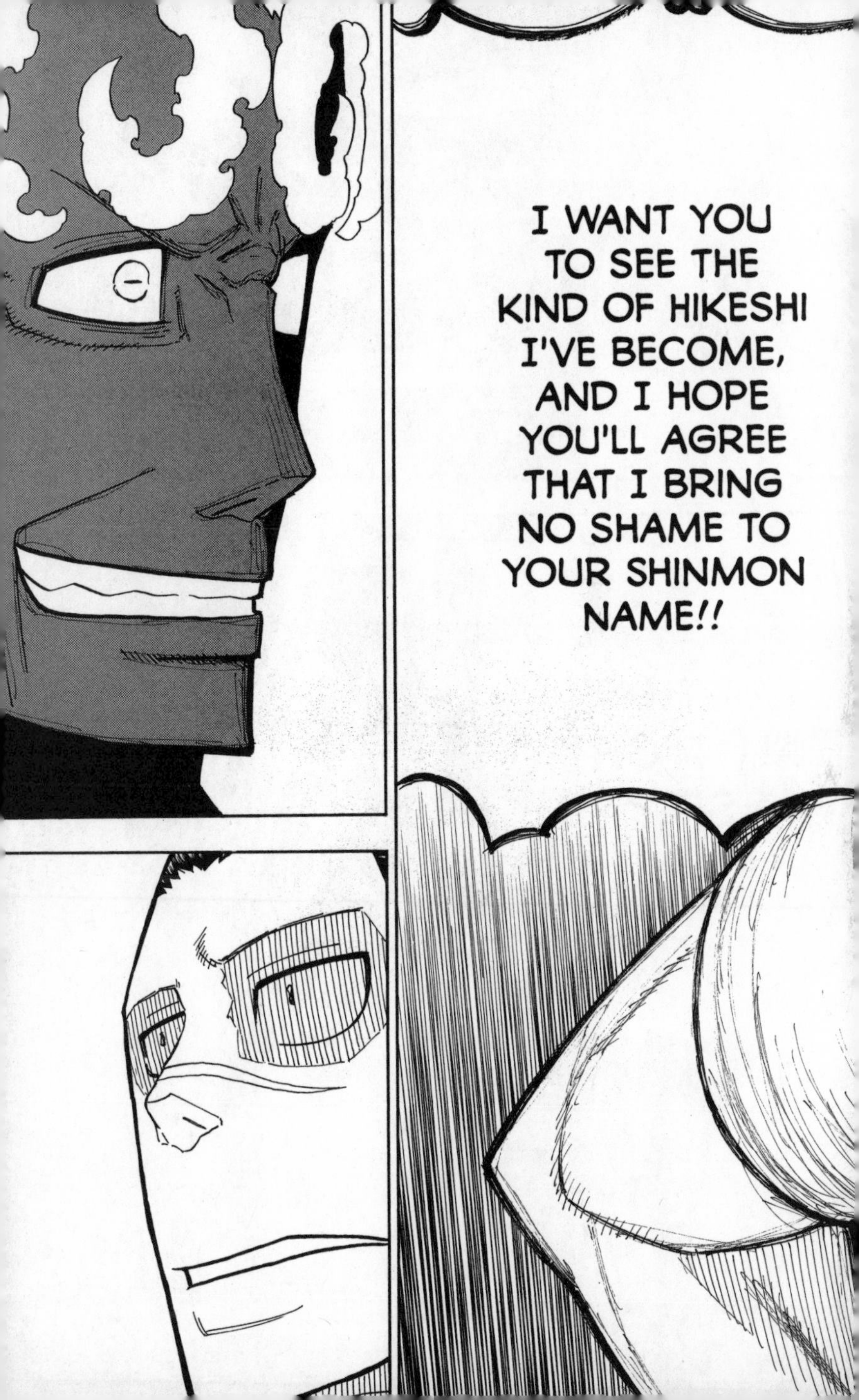
I WANT YOU TO SEE THE KIND OF HIKESHI I'VE BECOME, AND I HOPE YOU'LL AGREE THAT I BRING NO SHAME TO YOUR SHINMON NAME!!

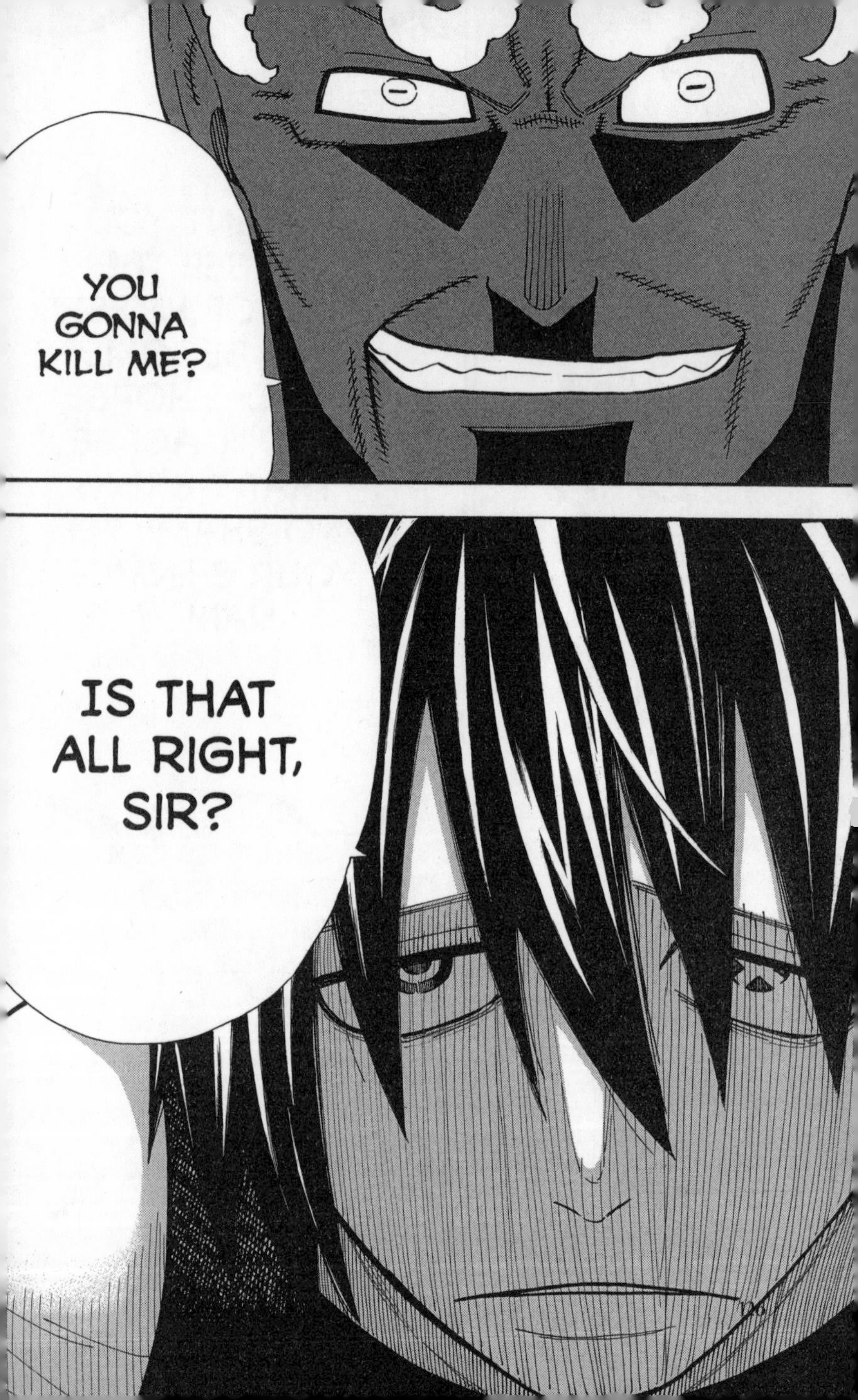
YOU GONNA KILL ME?
IS THAT ALL RIGHT, SIR?

FIRE FORCE

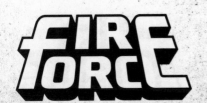

FIRE FORCE

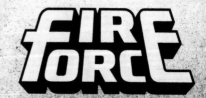

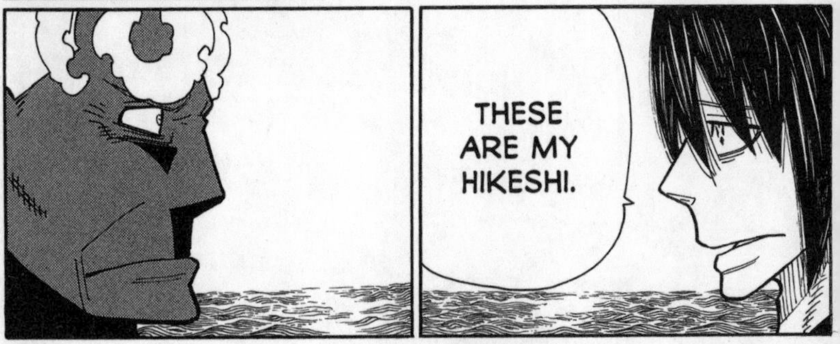
THESE ARE MY HIKESHI.

Banner: Seven

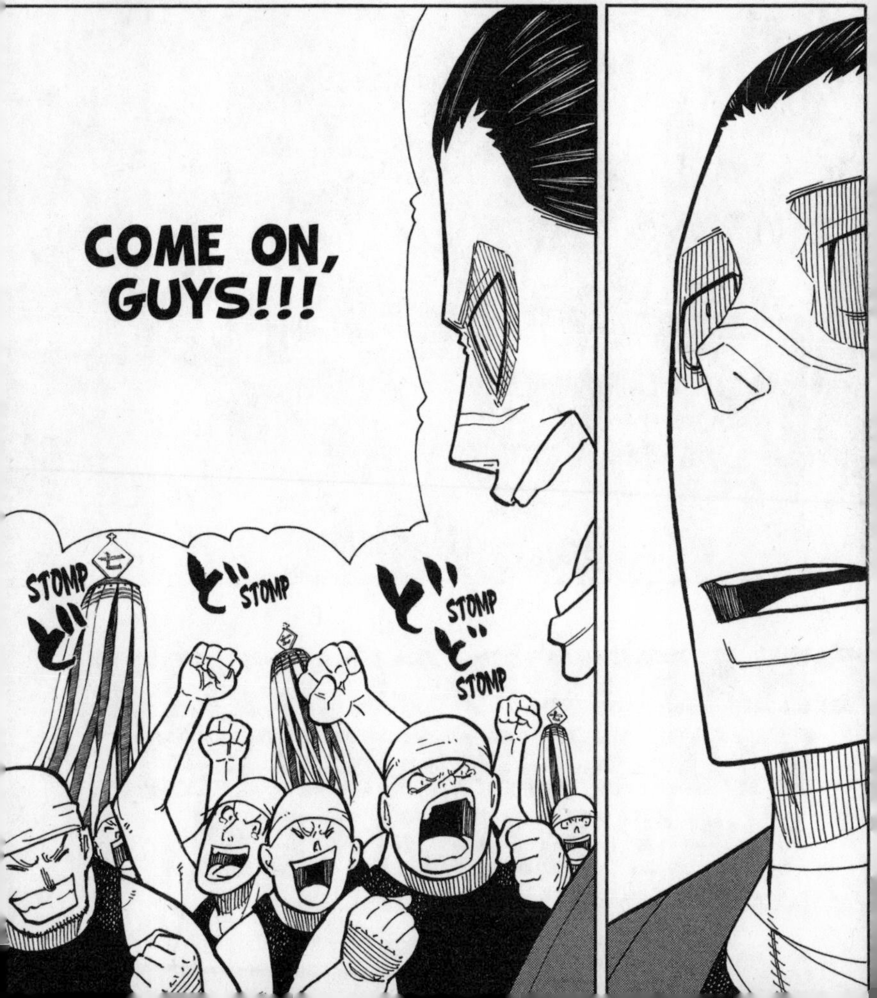
COME ON, GUYS!!!
ど STOMP
ど STOMP
ど STOMP
STOMP ど

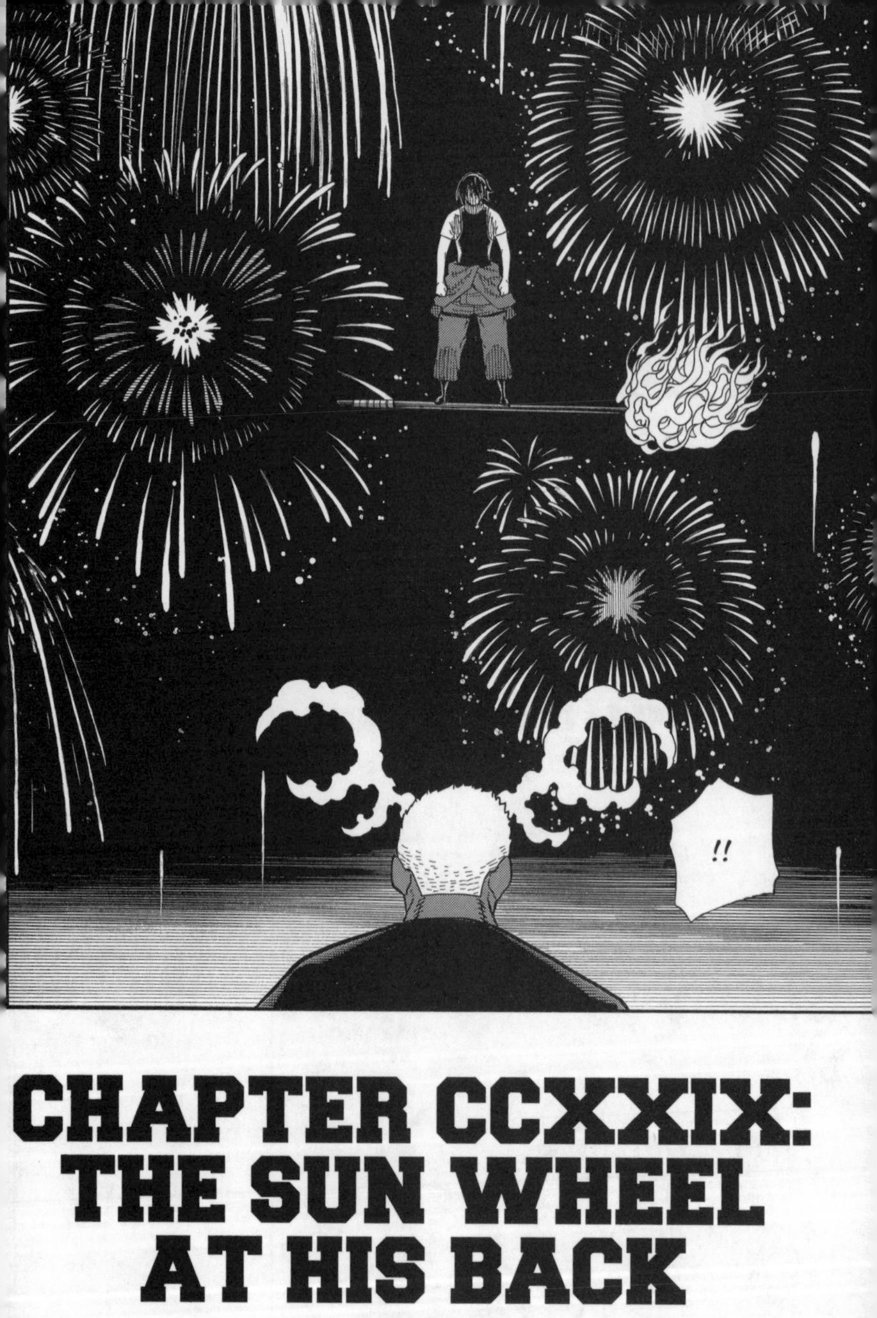
!!

CHAPTER CCXXIX: THE SUN WHEEL AT HIS BACK

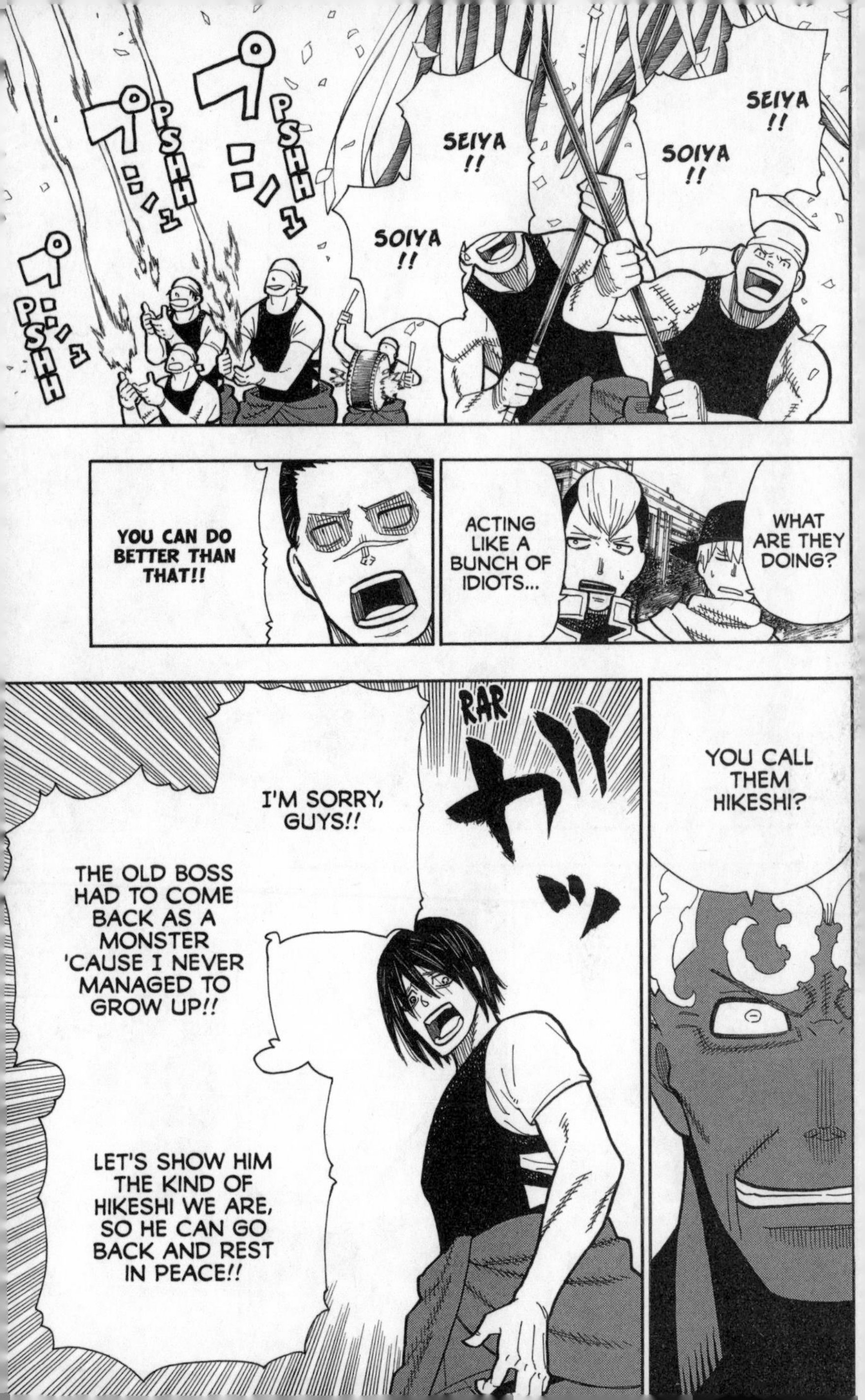
SEIYA!!
SOIYA!!
SEIYA!!
SOIYA!!
PSHH
PSHH
PSHH
WHAT ARE THEY DOING?
ACTING LIKE A BUNCH OF IDIOTS...
YOU CAN DO BETTER THAN THAT!!
YOU CALL THEM HIKESHI?
RAR
I'M SORRY, GUYS!!
THE OLD BOSS HAD TO COME BACK AS A MONSTER 'CAUSE I NEVER MANAGED TO GROW UP!!
LET'S SHOW HIM THE KIND OF HIKESHI WE ARE, SO HE CAN GO BACK AND REST IN PEACE!!

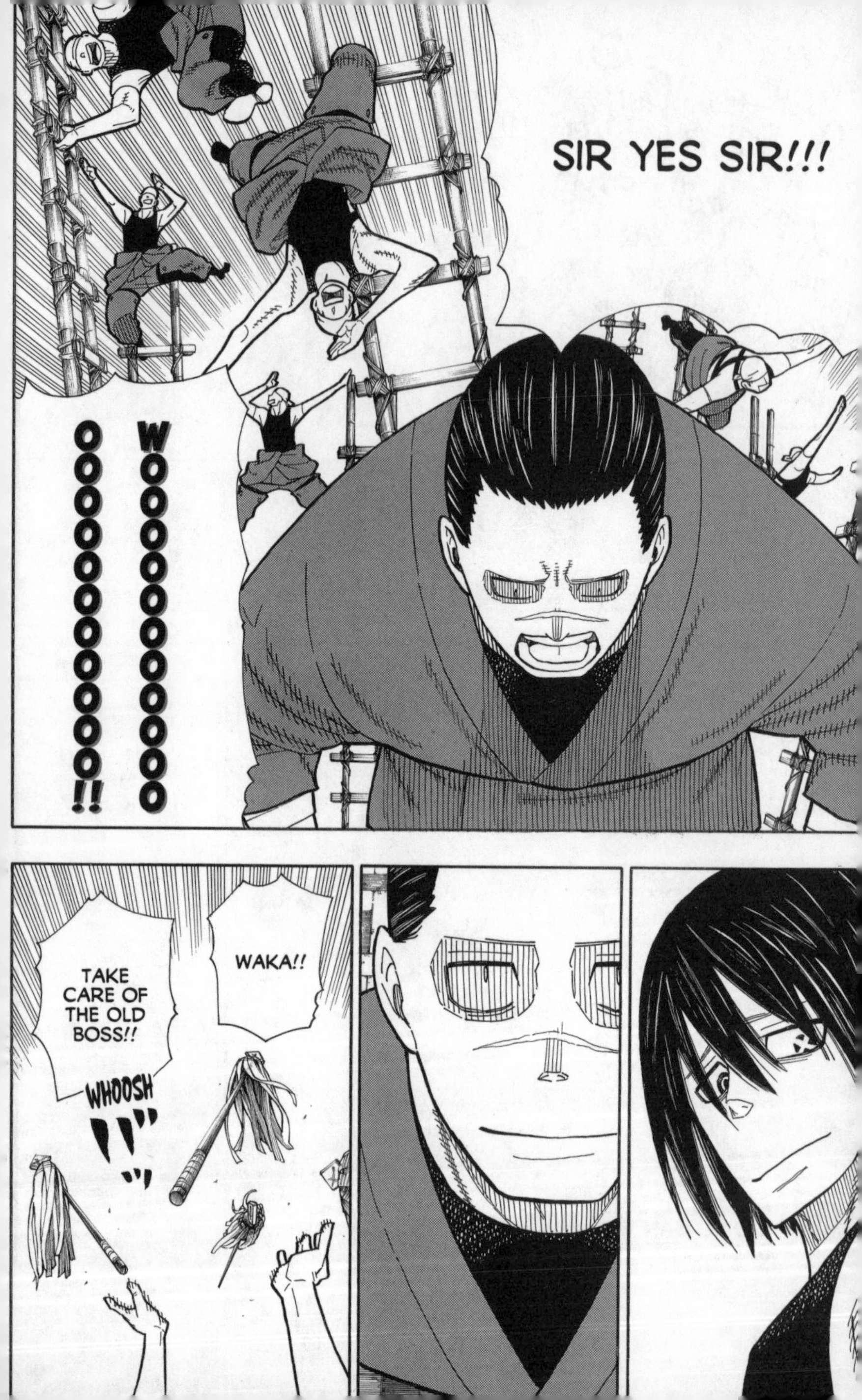
SIR YES SIR!!!
WOOOOOOOOOOOOOO
OOOOOOOOOOOOOOO!!
WAKA!!
TAKE CARE OF THE OLD BOSS!!
WHOOSH

WHAT TOMFOOLERY ARE YOU UP TO NOW, YOU PUNK KID?

I'M SORRY THIS TOOK SO LONG.

NOW HERE IT IS. MY NICHIRIN.

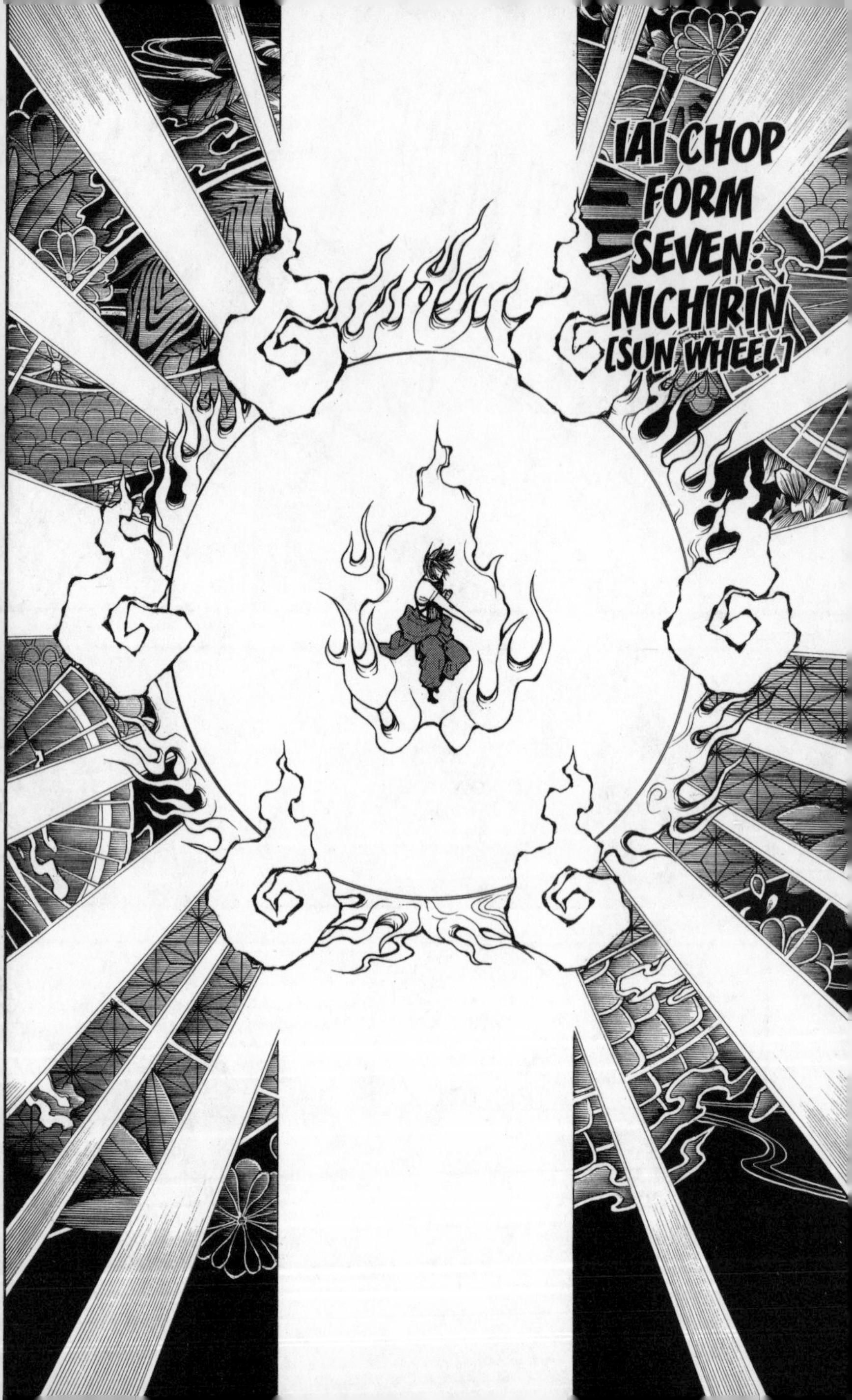
IAI CHOP FORM SEVEN: NICHIRIN [SUN WHEEL]

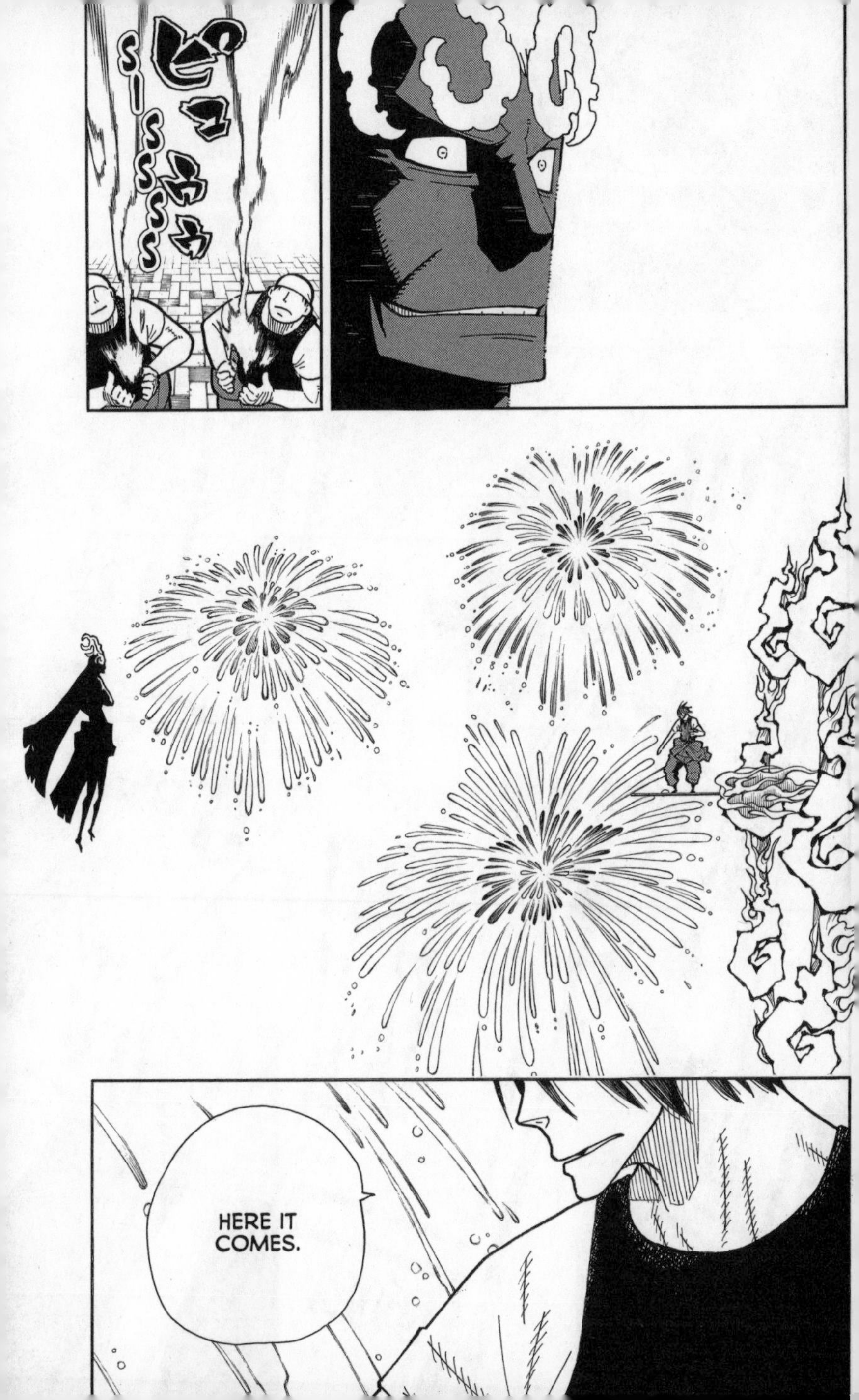
SISSSS
HERE IT COMES.

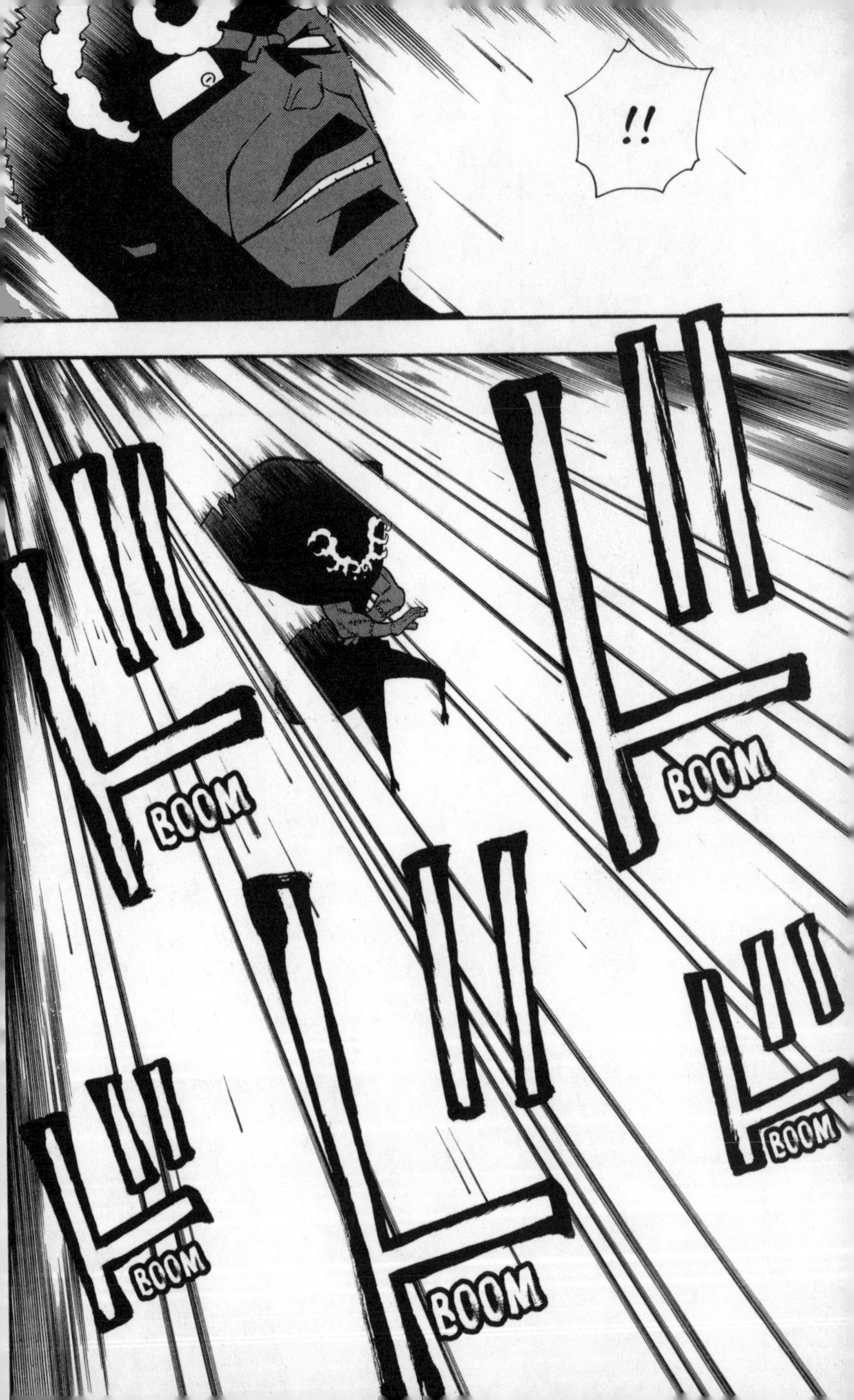
!!
BOOM
BOOM
BOOM
BOOM
BOOM
BOOM

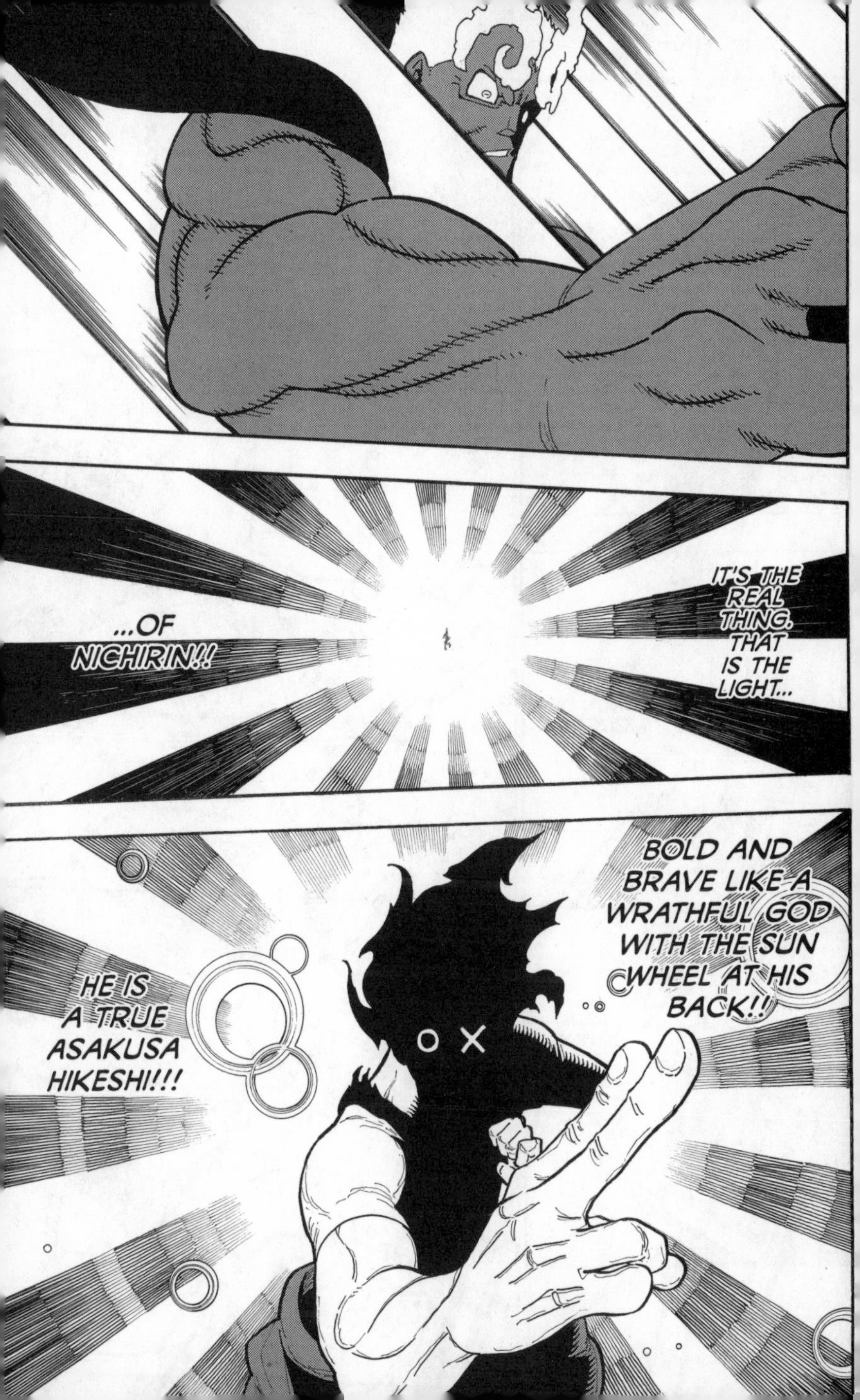
IT'S THE REAL THING. THAT IS THE LIGHT...
...OF NICHIRIN!!
BOLD AND BRAVE LIKE A WRATHFUL GOD WITH THE SUN WHEEL AT HIS BACK!!
HE IS A TRUE ASAKUSA HIKESHI!!!

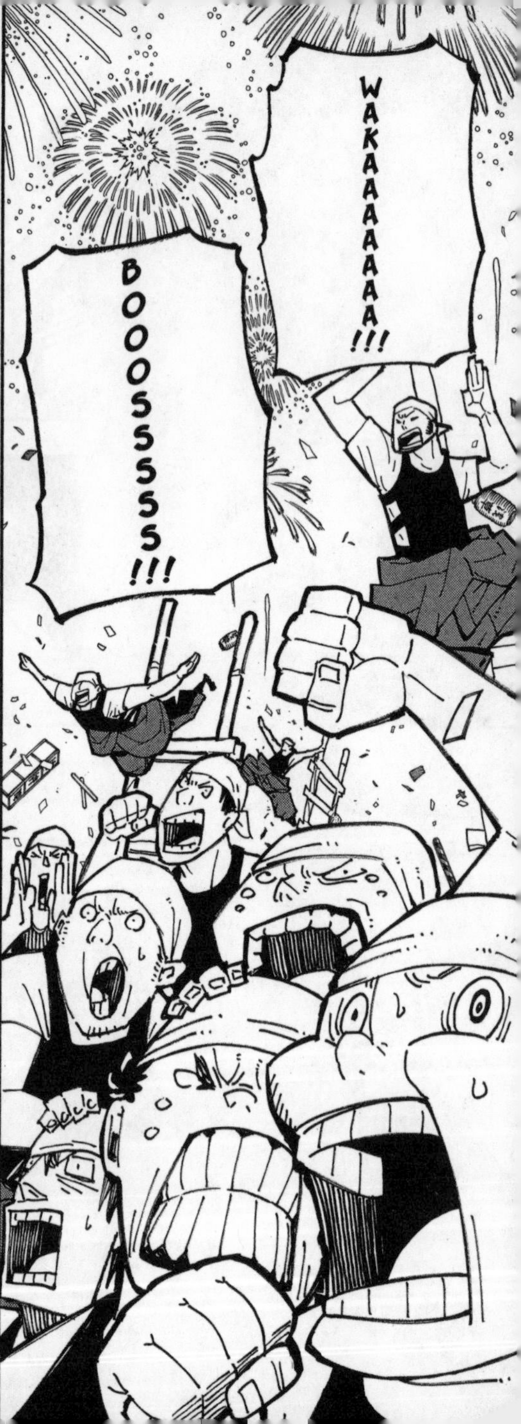

WAKAAAAAAAA!!!
BOOOSSSSS!!!

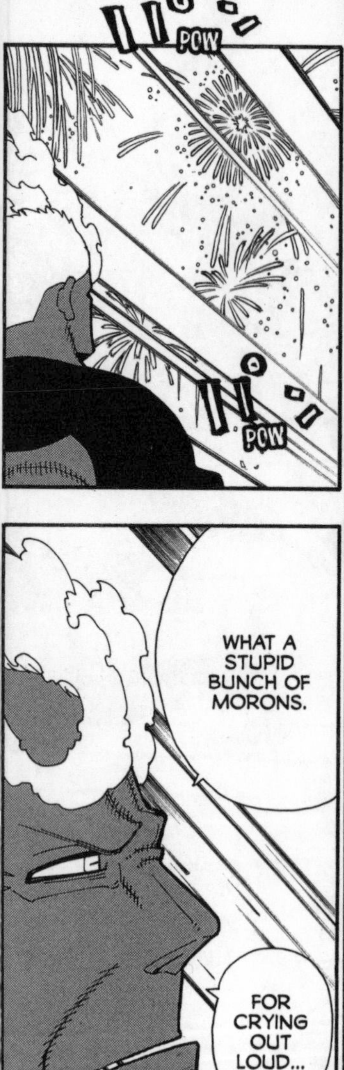

POW
POW
WHAT A STUPID BUNCH OF MORONS.
FOR CRYING OUT LOUD...

Lantern: Asakusa

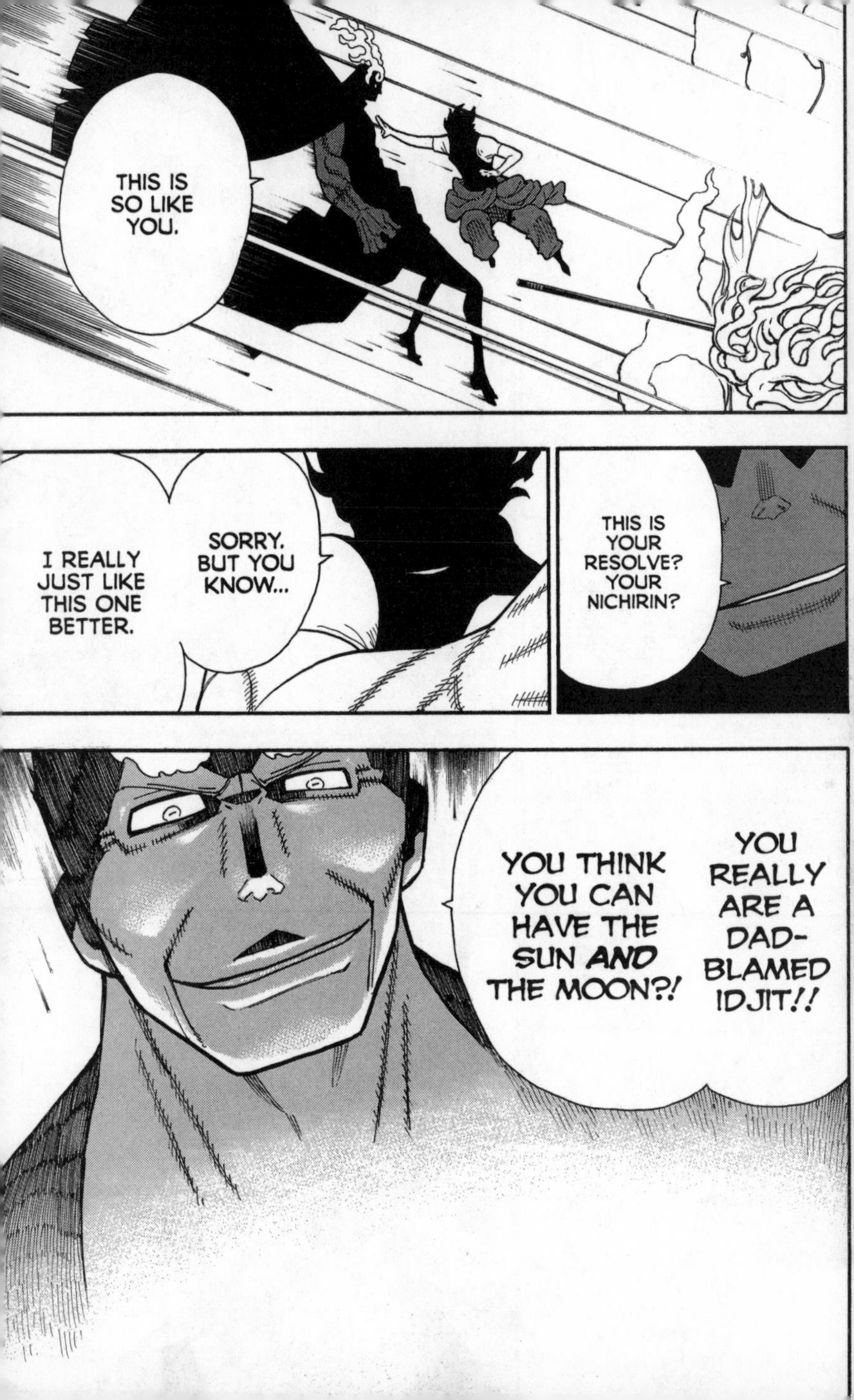
THIS IS SO LIKE YOU.
THIS IS YOUR RESOLVE? YOUR NICHIRIN?
SORRY. BUT YOU KNOW...
I REALLY JUST LIKE THIS ONE BETTER.
YOU REALLY ARE A DAD-BLAMED IDJIT!!
YOU THINK YOU CAN HAVE THE SUN *AND* THE MOON?!

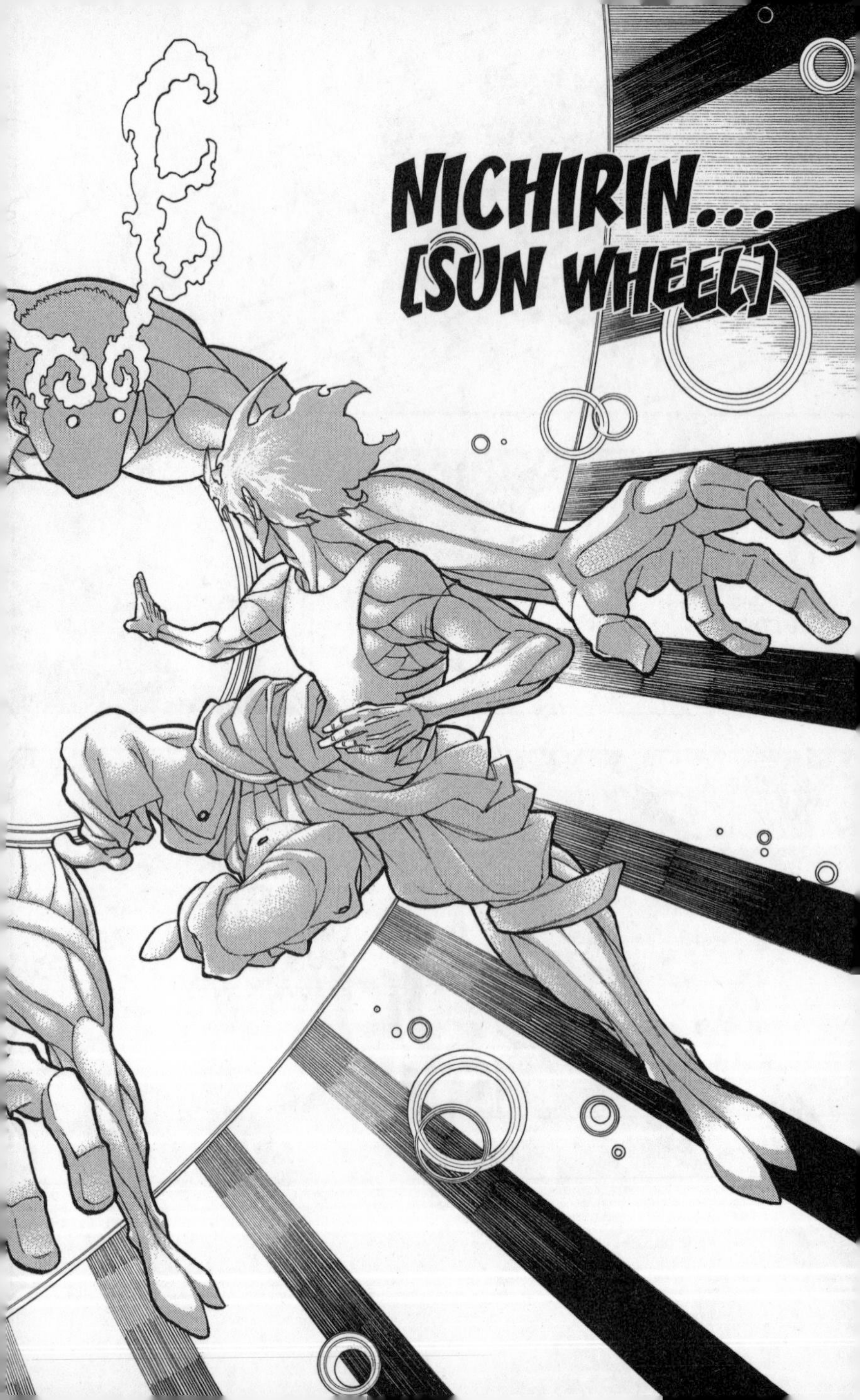
NICHIRIN...
[SUN WHEEL]

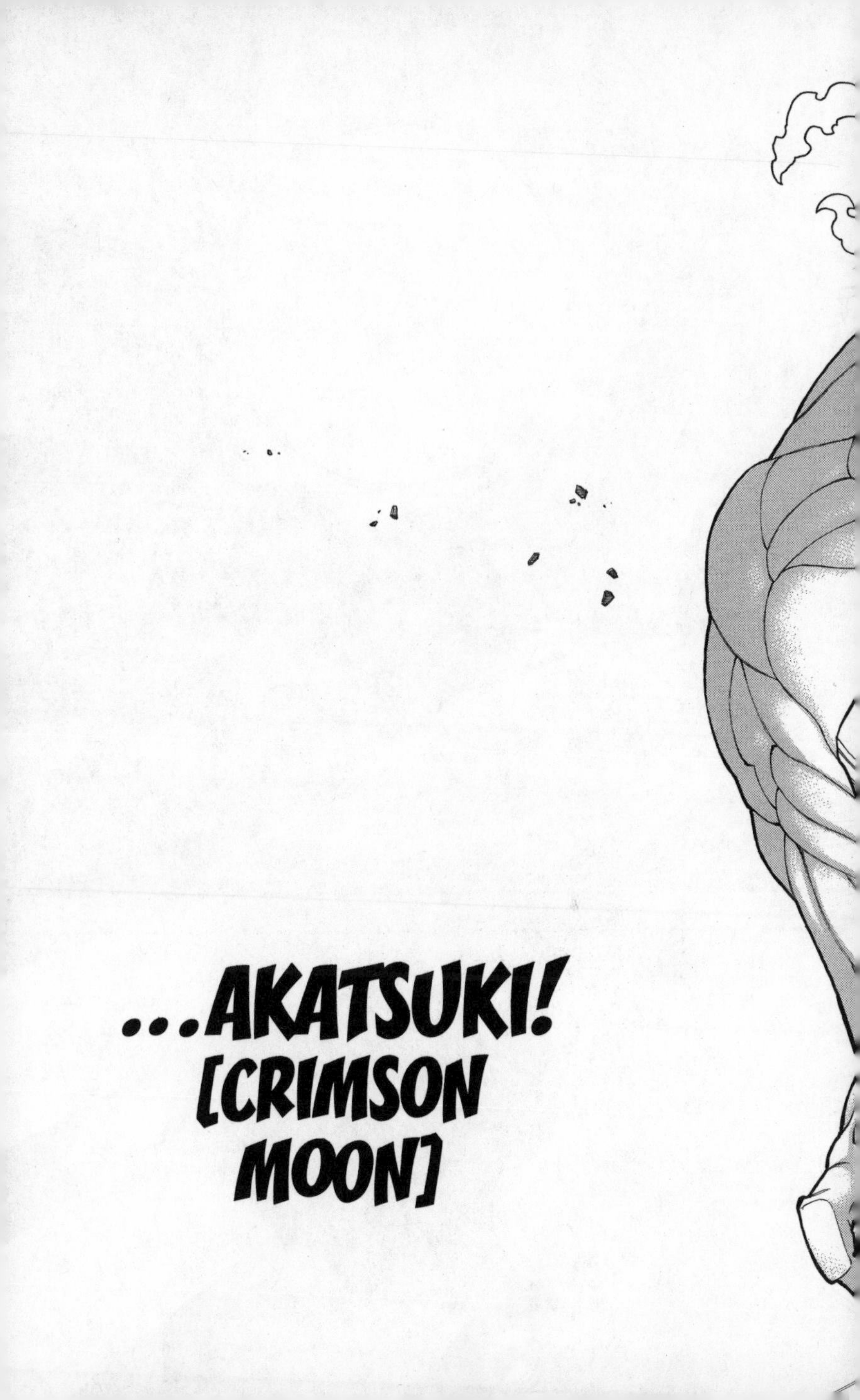
...AKATSUKI! [CRIMSON MOON]

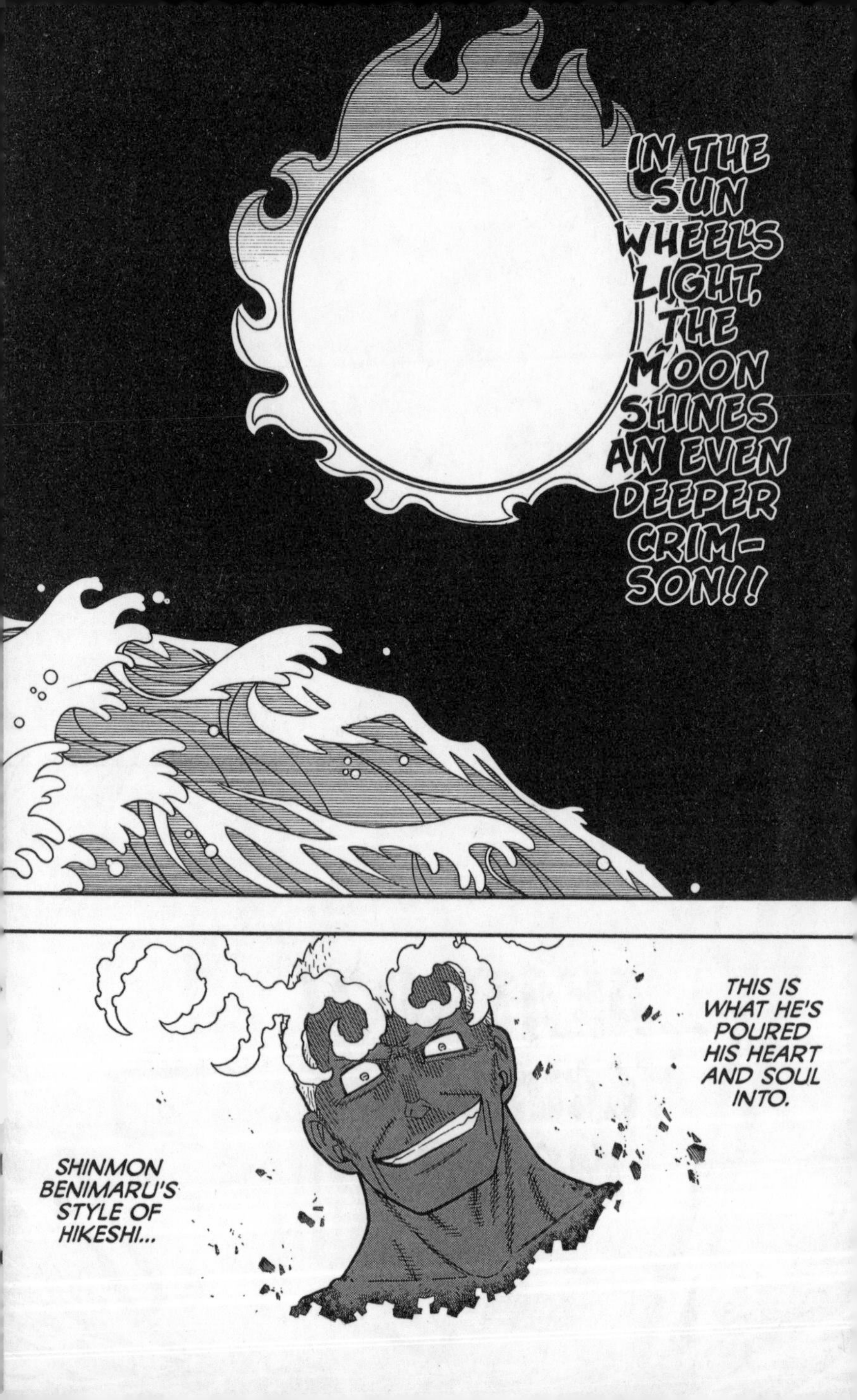
IN THE SUN WHEEL'S LIGHT, THE MOON SHINES AN EVEN DEEPER CRIM-SON!!
THIS IS WHAT HE'S POURED HIS HEART AND SOUL INTO.
SHINMON BENIMARU'S STYLE OF HIKESHI...

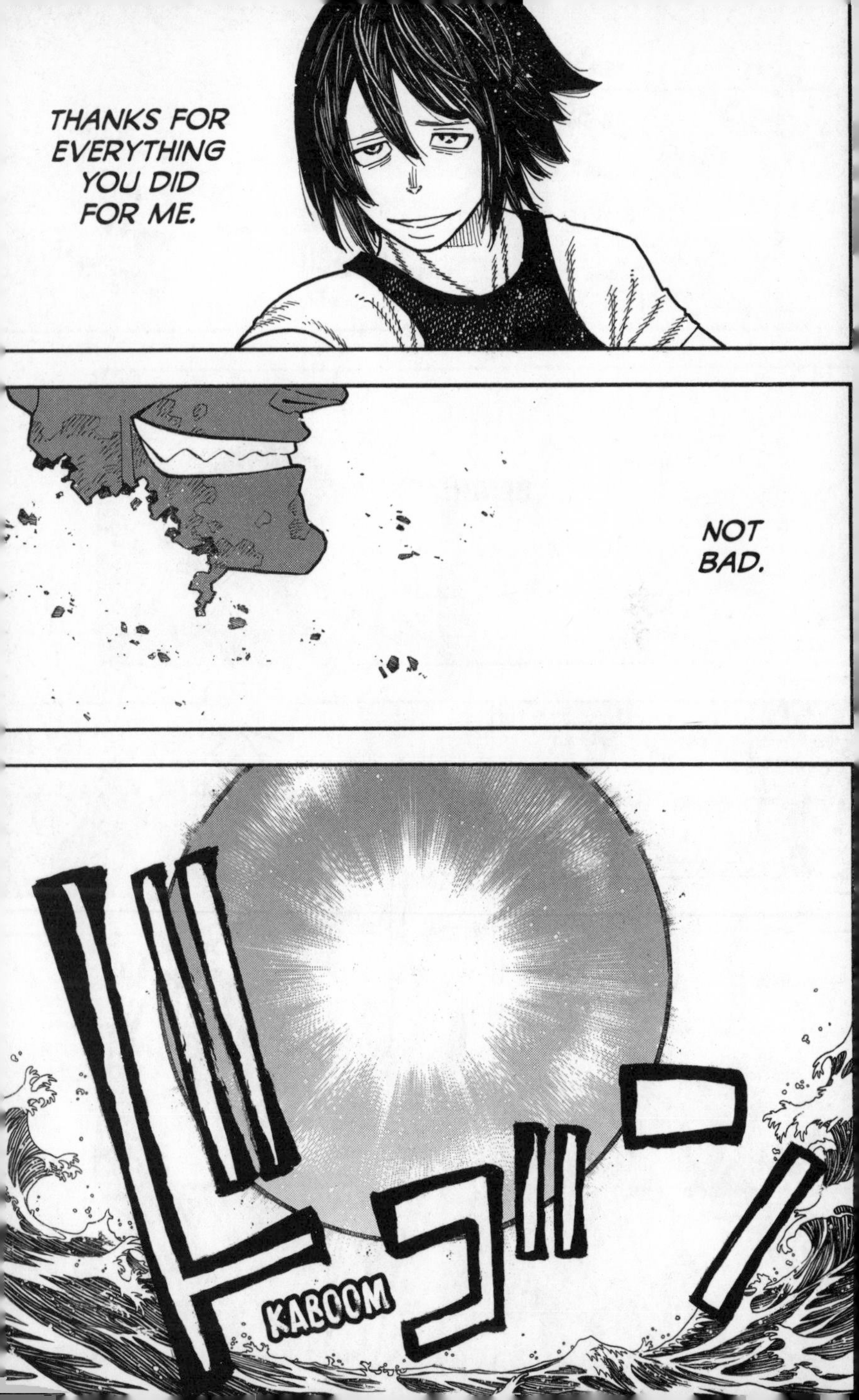
THANKS FOR EVERYTHING YOU DID FOR ME.
NOT BAD.
KABOOM

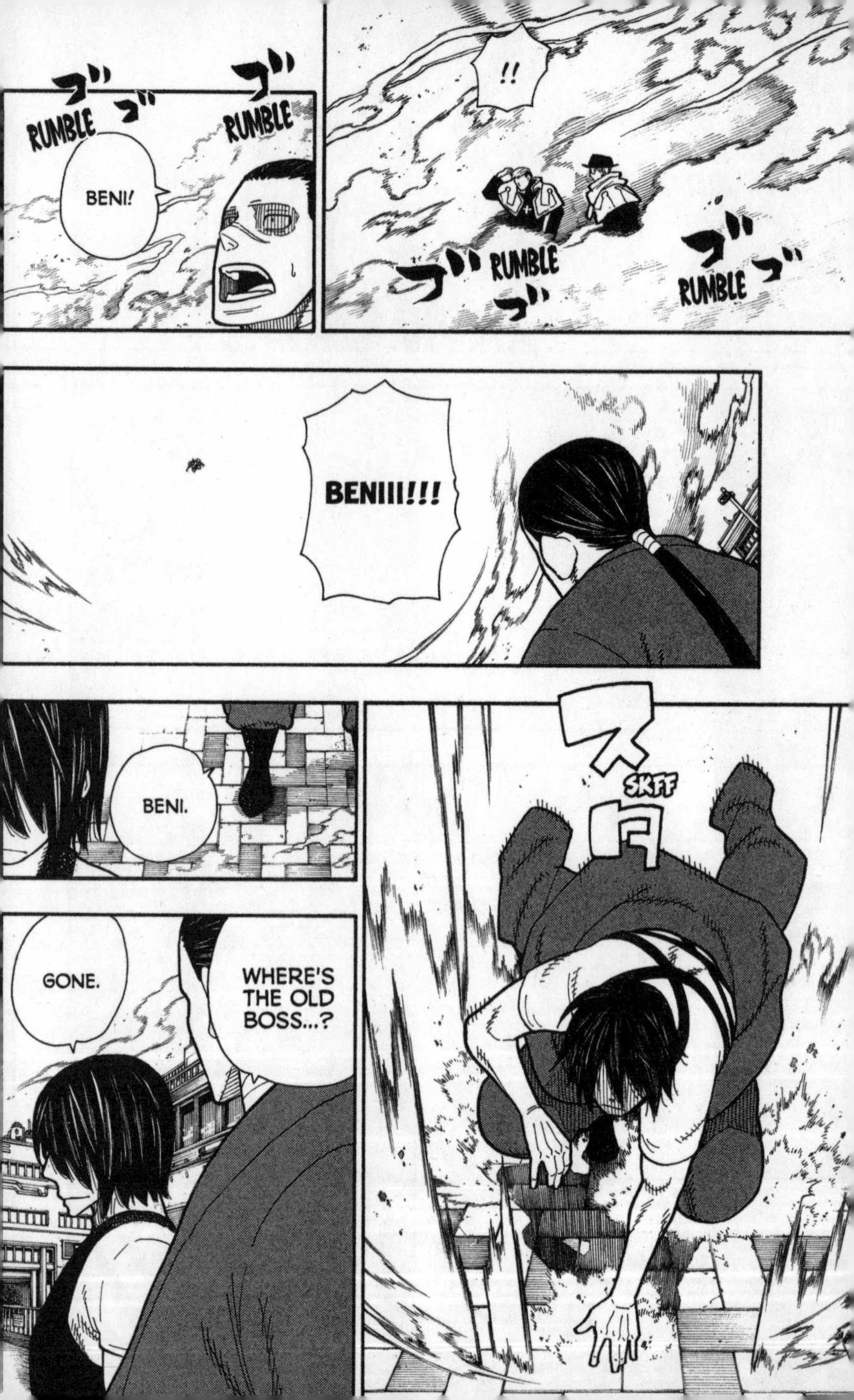

!!
ゴゴ
RUMBLE
ゴゴ
RUMBLE
ゴゴ
RUMBLE
ゴゴ
RUMBLE
BENI!
BENIII!!!
スタ
SKFF
BENI.
WHERE'S THE OLD BOSS...?
GONE.

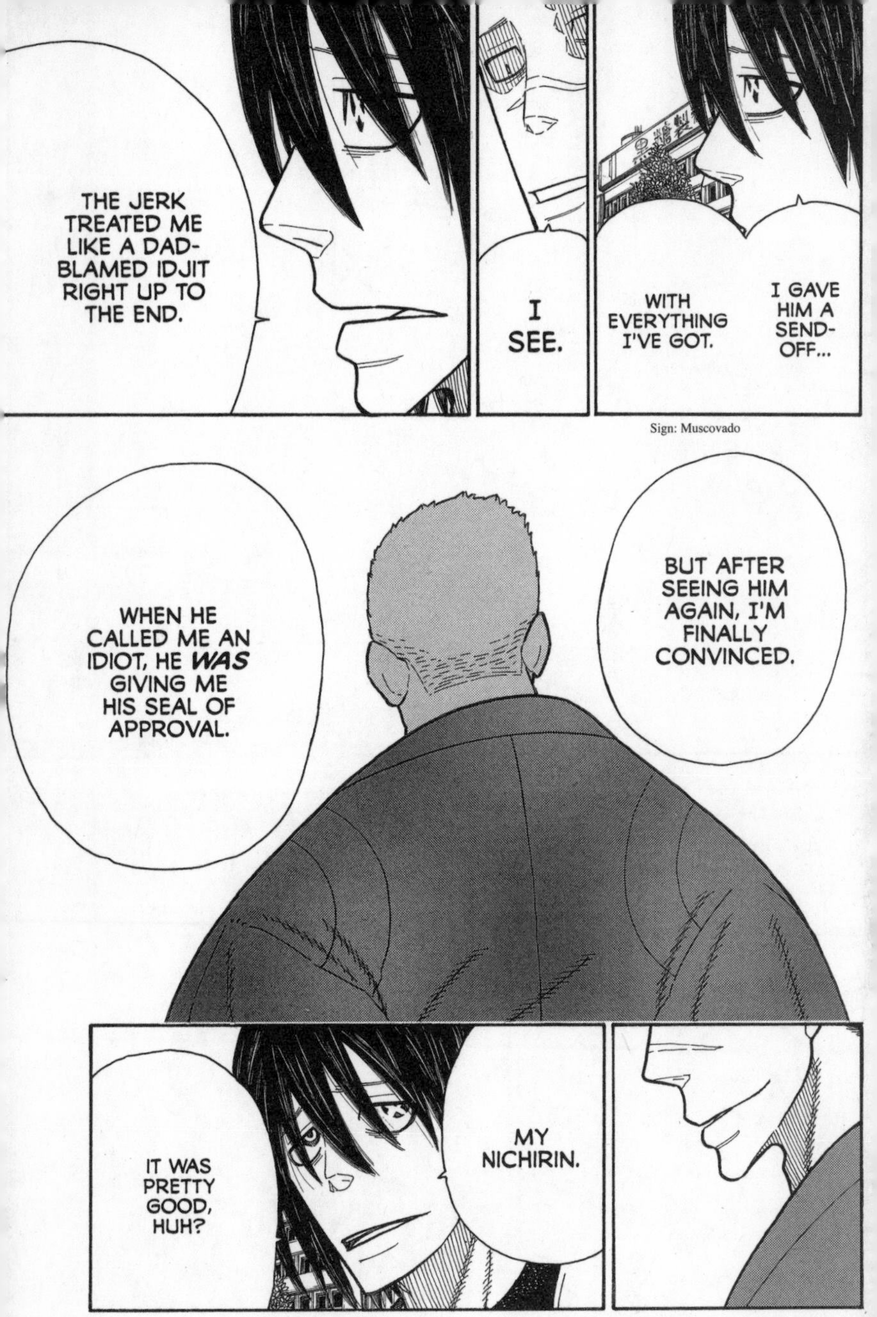
I GAVE HIM A SEND-OFF...
WITH EVERYTHING I'VE GOT.
I SEE.
THE JERK TREATED ME LIKE A DAD-BLAMED IDJIT RIGHT UP TO THE END.
BUT AFTER SEEING HIM AGAIN, I'M FINALLY CONVINCED.
WHEN HE CALLED ME AN IDIOT, HE *WAS* GIVING ME HIS SEAL OF APPROVAL.
MY NICHIRIN.
IT WAS PRETTY GOOD, HUH?
Sign: Muscovado

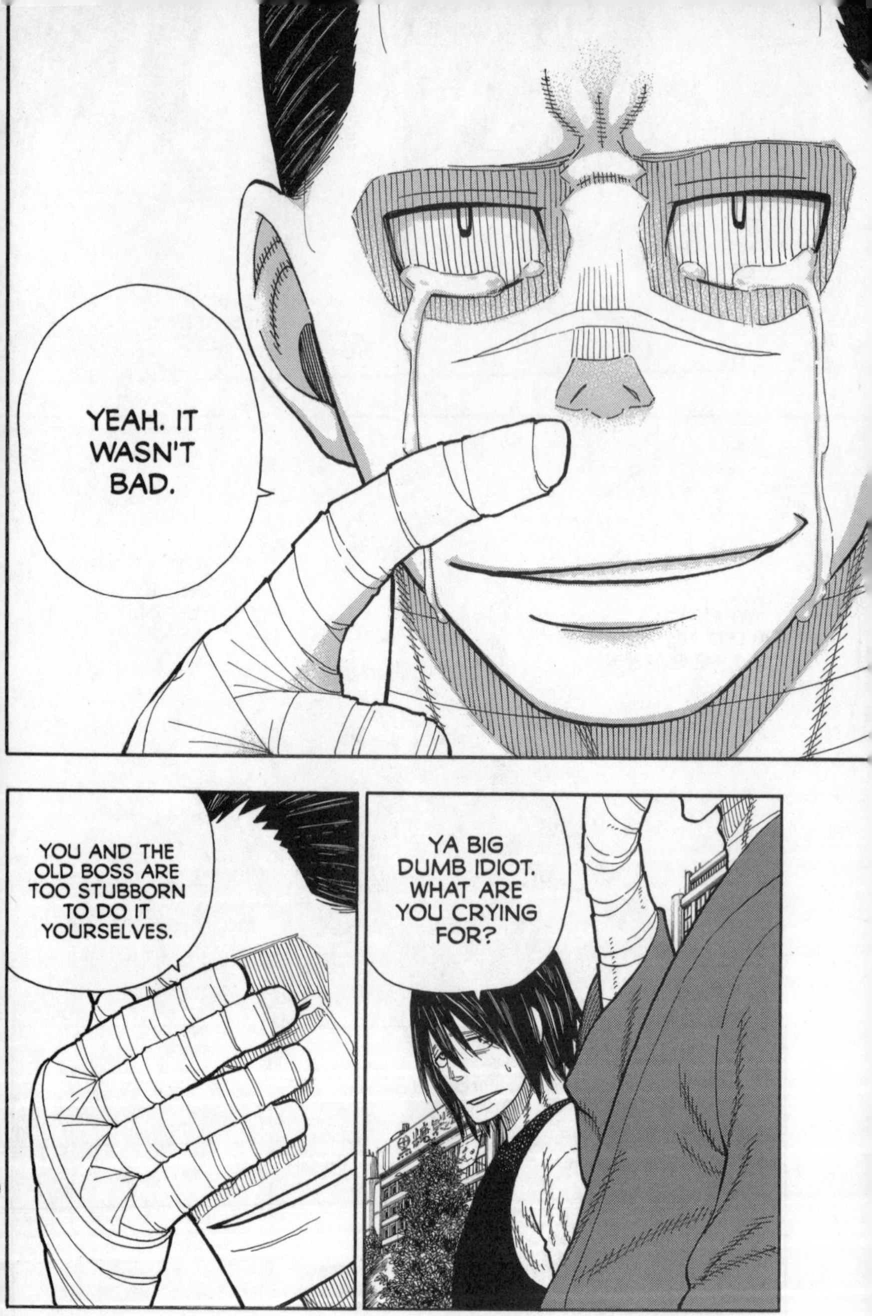
YEAH. IT WASN'T BAD.
YA BIG DUMB IDIOT. WHAT ARE YOU CRYING FOR?
YOU AND THE OLD BOSS ARE TOO STUBBORN TO DO IT YOURSELVES.

Sign: Muscovado

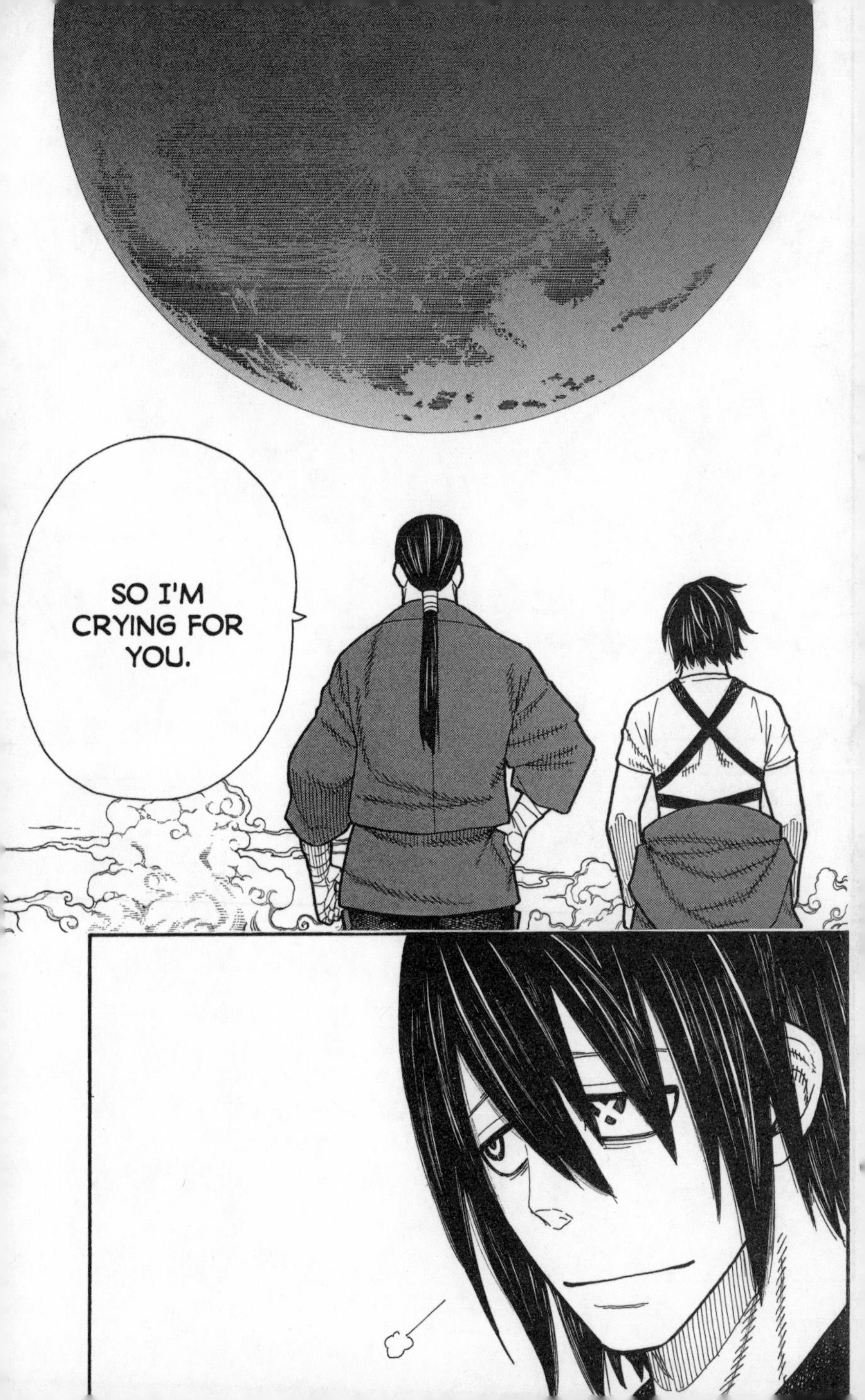
SO I'M CRYING FOR YOU.

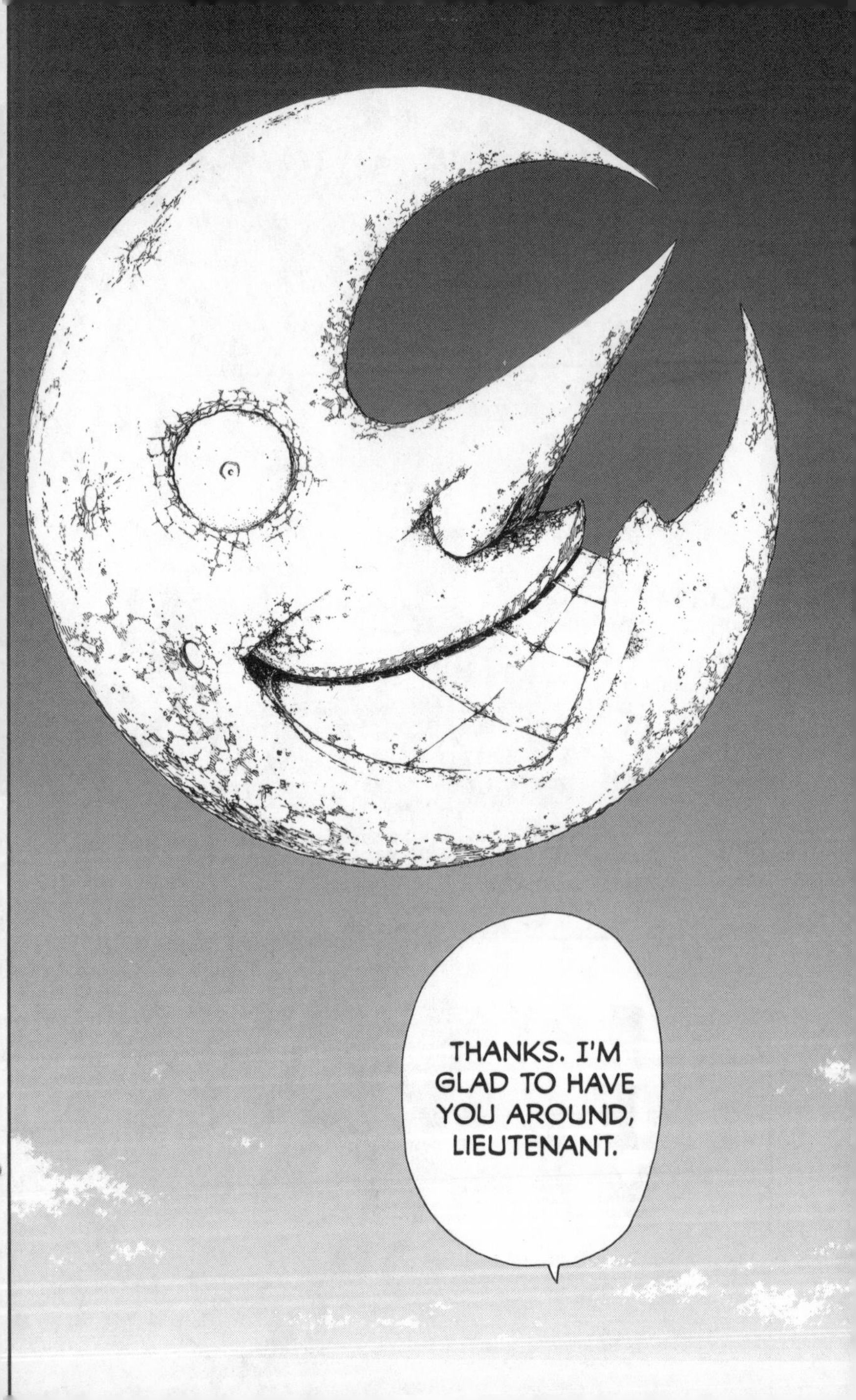
THANKS. I'M GLAD TO HAVE YOU AROUND, LIEUTENANT.

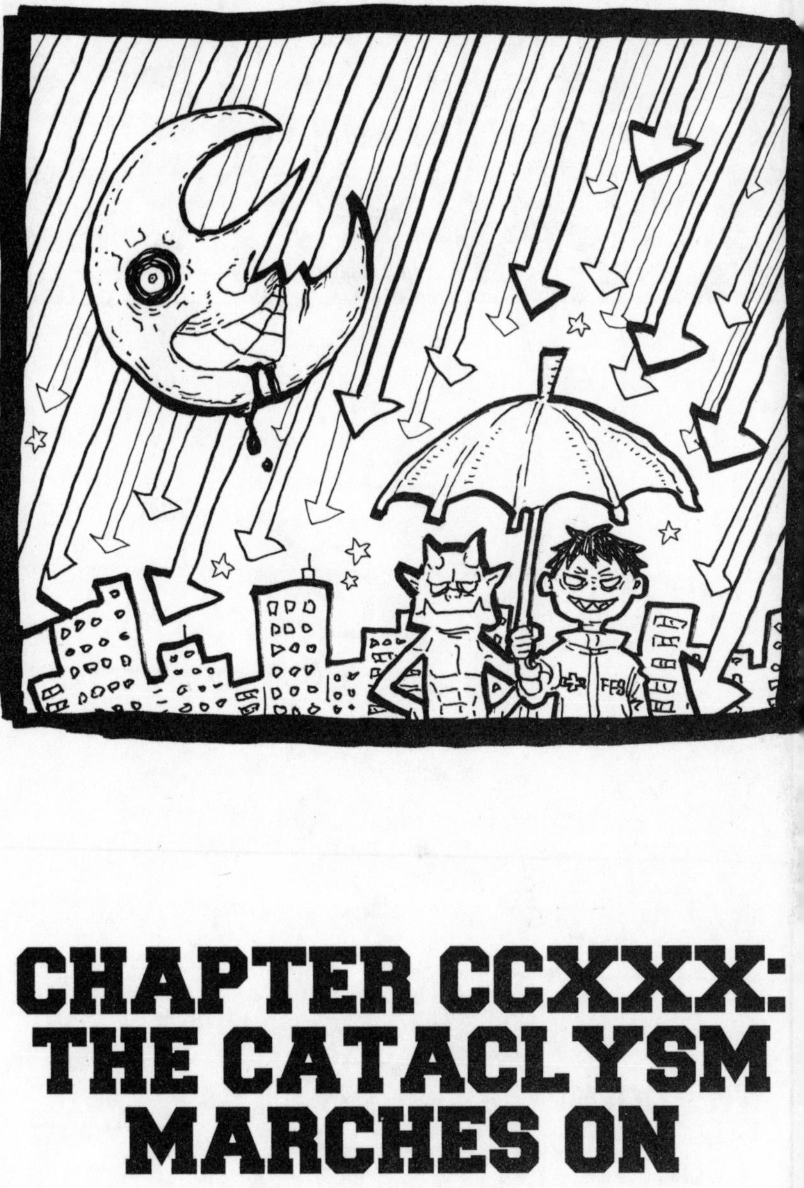
FFS

CHAPTER CCXXX: THE CATACLYSM MARCHES ON

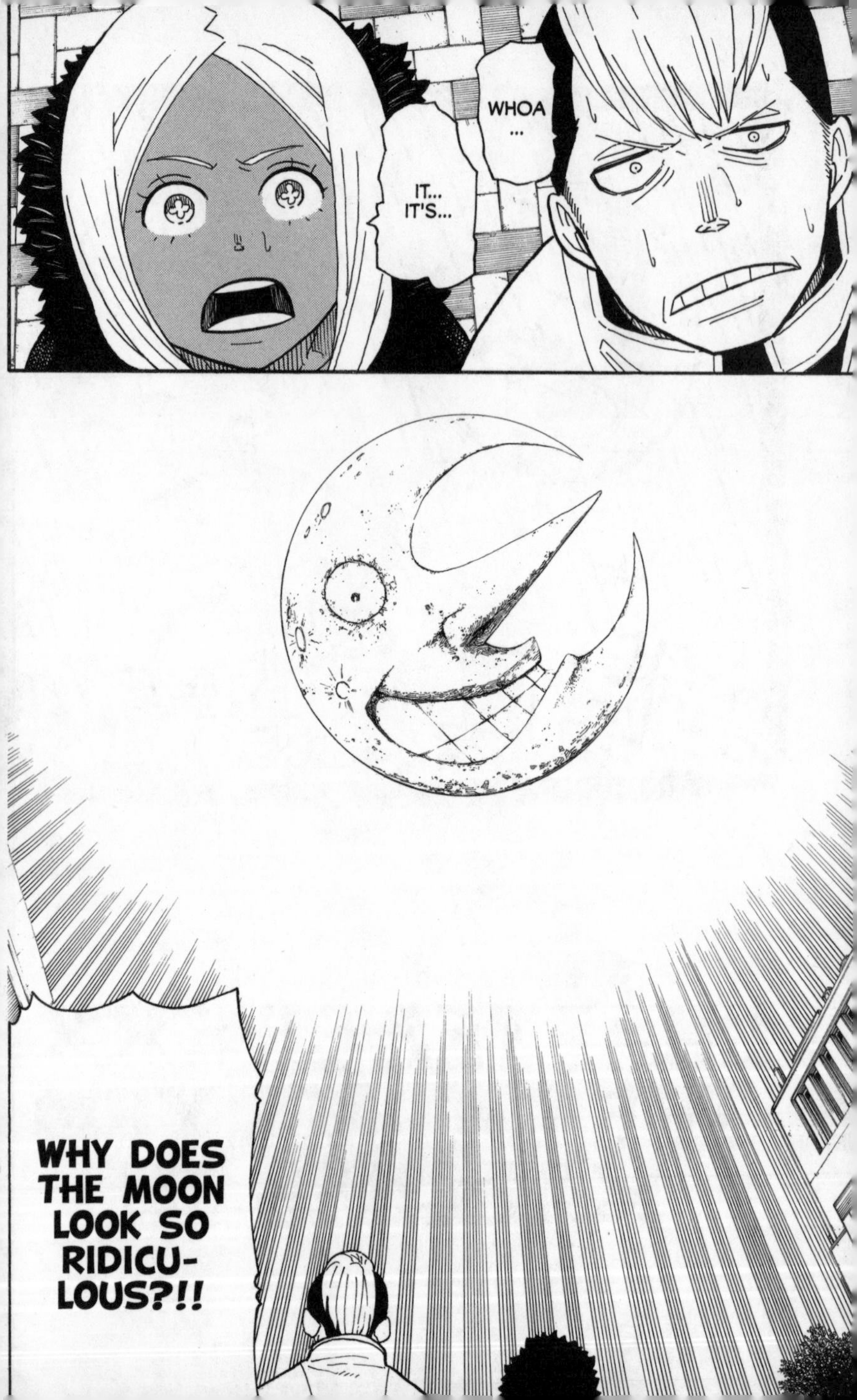
WHOA ...
IT... IT'S...
WHY DOES THE MOON LOOK SO RIDICU-LOUS?!!

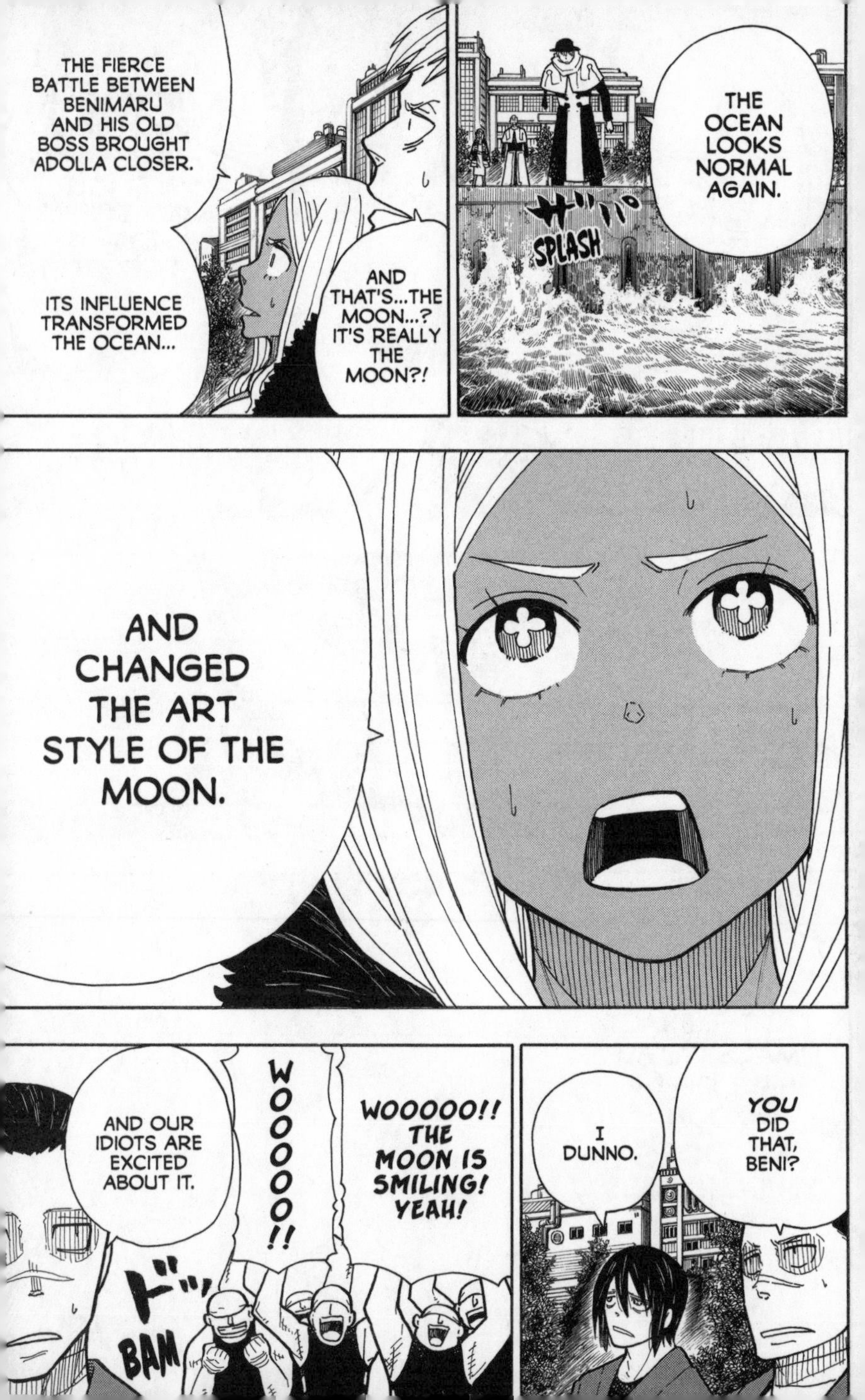

THE OCEAN LOOKS NORMAL AGAIN.
SPLASH
THE FIERCE BATTLE BETWEEN BENIMARU AND HIS OLD BOSS BROUGHT ADOLLA CLOSER.
AND THAT'S...THE MOON...? IT'S REALLY THE MOON?!
ITS INFLUENCE TRANSFORMED THE OCEAN...
AND CHANGED THE ART STYLE OF THE MOON.
YOU DID THAT, BENI?
I DUNNO.
WOOOOO!! THE MOON IS SMILING! YEAH!
WOOOOOO!!
AND OUR IDIOTS ARE EXCITED ABOUT IT.
BAM

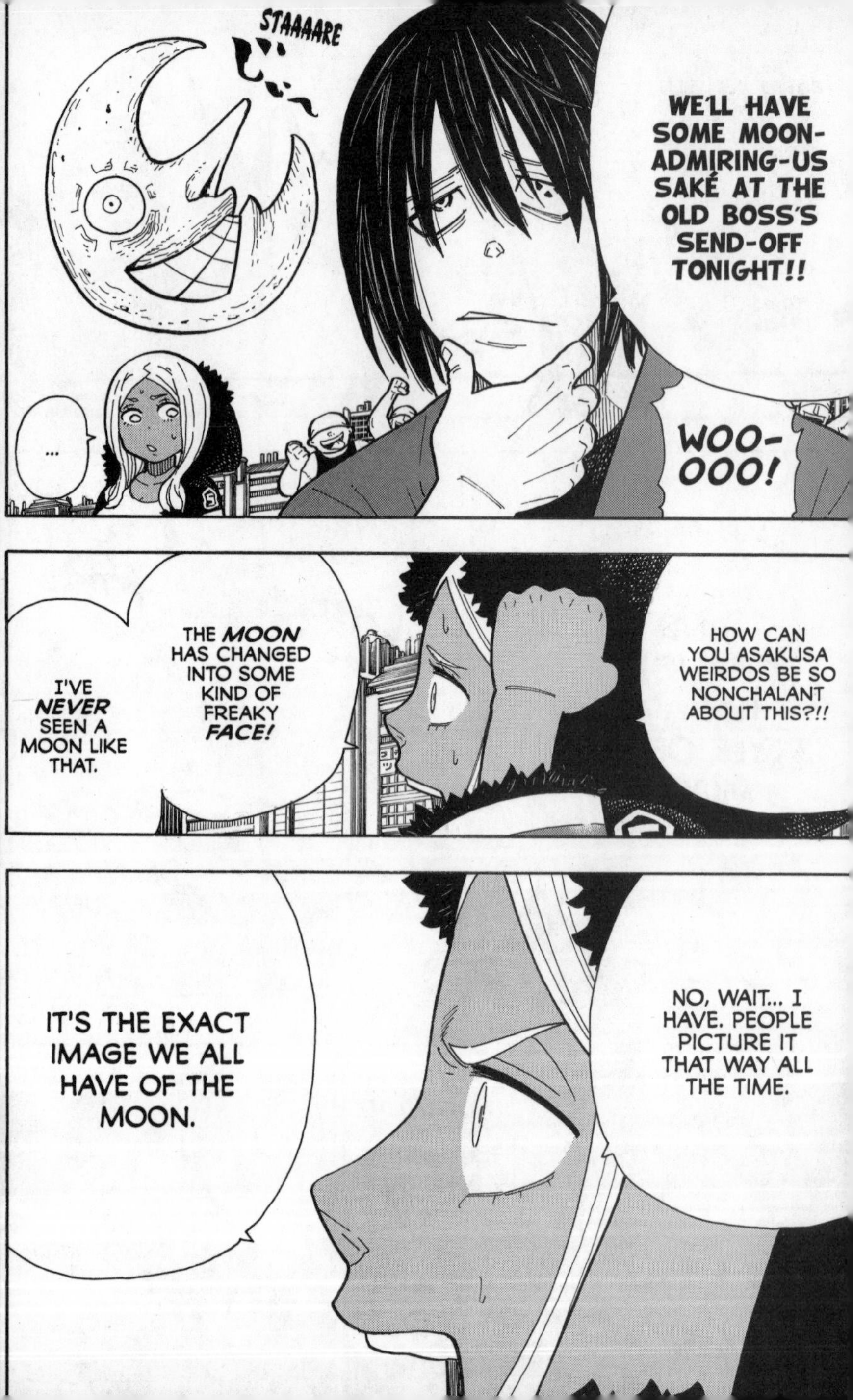
WE'LL HAVE SOME MOON-ADMIRING-US SAKÉ AT THE OLD BOSS'S SEND-OFF TONIGHT!!
STAAAARE
WOO-OOO!
...
HOW CAN YOU ASAKUSA WEIRDOS BE SO NONCHALANT ABOUT THIS?!!
THE MOON HAS CHANGED INTO SOME KIND OF FREAKY FACE!
I'VE NEVER SEEN A MOON LIKE THAT.
NO, WAIT... I HAVE. PEOPLE PICTURE IT THAT WAY ALL THE TIME.
IT'S THE EXACT IMAGE WE ALL HAVE OF THE MOON.

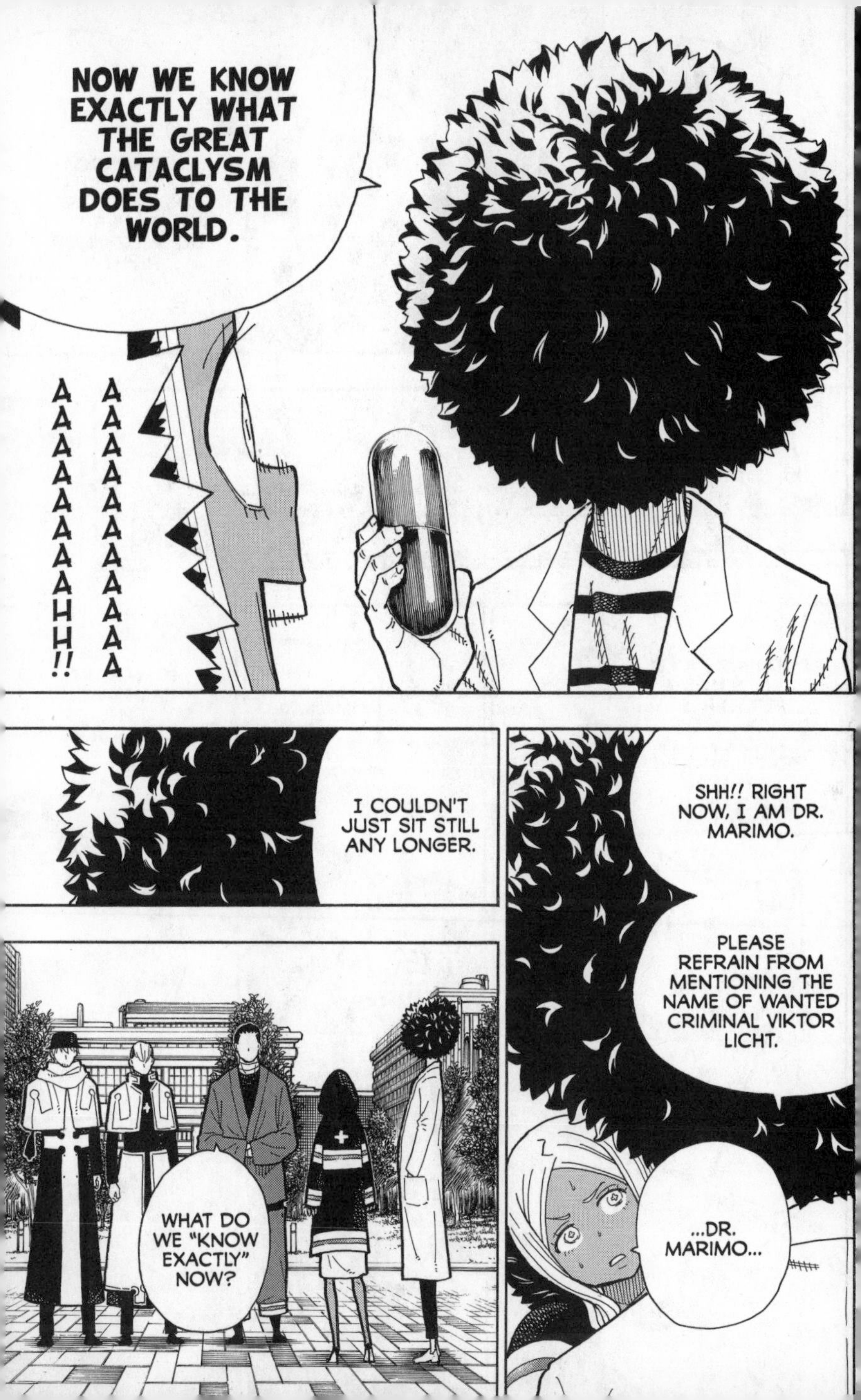
NOW WE KNOW EXACTLY WHAT THE GREAT CATACLYSM DOES TO THE WORLD.
AAAAAAAAAAA
AAAAAAAAHH!!
SHH!! RIGHT NOW, I AM DR. MARIMO.
PLEASE REFRAIN FROM MENTIONING THE NAME OF WANTED CRIMINAL VIKTOR LICHT.
...DR. MARIMO...
I COULDN'T JUST SIT STILL ANY LONGER.
WHAT DO WE "KNOW EXACTLY" NOW?

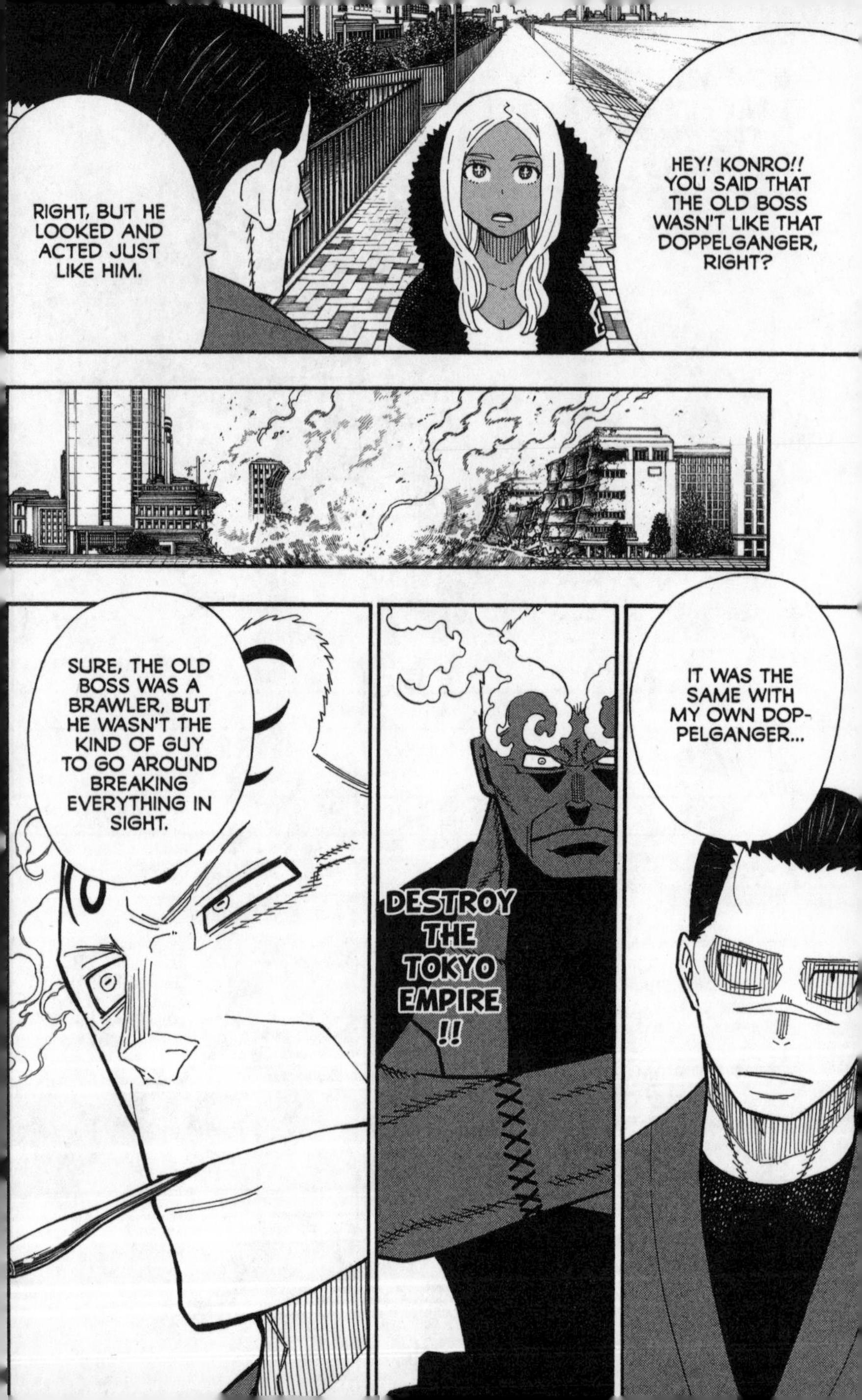
HEY! KONRO!! YOU SAID THAT THE OLD BOSS WASN'T LIKE THAT DOPPELGANGER, RIGHT?
RIGHT, BUT HE LOOKED AND ACTED JUST LIKE HIM.
IT WAS THE SAME WITH MY OWN DOP-PELGANGER...
DESTROY THE TOKYO EMPIRE !!
SURE, THE OLD BOSS WAS A BRAWLER, BUT HE WASN'T THE KIND OF GUY TO GO AROUND BREAKING EVERYTHING IN SIGHT.

THE GREAT CATACLYSM IS THE ASSIMILATION OF OUR WORLD WITH PEOPLE'S IMAGE OF IT... BUT THE WHITE CLAD CULT'S GOAL IS TO RETURN THIS WORLD TO FLAME.

THAT'S WHAT REKKA WAS SAYING, TOO.

OKAY, SO LET'S SAY THE GREAT CATACLYSM IS SUPPOSED TO *ALIGN THE ADOLLA FROM OUR IMAGININGS WITH REALITY.*

BUT IF THAT'S TRUE, THAT'S NOT WHAT THE WHITE CLAD GOONS ARE GOING FOR.

ADOLLA IS AN AMALGAMATION OF HUMAN IMAGININGS.

IF THE WHITE CLAD CULT WANTS TO GET US TO THE FINAL DESTINATION OF THOSE IMAGININGS, THAT WOULD TAKE US TO...

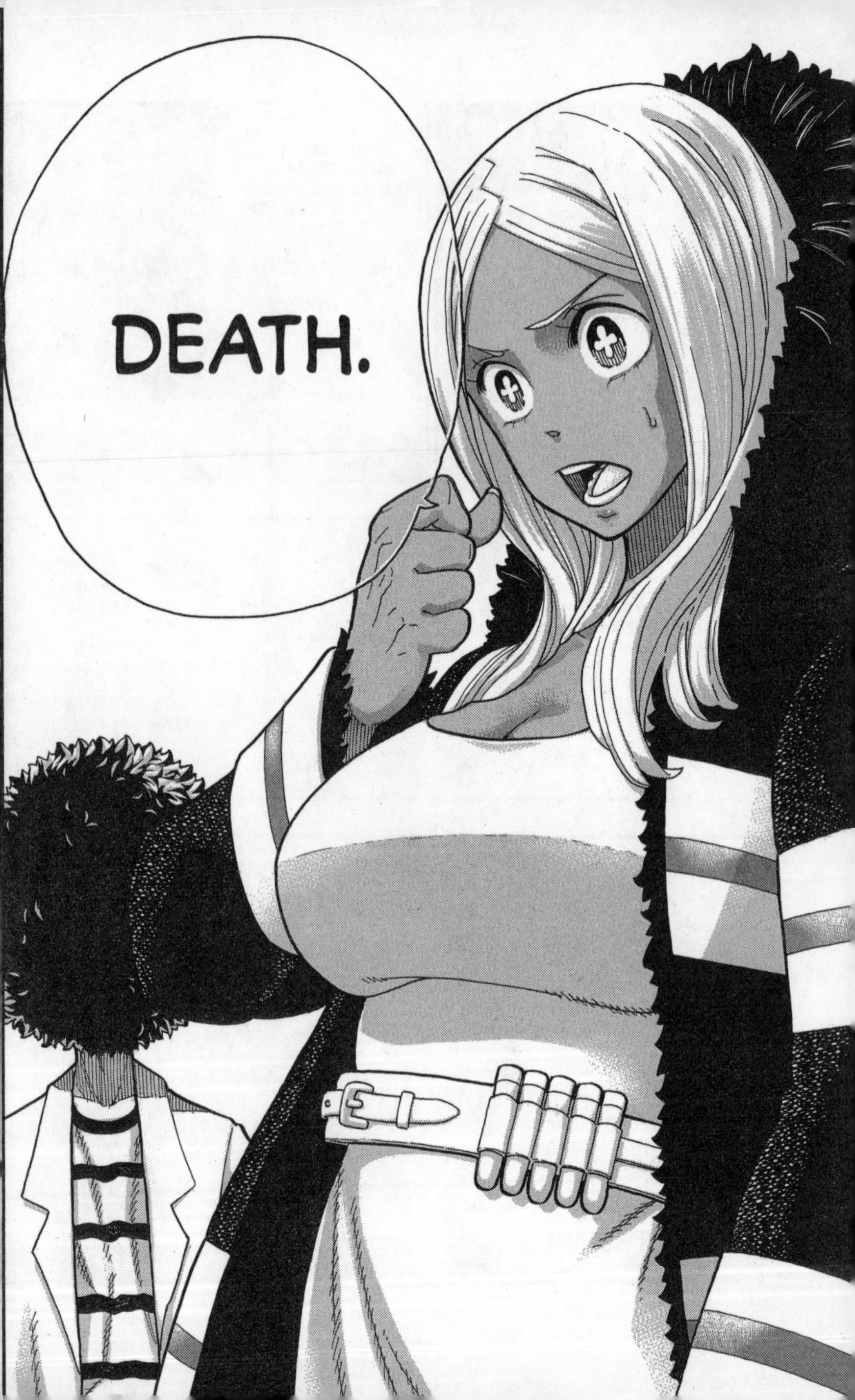
DEATH.

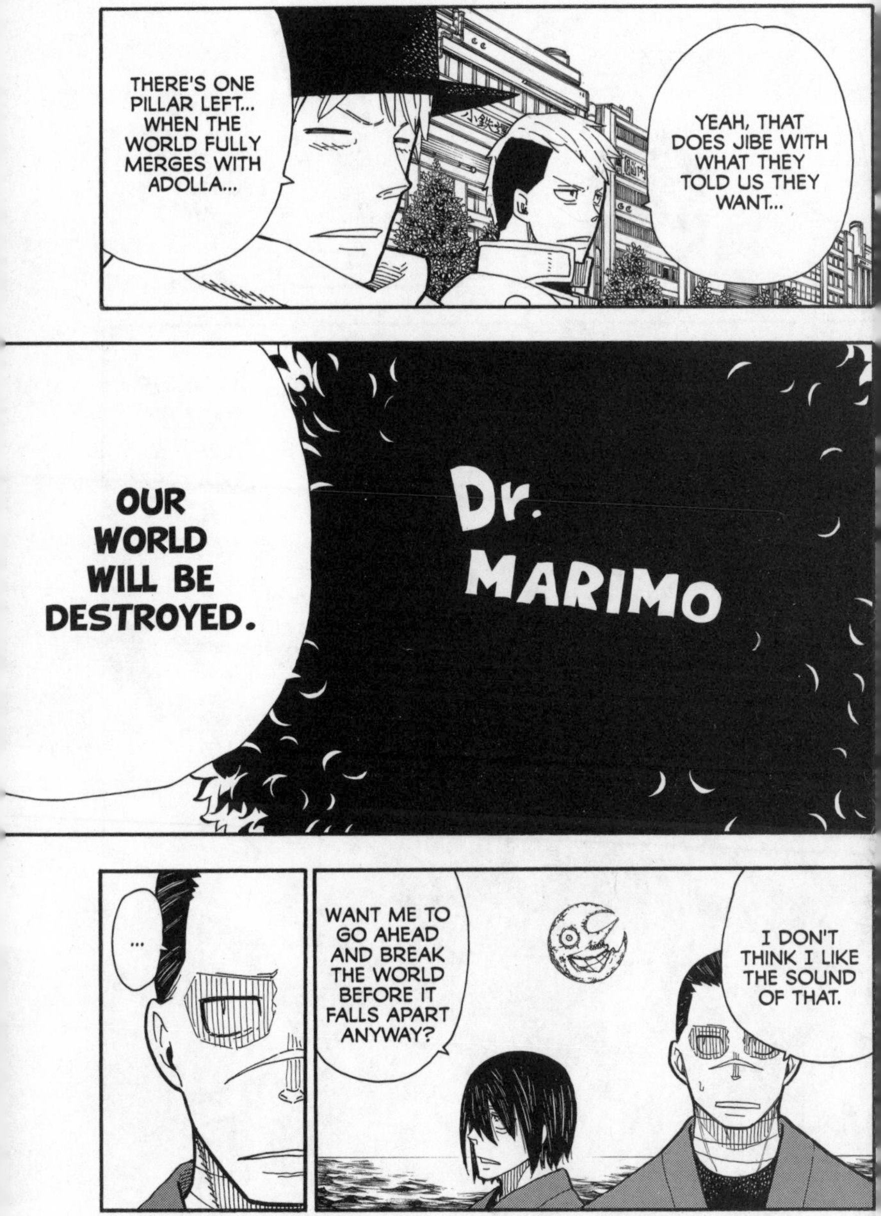
YEAH, THAT DOES JIBE WITH WHAT THEY TOLD US THEY WANT...
THERE'S ONE PILLAR LEFT... WHEN THE WORLD FULLY MERGES WITH ADOLLA...
Dr. MARIMO
OUR WORLD WILL BE DESTROYED.
I DON'T THINK I LIKE THE SOUND OF THAT.
WANT ME TO GO AHEAD AND BREAK THE WORLD BEFORE IT FALLS APART ANYWAY?
...

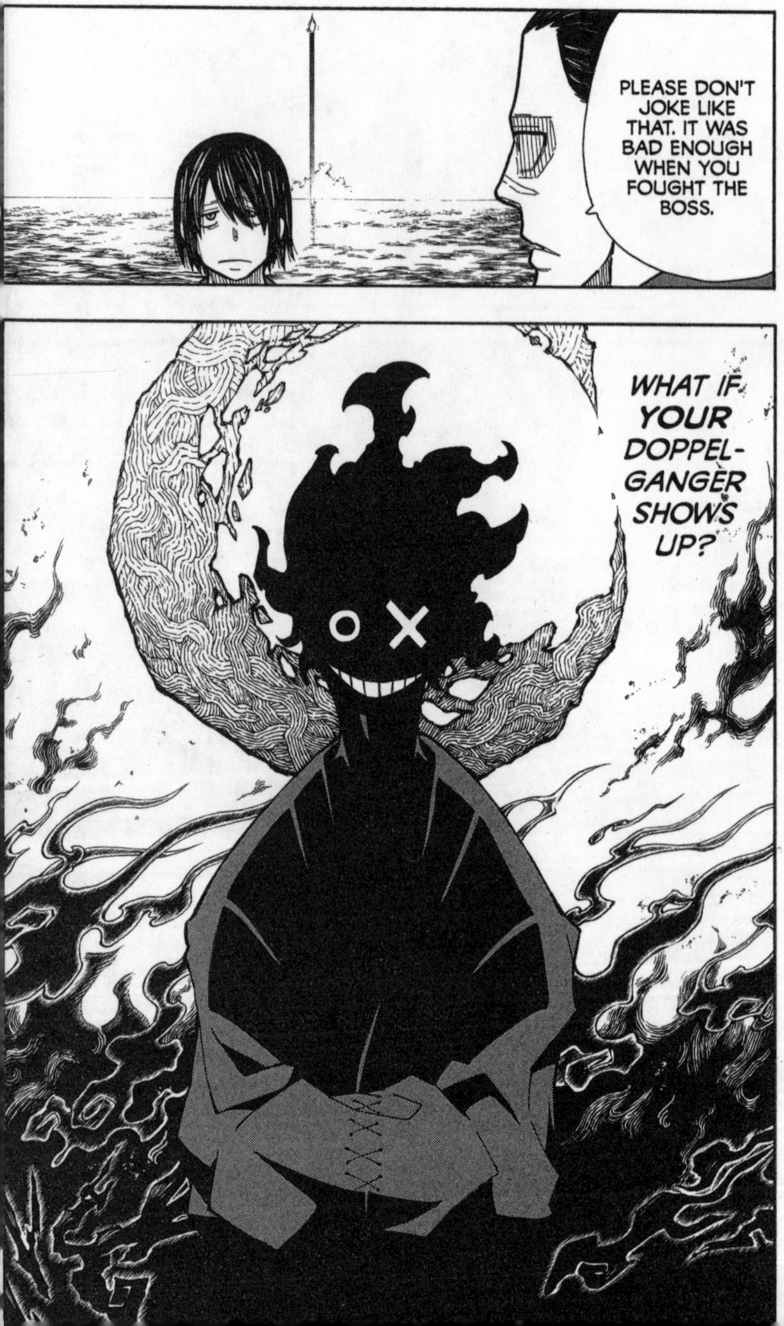
PLEASE DON'T JOKE LIKE THAT. IT WAS BAD ENOUGH WHEN YOU FOUGHT THE BOSS.
WHAT IF YOUR DOPPEL-GANGER SHOWS UP?

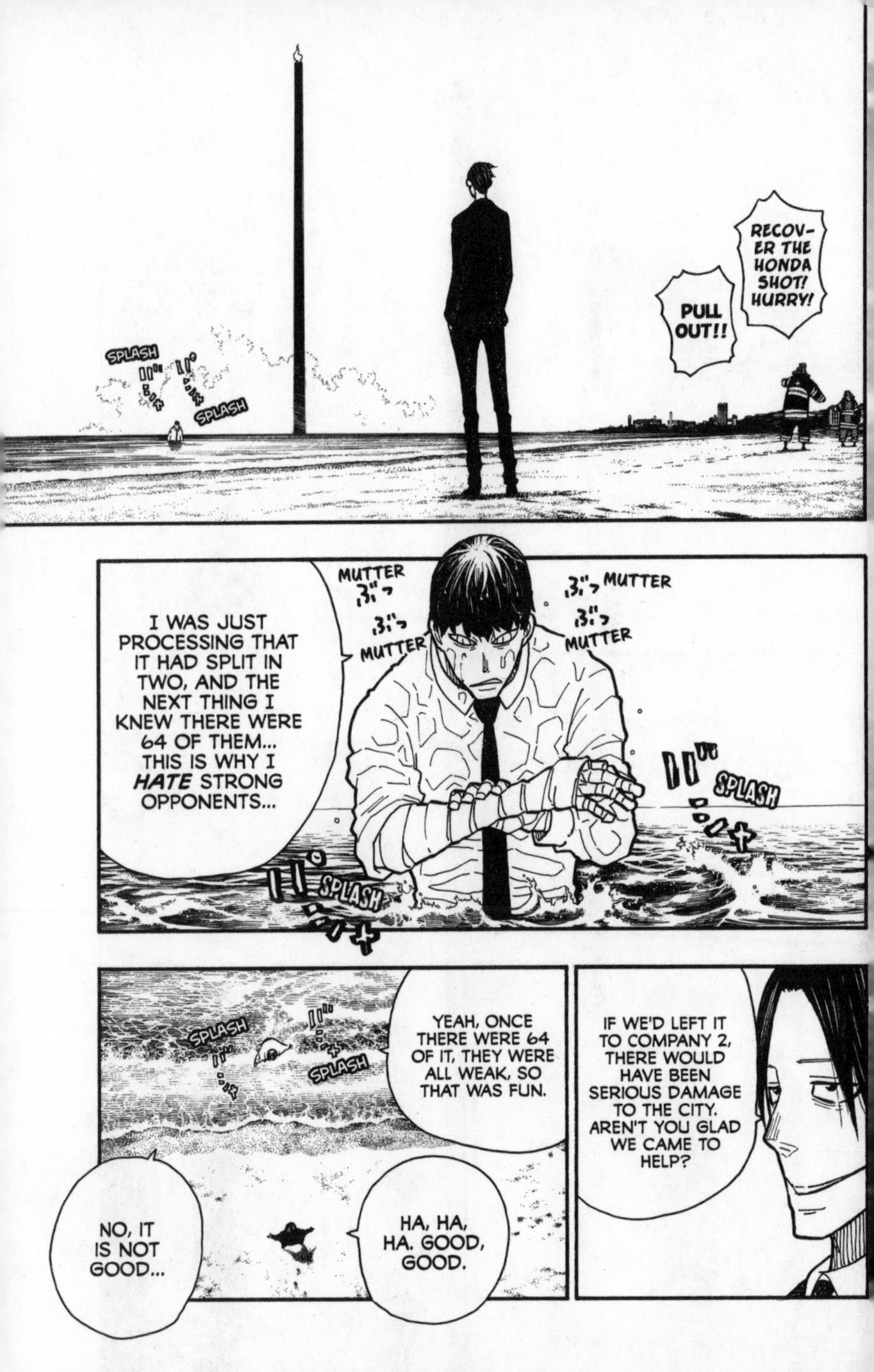
RECOV-ER THE HONDA SHOT! HURRY!
PULL OUT!!
SPLASH
SPLASH
MUTTER
MUTTER
MUTTER
MUTTER
I WAS JUST PROCESSING THAT IT HAD SPLIT IN TWO, AND THE NEXT THING I KNEW THERE WERE 64 OF THEM... THIS IS WHY I *HATE* STRONG OPPONENTS...
SPLASH
SPLASH
IF WE'D LEFT IT TO COMPANY 2, THERE WOULD HAVE BEEN SERIOUS DAMAGE TO THE CITY. AREN'T YOU GLAD WE CAME TO HELP?
SPLASH
SPLASH
YEAH, ONCE THERE WERE 64 OF IT, THEY WERE ALL WEAK, SO THAT WAS FUN.
HA, HA, HA. GOOD, GOOD.
NO, IT IS NOT GOOD...

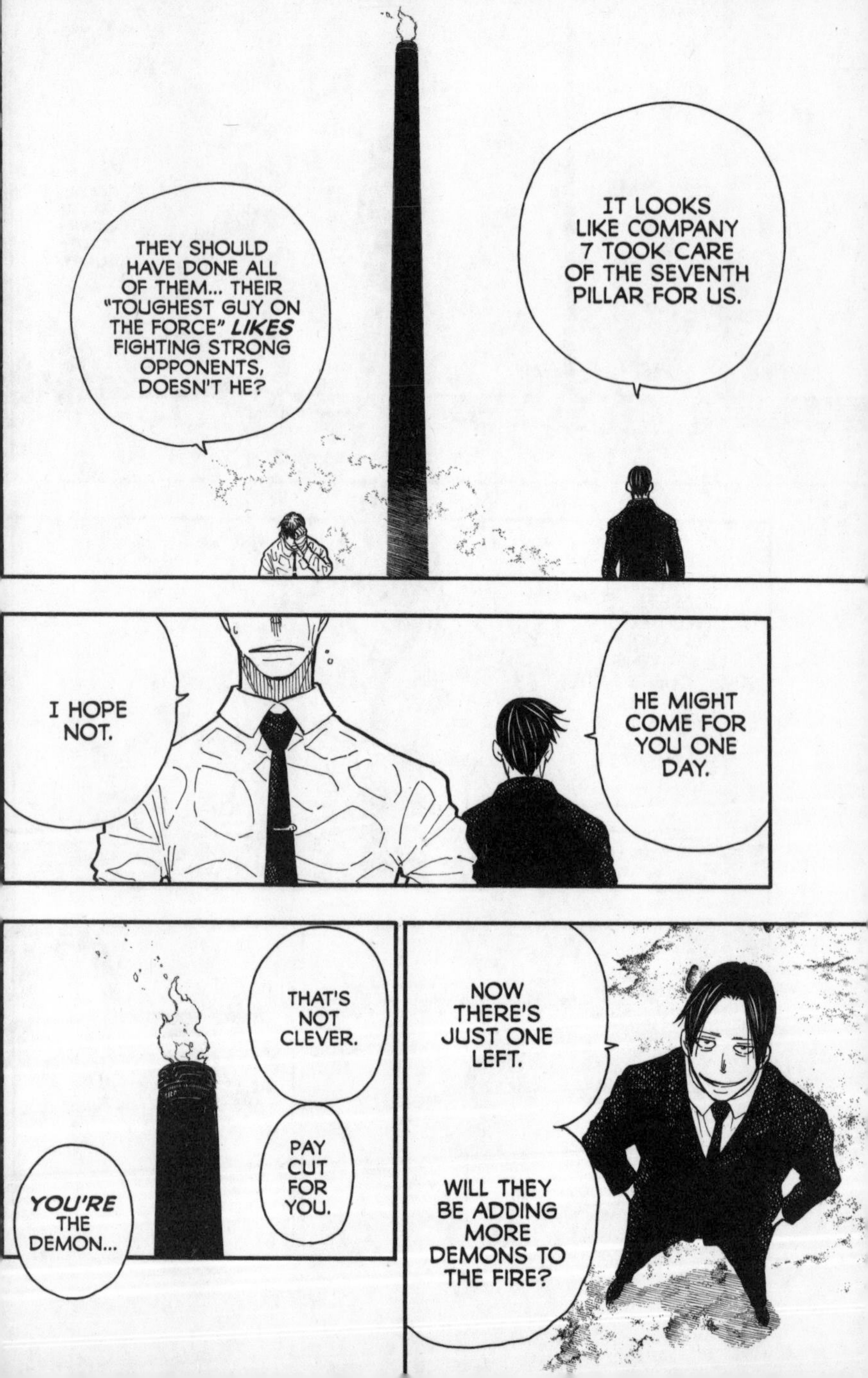
IT LOOKS LIKE COMPANY 7 TOOK CARE OF THE SEVENTH PILLAR FOR US.
THEY SHOULD HAVE DONE ALL OF THEM... THEIR "TOUGHEST GUY ON THE FORCE" *LIKES* FIGHTING STRONG OPPONENTS, DOESN'T HE?
HE MIGHT COME FOR YOU ONE DAY.
I HOPE NOT.
NOW THERE'S JUST ONE LEFT.
WILL THEY BE ADDING MORE DEMONS TO THE FIRE?
THAT'S NOT CLEVER.
PAY CUT FOR YOU.
YOU'RE THE DEMON...

Sign: Karaoke
Sign: Pachinko 666
Sign: 666 Pachinko
Sign: Seikoku Coffee

Sign: Arisa
Sign: Like
Sign: Karaoke
Sign: Black

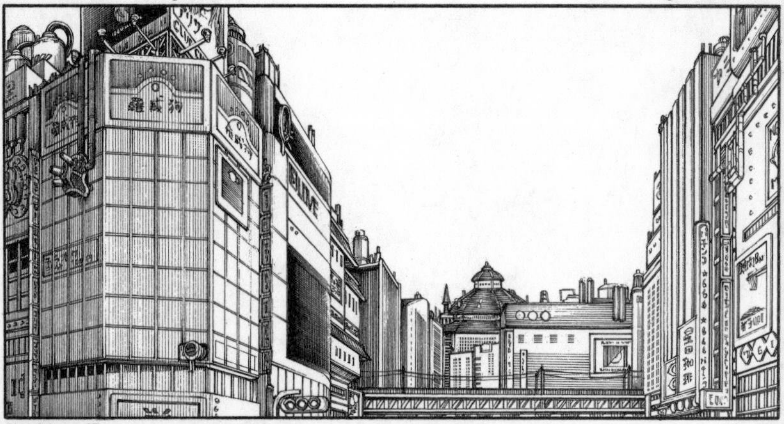

Sign: Sakuraya 2F
Sign: yaki

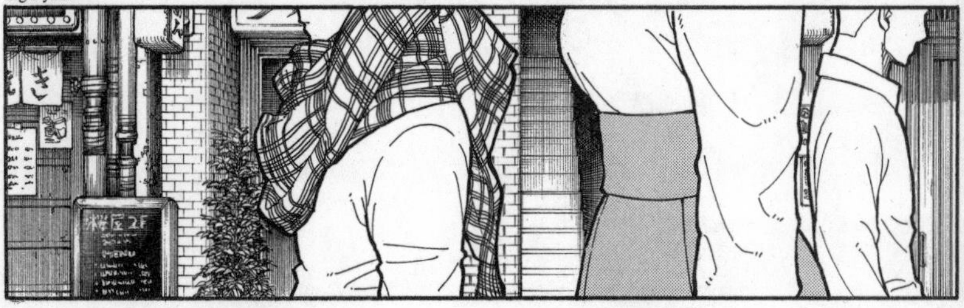

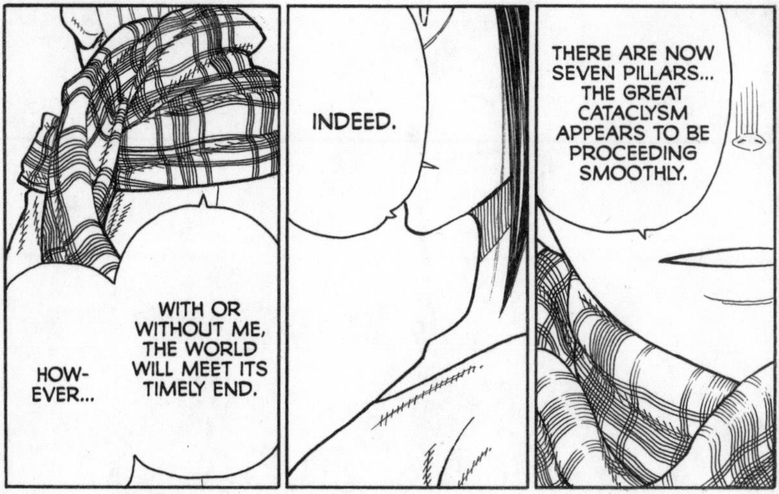
THERE ARE NOW SEVEN PILLARS... THE GREAT CATACLYSM APPEARS TO BE PROCEEDING SMOOTHLY.
INDEED.
WITH OR WITHOUT ME, THE WORLD WILL MEET ITS TIMELY END.
HOW-EVER...

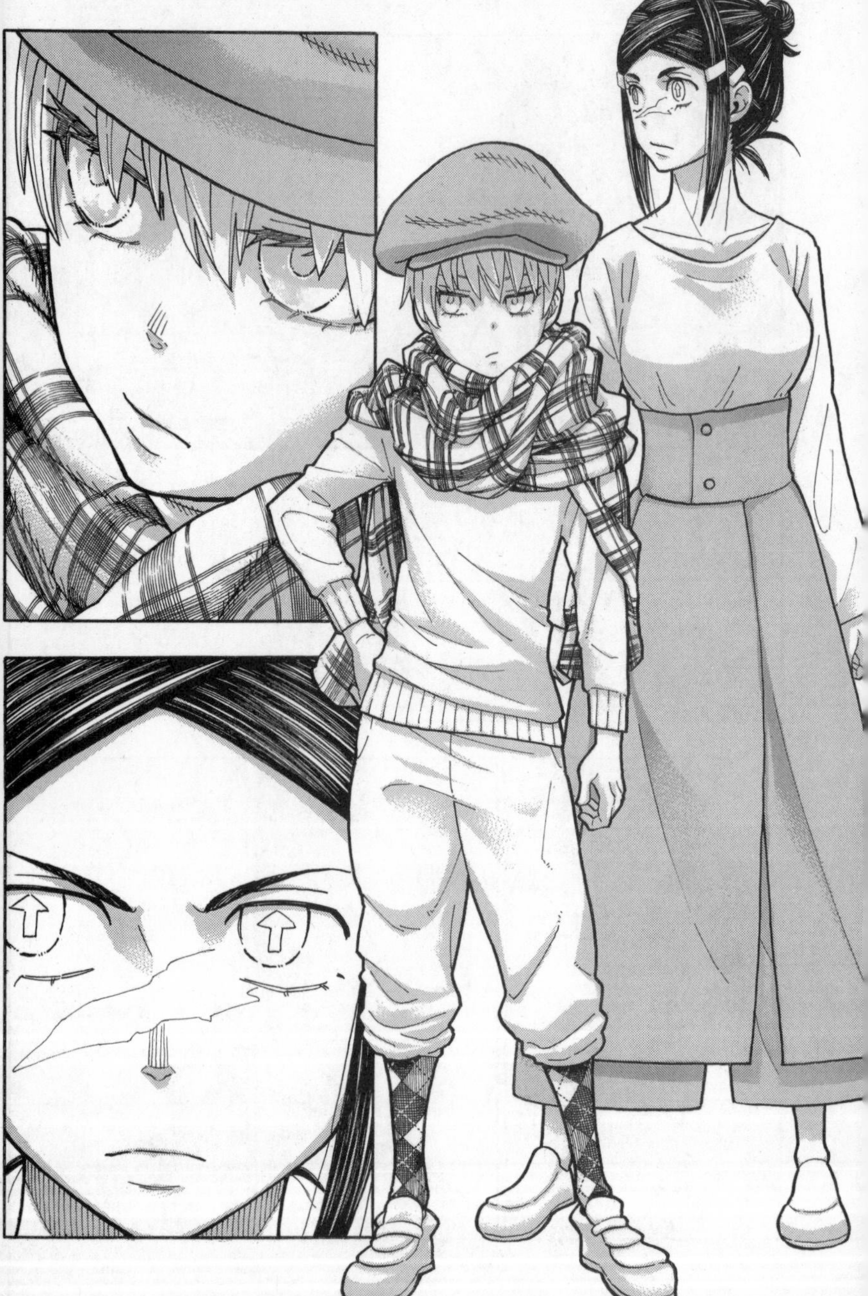

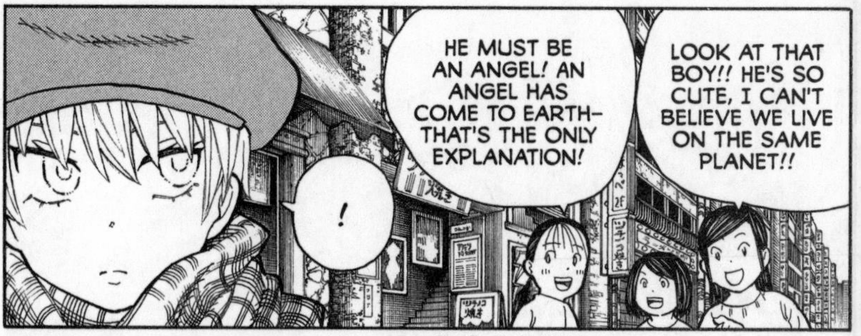
LOOK AT THAT BOY!! HE'S SO CUTE, I CAN'T BELIEVE WE LIVE ON THE SAME PLANET!!
HE MUST BE AN ANGEL! AN ANGEL HAS COME TO EARTH–THAT'S THE ONLY EXPLANATION!
!

Sign: Tsuchinokoyaki (x3)

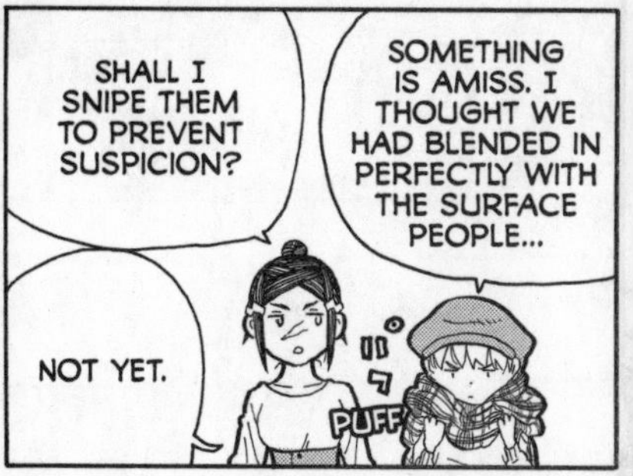
SOMETHING IS AMISS. I THOUGHT WE HAD BLENDED IN PERFECTLY WITH THE SURFACE PEOPLE...
SHALL I SNIPE THEM TO PREVENT SUSPICION?
PUFF
NOT YET.

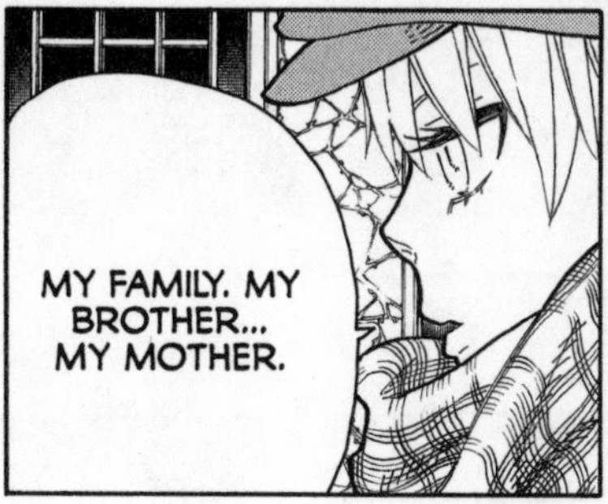
MY FAMILY. MY BROTHER... MY MOTHER.

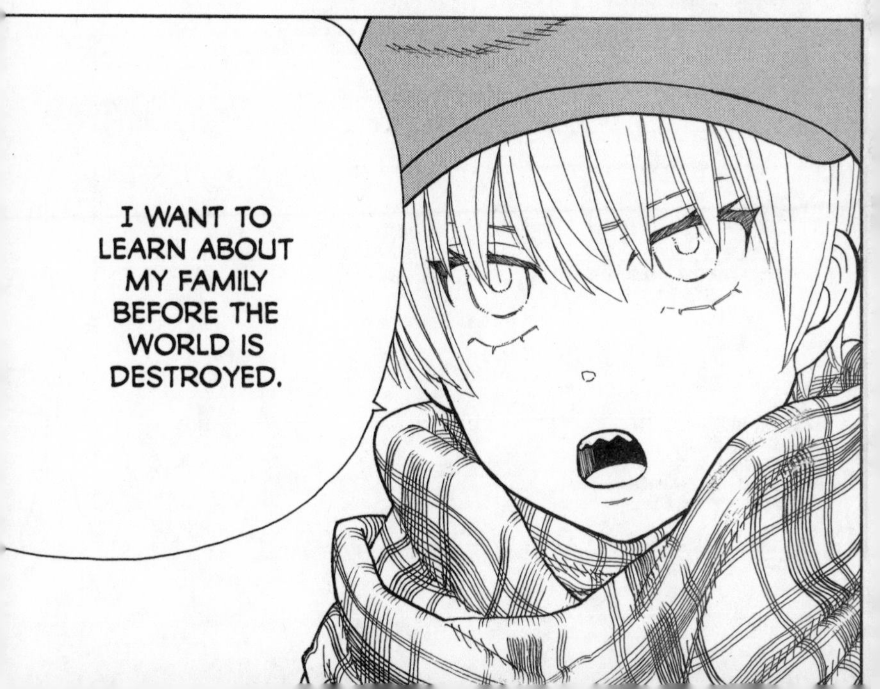
I WANT TO LEARN ABOUT MY FAMILY BEFORE THE WORLD IS DESTROYED.

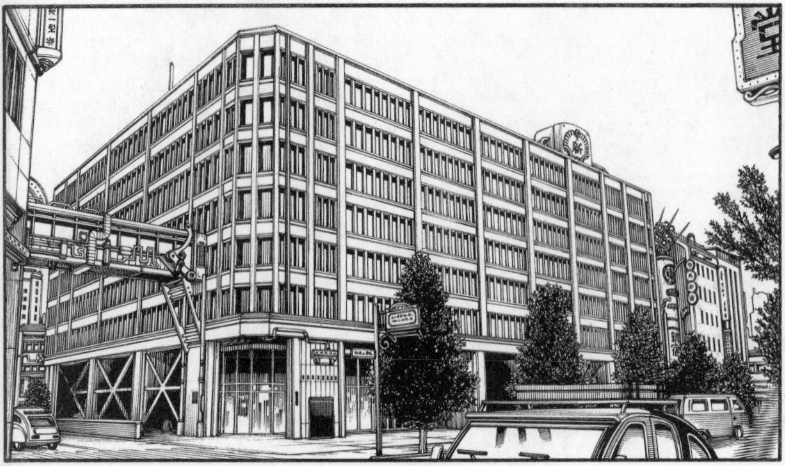

Sign: Hall

Sign: Ichikata

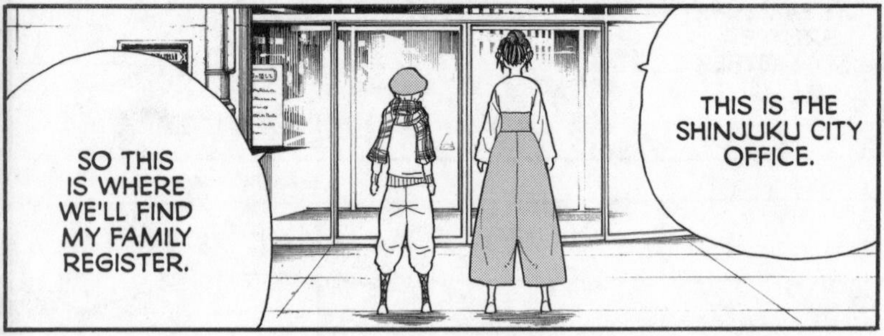
THIS IS THE SHINJUKU CITY OFFICE.
SO THIS IS WHERE WE'LL FIND MY FAMILY REGISTER.

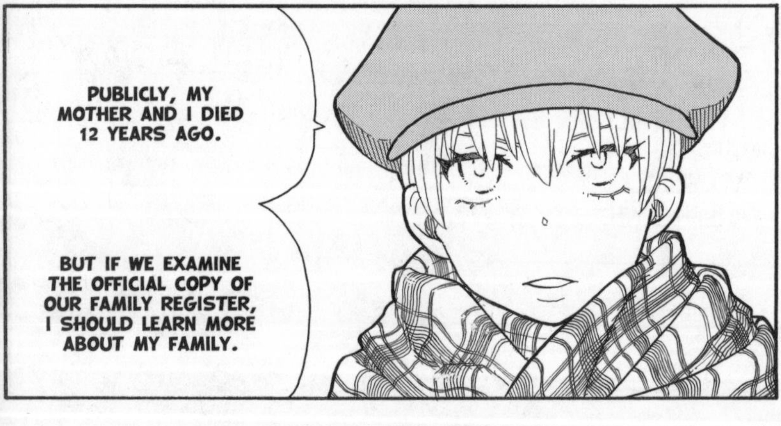
PUBLICLY, MY MOTHER AND I DIED 12 YEARS AGO.
BUT IF WE EXAMINE THE OFFICIAL COPY OF OUR FAMILY REGISTER, I SHOULD LEARN MORE ABOUT MY FAMILY.

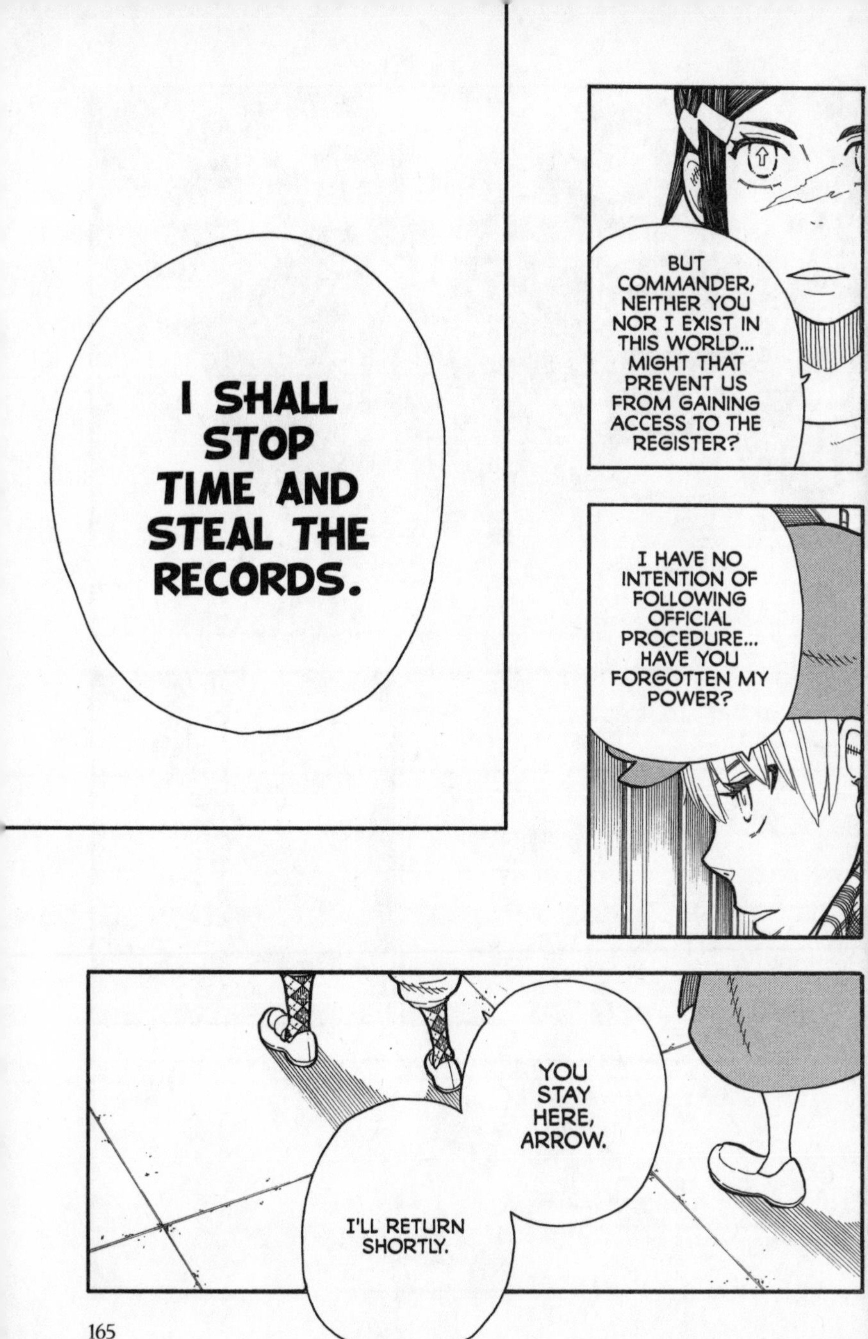
BUT COMMANDER, NEITHER YOU NOR I EXIST IN THIS WORLD... MIGHT THAT PREVENT US FROM GAINING ACCESS TO THE REGISTER?
I HAVE NO INTENTION OF FOLLOWING OFFICIAL PROCEDURE... HAVE YOU FORGOTTEN MY POWER?
I SHALL STOP TIME AND STEAL THE RECORDS.
YOU STAY HERE, ARROW.
I'LL RETURN SHORTLY.

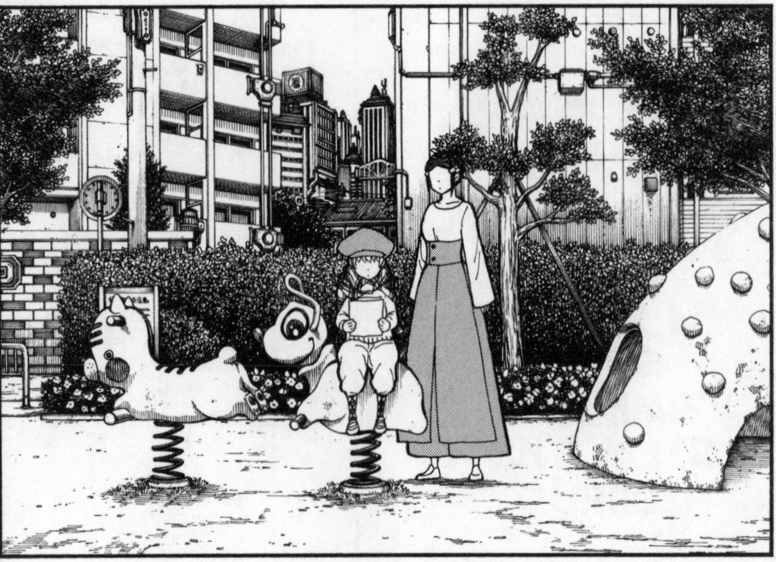

Sign: Warning

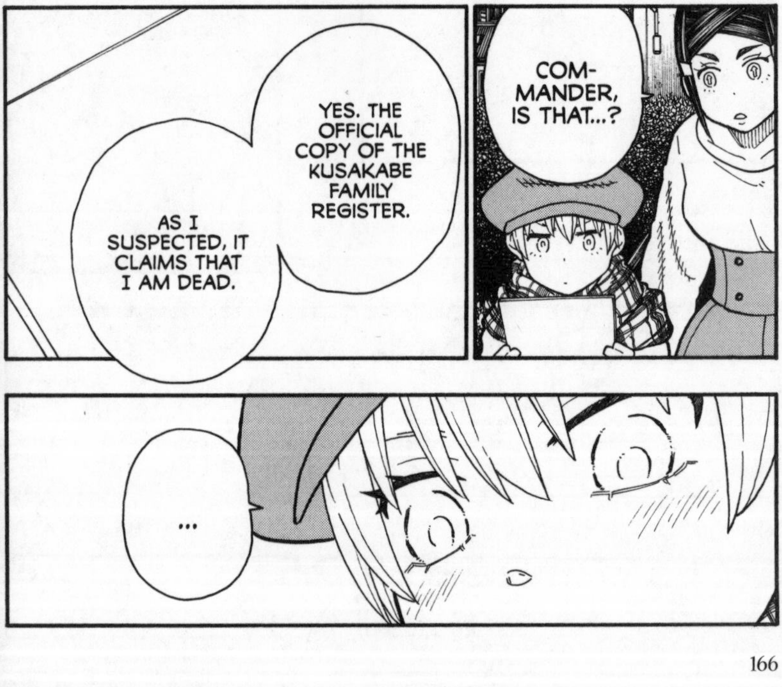
COM-MANDER, IS THAT...?
YES. THE OFFICIAL COPY OF THE KUSAKABE FAMILY REGISTER.
AS I SUSPECTED, IT CLAIMS THAT I AM DEAD.
...

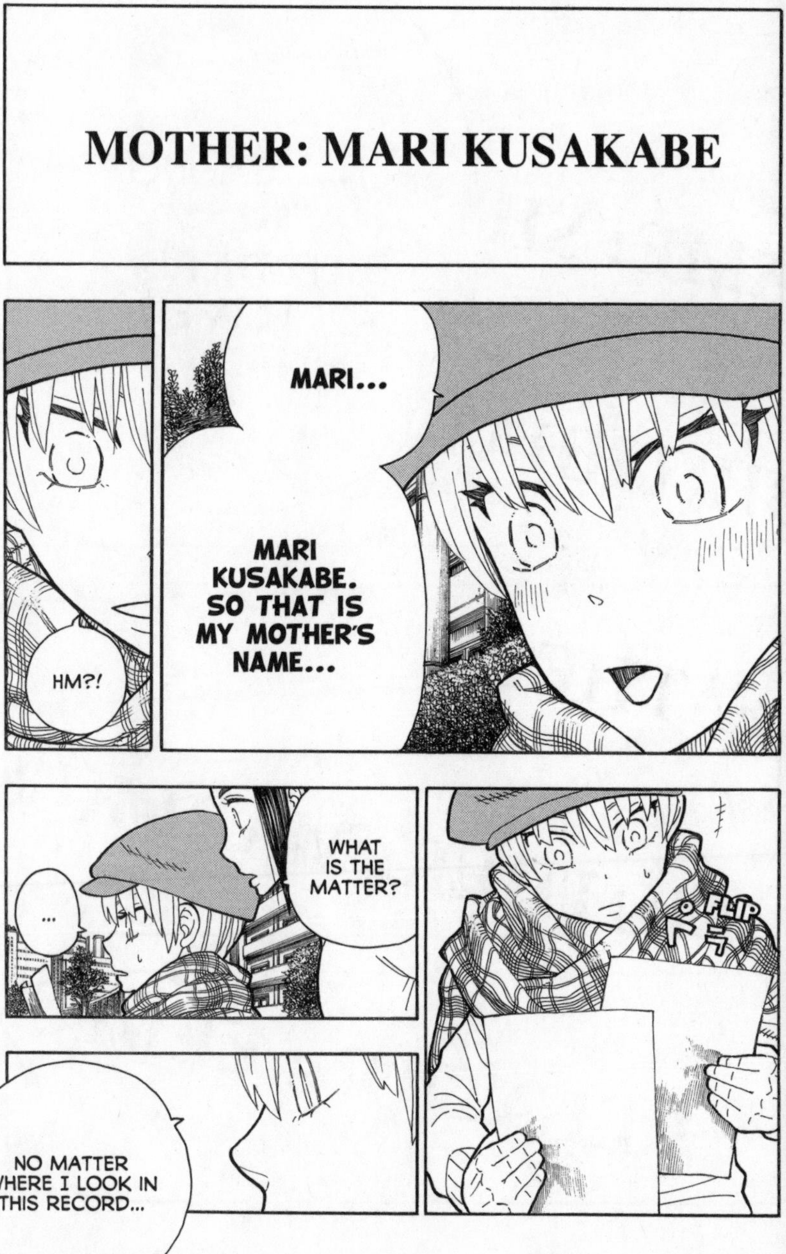
MOTHER: MARI KUSAKABE
MARI...
MARI KUSAKABE. SO THAT IS MY MOTHER'S NAME...
HM?!
FLIP
WHAT IS THE MATTER?
...
NO MATTER WHERE I LOOK IN THIS RECORD...

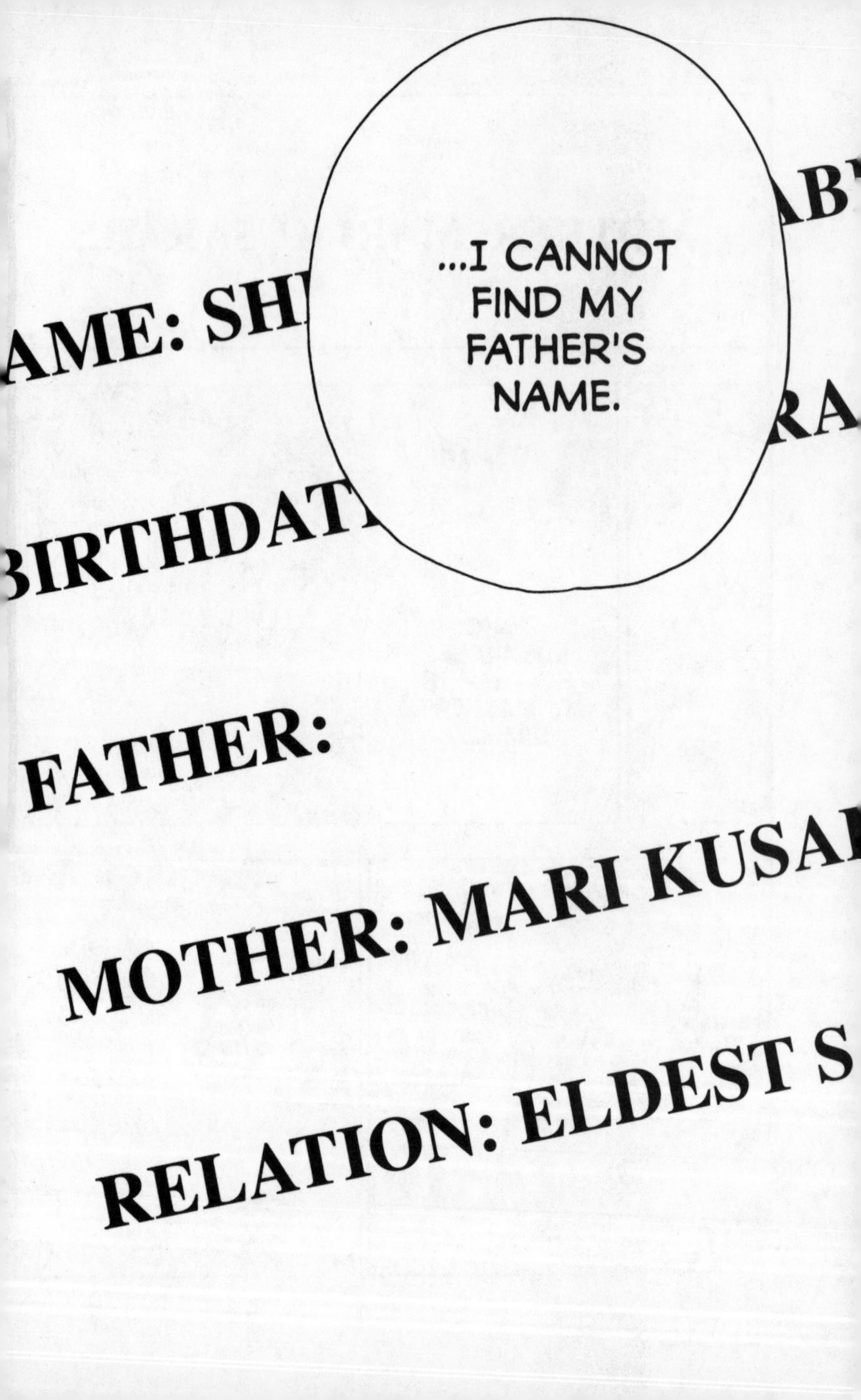
...I CANNOT FIND MY FATHER'S NAME.
AME: SH
AB
RA
BIRTHDAT
FATHER:
MOTHER: MARI KUSA
RELATION: ELDEST S

Instagram ID
ohkubo_a

CHAPTER CCXXXI: ORIGINS

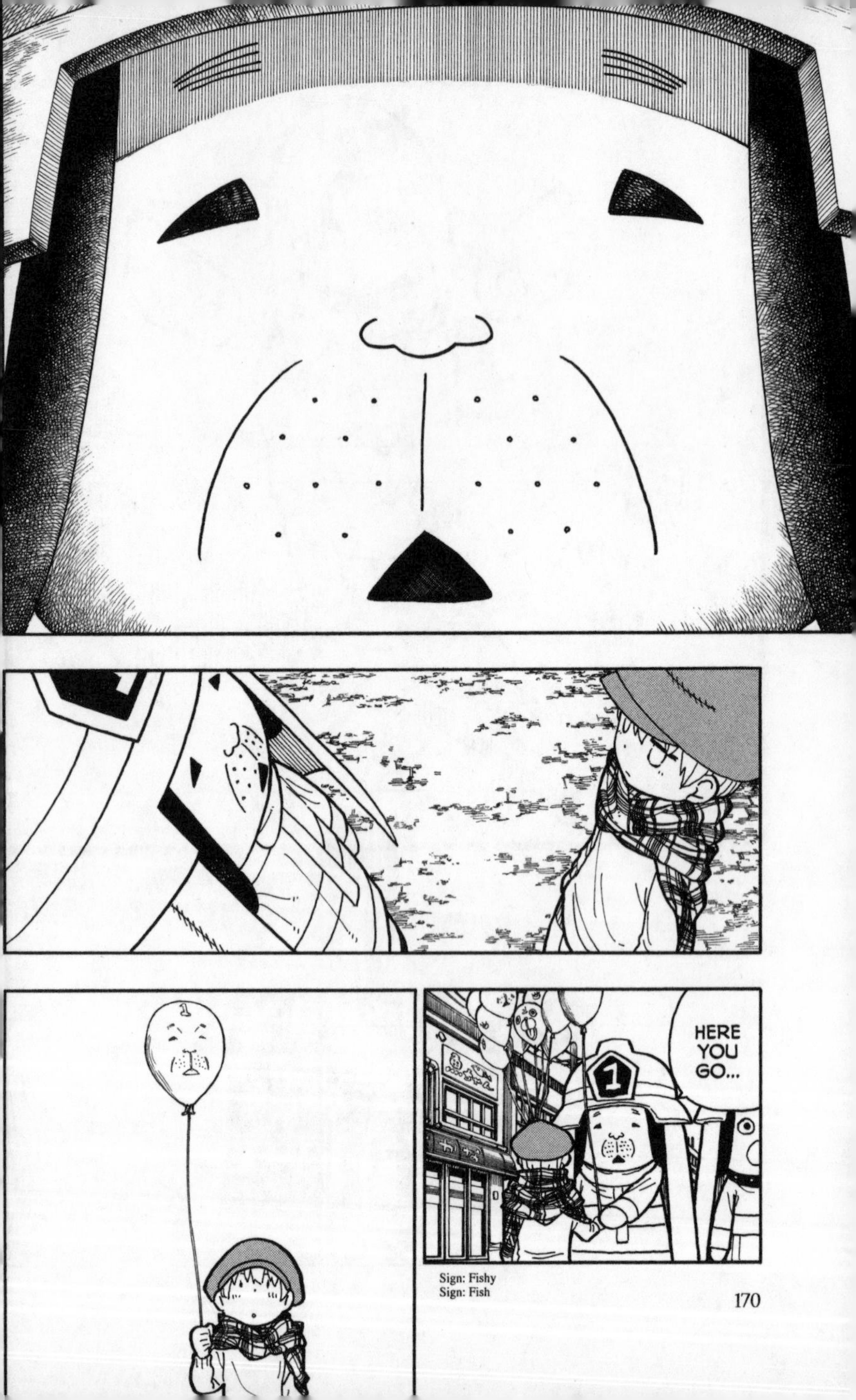
HERE YOU GO...
Sign: Fishy
Sign: Fish

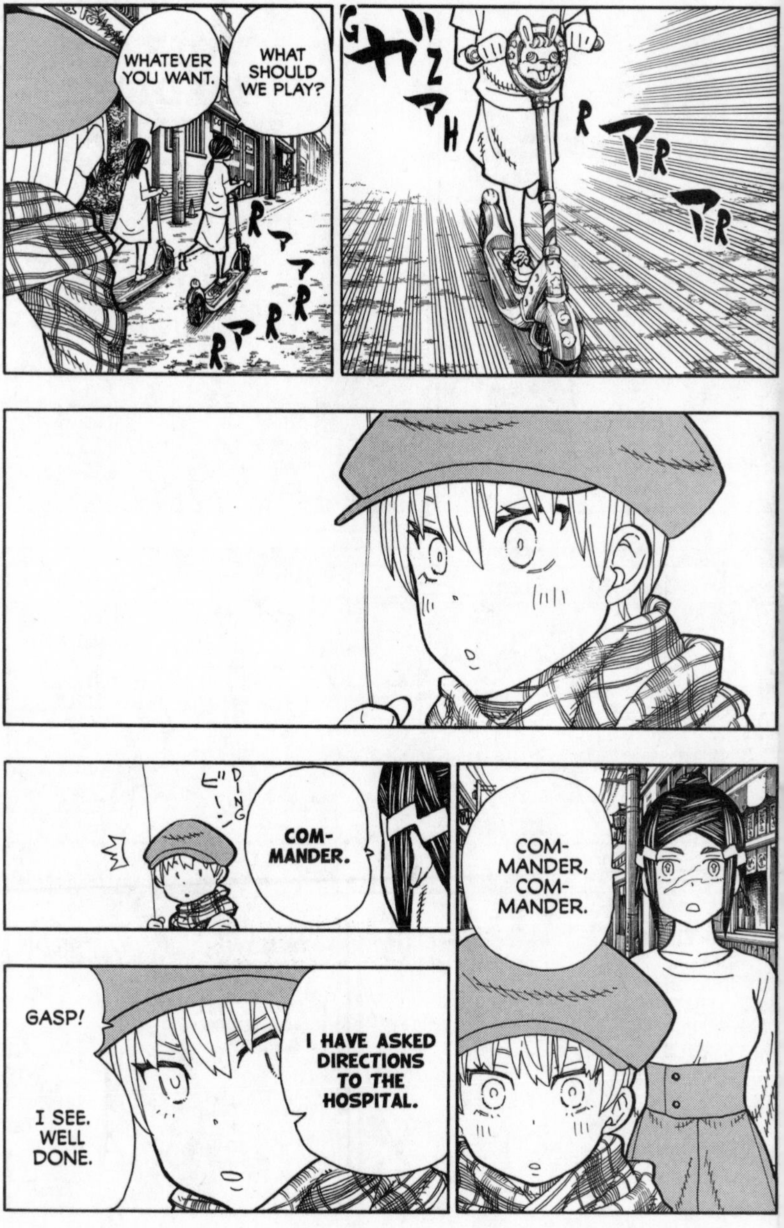
GZH
RRRR
WHAT SHOULD WE PLAY?
WHATEVER YOU WANT.
RRRRR
COMMANDER, COMMANDER.
DING
COMMANDER.
I HAVE ASKED DIRECTIONS TO THE HOSPITAL.
GASP!
I SEE. WELL DONE.

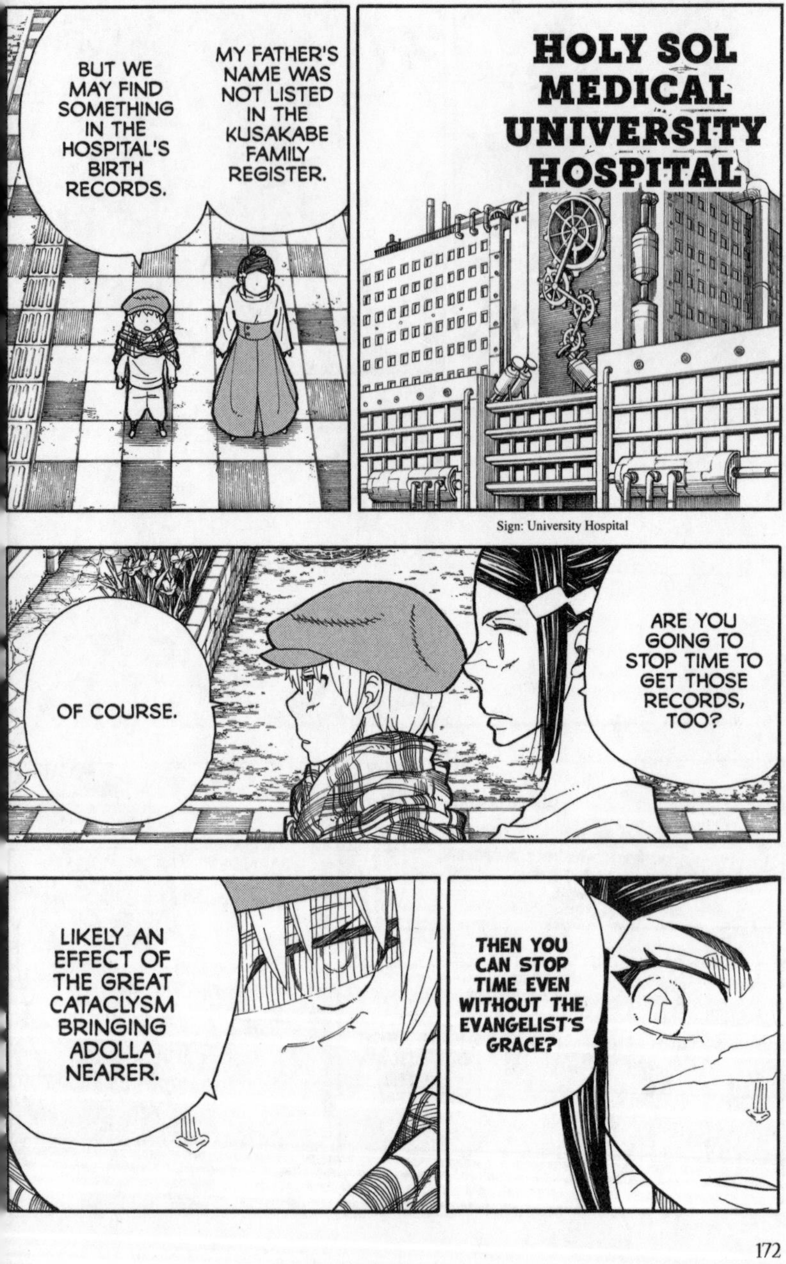
HOLY SOL MEDICAL UNIVERSITY HOSPITAL
MY FATHER'S NAME WAS NOT LISTED IN THE KUSAKABE FAMILY REGISTER.
BUT WE MAY FIND SOMETHING IN THE HOSPITAL'S BIRTH RECORDS.
ARE YOU GOING TO STOP TIME TO GET THOSE RECORDS, TOO?
OF COURSE.
THEN YOU CAN STOP TIME EVEN WITHOUT THE EVANGELIST'S GRACE?
LIKELY AN EFFECT OF THE GREAT CATACLYSM BRINGING ADOLLA NEARER.
Sign: University Hospital

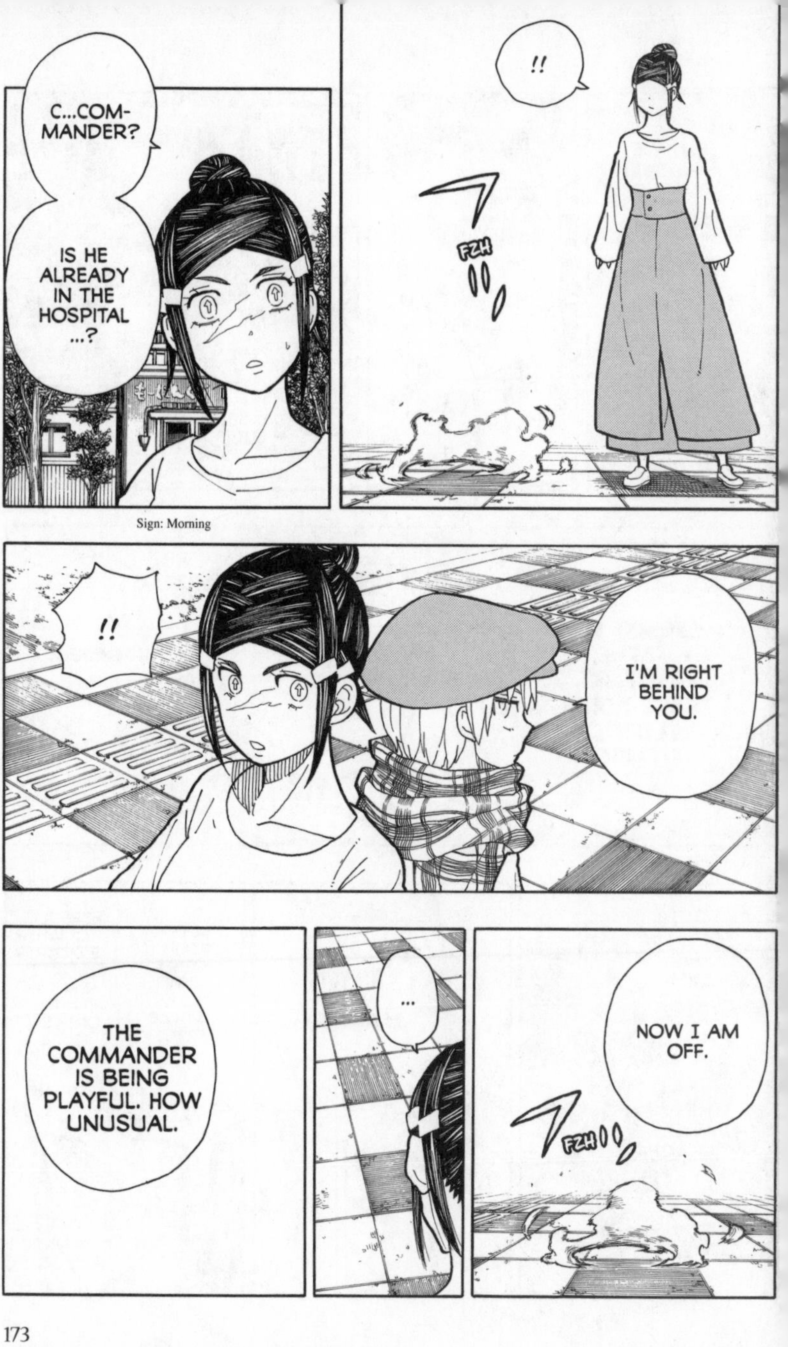
!!
FZH
C...COM-MANDER?
IS HE ALREADY IN THE HOSPITAL ...?
I'M RIGHT BEHIND YOU.
!!
NOW I AM OFF.
FZH
...
THE COMMANDER IS BEING PLAYFUL. HOW UNUSUAL.

Sign: Morning

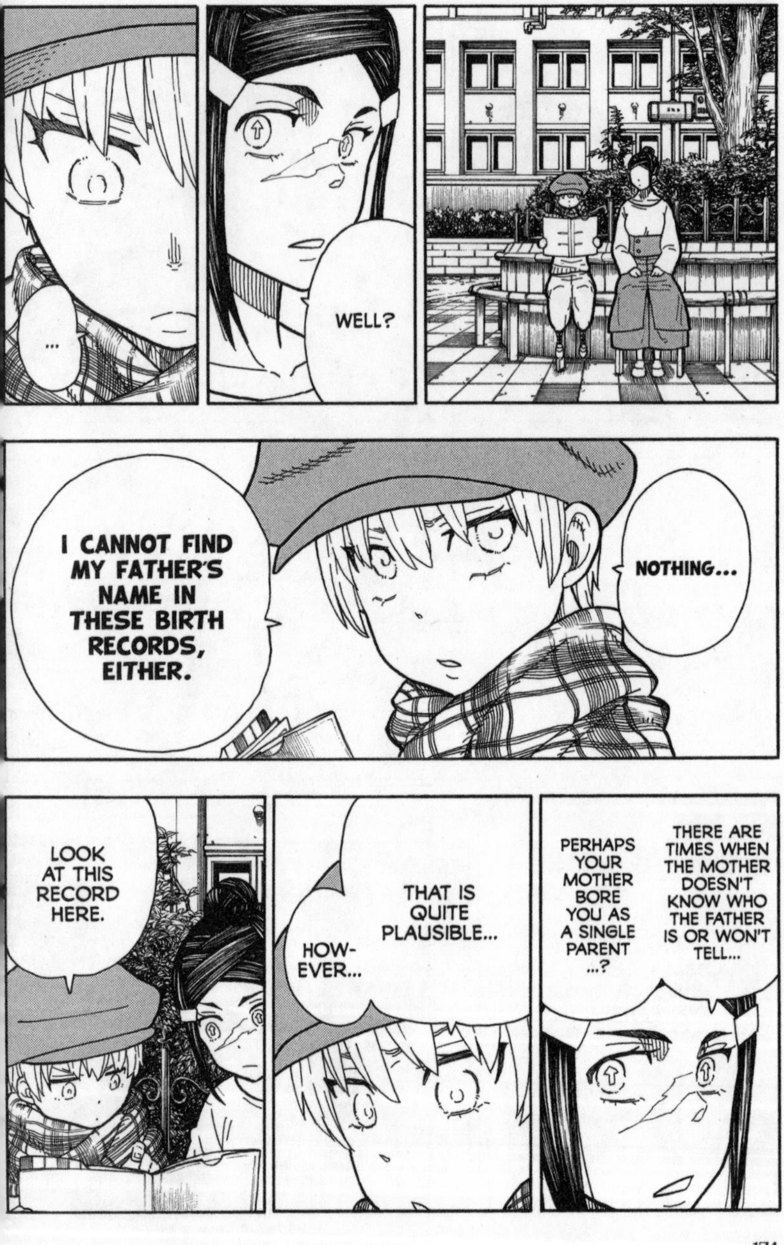
WELL?
...
NOTHING...
I CANNOT FIND MY FATHER'S NAME IN THESE BIRTH RECORDS, EITHER.
THERE ARE TIMES WHEN THE MOTHER DOESN'T KNOW WHO THE FATHER IS OR WON'T TELL...
PERHAPS YOUR MOTHER BORE YOU AS A SINGLE PARENT ...?
THAT IS QUITE PLAUSIBLE...
HOW-EVER...
LOOK AT THIS RECORD HERE.

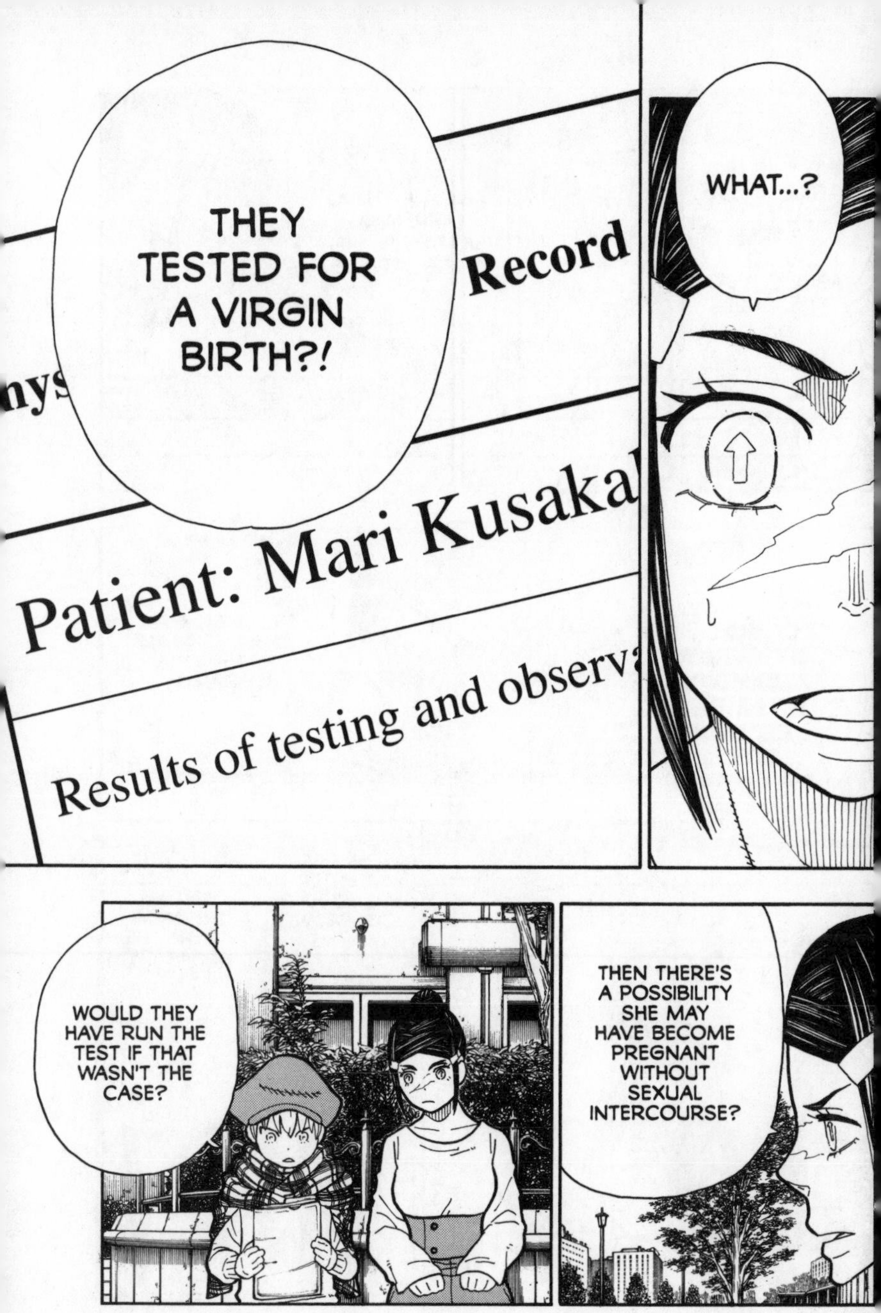
WHAT...?
Record
Patient: Mari Kusaka
Results of testing and observa
THEY TESTED FOR A VIRGIN BIRTH?!
THEN THERE'S A POSSIBILITY SHE MAY HAVE BECOME PREGNANT WITHOUT SEXUAL INTERCOURSE?
WOULD THEY HAVE RUN THE TEST IF THAT WASN'T THE CASE?

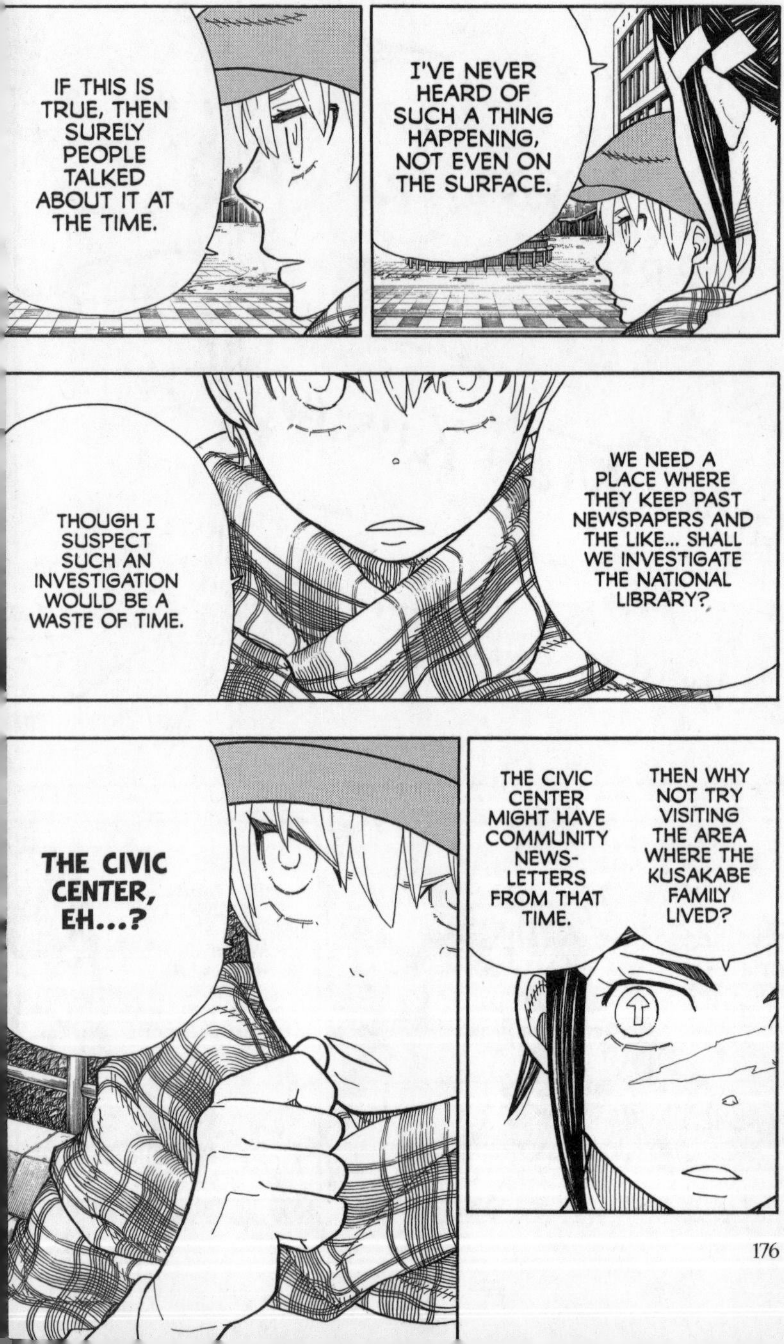
I'VE NEVER HEARD OF SUCH A THING HAPPENING, NOT EVEN ON THE SURFACE.
IF THIS IS TRUE, THEN SURELY PEOPLE TALKED ABOUT IT AT THE TIME.
WE NEED A PLACE WHERE THEY KEEP PAST NEWSPAPERS AND THE LIKE... SHALL WE INVESTIGATE THE NATIONAL LIBRARY?
THOUGH I SUSPECT SUCH AN INVESTIGATION WOULD BE A WASTE OF TIME.
THEN WHY NOT TRY VISITING THE AREA WHERE THE KUSAKABE FAMILY LIVED?
THE CIVIC CENTER MIGHT HAVE COMMUNITY NEWS-LETTERS FROM THAT TIME.
THE CIVIC CENTER, EH...?

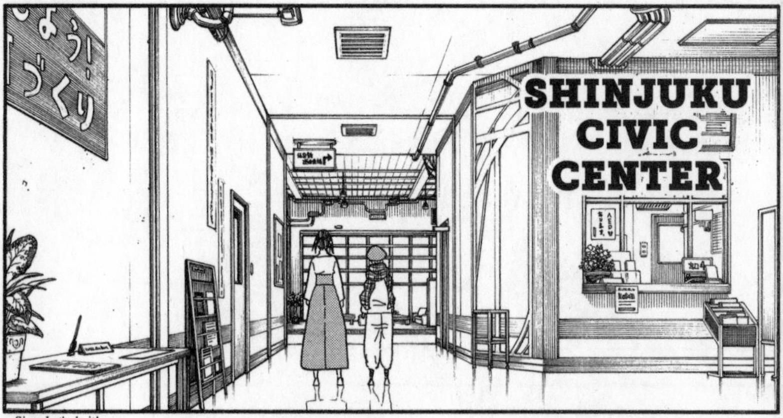
SHINJUKU CIVIC CENTER

Sign: Let's do it! Crafts

Sign: AED Available

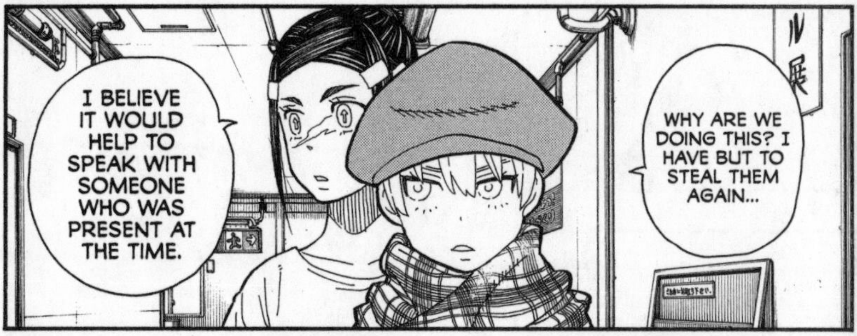
WHY ARE WE DOING THIS? I HAVE BUT TO STEAL THEM AGAIN...
I BELIEVE IT WOULD HELP TO SPEAK WITH SOMEONE WHO WAS PRESENT AT THE TIME.

Sign: Please Take One

Sign: Exhibit

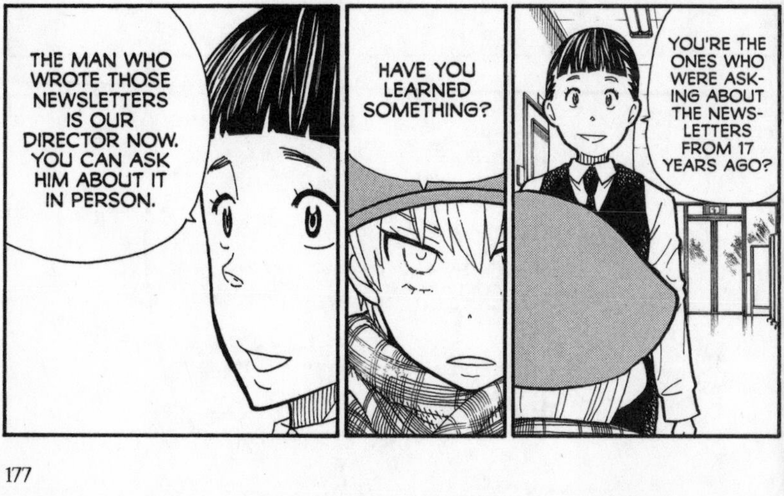
YOU'RE THE ONES WHO WERE ASK-ING ABOUT THE NEWS-LETTERS FROM 17 YEARS AGO?
HAVE YOU LEARNED SOMETHING?
THE MAN WHO WROTE THOSE NEWSLETTERS IS OUR DIRECTOR NOW. YOU CAN ASK HIM ABOUT IT IN PERSON.

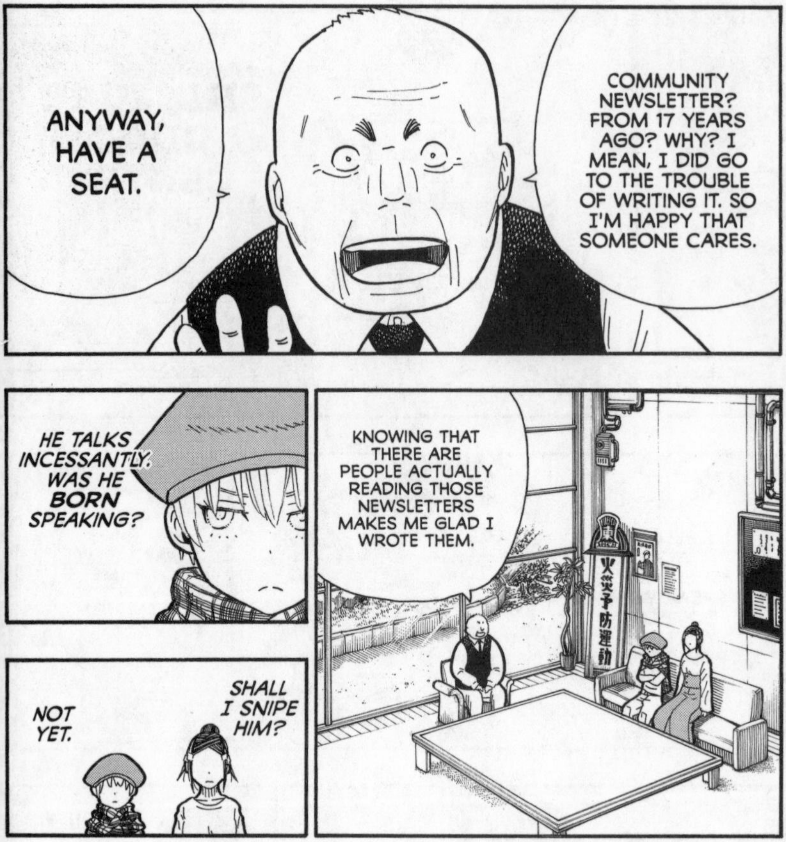
COMMUNITY NEWSLETTER? FROM 17 YEARS AGO? WHY? I MEAN, I DID GO TO THE TROUBLE OF WRITING IT. SO I'M HAPPY THAT SOMEONE CARES.
ANYWAY, HAVE A SEAT.
KNOWING THAT THERE ARE PEOPLE ACTUALLY READING THOSE NEWSLETTERS MAKES ME GLAD I WROTE THEM.
火災予防運動
HE TALKS INCESSANTLY. WAS HE BORN SPEAKING?
SHALL I SNIPE HIM?
NOT YET.
Sign: Tokyo Fire Prevention Exercises

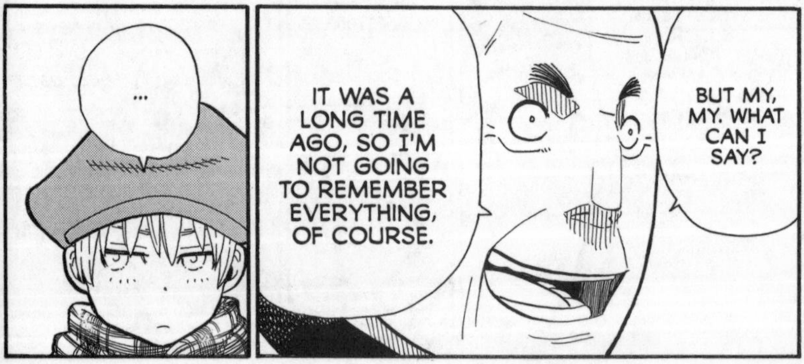
BUT MY, MY. WHAT CAN I SAY?
IT WAS A LONG TIME AGO, SO I'M NOT GOING TO REMEMBER EVERYTHING, OF COURSE.
...

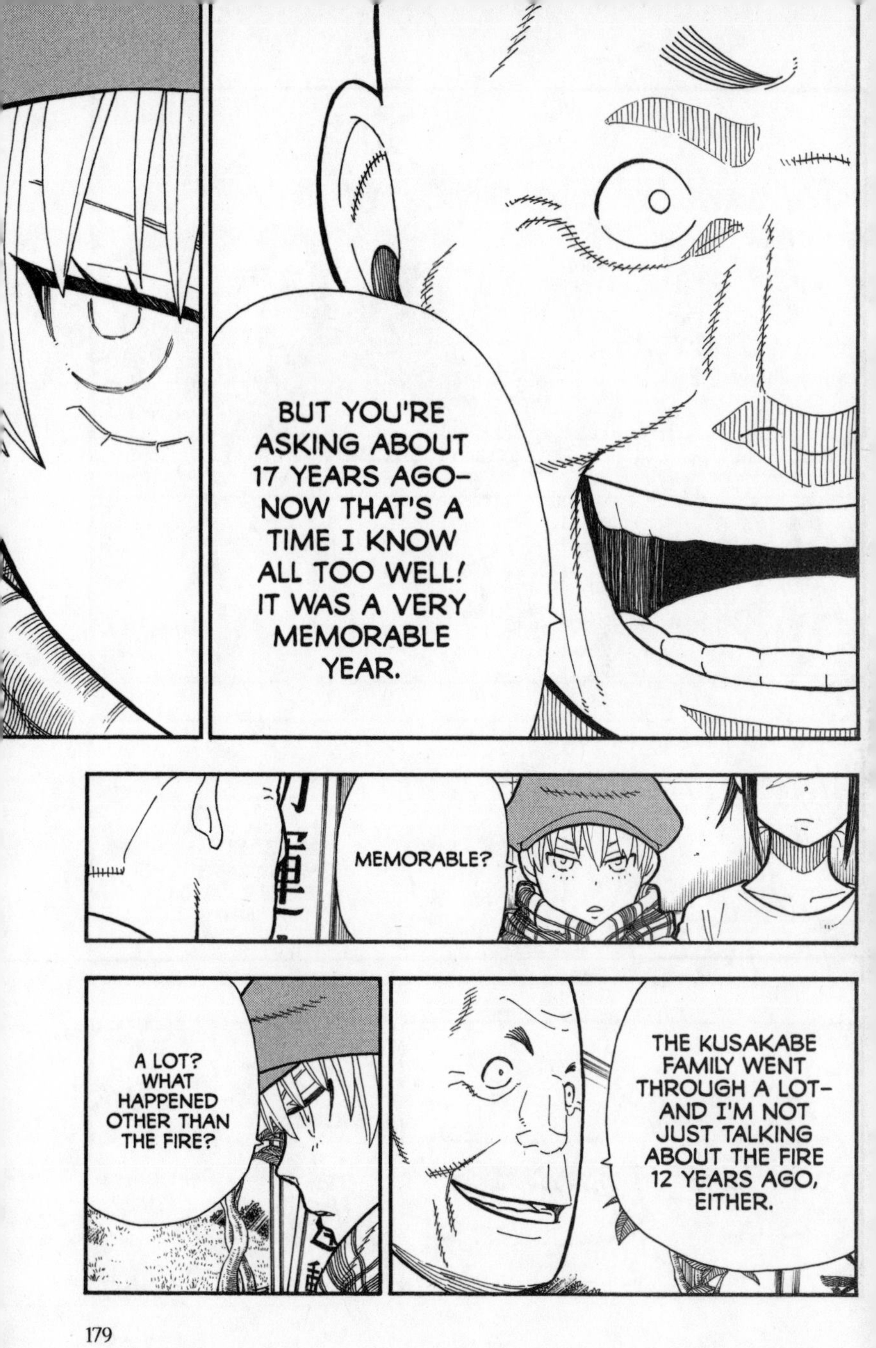
BUT YOU'RE ASKING ABOUT 17 YEARS AGO– NOW THAT'S A TIME I KNOW ALL TOO WELL! IT WAS A VERY MEMORABLE YEAR.
MEMORABLE?
THE KUSAKABE FAMILY WENT THROUGH A LOT– AND I'M NOT JUST TALKING ABOUT THE FIRE 12 YEARS AGO, EITHER.
A LOT? WHAT HAPPENED OTHER THAN THE FIRE?

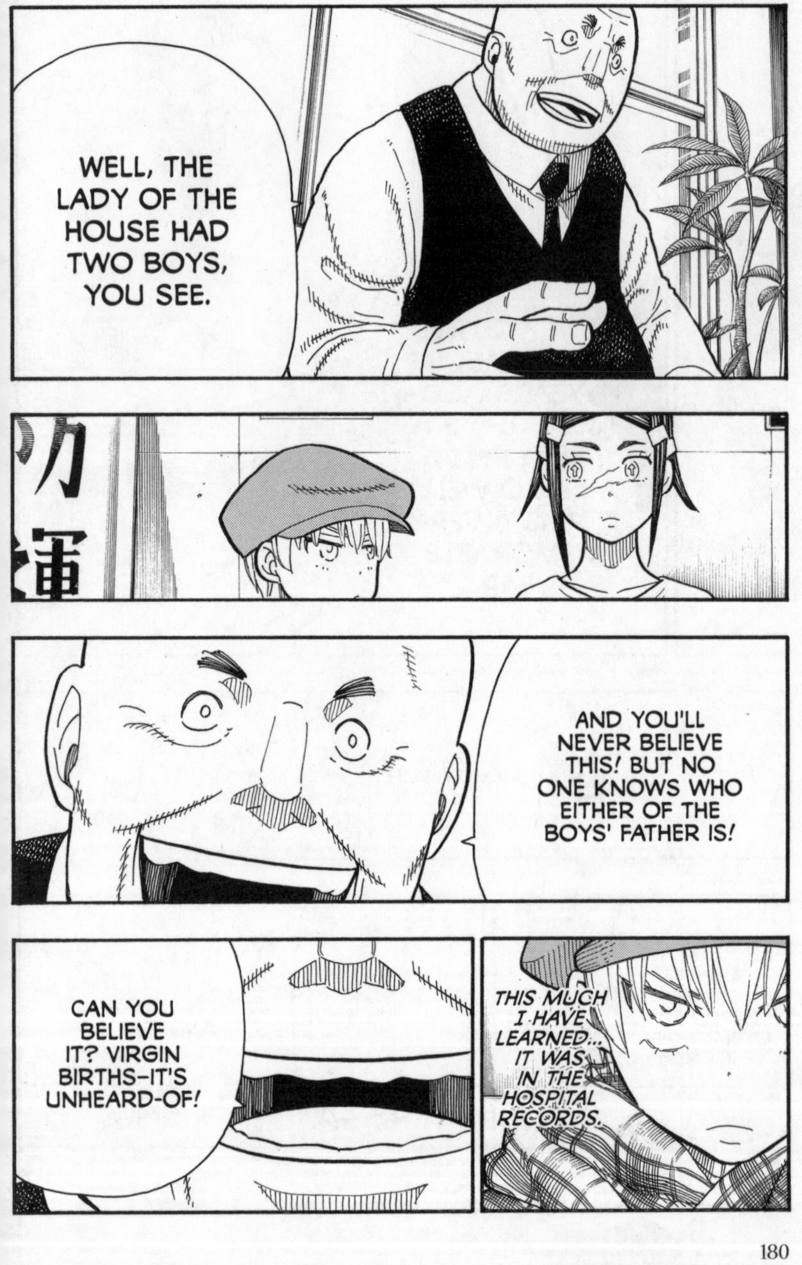
WELL, THE LADY OF THE HOUSE HAD TWO BOYS, YOU SEE.
AND YOU'LL NEVER BELIEVE THIS! BUT NO ONE KNOWS WHO EITHER OF THE BOYS' FATHER IS!
THIS MUCH I HAVE LEARNED... IT WAS IN THE HOSPITAL RECORDS.
CAN YOU BELIEVE IT? VIRGIN BIRTHS—IT'S UNHEARD-OF!

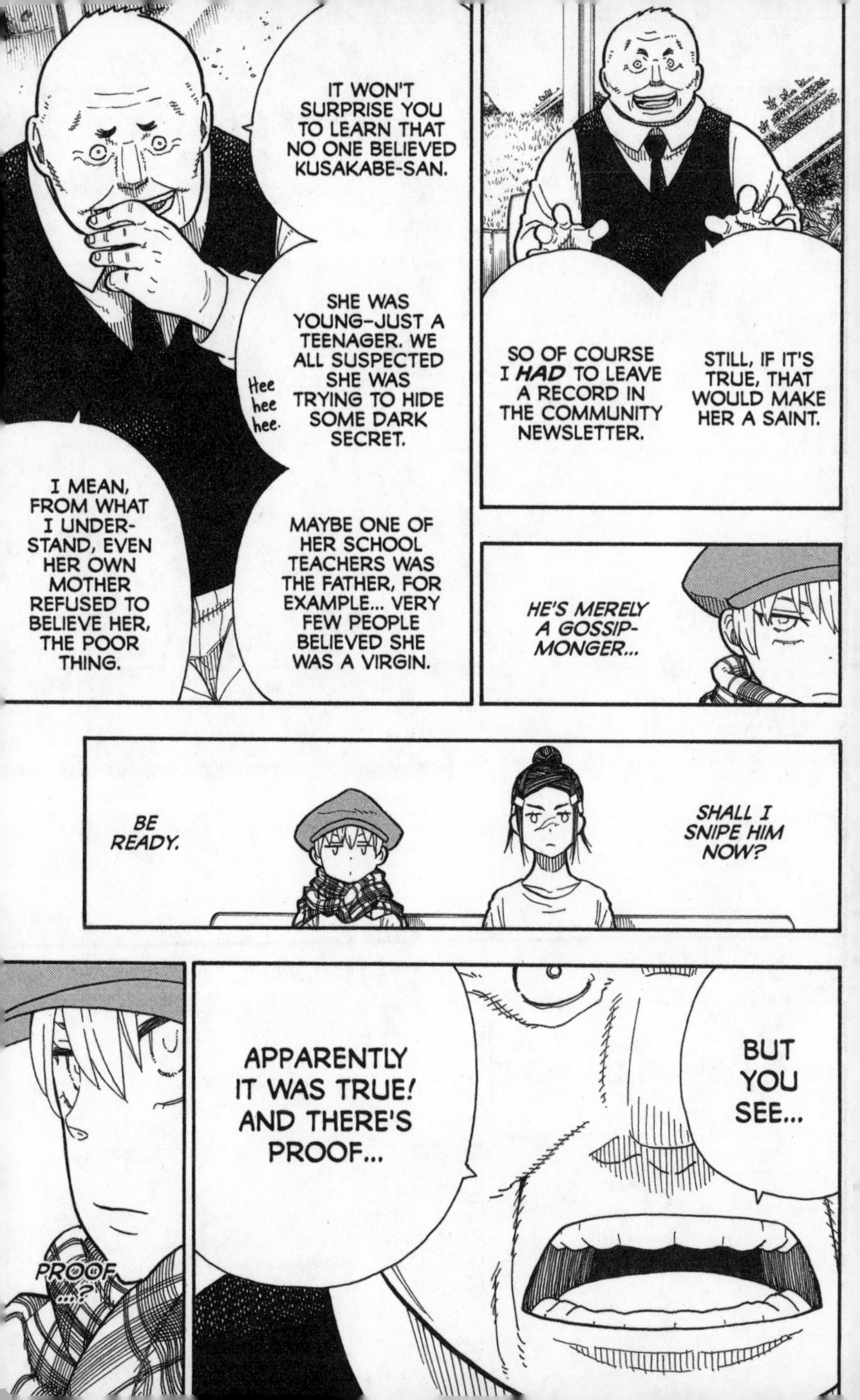
STILL, IF IT'S TRUE, THAT WOULD MAKE HER A SAINT.
SO OF COURSE I *HAD* TO LEAVE A RECORD IN THE COMMUNITY NEWSLETTER.
HE'S MERELY A GOSSIP-MONGER...
IT WON'T SURPRISE YOU TO LEARN THAT NO ONE BELIEVED KUSAKABE-SAN.
SHE WAS YOUNG—JUST A TEENAGER. WE ALL SUSPECTED SHE WAS TRYING TO HIDE SOME DARK SECRET.
Hee hee hee.
MAYBE ONE OF HER SCHOOL TEACHERS WAS THE FATHER, FOR EXAMPLE... VERY FEW PEOPLE BELIEVED SHE WAS A VIRGIN.
I MEAN, FROM WHAT I UNDER-STAND, EVEN HER OWN MOTHER REFUSED TO BELIEVE HER, THE POOR THING.
SHALL I SNIPE HIM NOW?
BE READY.
BUT YOU SEE...
APPARENTLY IT WAS TRUE! AND THERE'S PROOF...
PROOF ...?

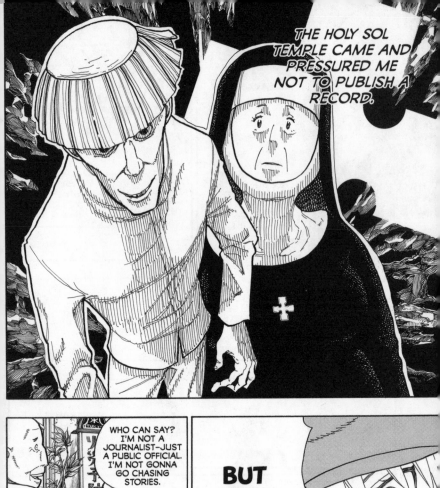

THE HOLY SOL TEMPLE CAME AND PRESSURED ME NOT TO PUBLISH A RECORD.

WHO CAN SAY? I'M NOT A JOURNALIST—JUST A PUBLIC OFFICIAL. I'M NOT GONNA GO CHASING STORIES.

I DON'T NEED TO KNOW WHY. IF THEY'RE TELLING ME TO STOP, THAT'S WHAT I'M GOING TO DO.

Sign: Fire Prevention Exercises

BUT WHY ?!

...

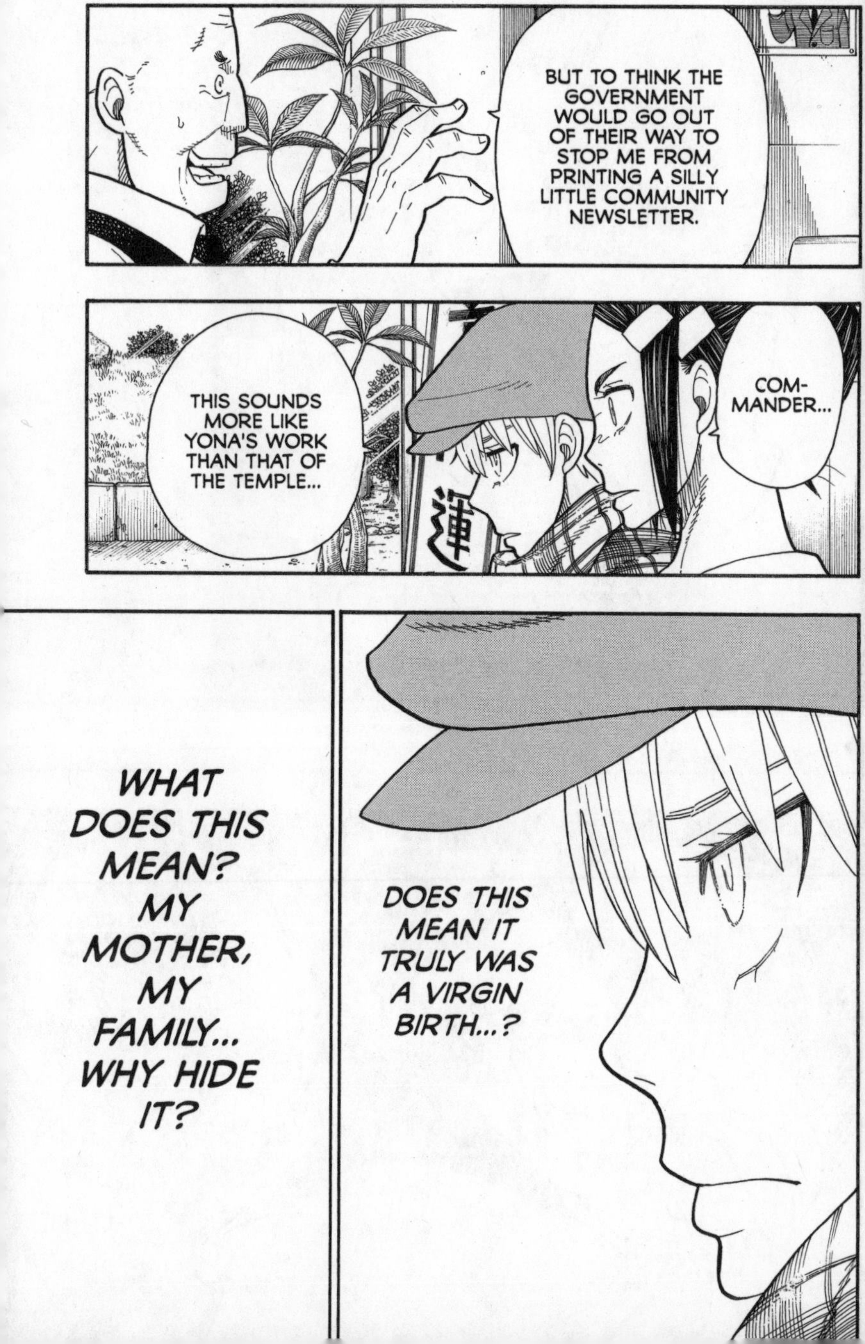
BUT TO THINK THE GOVERNMENT WOULD GO OUT OF THEIR WAY TO STOP ME FROM PRINTING A SILLY LITTLE COMMUNITY NEWSLETTER.
COM-MANDER...
THIS SOUNDS MORE LIKE YONA'S WORK THAN THAT OF THE TEMPLE...
DOES THIS MEAN IT TRULY WAS A VIRGIN BIRTH...?
WHAT DOES THIS MEAN? MY MOTHER, MY FAMILY... WHY HIDE IT?

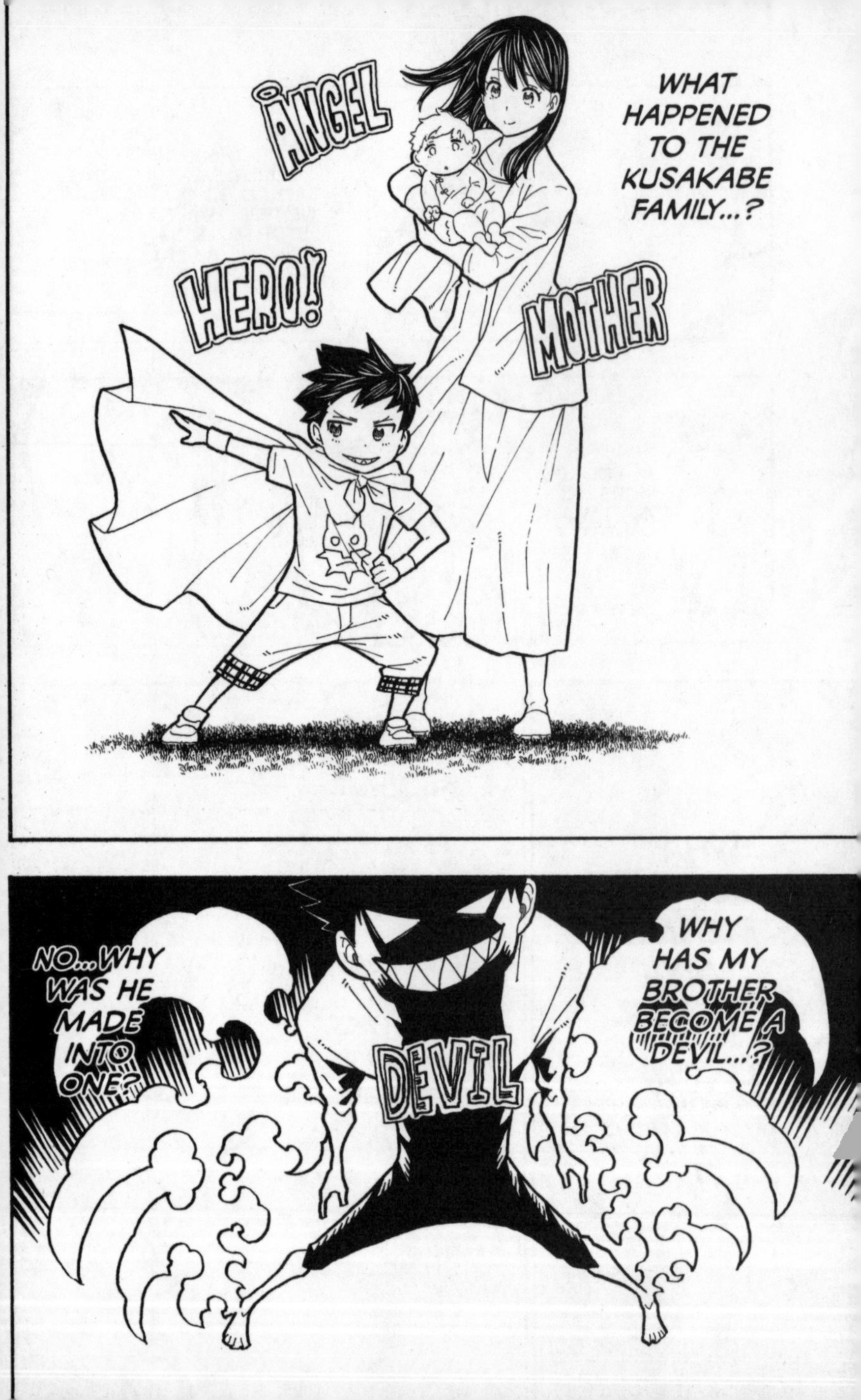
WHAT HAPPENED TO THE KUSAKABE FAMILY...?
ANGEL
MOTHER
HERO!
WHY HAS MY BROTHER BECOME A DEVIL...?
DEVIL
NO...WHY WAS HE MADE INTO ONE?

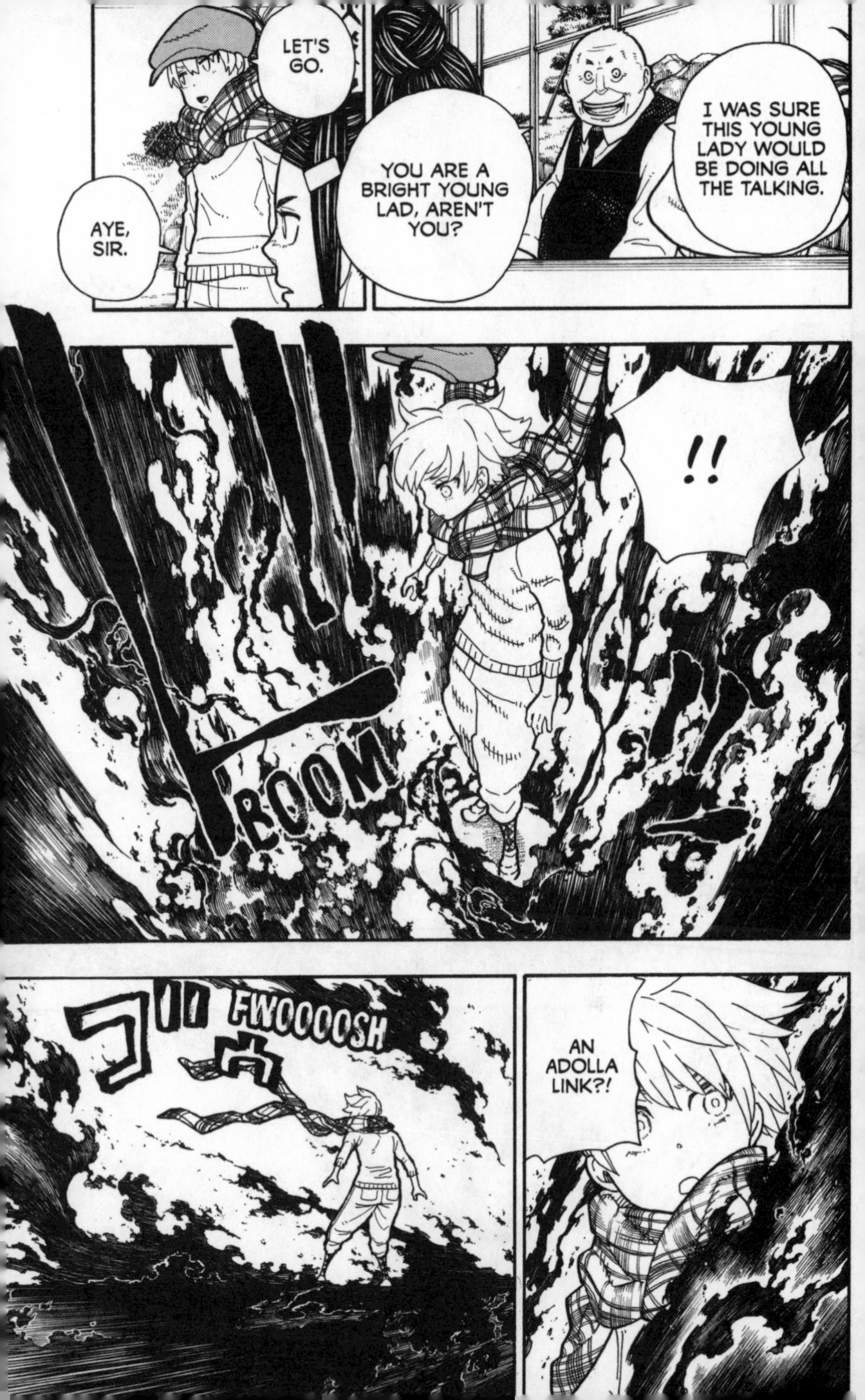
I WAS SURE THIS YOUNG LADY WOULD BE DOING ALL THE TALKING.
YOU ARE A BRIGHT YOUNG LAD, AREN'T YOU?
LET'S GO.
AYE, SIR.
!!
BOOM
AN ADOLLA LINK?!
FWOOOOOSH

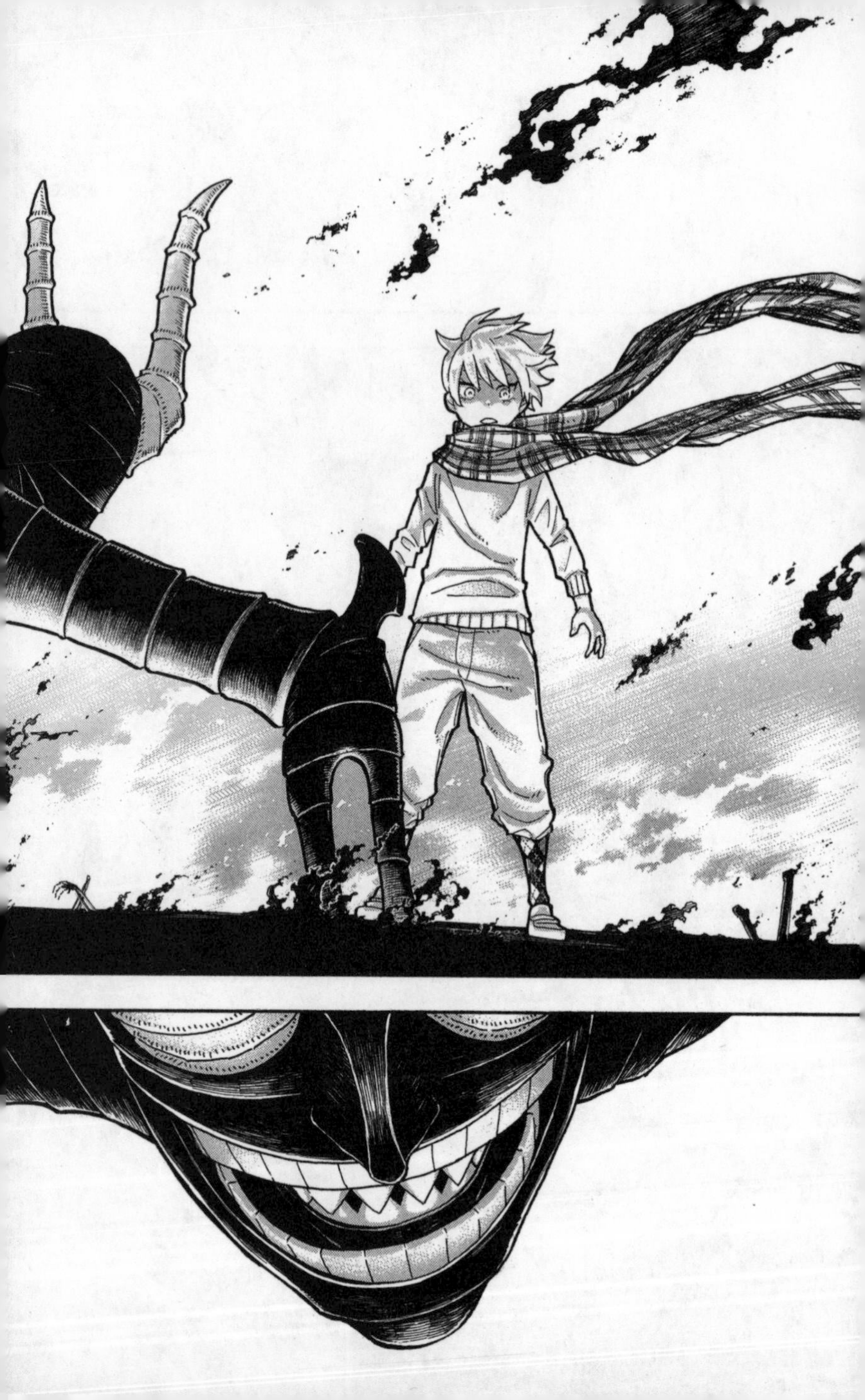

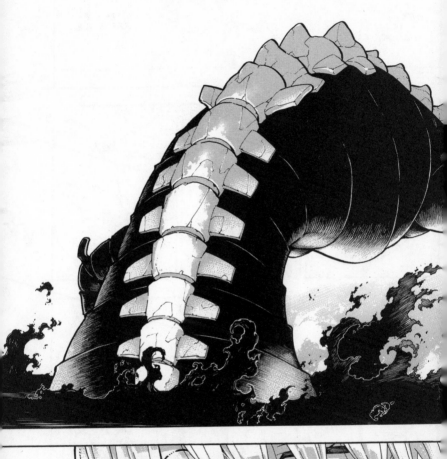

YOU'RE...

MY MOTHER...

TO BE CONTINUED IN VOLUME 27!!

AFTERWORD MANGA: ATSUSHIYA

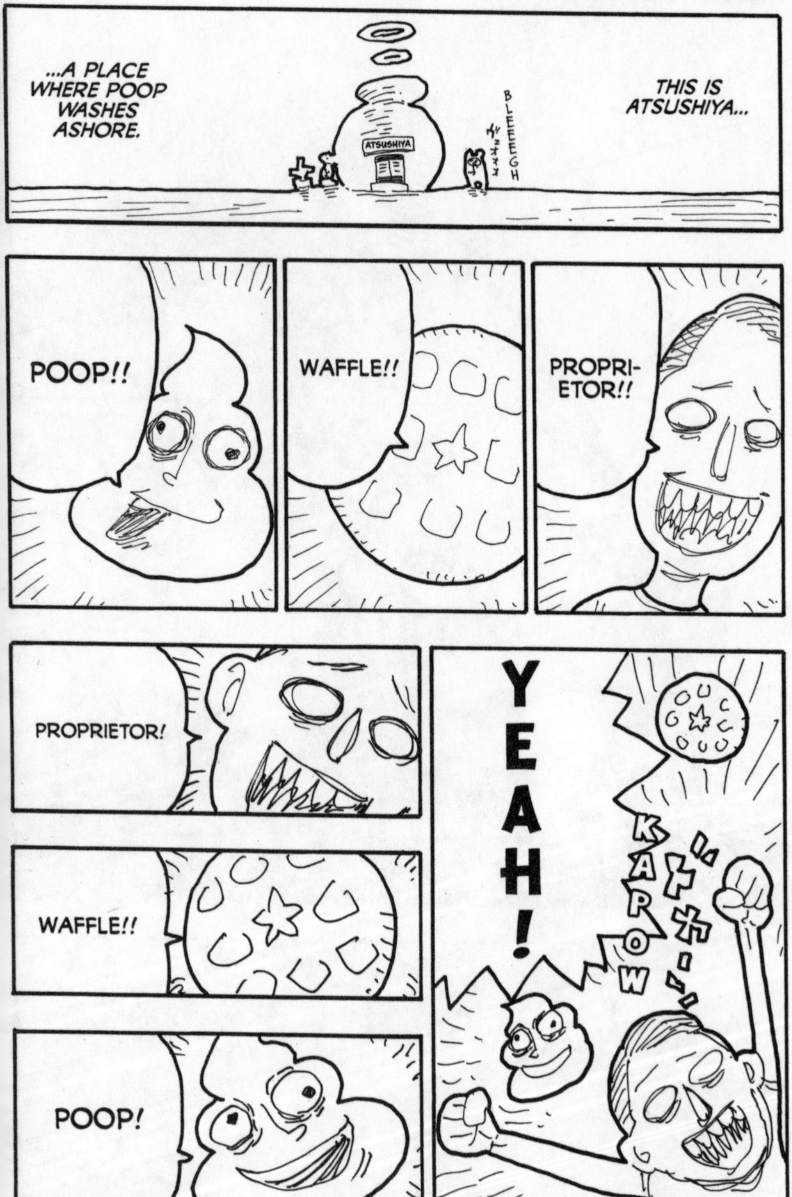

THIS IS ATSUSHIYA...
ATSUSHIYA
BLEEEGH
...A PLACE WHERE POOP WASHES ASHORE.
PROPRI-ETOR!!
WAFFLE!!
POOP!!
YEAH!
KAPOW
PROPRIETOR!
WAFFLE!!
POOP!

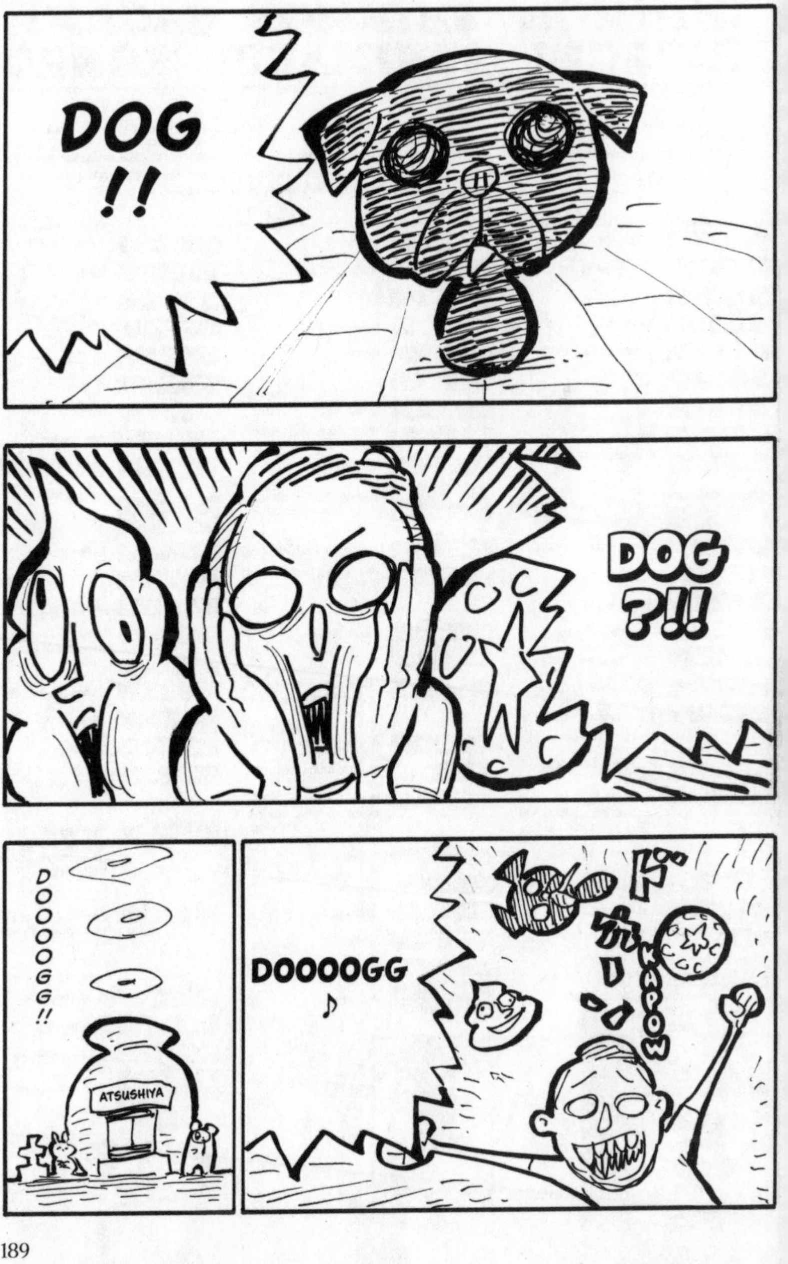
DOG !!
DOG ?!!
DOOOOGG ♪
KAPOW
DOOOOOGG!!
ATSUSHIYA

CHARACTER PROFILE

SHINMON HIBACHI

AFFILIATION: **ASAKUSA HIKESHI**
RANK: **CHIEF**
ABILITY: **THIRD GENERATION PYROKINETIC**

Height	177cm [5'10"]
Weight	83kg [183lbs.]
Age	58
Birthday	January 8
Sign	Capricorn, I think?
Blood Type	O
Nickname	I guess people call me Boss
Self-Proclaimed	I'm me
Favorite Foods	Flavorful sukiyaki, the old bat's daifuku
Least Favorite Food	Green onions, except in sukiyaki
Favorite Music	Taiko drums
Favorite Animal	Dogs
Favorite Color	Red, navy blue
Favorite Type of Girl	My wife, obviously
Who He Respects	The old boss
Who He Hates	Spineless cowards
Who He's Afraid Of	Ain't nobody scares me
Hobbies	Collecting crazy-shaped pipes
Daily Routine	Puttering around the garden
Dream	I'd love to get my wife something good to eat one more time
Shoe Size	27cm [10]
Eyesight	1.5 [20/12.5]
Favorite Subject	I was never good at studying
Least Favorite Subject	But I don't hate it

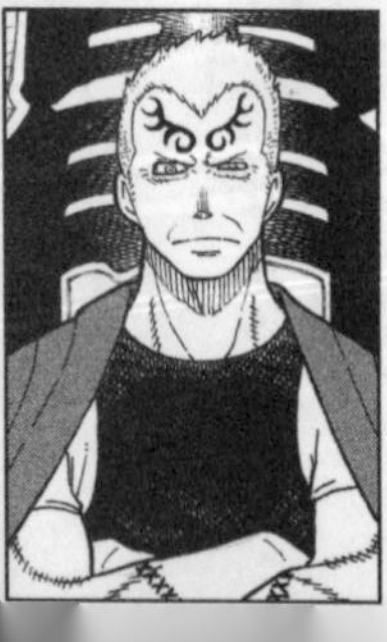

SHINMON BENIMARU

AFFILIATION: **ASAKUSA HIKESHI**
RANK: **TRAINEE**
ABILITY: **COMPOSITE PYROKINETIC**
Can use the ignition powers of a Third Gen and the fire manipulation powers of a Second Gen.

Height	157cm [5'2"]
Weight	50kg [110lbs.]
Age	13
Birthday	February 20
Sign	Pisces
Blood Type	A
Nickname	Stray dog
Self-Proclaimed	What does that mean, "self-proclaimed"?
Favorite Foods	Mild sukiyaki
Least Favorite Food	The old bat's daifuku. She makes too many
Favorite Music	Japanese festival music
Favorite Animal	Foxes and those dogs that are black around the eyes
Favorite Color	Black, blue
Favorite Type of Girl	I dunno
Who He Respects	The Boss who took me in and Konro, I guess
Who He Hates	Anybody who pisses me off
Who He's Afraid Of	I'm not scared of anything
Hobbies	Betting on stuff like beigoma tops and the menko card-slapping game
Daily Routine	Fighting
Dream	To be the Asakusa Hikeshi boss
Shoe Size	24cm [6.5]
Eyesight	2.0 [20/10]
Favorite Subject	Martial arts
Least Favorite Subject	Arithmetic

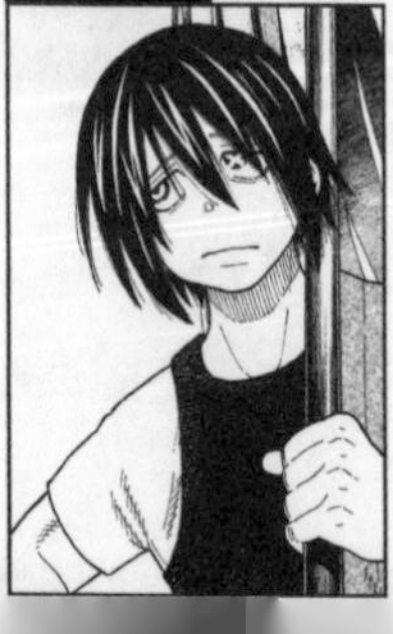

SAGAMIYA KONRO

AFFILIATION: **ASAKUSA HIKESHI**
RANK: **UNDERBOSS**
ABILITY: **THIRD GENERATION PYROKINETIC**
Can't use powers adequately due to tephrosis

Height	188cm [6'2"]
Weight	92kg [203lbs.]
Age	29
Birthday	May 6
Sign	Taurus
Bloodt Type	B
Nickname	Kon-san
Self-Proclaimed	Tea server
Favorite Foods	Tsukudani [seafood simmered in soy sauce and sugar], saketoba salmon jerky, unaju [eel served on rice], anmitsu
Least Favorite Food	None
Favorite Music	Folk music
Favorite Animal	River otters, dogs
Favorite Color	Black, red
Favorite Type of Girl	A pretty broad with a nice set of gams.
Who He Respects	The old boss, Beni
Who He Hates	No one
Who He's Afraid Of	Ghosts
Hobbies	Making soba, pickling, photography
Daily Routine	Making Beni lose at bets. I hope he doesn't get addicted to gambling
Dream	I hope Asakusa stays in as good shape as it's in now
Shoe Size	29cm [13]
Eyesight	1.5 [20/12.5]
Favorite Subject	Don't have one
Least Favorite Subject	Don't have one

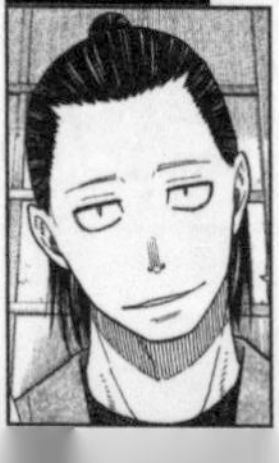

Translation Notes:

Kagutsuchi, page 120

HE IS THE CHILD OF FLAME...
...KAGUTSUCHI.

Here Konro compares Benimaru to Kagutsuchi, the god of fire in Japanese mythology, whose heat is so intense that his mother burned to death while giving birth. The word Konro uses when he calls Benimaru the child of flame is *moshigo*, which is a child who is born as an answer to his or her parents' prayers. This implies that Benimaru is a gift to Asakusa, given by the flames.

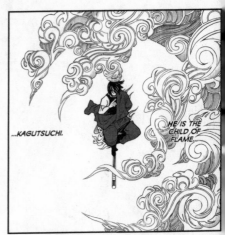

Wrathful god, page 137

BOLD AND BRAVE LIKE A WRATHFUL GOD WITH THE SUN WHEEL AT HIS BACK!!
HE IS A TRUE ASAKUSA HIKESHI!!!

Specifically, Hibachi compares Benimaru to a *Myo-o*, or Wisdom King, like Acala (see volume 20). These Wisdom Kings are wrathful manifestations of Buddhas, and are often portrayed with fiery circles behind their backs.

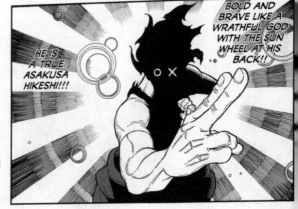

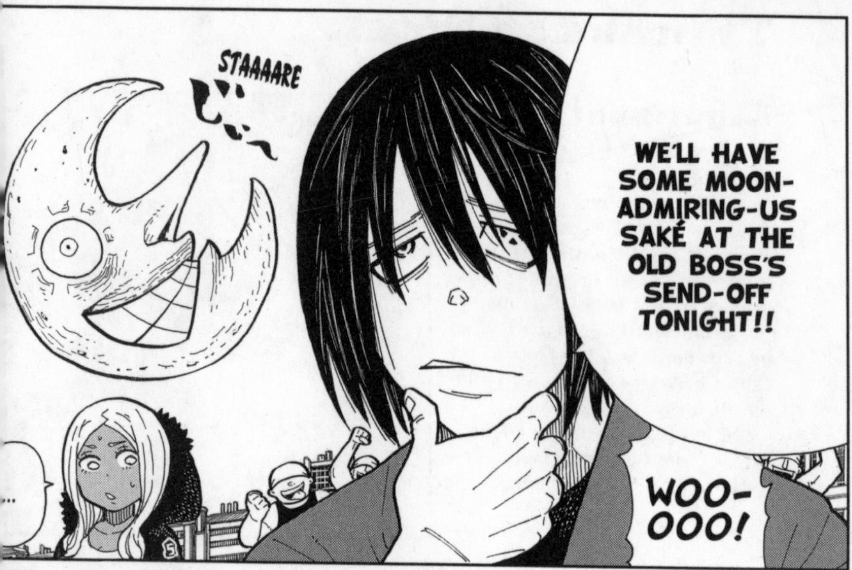
WE'LL HAVE SOME MOON-ADMIRING-US SAKÉ AT THE OLD BOSS'S SEND-OFF TONIGHT!!
WOO-OOO!
STAAAARE
...

Moon-admiring-us, page 152

A traditional Japanese activity is to go out at night to admire the moon while enjoying a cup of saké. This is called *tsukimi*, or "moon viewing." Here Benimaru suggests they should have *tsukimirare saké*, where *tsukimirare* still technically means "moon viewing," only this time the moon is the one doing the viewing.

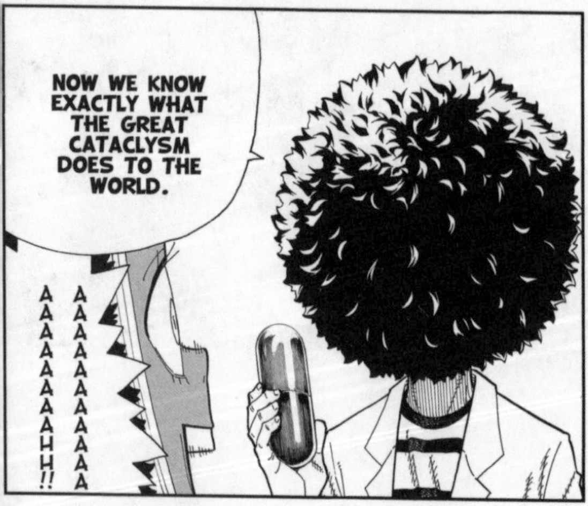
NOW WE KNOW EXACTLY WHAT THE GREAT CATACLYSM DOES TO THE WORLD.
AAAAAAAAAAA
AAAAAAAAHH!!

Dr. Marimo, page 153

A marimo, also known as a moss ball, is a type of algae that grows in lakes and forms into green velvety balls, much like "Dr. Marimo"'s head. Surely the name's resemblance to that of a video puzzle game doctor who uses two-toned medicinal capsules like the one in Marimo's hand is purely coincidental...

MOTHER: MARI KUSAKABE

Mari Kusakabe, page 167

The reader may remember Shinra's determination to called himself Whatever-Is-Currently-Relevant Man. As he explained back in volume nine, this determination comes from the term *Shinra Bansho*, which means "all creation." The Chinese character for *ban* can also be pronounced *man*, so when Shinra calls himself Shinra Man, it leads straight to his brother Sho, and thus "*man*" connects the two of them. The translators bring this up because the *ma* in Mari Kusakabe uses the very same Chinese character as *ban* and *man*, making her another link between the brothers.

Young characters and steampunk setting, like *Howl's Moving Castle* and *Battle Angel Alita*

Beyond the Clouds © 2018 Nicke / Ki-oon

A boy with a talent for machines and a mysterious girl whose wings he's fixed will take you beyond the clouds! In the tradition of the high-flying, resonant adventure stories of Studio Ghibli comes a gorgeous tale about the longing of young hearts for adventure and friendship!

A SMART, NEW ROMANTIC COMEDY FOR FANS OF *SHORTCAKE CAKE* AND *TERRACE HOUSE!*

A romance manga starring high school girl Meeko, who learns to live on her own in a boarding house whose living room is home to the odd (but handsome) Matsunaga-san. She begins to adjust to her new life away from her parents, but Meeko soon learns that no matter how far away from home she is, she's still a young girl at heart — especially when she finds herself falling for Matsunaga-san.

PERFECT WORLD

Rie Aruga

A TOUCHING
NEW SERIES
ABOUT LOVE AND
COPING WITH
DISABILITY

An office party reunites Tsugumi with her high school crush Itsuki. He's realized his dream of becoming an architect, but along the way, he experienced a spinal injury that put him in a wheelchair. Now Tsugumi's rekindled feelings will butt up against prejudices she never considered — and Itsuki will have to decide if he's ready to let someone into his heart...

"Depicts with great delicacy and courage the difficulties some with disabilities experience getting involved in romantic relationships... Rie Aruga refuses to romanticize, pushing her heroine to face the reality of disability. She invites her readers to the same tasks of empathy, knowledge and recognition."
—Slate.fr

"An important entry [in manga romance]... The emotional core of both plot and characters indicates thoughtfulness... [Aruga's] research is readily apparent in the text and artwork, making this feel like a real story."
—Anime News Network

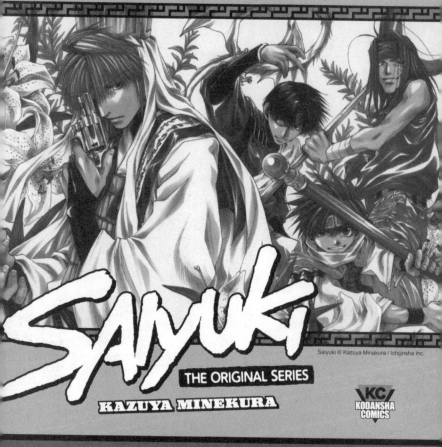

Something's Wrong With Us

NATSUMI
ANDO

The dark, psychological, sexy shojo series readers have been waiting for!

A spine-chilling and steamy romance between a Japanese sweets maker and the man who framed her mother for murder!

Following in her mother's footsteps, Nao became a traditional Japanese sweets maker, and with unparalleled artistry and a bright attitude, she gets an offer to work at a world-class confectionary company. But when she meets the young, handsome owner, she recognizes his cold stare...

THE SWEET SCENT OF LOVE IS IN THE AIR! FOR FANS OF OFFBEAT ROMANCES LIKE *WOTAKO!*

Sweat and Soap © Kintetsu Yamada / Kodansha Ltd.

In an office romance, there's a fine line between sexy and awkward... and that line is where Asako — a woman who sweats copiously — meets Koutarou — a perfume developer who can't get enough of Asako's, er, scent. Don't miss a romcom manga like no other!

KC
KODANSHA COMICS

CUTE ANIMALS AND LIFE LESSONS, PERFECT FOR ASPIRING PET VETS OF ALL AGES!

For an 11-year-old, Yuzu has a lot on her plate. When her mom gets sick and has to be hospitalized, Yuzu goes to live with her uncle who runs the local veterinary clinic. Yuzu's always been scared of animals, but she tries to help out. Through all the tough moments in her life, Yuzu realizes that she can help make things all right with a little help from her animal pals, peers, and kind grown-ups.

Every new patient is a furry friend in the making!

Chobits © CLAMP·ShigatsuTsuitachi CO.,LTD./Kodansha L

THE WORLD OF CLAMP!

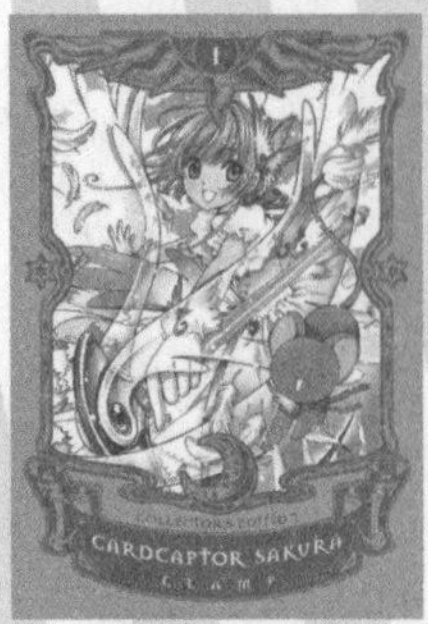
CARDCAPTOR SAKURA
CLAMP
Cardcaptor Sakura
Collector's Edition

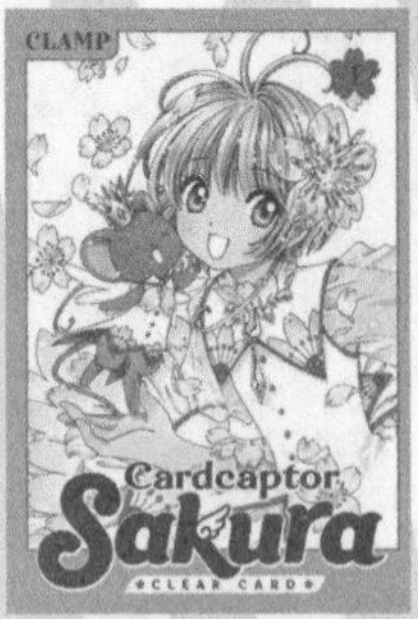
CLAMP
Cardcaptor Sakura
CLEAR CARD
Cardcaptor Sakura:
Clear Card

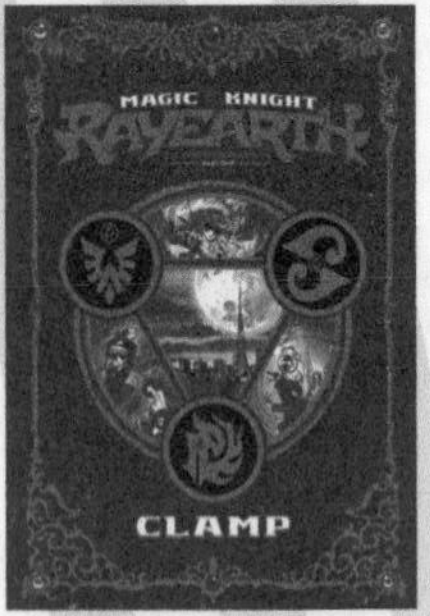
MAGIC KNIGHT
RAYEARTH
CLAMP
Magic Knight Rayearth
25th Anniversary Box Set

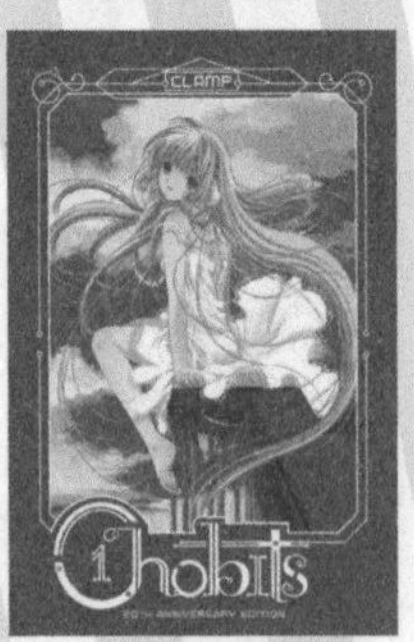
CLAMP
1
Chobits
Chobits

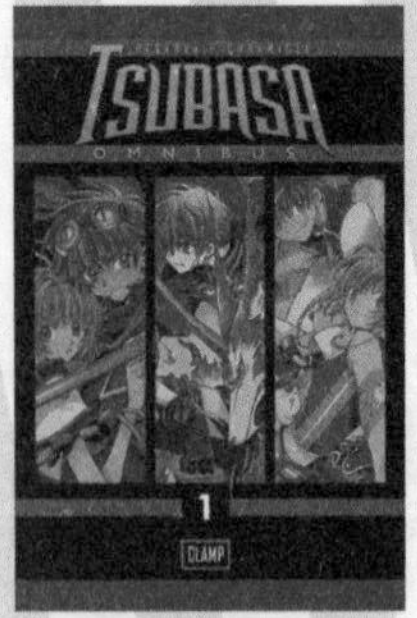
TSUBASA
OMNIBUS
1
CLAMP
TSUBASA Omnibus

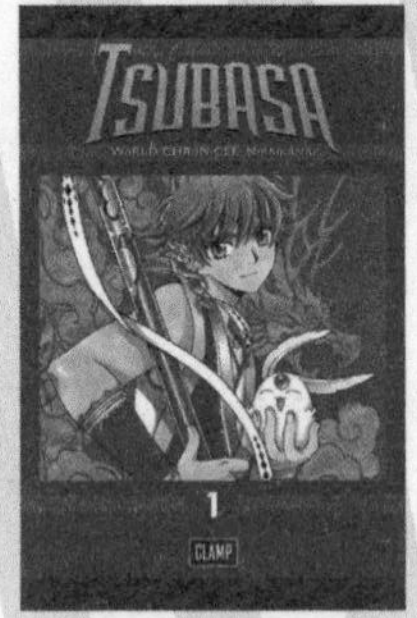
TSUBASA
1
CLAMP
TSUBASA WoRLD CHRoNiCLE

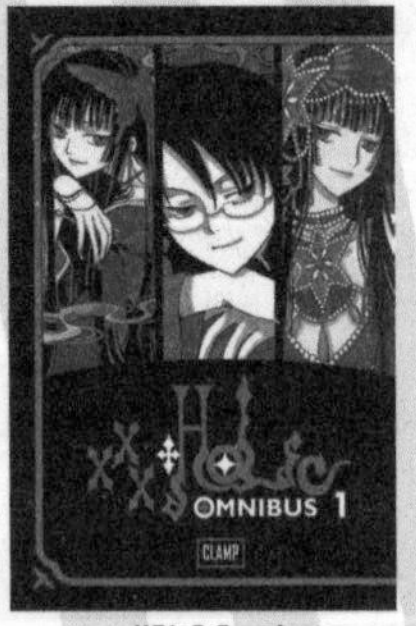
xxxHOLiC
OMNIBUS 1
CLAMP
xxxHOLiC Omnibus

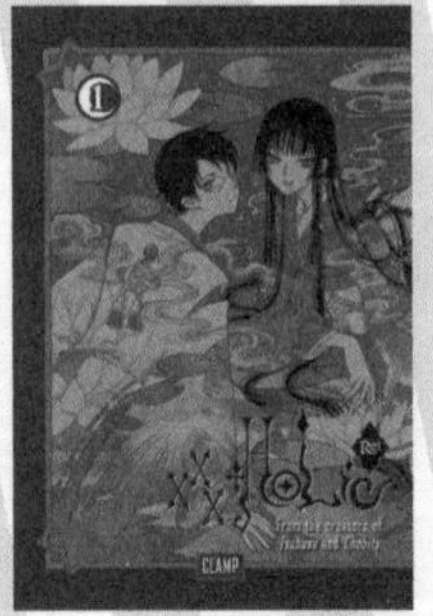
1
xxxHOLiC
CLAMP
xxxHOLiC Rei

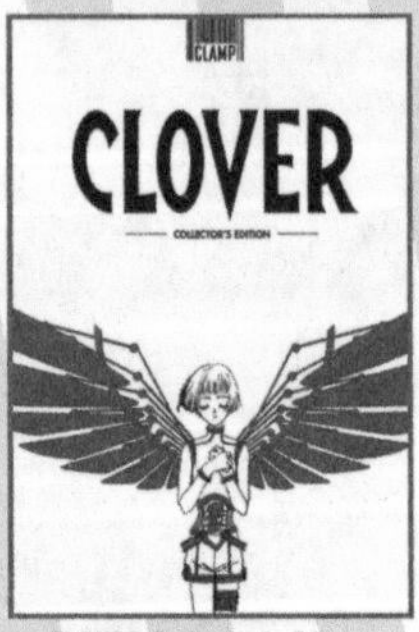
CLAMP
CLOVER
COLLECTOR'S EDITION
CLOVER Collector's Edition

KC KODANSHA COMICS

Kodansha Comics welcomes you to explore the expansive world of CLAMP, the all-female artist collective that has produced some of the most acclaimed manga of the century. Our growing catalog includes icons like *Cardcaptor Sakura* and *Magic Knight Rayearth*, each crafted with CLAMP's one-of-a-kind style and characters!

The art-deco cyberpunk classic from the creators of *xxxHOLiC* and *Cardcaptor Sakura*!

"Starred Review.
This experimental
sci-fi work from
CLAMP reads like a
romantic version of
AKIRA."
—Publishers Weekly

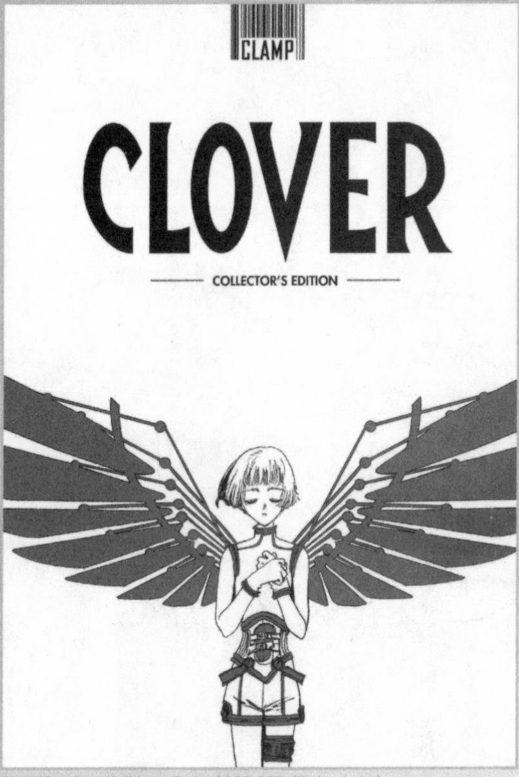

CLAMP

CLOVER

— COLLECTOR'S EDITION —

CLOVER © CLAMP-ShigatsuTsuitachi CO.,LTD./Kodansha Ltd.

Su was born into a bleak future, where the government keeps tight control over children with magical powers—codenamed "Clovers." With Su being the only "four-leaf" Clover in the world, she has been kept isolated nearly her whole life. Can ex-military agent Kazuhiko deliver her to the happiness she seeks? Experience the complete series in this hardcover edition, which also includes over twenty pages of ravishing color art!

KC
KODANSHA
COMICS

MAGIC KNIGHT RAYEARTH
25TH ANNIVERSARY EDITION
CLAMP

A BELOVED CLASSIC MAKES ITS STUNNING RETURN IN THIS GORGEOUS, LIMITED EDITION BOX SET!

his tale of three Tokyo teenagers who cross through a magical
ortal and become the champions of another world is a modern
manga classic. The box set includes three volumes of manga
overing the entire first series of *Magic Knight Rayearth*, plus the
eries's super-rare full-color art book companion, all printed at a
arger size than ever before on premium paper, featuring a newly-
evised translation and lettering, and exquisite foil-stamped covers.
strictly limited edition, this will be gone in a flash!

KC KODANSHA COMICS

The beloved characters from *Cardcaptor Sakura* return in a brand new, reimagined fantasy adventure!

"[*Tsubasa*] takes readers on a fantastic ride that only gets more exhilarating with each successive chapter." —Anime News Network

In the Kingdom of Clow, an archaeological dig unleashes an incredible power, causing Princess Sakura to lose her memories. To save her, her childhood friend Syaoran must follow the orders of the Dimension Witch and travel alongside Kurogane, an unrivaled warrior; Fai, a powerful magician; and Mokona, a curiously strange creature, to retrieve Sakura's dispersed memories!

A Kodansha Comics Trade Paperback Original
Fire Force 26 copyright © 2020 Atsushi Ohkubo
English translation copyright © 2021 Atsushi Ohkubo

All rights reserved.

Published in the United States by Kodansha Comics, an imprint of Kodansha USA Publishing, LLC, New York.

Publication rights for this English edition arranged through Kodansha Ltd., Tokyo.

First published in Japan in 2020 by Kodansha Ltd., Tokyo.

ISBN 978-1-64651-419-9

Printed in the United States of America.

www.kodansha.us

9 8 7 6 5 4 3 2 1
Translation: Alethea Nibley & Athena Nibley
Lettering: AndWorld Design
Editing: Greg Moore
Kodansha Comics edition cover design by Phil Balsman

Publisher: Kiichiro Sugawara

Director of publishing services: Ben Applegate
Associate director, publishing operations: Stephen Pakula
Publishing services managing editors: Madison Salters, Alanna Ruse
Production managers: Emi Lotto, Angela Zurlo